CKBS '90

Proceedings of the International
Working Conference on Cooperating
Knowledge Based Systems

3–5 October 1990
University of Keele, UK

CKBS '90

Proceedings of the International
Working Conference on Cooperating
Knowledge Based Systems

3–5 October 1990
University of Keele, UK

Edited by S.M. Deen

Organiser: DAKE Centre
University of Keele

Sponsors: Information Technology Division of the
Department of Trade and Industry

BCS Data Management and
Expert Systems Specialist Groups

US Air Force European Office of
Aerospace Research and Development

European Research Office of the US Army

EEC ESPRIT

Springer-Verlag
London Berlin Heidelberg New York
Paris Tokyo Hong Kong
Barcelona Budapest

S.M. Deen, MSc, PhD, DIC, FBCS, C.Eng.,
DAKE Centre
University of Keele, Keele,
Staffordshire, ST5 5BG, UK

ISBN-13:978-3-540-19649-5   e-ISBN-13:978-1-4471-1831-2
DOI: 10.1007/978-1-4471-1831-2

British Library Cataloguing in Publication Data
CKBS '90
CKBS '90: proceedings of the international working conference on cooperating
knowledge based systems, held at the University of Keele, England,
October 3–5, 1990
1. Expert systems
I. Title   II. Deen, S. M. (S. Misbah)
006.33
ISBN-13:978-3-540-19649-5

Library of Congress Cataloging-in-Publication Data
International Working Conference on Cooperating Knowledge Based Systems
(1990: University of Keele)
CKBS '90: proceedings of the International Working Conference on
Cooperating Knowledge Based Systems, held at the University of Keele,
England, October 3–5, 1990 / editor, S.M. Deen : [organizer, DAKE Centre,
University of Keele : sponsors, Information Technology Division of the
Department of Trade and Industry ... et al.].
p. cm.
Includes index.
ISBN-13:978-3-540-19649-5
1. Expert systems (Computer science) – Congresses.   I. Deen, S.M. (Sayyed M.)
II. Great Britain. Dept. of Trade and Industry. Information Technology
Division.   III. Title.
QA76.76.E951584   1990   91–7456
006.3'3–dc20   CIP

34/3830–543210 Printed on acid-free paper.

PREFACE

This is the first international conference aimed at bringing the distributed database and distributed AI (DAI) experts together, from both academia and industry, in order to discuss the issues of the next generation of knowledge based systems, namely Cooperating Knowledge Based Systems or CKBS for short. As the area of CKBS is new, we intended it to be an ideas conference – a conference where interesting new ideas, rather than results from completed projects, are explored, discussed, and debated.

The conference was organised by the DAKE Centre. This is an interdisciplinary centre at the University of Keele for research and development in Data and Knowledge Engineering (DAKE). The Centre draws most of its strength from the Department of Computer Science which also provides administrative support for the activities of the Centre, although its membership is spread over several departments. The Centre has three main streams of research activities, namely:

Large Knowledge Bases
Software Engineering
Neural Networks

The Large Knowledge Base group, which provided the focus for this conference, is active in a number of research areas relating to data and knowledge bases, spanning from distributed databases to cooperations among data and knowledge bases. The current research topics include integration of data and knowledge bases and cooperating knowledge based systems, with several major projects in the latter (see the entries under the Poster Session given below). The Software Engineering group has provided strong support for this conference, and it is well-known for its work in logic-based software configuration management and software re-use. The Neural Network group specialises in speech and image recognition areas.

In order to provide a conducive atmosphere for in-depth discussions, we restricted attendance at the conference to those who have a genuine interest in this new area. Even then we had over 80 participants from 15 countries. To facilitate discussion, we made the conference residential, and allowed plenty of time after each presentation for discussion, in which both DDB and DAI researchers participated. We taped these discussions, and their selected transcripts are included in this book, following each paper.

There were over 80 extended abstracts submitted to this conference of which less than half were selected by the Programme

Committee for presentation. Following the conference, a second review was carried out, this time on full papers, from which 17 papers were selected for publication in this book. Each abstract/paper was reviewed, as usual, by several referees at each stage. The selection was based on the usual criteria of originality, significance, research content, readability and finally relevance. A paper was deemed relevant if it was considered to be of interest to both the communities.

The conference was run in two parallel sessions, with some joint sessions for reporting from the parallel session by the Session Chairmen. These joint sessions proved very stimulating, mainly because of the succinct summaries and perceptive comments made by the Session Chairmen.

The conference also had a poster session, in which the following posters on some current projects were presented:

The Consensus Project
P.J. Kearney, D.H. Walburn, A.A. Clark, S.C. Martin, A.J. Slade, D.P.M. Wills, P.A.Read (British Aerospace (Military Aircraft) Ltd, UK)

Cooperating Expert Systems in Risk and Reliability Assessment
Neil Mitchison, Andre Poucet (Institute for Systems Engineering and Informatics (EEC), Ispra, Italy)

COSMOS (Co-Ordination Strategies for Multi-Object Systems)
Collaborators are: Universities of Keele, Leicester and Ulster, UMIST, Dundee College of Technology and Teeside Polytechnic

Demonstration of Planning Operator Induction in a Multi-agent System
T.J. Grant (BSO & Aerospace Systems, Netherlands)

IMAGINE Project (ESPRIT Project)
Partners are: Imperial College London, Intrasoft (Greece), Plessey (UK), Siemens (Germany – Coordinator), Steria (France), University of Keele, University of Leiden

Interfacing Expert Systems with Databases and Simulation
Esko K. Juuso and Kauko Leiviska (University of Oulu, Finland)

MIRAGE (A Model for the Interaction of Routing Agents in a Global Environment)
S.M. Deen, N.A. Al-Samarraie, H.M.A.C. Herath, B. Ndovie, (University of Keele)

The final session of the conference was a panel discussion with the title "Any Lessons"?. The idea was to explore if, in this conference, the DDB researchers had learnt anything from the DAI researchers, and *vice versa*. This session was naturally the culmination of the whole proceedings, in which Panel Members from both sides, with lively contributions from the floor, elaborated on how they benefited from discussions with each other and how they felt that this dialogue between the two sides should continue. After this, it was not surprising that there was a unanimous agreement to repeat the conference, once every two to three years. The University of Florida was offered as a possible venue for 1992, failing that, it will probably be held at the University of Keele in 1993.

The conference also agreed to establish an International Special Interest Group on CKBS, which is currently being administered by the DAKE Centre. If you are:

(i)   a DDB researcher with interests in DAI research, or

(ii)   a DAI researcher with interest in DDB research, or

(iii)   interested in CKBS applications

then this is the SIG for you. This SIG is run largely through email. If you wish to have further information on this SIG, please contact me.

I now return to the 17 selected papers included in this book. These papers are grouped under six heading as follows:

> Cooperation Framework: DB Perspectives (3 papers)
> Cooperation Framework: AI Perspectives (3 papers)
> Knowledge Revision (3 papers)
> Conflict Resolution Strategies (2 papers)
> Multi-agent Development Model (2 papers)
> Interactions in Data/Knowledge Bases (4 papers)

Cooperation Framework: DB Perspectives

Cooperating Agents – A Database Perspective
S.M. Deen

Meeting the Cooperative Problem Solving Challenge: A Database-Centered Approach
S. Chakravarthy, S.B. Navathe, K. Karlapalem, A. Tanaka

Intelligent Agents in Federative Expert Systems: Concepts and Implementation
St. Kirn, G. Schlageter

As recommended by the Programme Committee this book starts with my paper since it attempts to give a database view of what we called CKBS, and explains the need (as viewed by the Conference Chairman) to bring the DDB and DAI experts together – the principal motivation behind this conference. The paper also presents an agent and a cooperation model, the latter based on distributed transaction as a general facility for cooperative problem solving. In the second paper, Chakravarthy et al provide an alternative view of what cooperation might mean in a database context, and suggest a framework to support a blackboard model. The third paper, by Kirn and Schlageter, describes a federative cooperation among intelligent agents and discusses features needed to make expert systems really competent for cooperative problem solving.

Cooperation Framework: AI Perspectives

Diffusing Inference: An Inference Method for Distributed Problem Solving
Y. Kitamura, T. Okumoto

ARCHON: A Cooperation Framework for Industrial Process Control
C. Roda, N.R. Jennings, E.H. Mamdani

Collaboration of Knowledge Bases via Knowledge Based Coordination
Donald E. Steiner, Dirk E. Mahling, Hans Haugeneder

Kitamura proposes an intermediate problem solving strategy that bridges the gap between task and result sharing approaches by using local knowledge to reduce the search space. The second paper in this group, by Roda et al, is from the ARCHON project (of EEC ESPRIT), and it describes a pragmatic cooperation strategy for industrial process control. Steiner et al in the third paper propose an agent model and a set of cooperation strategies for applications, which could permit human agents as well. In a curious way all these three cooperation frameworks have a close proximity to the one proposed by Deen from a database perspective. Perhaps this is an indication of a convergence between some DAI and DDB approaches – an objective of this conference.

Knowledge Revision

Distributed Truth Maintenance
Michael N. Huhns, David M. Bridgeland

Cooperative Interaction as Strategic Belief Revision
Julia Rose Galliers

The Role of Cooperation in Multi-Agent Learning
Sati S. Sian

Huhns and Bridgeland present an innovative approach which includes an algorithm for truth maintenance that guarantees local consistency for each agent and global consistency for data shared by agents. Galliers proposes a model of automatic belief revision, in which each agent decides if and how to revise its belief on recognition of the wish of another that it should do so. In contrast,

Sian presents a multi-agent learning model in which an agent can learn (update its own experience) from the experiences of others through cooperation.

Conflict Resolution Strategies

Conflict Resolution Strategies for Cooperating Expert Agents
Susan Lander, Victor R. Lesser, Margaret E. Connell

A Computational Model for Conflict Resolution in Cooperative Design Systems
Mark Klein, Arthur B. Baskin

Lander and Lesser present a cooperating experts framework in which local strategies are invoked selectively with trade offs between quality of solutions, processing required and effect on the global solution. In contrast, Klein and Baskin advocate a conflict resolution strategy modelled on human-group problem-solving, in which each agent represents a domain of expertise which includes its own technique of conflict resolution.

Multi-agent Development Model

Modeling Concurrency in Rule-Based Development Environments
Naser S. Barghouti, Gail E. Kaiser

The MCS Multi-Agent Testbed: Developments and Experiments
James Doran, Horacio Carvajal, Y.J. Choo, Yueling Li

Barghouti and Kaiser propose a multi-agent expert system for software development and focus on the resolution of update conflict by a preclaim (database term) strategy. In the second paper J. Doran et al describe a multi-agent test-bed, which uses a complex planner as an interface engine and has been used to study human social systems.

Interactions in Data/Knowledge Bases

Epistemic Logic as a Framework for Federated Information Systems
Magnus Boman, Paul Johannesson

Cooperative Query Answering via Type Abstraction Hierarchy
Wesley W. Chu, Qiming Chen, Rei-Chi Lee

Contracts in Database Federations
Matts Ahlsén, Paul Johannesson

Object Recognition and Retrieval in the Back System
Carsten Kindermann, Paolo Randi

Some database experts interpret the term cooperation more widely than is done in DAI, to include interaction in data/knowledge as a form of cooperation. This view has been represented in the four papers of this section.

Boman and Johannesson describe a cooperation model based on epistemic logic for federated information systems, whereas Chu et al provide a scheme to employ domain knowledge at different data abstraction levels, in cooperation, to answer inexact database queries.

Ahlsén and Johannesson advocate a model for information sharing in data/knowledge bases in which the cooperation is specified through bilateral contracts. Kindermann and Randi discuss integration issues between data and knowledge bases as a form of a cooperative integration.

Acknowledgements

Finally it is my great pleasure to acknowledge the generous assistance I received from so many people who helped to make this conference a great success. First, my thanks to all the members of the organising and programme committees for their assistance, with special thanks to Dr. O.P. Brereton, conference secretary, without whose assistance I could not have staged this conference. I am also thankful to the session chairmen and the referees for their invaluable help. Persons whose names do not appear in any official committees, but nevertheless provided essential services included Najib Al-Sammaraie, Mike Green, Athula Herath, Yufan Hu, Baird Ndovie and Andy Seddon – all doctoral students. Thanks are also due to our secretaries Kendal Allen and Jayne Beardmore, technicians Rob Ankers and Ian Marr and, of course, to the Head of the Department of Computer Science, Alan Treherne. I must also mention the authors, presenters and the delegates for making the conference a professionally stimulating event.

Although unusual, I should also thank the Keele University Hospitality for accommodation and excellent catering services, particularly the grand conference dinner which every delegate enjoyed so much.

I am also very grateful to all the sponsors, particularly to the Information Technology Division of the Department of Trade and Industry, the US Air Force European Office of Aerospace Research and Development, and the European Research Office of the US Army, for their financial supports.

Finally, I trust the readers will find the papers in this book as stimulating as the participants found their presentation at the conference.

March 1991   S.M. Deen
                                                          Conference Chairman

CKBS '90

List of Referees

In addition to the Programme Committee Members, the following
persons also reviewed papers.

H.D. Boecker
O.P. Brereton
B. Ergin
Fankhauser
H.M.A.C. Herath
N.R. Jennings
W. Klaus
B. Ndovie
T.C. Rakow
C. Roda

Contents

Conflict Resolution Strategies

Multi-agent Development Model

Interactions in Data/Knowledge Bases

Cooperation Framework: DB Perspectives

COOPERATING AGENTS - A DATABASE PERSPECTIVE

S.M. Deen

DAKE Centre

University of Keele

England

ABSTRACT

A Cooperating Knowledge Based System (CKBS) is a collection of autonomous and potentially heterogeneous, objects (or units) which cooperate together in solving problems. An object can be a data/rule base or an agent which can be intelligent or unintelligent. The paper investigates the issues in CKBS from a database perspective, which is distinguished from the AI perspective by its emphasis on a common architecture with well-defined components and interfaces, performance efficiency and concurrency/reliability/recovery. The paper describes a generic object model, and also a hybrid cooperation model which incorporates the blackboard approach within the framework of a distributed transaction. The object model has a layered structure, complete with the necessary software components for run-time execution. The hybrid cooperation model is claimed to reduce unnecessary communications, while retaining the effectiveness of a blackboard approach. Three exploratory applications - travel planning, image recognition and air-traffic control - have been used to illustrate this approach.

The concepts presented in this paper are being further developed in the COSMOS project, in which a number of British Universities and Polytechnics, collaborate.

1 INTRODUCTION

Recent research activities in AI and databases seem to have established two important facts: (i) there are some common problem domains where a dialogue between AI and DB communities is fruitful, and (ii) there are many industrial applications of AI where some database facilities are required. Several workshops organised by M. Brodie et al [1] and the numerous research projects on data/knowledge base integration [2] bear testimony to these twin assertions. It would appear to us that the topic of Cooperating Knowledge Based Systems (CKBSs) as defined below, constitutes a further common domain where both the communities, particularly the researchers in distributed AI (DAI) and distributed databases (DDBs) can fruitfully cooperate. There is a close parallel between the issues in distributed databases and multi-agent systems (MAS)[3] of DAI.

Two autonomous systems (as nodes) may be said to cooperate in problem solving if both have to exchange intermediate results in solving the problem. Since many such systems require volume processing of data and rules, they are of interest to database researchers. From the database perspective, we are interested in the following three issues:

1. General Architecture

   We would like to develop a general architecture with well-defined interfaces, abstraction levels and components, so that such a system can be used for a class of applications, rather than a single application. A formal framework will allow the development of standardised facilities.

2. System Performance

   Within this general framework we would like to design a system that is operationally efficient. A cooperating system is expensive in communications terms. The need to exchange partial results can be reduced by providing each node with some basic information about the other, and by pre-planning the solution steps. This is a strategy we generally follow in distributed databases; however it may not be necessarily consistent with a pure AI approach. There is however a class of problems, such as in image recognition from raw data (signals from sensors), where complete global information cannot be realistically supplied to each node. Sensor data have to be divided into subareas and possibly abstracted for data reduction, and this leads to what we would refer to as *boundary problems*. Heuristics or some other algorithms will be required to resolve these conflicts, possibly using data from overlapping subareas. While the design of the these algorithms may not be considered as database research, we must provide anchor points in our architecture where these algorithms can be hooked.

   Another possibility that one might explore is to design nodes in such a way that refinements of intermediate results are carried out by higher-level nodes, thus reducing internodal communications. In that event the problem will be similar to that of distributed databases, but it is not a practicable proposition in many applications.

3. Concurrency, reliability and recovery

   These are essential facilities that an operational system must have, and for which a proper architectural framework is needed, as proposed in this paper. Apart from this architectural framework, we shall not consider these issues explicitly.

Having indicated our database perspective, we would define a Cooperating Knowledge Based System (CKBS) as a collection of autonomous, potentially heterogeneous and possibly pre-existing, objects (or units) which cooperate in problem solving in a decentralised environment. The term object used here should not be confused with the concept of object in object oriented programming, although our objects could also be encapsulated. An object can be a knowledge server (a data/rule base, sometimes referred to here as knowledge base) or an agent, such as a financial adviser or an intelligent robot. While an agent may have its own private belief, a knowledge server holds shared knowledge. In our approach a CKBS, like a database, is more concerned with practical usability and performance as outlined earlier, rather than the purity of ideas and their faithful representation; this apart, a CKBS is similar to Cooperative Distributed Problem Solving (CDPS) systems of Durfee et al [4]. Our reason for the definition of CKBS is not to re-invent the wheel, but to establish a context for this paper, independent of the DAI concepts of CDPS. We would like to thinks that the relationship of CKBS to distributed databases is similar to that of CDPS to muti-agent systems. We believe that some of the concepts developed in distributed databases could be useful to MAS in general, and CKBS in particular.

We have recently undertaken a project called Coordination Strategies for Multi-object Systems (COSMOS) to explore this area. *Cooperation* may be viewed as a special case of *coordination* where the objects interact in a friendly rather than in a hostile environment. Our approach in COSMOS is based on a generic object (agent) model and a hybrid co-operation framework which incorporates blackboard ideas within a concept of distributed transaction[20], as discussed in this paper.

However we shall begin with a review of current research and our own ideas in section 2, followed by our object (agent) model in section 3 and hybrid cooperation framework in section 4. The effectiveness of our approach will be illustrated in section 5, with a number of diverse but exploratory applications: one main application from travel services and two supporting applications from air-traffic control and image recognition. A conclusion is given in section 6.

2 REVIEW

Research in distributed Artificial Intelligence (DAI) began in earnest from 1980 with some projects based on earlier prototypes, such as the HEARSAY speech system [5]. Recently a number of prototypes have been proposed in multi-agent systems: among these are the DVMT of Durfee et al [6,7], Contract-Net of Davies and Smith [8,9], Actors model of Agha et al [10,11], Air-traffic control models of Steeb et al [12-14], MACE system of Gasser et al [15], and Agora of Bisiani et al [16]. Many of them are based on the blackboard architecture [17] for cooperation.

Despite this large number of systems there has not been much attempt to unify the field of MAS with an integrated perspective [3], except some generalised blackboard models [27-29]. Agent modeling is a case in point. Although many of these researchers employ some form of agent descriptions, they do not propose any comprehensive model of an agent; instead they often represent only the agent's actions. Kamel and Syed [18], discuss an interesting object-oriented approach for MAS, but do not suggest any agent models; likewise Bond [19] indicates some behavioral characteristics of agents, but does not go any further.

Major achievements in heterogeneous distributed databases have been the development of homogenisation and integration facilities [21,25,26] backed by a sound transaction model[20], to an extent that commercial products can now be built, and are indeed appearing on the market [23]. Although a node in a distributed database is assumed to be autonomous, and sometimes heterogeneous, there is no active cooperation even in subquery executions and onward transmission of results. The characteristics of a DDB are:

1. A DDB handles only knowledge servers but not agents (as defined earlier).

2. A DDB is a general purpose facility to retrieve and update data in the knowledge servers; it does not automatically produce global solutions purely from local com-putation without a global schema (or equivalent tables). An exception to this is a multi-database system where there is no global schema, but the user is assumed to provide the link [22, 25].

3. There is a unique answer to a query.

In contrast, we may define the characteristics of our CKBS, borrowing some ideas from [13], as:

1. It handles both agents and knowledge servers, which are generally heterogeneous.

2. Objects and skills may display many to many relationships, with some objects having overlapping, even identical, capabilities.

3. Each object has an immediate circle of acquaintances which may be different from those of another object of even the same type. Its acquaintances may be different from those of another object.

4. An agent may have both private and shared knowledge.

5. An object decomposes a problem on the basis of some knowledge of the environment and it allocates the tasks on the basis of its knowledge of its immediate acquaintances. However, this knowledge of the environment and the acquaintances may not be complete or up-to-date.

6. If a receiving agent is unable to solve an allocated problem, it may pass it to an acquaintance who can. This implies that *both the task decomposition and allocation processes are wholly dynamic.*

7. A receiving agent may reason about the information it has received and enter into a dialogue with the sender or other relevant agents, in order to resolve conflicts (i.e. *dynamic negotiation*).

8. The agents must produce a globally coherent solution in accordance with specified criteria.

9. There may not be any unique solution to a problem.

Three interesting criteria of a multi-agent system (apart from decentralised control and potential heterogeneity) seem to be:

1. Each suitable agent should be able to solve its problem in consultation with other agents as needed.

2. There is no centralised global view point[3].

3. Globally coherent solutions must be obtained through local computation alone [3].

These characteristics have a number of consequences. The limitation of partial global knowledge is generally offset by increased inter-agent communications. The less the global knowledge, the more is the need for communications, but the communication cost can be unacceptably high[13].

We, however, accept these criteria except that we would like to feel free to include a comprehensive global view point (as in distributed databases) as part of each object model, if this improves the overall system performance (taking the resultant update overheads into account). To reduce inter-object communications, particularly when there are too many objects communicating with each other, we use superior objects (in an aggregation hierarchy) to control this communication cost where appropriate. This hierarchy is problem-dependent, and can be defined automatically during the task decomposition/allocation stage of each new problem as needed. Reasoning can be carried out in two stages: at the task allocation stage (pre-event), and at the acceptance stage, i.e. when the result is presented (post-event). Whenever possible, we opt for pre-event reasoning (with the help of global information), as it reduces communication cost.

We support global information in a decentralised form; each object can learn and retain its new knowledge, although the global knowledge may not be identical in each case. There is an associated update problem which we view as minor compared to the improvement in performance this offers. We also recognise that all the necessary information (as global knowledge) on other objects (foreign objects) may not be always available, and this might require a search to locate a suitable foreign object, with additional communication overheads.

In our case all computations are object-based (i.e. local) and global coherence is partly enforced by pre-event reasoning during the task decomposition process, subject to some final confirmation by post event reasoning, where relevant. In a hierarchic structure, each higher-level object is responsible for the subsequent decomposition of its task into subtasks for its lower-level objects. In this scheme the resolution of *boundary problems* , as indicated earlier, is left to the individual applications, where appropriate objects will invoke suitable algorithms as needed. The task execution plan (see later) will ensure that an object gets the partial results it needs from other relevant objects, at a minimal communication cost.

3 OBJECT MODEL

We propose a generic framework for an object model (figure 1), based on our earlier work in distributed databases [22]. In this framework each object contains a base which is the basic autonomous system and a head which provides the additional facility needed for cooperation . The head has three main components as listed below:

1. Global Support Facilities

   - Global Module (run-time software)
   - Auxiliary Database System (metadata and supplementary functions)

2. Global Models

   - User Model (facilities visible to end user)
   - Environment Model (the model of the operational environment)
   - Participation Model (models of the participating objects)

Object Module (Figure -1)

3. Basic Facilities

- Communication facility (to communicate with other objects)
- Home Model (the model of this object)

Each object in our scheme is autonomous and reusable, with an open interface, which enables it to participate in more than one cooperating system with appropriate upper levels. An object must also support inter-operability. Each object (the home object), has an immediate circle of acquaintances (foreign objects); the home and the foreign objects together participate, as participating objects, in cooperating problem solving. Although an object can be the duplicate of another object, it may not necessarily have the same set of acquaintances. Each acquaintance, in its turn as a home object, may have a different set of acquaintances. There could be many levels of cooperation in which an object can participate. In addition, an object can be hierarchic (as in aggregation): an object (superobject) being made up of other objects (subobjects). For instance in air-traffic control, regional controllers cooperate together, but a regional controller itself could represent a lower-level cooperative system among flight-path allocators, transit controllers, airport-arrival/departure controllers and monitoring stations. A monitoring station could be a hierarchic object consisting of a collection of radars and other monitoring equipment.

Global Support Facilities

The Global Module consists of the software needed for the global operation, whereas the private auxiliary database system (ADBS) (figure 2) holds the directory information and supplementary operational facility. This facility is essential if we are to provide open

9

interfaces to support pre-existing objects. For instance if a travel agent (software) X can yield all the flights between points A and B in a single query, and another travel agent Y can yield only one flight per query, then the ADBS of Y could simulate the capability of X by generating one query per flight from the original single query.

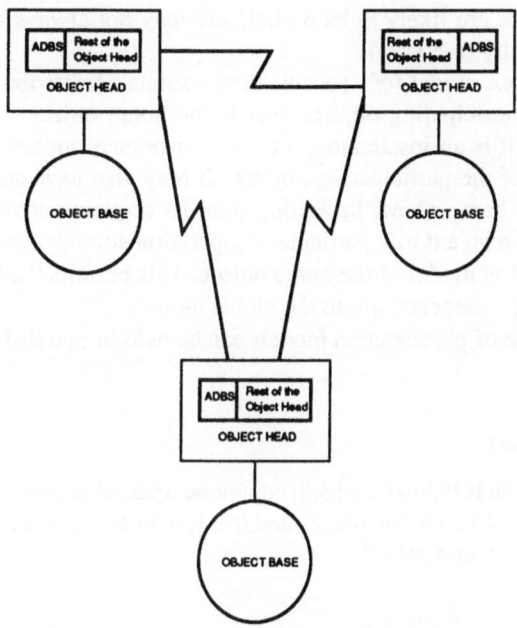

The Auxiliary Database System (ADBS) supplement the capability of the Object (Figure - 2)

The global module is equivalent to the run-time control system of the DDB, and will include all the necessary software to make the cooperating system work. The facilities supported by the auxiliary database system include:

- global models descriptions
- cached data/knowledge from knowledge servers
- replicated data/knowledge for knowledge servers
- integration information and integration facilities[21]
- special operations to cater for operations that are not available at this object

In a distributed database this role is fulfilled by a supplementary or subsidiary database[22]. Integration information will provide missing information backed by integration facilities as elaborated in the next section.

Global Models

The *user model* specifies the facilities of the cooperating system visible to an end-user; the user-task is specified in terms of these facilities. A user model has two parts: a task specification model, which is used to specify a task, and a response presentation model, which is used to present responses to the end user. All user queries are validated against this model.

The *environment model* provides a description of the operational environment which consists of object classes, their inter-relationships and capabilities, including functions and procedures that can be invoked for integration. The contents of both the environment and participation models are likely to be partial, and may not always be up-to-date; they can also vary dynamically (see later).

The *participation model* (*cf.* participation schema of distributed databases) consists of entries for all participating objects, that is the home object and its immediate circle of acquaintances. It is an instantiation of the environment model, with items taken from the home models of the participating objects. It may also have special fields which hold experiences of the home object in dealing with its acquaintances. All items of a home model may not be relevant to a particular cooperation strategy, and therefore we insist in having a participation model of the home object. This permits the home model of a home object to be defined independently to the global models.

The information of participation models can be held in two different ways[24]:

- Cache

- Replicated data

If the information is held as cache, it cannot be updated automatically, except through a cache update policy[24]. On the other hand if it is held as replicated data, then one can use a weak consistency in update[22].

Basic Facilities

The communication facility consists of a set of protocols, appropriate to the object and coordination model. These protocols should be designed as standard, to be transmitted over a file server within the ISO/OSI framework.

The home model is an abstract description of an object and its characteristics, and all access to the object is directed only through this home model, which acts as the encapsulation barrier. The home model is equivalent to local (nodal) schema of a distributed database and it contains data types for the properties and information content of the object concerned. Normally only a subset of these properties appear in the participation model.

The home model of a hardware based agent will contain all its relevant physical properties, including information on its skills, performance, techniques it uses, reliability, faults, faults diagnostics, potential application environment, and relationships to other agents (e.g. duplicate capability).

An object base along with its home model and the communication facility is known as a basic object, and is independent of any specific coordination environment. A basic object can participate in any suitable cooperating system, with appropriate upper levels (global models and global support facility). A basic object may also represent, hidden from the upper layers, a hierarchy or another level of cooperation, in which case its home model will act as the global model of the lower-level objects. A lower-level object can sometimes be a pure basic object, without the upper layers, e.g, a sensor.

An agent may or may not be intelligent, depending on the content of its head, which may vary from agent to agent. Typically a sensor as an agent is unlikely to be intelligent.

4 COOPERATION FRAMEWORK

We would like to group the cooperation strategies for the application domains of our interest into the following classes:

- Transaction oriented strategy

- Recognition oriented strategy

- Control oriented strategy

Although carried out independently, our classification is very similar to the one given in ref [4]. In a transaction oriented strategy, the objective is to produce new information, such as data, rules, text or images, using a top-down approach , in which each task is decomposed into subtasks recursively - finally into small granules that can be executed by an object. Any appropriate object can initiate the processing. Some examples of a transaction oriented strategy are: a complex query, such as a travel plan where several expert systems cooperate to produce the answer; response integration where several expert systems discuss an issue to reach a consensus; and iterative design where several expert systems cooperate in producing a final design by iterative refinement from a rough plan.

In a recognition oriented strategy, the objective is to identify/recognise patterns from some input which could be raw data or monitoring data. This strategy uses a bottom-up approach, in contrast to the transaction oriented strategy; it also causes the boundary conflicts mentioned earlier. An example of this strategy can be found in the DVMT project of Durfee et al [6].

A control oriented strategy differs from a transaction strategy in that its objective is to control an operation so that it can be completed successfully, despite potential distractions, possibly in a hostile environment. It often involves planning and sometimes forecast and negotiation. Typical examples are: air-traffic control, network traffic management, automated process control (with robots) and guided missiles.

Although these strategies are diverse requiring different types of solution, we claim that the agent model proposed earlier can be used as a general facility in all of these. Following this idea of generalisation we present below a hybrid cooperation framework which also can be used by all three strategies. We shall first develop this framework in terms of the transaction-oriented strategy alone, and then in the next section we shall show how it can be adapted for the other two strategies as well.

The blackboard framework represents a general technique for task decomposition, scheduling and inter-agent information exchange, but it is communication-intensive[3], even in a multi-panel scenario, since the agents have to communicate through their respective panels. In contrast in a transaction model of a DDB the decomposed tasks are allocated to appropriate nodes depending on their abilities. These nodes can use other nodes if needed, in a number of ways [22]. This is achieved in a DDB by holding the complete global knowledge in the form of a global schema (or equivalent), but in a CKBS we do not have a complete global view.

We propose here a hybrid scheme, incorporating ideas from both the blackboard framework and transaction models with the following main changes to the blackboard approach:

1. A tentative schedule (an execution plan) is prepared in an optimal manner by using the partial global information available. A dynamic strategy stipulates subsequent

12

actions, where to find/send intermediate results, and what to do if the allocation is incorrect.

2. The relevant acquaintances communicate with one another directly (bypassing their panel), guided by the specification in the schedule.

3. A low-cost facility exists for each object to learn more about the environment and acquaintances, and thus to update the global knowledge. This allows the object to offset the effect of partial and out of date global information.

Our main objective above is to reduce the communication cost of the blackboard framework, while retaining its flexibility. We view the communication network as a black box, as assumed in distributed databases. Since each object is encapsulated with possibly private knowledge, we do not need to provide any facility for the preservation of global consistency in updates for these objects. A diagram for our hybrid model is given in figure 3, which is explained below briefly.
The model has the following components:

1. The **Task Manager** which manages a task (i.e. a user request or query) and is in overall control. It may support different coordination strategy for specific situations.

2. The **Higher Decomposer** which decomposes a task into subtasks using the environmental model. Here only object types are used.

3. The **Higher Recomposer** which produces a presentation format for the final answer.

4. The **Lower Decomposer** which decomposes the subtasks into nodal tasks, using the participation models. Here object types are instantiated by actual objects.

5. The **Lower Recomposer** produces a recomposition and response plans, using integration tools. It describes how the final result is produced.

6. The **Allocator** produces an execution plan (made up of many subplans) and allocates nodal tasks optimally, taking network performance into account.

7. The **Communicator** supports protocols and provides the inter-object communication facility with a time-out condition. A message may include a dynamic coordination plan if supported by the Task Manager.

8. There are a number of **Learners** at various levels which are invoked if a decomposition is unsuccessful and also if a task (or its decomposed components) succeeds/fails (to acquire experiences).

9. Integration facilities consists of an **Integrator** for data/knowledge integration and conflict resolution. An integrator produces a final form of the integrated results using converters and mediators. A converter is a simple function which carries out reversible conversions, such as mile to kilometer, while a mediator is a complex procedure which might lead to a compromise solution. It may not have a inverse.

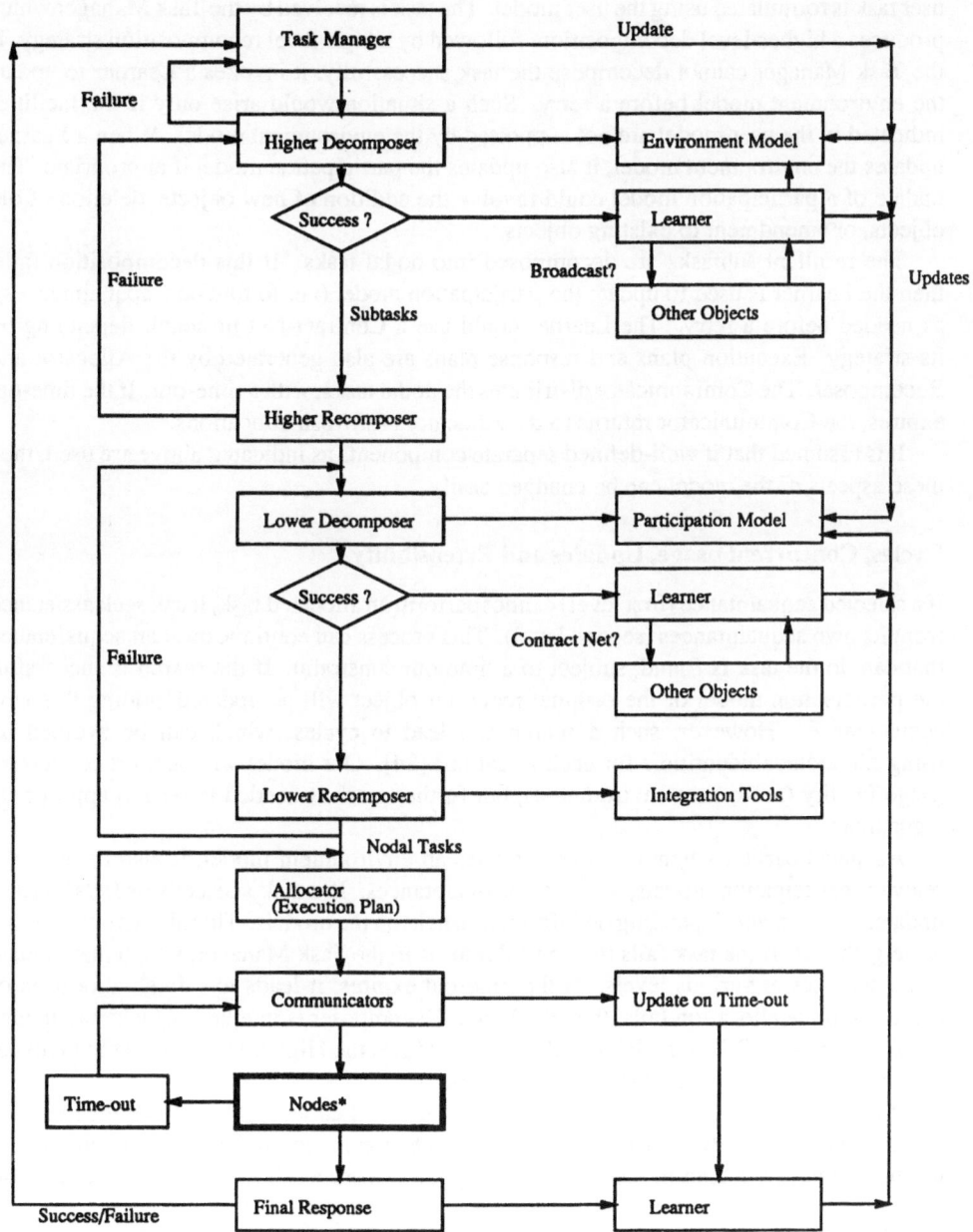

Hybrid Cooperation Strategy (Figure -3)

Learning at the decomposition stage can be accomplished either by a cache or replication policy. In this paper we assume learning by cache which requires re-cacheing. In this case, data can become out of date, and a periodic re-cacheing policy is needed. However, if replication is used instead, the owner nodes (from which data are copied) will automatically send out update messages whenever any change has occurred. Returning to the diagram, the user task is formulated using the user model. The task is received by the Task Manager which produces a higher-level decomposition, followed by a high-level recomposition strategy. If the Task Manager cannot decompose the task successfully, it invokes a Learner to update the environment model before a retry. Such a situation would arise only if the facilities indicated in the user model are not supported by the environment model. When a Learner updates the environment model, it also updates the participation model if appropriate. The update of a participation model could involve the addition of new objects, deletion of old objects, or amendment to existing objects.

The resultant subtasks are decomposed into nodal tasks. If this decomposition fails, then the Learner is used to update the participation model (i.e. to find new acquaintances), as needed before a retry. The Learner could use a Contract-Net protocol, depending on its strategy. Execution plans and response plans are also generated by the Allocator and Recomposer. The Communicator distributes the nodal tasks, with a time-out. If the time-out expires, the Communicator returns to the Allocators for fresh allocations.

It is assumed that if well-defined separate components as indicated above are used, then these aspects of the model can be changed easily.

Cycles, Concurrent usage, Updates and Extensibility

If a selected acquaintance (first level) cannot perform an allocated task, it can seek assistance from its own acquaintances (second level). This process can continue until an acquaintance that can do the task is found, subject to a time-out constraint. If the search is successful, the participation model of the original requester object will be updated, adding this new acquaintance. However, such a search can lead to cycles, which can be avoided by using hierarchical identifiers for each nodal task[24]. Our model will support concurrent usage facility (multi-user environment), but further work is needed to design appropriate algorithms.

As stated earlier, when a Learner updates an environment model, it also updates the relevant participation models, with new acquaintances. If a task succeeds or fails, further updates can be made depending on information held on the models. This allows experiences to be gathered. If the task fails the control returns to the Task Manager, which may update some statistics at various levels. If the time-out expires, it leads to a fresh allocation of tasks, but if the allocation fails, then the Lower Decomposer is invoked, which may in turn invoke a Learner. When the Higher Recomposer fails, the Higher Decomposer is invoked, which in turn might invoke the Higher Learner.

It may be observed that the communication cost for Learning is low, since the Learners are invoked only rarely at task decomposition. The total communication cost could be up to 50 percent lower than in the corresponding framework as shown in figure 5 of section 5.1.

The user should be able to define new data types and functions (abstract data types) with the help of those available in the user, environment and participation models. It should also be possible to create new agents dynamically.

5 APPLICATION EXAMPLES

We shall illustrate the use of the agent and cooperation frameworks proposed above by considering three examples, one from each of the cooperation strategies discussed earlier:

one example from an ubiquitous travel service, one from image recognition and the final one from air-traffic control; the last two examples will be only cursory.

5.1 Travel Plan (Transaction-oriented Strategy)

Let us consider a simplified model of a travel service where there are a number of agents who cooperate together for booking plane tickets with hotel reservation and car hire. This example has four useful characteristics for our present purposes:

1. There is a need, at least in some queries, to exchange partial results.

2. The objects are heterogeneous.

3. The objects display overlapping, in some cases identical, capabilities.

4. The relationships between objects and skills are many to many.

We begin with a user model:

User Model

As stated earlier the user model has a task formulation model for the specification of tasks, and a response presentation model for response presentation, as shown below:

Task formulation model

```
Single (Cno, Source, Destination, Apdep, Quality)
where [condition (...)]

Return (Cno, Source, Destination, Apdep, Apret, Quality)
where [condition (...)]

Hotel (Cno,Area,Location,Asdate,Addate,Price-range,Unit,Rating,
                                                         Quality)
where [condition (...)]

Car (Cno, Area, Location, Asdate, Addate, Model, Quality)
where [condition (...)]
```

Response Presentation Model

```
Single (Cno, Source, Destination, Carrier Flight, Depdate,
Deptime, Arrdate, Price Unit, Quality, Condition)

Return (Cno, Source, Destination, Carrier Flight, Depdate,
        Deptime, Arrdate, Carrier Flight, Retdate, Rettime,
        Price Unit, Quality, Condition)

Hotel (Cno, Area, Location, Sdate, Ddate, Rating, Price Unit,
        Quality)
```

```
Car (Cno, Area, Location, Sdate, Ddate, Model, Price Unit,
     Quality)
```

We assume the item Quality holds a quality rating of the agent as perceived by this home agent.

Environment Model

The environment model consists of object classes, class-relationships, and function list (which includes all functions and procedures for invocation) The object classes are:

```
Airline (Name, Area, Quality, Last-used, Last-changed)

Trag    (Name, Area, Quality, Last-used, Last-changed)

Bucket  (Name, Area, Quality, Last-used, Last-changed)

Tbureau (Name, Area, Quality, Last-used, Last-changed)

Car-rentals (Name, Area, Quality, Last-used, Last-changed)
```

Trag stand for general high street travel agents, Bucket for cheap ticket agents and Tbureau for Tourist bureaus which specialise in hotel booking.

Class-link (Obname	Service	Last-used	Last-changed	Home)
Airline	Single	-	-	-
Airline	Return	-	-	-
Airline	Hotel	-	-	-
Airline	Car	-	-	-
Bucket	Return	-	-	-
Trag	Single	-	-	-
Trag	Return	-	-	-
Trag	Hotel	-	-	-
Trag	Car	-	-	-
Tbureau	Hotel	-	-	-

```
Regions (Area, Location, Last-used, Last-changed, Home)

Functions (Name, Tuple, Inverse, Parameters, Comments)
```

New or user-defined functions are added from the top and all functions are searched from the top, so that a user can over-ride an existing function by adding a new function of the same name. The Class-link relation lists skills of agent classes, Region yields location of places, and Functions lists library functions that are available.

Participation Model

Some examples of a participation model are:

Airline	(Name	Area	Quality	Last-Used	Last-Changed)
	BA	Europe	0.6		
	BA	World	0.5		
	BA	Germany	0.6		
	LH	Germany	0.6		
	AF	France	0.5		

Trag	(Name	Area	Quality	Last-Used	Last-Changed)
	Cook	Belgium			
	Cook	France			
	Cook	Japan			

Bucket	(Name	Area	Quality	Last-Uned	Last-Changed)
	Stravel	Europe			
	UST	USA			

Tbureau	(Name	Area	Quality	Last-used	Last-Changed)
	Cook	Europe			
	Amex	USA			
	Ytour	Yugoslavia			

Car-hire	(Name	Area	Quality	Last-Used	Last-Changed)
	Alamo	Atlanta			
	Budget	Atlanta			
	Budget	London			

Regions	(Area	Location	Last-used	Last-changed	Home)
	Africa	Nairobi			
	France	Paris			
	Europe	Brussels			
	USA	Atlanta			
	USSR	Moscow			

Home Model and Communication Facility

The home model consists of the description of the home object, which is transparent to the global operations. For an airlines agent, such a model is likely to include items such as Start-city, Destination-city, Flight-no, Aircraft, Start-time, Destination-time, days and dates in which the flights are available, Price calculation procedure, etc. Since the specifications of the home model and communication facility are not needed to appreciate our presentation, we shall not discuss them any further here, except to point out that we assume the basic objects to be capable of performing their tasks.

Tasks

Consider the following user tasks

```
Return  (Cno Source      Destination Apdep         Apret          Qualit
Return  [C10 London      Atlanta     Oct 12 ± 3    Oct 20 ± 3     > 0.4]
Where  [Retdate - Depdate] = 8

Hotel    (Cno   Area    Location    Asdate    Addate    ...Rate
Hotel    [C10   USA     Atlanta     X         Y         ***]
Where  [x = Return.Arrdate AND Y = (Return.Retdate-1)]

Car      (Cno   Area    Location    Asdate    Addate    %...)
Car      [C10   USA     Atlanta     X    Y
Where  [X=Return.Arrdate AND Y = (Return.Retdate)]
```

Processing

This query is decomposed into three subtasks. Return, Hotel and Car, and the appropriate answer form produced. Converter for ratings and currency are also invoked. These subtasks can be executed three separate ways.

1. By Airline alone

2. By Trag alone

3. By Tbureau, Bucket and Car-hire in cooperation, as shown in figure 4.

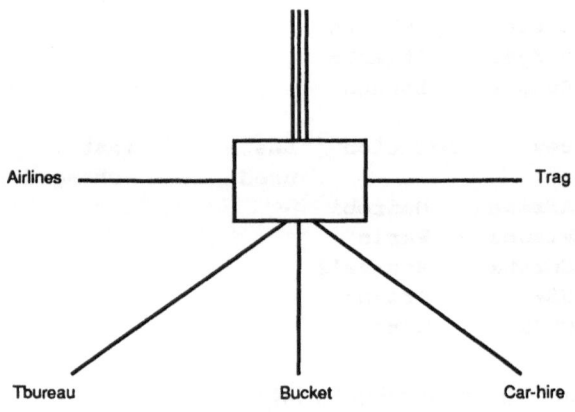

Query Tree (Figure - 4)

Assume we wish to find the minimum cost by exploring all three approaches. The Allocator will select suitable agents for the task/subtasks. The Airline and Trag agents will evaluate their response and return them to the requester node. For the third approach, which is more interesting to us, the agents must work in cooperation in two phases.

Phase (i): determination of the common dates for which flight, hotel and car are available.

Phase (ii): calculating the traveling costs for these common dates.

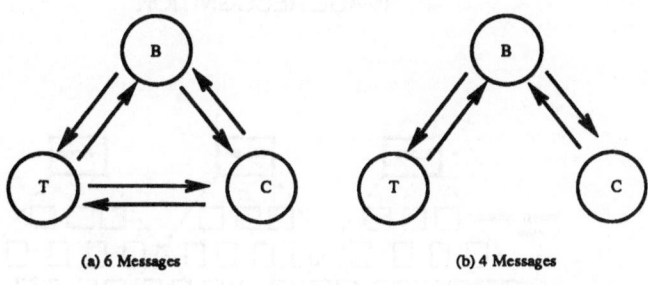

(a) 6 Messages   (b) 4 Messages

(Figure - 5)

In **Phase (i)** there are two ways in which the agents can communicate the common dates as shown in figure 5(a) and 5(b). In 5(a) each agent communicates with the others involving 6 messages, while in 5(b) T (Tbureau) and C (Car hire) communicate to B (Bucket), and the Bucket forwarding the final dates to T and C, with a total of 4 messages. We choose 5(b) to minimise the number of messages.

Once the **Phase (i)** is completed, the results are sent to the originating node. If any of the above agents are unable to perform the action, they can invoke others in turn, as explained earlier. The originating node will produce the final answer for minimum traveling cost, with help of the Lower Recomposer and appropriate converters.

If the task was for a World Tour rather than a return flight, then the environment model would have been updated, as it does not have an entry for World (Cno.....). If the Bucket shop UST does not cover Atlanta, it will invoke its known acquaintances and if successful, the participation model of the requester node, will be updated accordingly. On the other hand if the flight is for a city in the USSR, the Learner will be invoked to update the participation model with new agents, since none of the flight agents in the present participation model for the requester node covers USSR.

5.2 Image Recognition (Recognition-oriented Strategy)

We assume a general case of a number of first level objects (nodes) which are capable of recognising patterns of interest from raw sensor data. The capabilities of the objects may vary, and therefore the first task in a recognition process is the selection of an appropriate set of objects. We also assume that there are a large number of sensors, some or all of them may be required in a recognition process; sensors may be dynamically linked to nodes and shared by nodes, since the nodes cover overlapping sensed-areas, to reduce the boundary effects. Each node sits at the top of a hierarchical set of objects (generally nondisjoint) with sensors lying at the lowest level, as in figure 6.

There are two possible ways of linking the nodes, as shown in figure 7(a) and (b); 7(a) is communication intensive, while 7(b) is application dependent. Unless there is an

20

over-riding reason to the contrary, we advocate (b) as it is more efficient. We assume that wherever useful (at any level of the hierarchy), a superior object will be created for each application by the execution plan to reduce inter-object communications.

IMAGE RECOGNITION

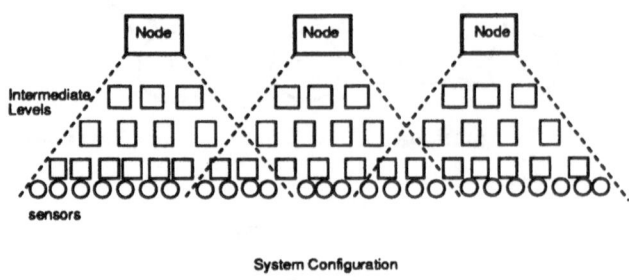

System Configuration
(Figure - 6)

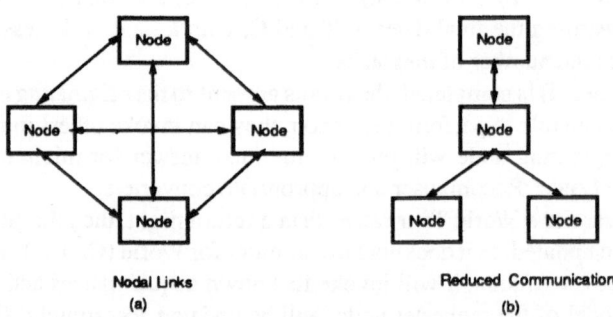

Nodal Links
(a)

Reduced Communication
(b)

(Figure - 7)

Image recognition is a bottom-up approach, since the raw data from sensors is processed upward leading to the recognition of the pattern. However, if we separate the preparation and execution stages, then we can generalise it with a top-down preparation phase backed by a bottom-up recognition phase. Furthermore, if we allow user-queries on recognised patterns, then we can treat this processing like a transaction model, where the pattern is a virtual item to be generated like a relational view facility. Thus, we can use the generalised transaction model given earlier. Consider the following skeleton for environment and participation models:

Environment Model

`Patterns (name,  identifier)`

`Object (pattern-id,  node-id)`

`Nodes (node-id,pattern,reliability,coverage,version parameter)`

Participation Model

Nodes (node-id,	pattern,	reliability,	coverage,	version	parameter)
N11	face	0.5	a12	3.6	. . . . . .
N12	face	0.6	a12	3.7	. . . .
N21	face	0.6	a13	2.1	. . . .

Task Processing Steps

1. The query from a pattern is validated against the expected structure and content of a pattern. The rest of the processing concerns the determination of the presence of a pattern.

2. The environmental model of the local node is used to identify the nodes of interest. If these nodes are not available, then the Learner will be invoked, thus leading to some updates of the environment and participation models. This stage will provide general information for decomposing the area to be sensed (Higher Decomposer).

3. In the next level the participation models are invoked, and if they are out of date, then the foreign nodes concerned can be contacted for their updated versions. Nodes are selected along with a recomposition strategy (which might include integrators to resolve the boundary problems). The execution strategy will indicate which node will communicate with which other node(s).

4. Each node considers its part of the task and decomposes it further, again using some decomposition strategy. The process continues until the sensors (lowest level) are reached.

5. When all decompositions are completed, the executions can begin, following the plans prepared.

Given an object at any level of the hierarchy, it will treat the cooperation model of its lower-level objects as a black box; however, a subordinate object can contribute to more than one superior object, if so specified at the setup stage. The global coherence (resolution of boundary problems) will be achieved with appropriate integrators at each level; this we would view to be an application-dependent function, which we do not consider here.

5.3 Air-traffic Control (Control-oriented Strategy)

We shall select air-traffic as an example of control-oriented strategy. We consider a simplified model where the world is divided into regions, each region having a set of airports as shown in figure 8.

22

The regional controllers provide flight paths and exercise transit controls, while airport controllers supervise the take-offs and landings of planes. An appropriate authority requests for a flight plan which is passed to the local regional controller who consults with the controller of the destination region and those of the intervening regions, if any. Each regional controller in turn may have to consult the relevant airports. Once everyone agrees, the aircraft may take off. In a changeover from one region to another, there will be a standard protocol, which might require the aircraft (another agent) to change position, height, direction and speed.

Skeletal environment and participation models will be:

Environment model

```
Region-map ( Source-reg,   Dest-reg,   Int-reg,   Quality)
             UK             Italy       France
             UK             Italy       Spain
             UK             USSR        France, Germany ...
```

Participation Model

```
Regports ( Region,    Airport,     Restriction, Communication point)
           UK         Heathrow
           UK         Manchester
           France     Paris
```

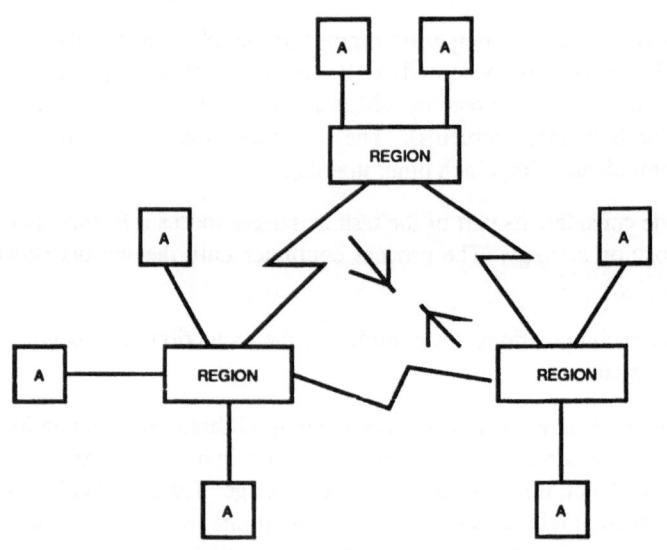

Air-Traffic Control

A is an airport

(Figure - 8)

Task Processing (Flying)

1. A requested route is passed to the Task Manager which invokes the Higher Decomposer to determine intervening regions on the route. The environment model of the local region is searched, and if the destination region is absent the learner is invoked, which may broadcast for assistance, resulting in the update of the environment and participation models. The process may lead to several sets of possible intervening regions. The Higher Decomposer invokes the appropriate structure for the result presentation.

2. The Lower Decomposer invokes the most convenient set of regions, following a decomposition strategy, extracts their contact addresses, and passes them to the proposed schedule. If the answer is unfavorable, it may choose another set of intervening regions, again following a decomposition strategy. If the destination airport is busy, and if the original requester is happy with a nearby airport, the Decomposer will select one. The integrator will be invoked for sector-change protocols. If the process is successful, a route plan will then be ready. The success/failure is communicated to the requester. If the route is for a regular flight (equivalent to a repeated query), a route plan will probably be already in existence. In this case, the Task Manager will communicate to the appropriate regions for clearance. Once the clearance is given, it is communicated to the requester.

Then the execution phase begins:

3. When the plane takes off, the communicator communicates the message to all the relevant air-traffic controllers; but no time-out is probably needed.

4. The execution proceeds according to the execution plan. Action within each region will be the next level of activities within the regional controller, where controls will be exercised in accordance with the regional rules. These will be specified in the execution plans prepared by the Lower Decomposer, mentioned earlier.

CONCLUSION

We have introduced the concept of a Cooperating Knowledge Based System to provide multi-agent processing with a database flavour, emphasising three items: a general architecture, performance efficiency and concurrency/ reliability/ recovery facilities, of which we have discussed first two in detail. We have presented a generic model for the representation of agents, more generally encapsulated objects, backed by a hybrid cooperation model which is expected to provide efficient performance. We have also shown how these ideas can be used to develop applications in a wide range of application domains. By and large the work presented here is an exercise of applying some ideas of distributed databases on multi-agent systems.

Despite our attempt to produce generic framework, we must admit that the world of CKBS is far too complex to be solved by a single unified implementation. On the other hand, the idea of a tailor-made system for every application is also unacceptable in terms of development cost. The generic framework we have developed is based on an inherent similarity in the CKBS application areas; and this strengthens our belief that it should be possible to design some general-purpose systems, each of which can meet the needs of a whole class of applications. The proposed framework also provides scope for standardisation and formalisation, as in databases.

The proposed object model creates an autonomous object with an open interface, permitting not only heterogeneous but also pre-existing systems to act as an object in a cooperative environment. However, not all the facilities of the object model will be needed by each potential object. Likewise, the hybrid cooperation strategy provides a framework for many types of cooperation; a specific application may not need all the facilities. This framework can also be used to describe further facilities such as concurrent usage, reliability, recovery, constraint propagation, reasoning and triggers. There are of course other issues, such as a high-level language for information exchange, which we have not addressed.

We are at the moment examining the following three applications, within the COSMOS project, which will use the ideas developed in this paper:

- Travel service

- Air-traffic control

- Network-traffic control

In due course, we also expect to improve the models in the light of our experience in these applications.

Acknowledgment

I would like to thank Athula Herath, Jim Longstaff, Baird Ndovie and Bill Samson for their invaluable comments and suggestions, and also for assistance with the production of the manuscript.

REFERENCES

[1] M. L. Brodie et al (editors): On conceptual Modeling: Perspectives from Artificial Intelligence, Databases, and Programming Languages, Springer-Verlag, 1984.

[2] S. M. Deen and G.P. Thomas (editors): Data and Knowledge Base Integration, Proc. of a working conference, Pitman, 1990.

[3] A.H. Bond and L. Gasser: "An analysis of Problems and research in DAI", Readings in Distributed Artificial Intelligence, edited by Bond and Gasser, Morgan Kaufman, 1988, pp 3-35 (This volume is strongly recommended to the new corners - this book reproduces important articles from past publications).

[4] E.H. Durfee et al: "Trends in Cooperative distributed problem solving", IEEE TKDE vol (1:1) pp 63-83, March 1989.

[5] L.D. Erman and V.R. Lesser: "A multi-level organisation for problem solving using many diverse cooperating sources of knowledge", Proc. International Joint Conf on AI, pp 483-490, 1975.

[6] E.H. Durfee, V.R. Lessor, D.D. Corkill: "Cooperation through Communications in a Distributed Problem Solving Network", Distributed Artificial Intelligence, edited by N. Huhns, Pitman 1987, pp 29-58. This book is also a recommended reading. A version of this work also appears on pp 268-284 in ref [3]. There are many papers on DVMT, we refer here only to some.

[7] E.H. Durfee and V.R. Lesser: "Negotiating task decomposition and allocation using partial global planning", Distributed Artificial Intelligence, vol II, edited by L. Gasser and M.N. Huhns, Pitman 1989, pp 229-244. This is another recommended volume.

[8] R. Davies and R.G. Smith: "Negotiation as a metaphor for distributed problem solving", Readings in Distributed Artificial Intelligence, edited by Bond and Gasser, Morgan Kaufman, 1988, pp 331-356.

[9] R.G. Smith "The Contract Net protocol: high level communication and control in a distributed problem solver", Readings in Distributed Artificial Intelligence, edited by Bond and Gasser, Morgan Kaufman, 1988, pp 357-366.

[10] G. Agha and C. Hewitt: "Concurrent programming using Actors ....", Readings in Distributed Artificial Intelligence, edited by Bond and Gasser, Morgan Kaufman, 1988, pp 398-407.

[11] C.E. Hewitt: "Offices are open systems", Readings in Distributed Artificial Intelligence, edited by Bond and Gasser, Morgan Kaufman, 1988, pp 321-330.

[12] R. Steeb et al: "Architectures for distributed air-traffic control" Readings in Distributed Artificial Intelligence, edited by Bond and Gasser, Morgan Kaufman, 1988, pp 90 - 101.

[13] S. Cammarata et al: "Strategies for cooperation in distributed problem solving", Readings in Distributed Artificial Intelligence, edited by Bond and Gasser, Morgan Kaufman, 1988, pp 102-105.

[14] N.V. Findler and R. Lo: "An examination of distributed planning in the World of air-traffic control", Readings in Distributed Artificial Intelligence, edited by Bond and Gasser, Morgan Kaufman, 1988, pp 617-627.

[15] L. Gasser et al: "MACE: A flexible test bed for distributed AI", Distributed Artificial Intelligence, edited by N. Huhns, Pitman 1987, pp 119 - 152.

[16] R. Bisiani et al: "The Architecture of the Agora Environment", Distributed Artificial Intelligence, edited by N. Huhns, Pitman 1987, pp 99-118.

[17] R. Engelmore and T. Morgan (editors): Blackboard systems, Addison-Wesley 1988. This edited volume contains a large number of systems that use the blackboard architecture.

[18] M. Kamel and A. Syed: "An object-oriented multiple agent planning system", Distributed Artificial Intelligence, vol II, edited by L. Gasser and M.N. Huhns, Pitman 1989, pp 259-290.

26

[19] A.H. Bond: "The cooperation of experts in engineering design", Distributed Artificial Intelligence, vol II, edited by L. Gasser and M.N. Huhns, Pitman 1989, pp 463-486.

[20] S. Ceri and G. Pelagatti: Distributed Databases - Principles and Systems, McGraw-Hill, 1985.

[21] S.M. Deen et al: "Data Integration in Distributed Databases", IEEE Transactions on SE, Vol (SE 13:7), July 1987, pp 860-864.

[22] S.M.Deen et al: "The architecture of a distributed database system - PRECI*", Computer Journal, Vol (28:3), Aug 1985, pp 282-290.

[23] S. Bhalla et al: "A technical comparison of heterogeneous distributed database management system," MIT technical report 1987 (copies from Dr. A. Gupta, Sloan School of Management, MIT, Cambridge, Mass 02139). This report reviews a number of major distributed database systems.

[24] S.M. Deen et al: "Distributed directory database system for telecommunication", Computer Journal, Vol (31:12), April 1988, pp 175-81.

[25] W. Litwin and A. Abdellatif: "Multidatabase interoperability", IEEE Computer Vol (19:12), Dec, 1986, pp 10-18.

[26] U. Dayal: "Query processing in multidatabase system", Query Processing in Database System, Springer-Verlag, 1985, pp 81-108.

[27] J.R. Ensor, J. D. Gable: "Transactional Blackboard", Blackboard Systems, R. Englemore and T. Morgan (editors), Addison-Wesley, 1988, pp 465-474. A recommended book to read.

[28] B. Hayes-Roth and M. Hewett: "BB1: An implementation of the Blackboard Control Architecture", Blackboard Systems, R. Englemore and T. Morgan (editors), Addison-Wesley, 1988, pp 297-315. The same authors have another article on BB* in the same book on pp543-560.

[29] D.D. Corkill et al: "GBB : A Generic Blackboard Development System", Blackboard Systems, R. Englemore and T. Morgan (editors), Addison-Wesley, 1988, pp 503-516.

DISCUSSION

Presenter: S. M. Deen.

Q. (L. Gasser, USC) : I support your call for some viewpoints on standardised agent architecture and standardised theories of computing AI, but I want to make an observation
on your particular proposal for an agent architecture. When thinking about the nature
of an agent we should think about something I'll call levels of analysis. We might
think about a particular single actor, like a human being, as an agent. But we might
also want to think about an entire organisation as an agent or we might want to think
about some small group of people within an organisation as an agent. So there's some
aspect of, I'll call it, compositionality. We need to be able to put things together and
call that an agent and would like to have, in a certain sense, a recursive or reducible or
composable structure that allows us to build agents at different levels of granularity.

A. (S. M. Deen) : It is in the paper but perhaps not using the same terms you have used.
What we assume is that an agent could be based on an abstraction (aggregation and
generalistation) hierarchy. An agent could be made of a number of other agents with
many levels. One can think of a monitoring station, which is made up of subordinate
agents which do not communicate among themselves, all communication is via the
monitoring station. This would be an example of an aggregation hierarchy.

Q. : I think, following on from the last question, it's not just a matter of being able to
represent a hierarchy. An organisation has many roles in consulting that organisation
in developing multiple agent systems. It can actually define the behaviour of agents
in a particular context, how they relate to the environment as well as to each other.
It's a much higher level concept than the one I think you were just suggesting, that
could be further represented in your model.

A. (S. M. Deen) : I'm not sure. If you are asking if I can visualise modelling a whole
organisation, then perhaps I cannot. I have a very modest aim: I wish to model
only classes of application but in very general terms. I view an agent either as a
stand-alone or a hierarchic object. In an aggregation hierarchy an agent is made up
of other agents in turn, but at each level of the hierarchy they communicate with one
another only via the higher level. In a generalistion hierarchy an agent can inherit,
possibly from multiple ancestors; thus it can acquire behaviour from contexts. In
addition, there could be many levels of cooperations, an agent feeding to a higher
level from the results it receives from its local lower level. In this case, unlike the
aggregation hierarchy, the agents at a given local (lower) level cooperate (and hence
also communicate) directly with one another. This is the general structure as I see it
and I can make the structure as deep as I like. I do not see why this framework is not
adequate for a large number of applications.

Q. (T. Brown, Brunel University) : My question is not directly related to what's in your
paper but in terms of a database perspective on multi-agent systems on DAI. Can you
say something more about how database technology could help? I'm thinking in particular in terms of distributed databases and maintaining consistency of information
in distributed databases in terms of perhaps say relational database technology. The

relationships you might see between an idea such as a relational table, and a class of objects, class of agents, any other kinds of comments you might have like that.

A. (S. M. Deen) : This question needs a long answer; and hence I am not sure where to begin. How does database technology help? I mentioned in my paper some of the ideas from distributed databases (DDBs). DDBs provide a fairly standard architecture, with cleanly defined interfaces. This helps future extensions and development of general algorithms for performance optimisation, concurrency control, and so on. DDBs also support recovery facilities, and standard user-interfaces. These are some of the techniques that can be useful to multi-agent systems in general.

Are relations useful in this context? A knowledge-server could be relation-based. There are also other cases where relations will be most appropriate. This will still leave a large area where the relational representation may not be adequate.

Q. (T. Brown) : That's at an implementation level. My question was more addressed to the conceptual level. Concepts from database technology.

A. (S. M. Deen) : The relational database technology is centred around the concept of data in the form of relation; some people are working on extended relational model which allows the representation of complex object. These are at concept level for knowledge representation. And then database research has contributed enormously in performance optimisation: the concepts developed there could be useful in multi-agent systems. In distributed databases, we regard the communications as a black box at a lower level, and it either fails or succeeds. This permits independence in design. The decomposition of the architecture into standard levels is very important in distributed databases, as it gives data transparency, which gives clarity, simplifies design and helps incorporation of changes easily. These are some of the ideas that can be introduced into the multi-agent world.

You mentioned consistency. There are three possible ways we can go about updating. The first is strong consistency, which is controlled by exclusive locking. This is not feasible in long transactions which are likely to dominate multi-agent systems. There are also some non-locking techniques available, which could be more appropriate. The second technique is weak consistency which is suitable for only the update of replicated data. In this case you update the home node of that data, leaving it to the home node to propagate the update to the replicated versions. But there may be a time lag before a node receives the request to update its replicated copy, and so this copy can become be out of step for a short while. In some applications this delay is acceptable, but not so in others. The third case is cached data, which is updated only on a demand basis. Thus, you can use different strategies in different situations. These techniques can be extended for multi-agent systems. So I think there are a number of concepts in distributed databases that can be useful to multi-agent systems.

Q. (W. Chu, UCLA) : I think the consistency shown in particular is very difficult when you go to the inhomogeneous environment because most of the similar database work has assumed an homogeneous underlying system. So in particular, I think all these comments are well-taken except the consistency. It's the most difficult one to manage

A. (S. M. Deen) : At one level it is quite simple, but at another it is quite complex. Since the agents are autonomous with private knowledge, there is no need to maintain consistency among them, save those cases mentioned in Mike Huhns's paper. So if I don't need every agent to be globally consistent, I do not have a global update problem, unlike in DDBs. I mentioned knowledge severs being present. Yes, information in the severs must be consistent but you do not have to have many different knowledge severs, you can do with only one. If there are more than one knowledge server, then they need to be consistent, in which case you may like to use techniques similar to those in DDBs.

Q. (W. Chu): I suggest we move a little bit more. I felt that the relational database we had was very limited in the cooperation we have and cannot be rich enough for the application to be easily extended further. Also the database people are starting to put rules into their system and use in commercial databases will have these kind of features. I think those are helpful but I worry that the database people do not know what they are doing. Handling the rules can be very fragile. I think it is time for the AI people to work very closely with the database people.

Q. (Probably S. Chakravarthy, Univ of Florida): There is one thought that occurred to me just now so I throw it out on the fly. This problem of consistency in our databases. In some ways it seems to be also language relative. So, if for example I'm engaged in a particular kind of world of activity where I will have a particular kind of vocabulary in that world, and the agents that interact within that world. Well, I want to have consistency with respect to that kind of activity but not necessarily a consistency with the whole thing. So, we might get a reduction in complexity in terms, and also, a reduction, in terms of updating the databases, if we introduce some kind of notion of relevance. Relevance relative to the language and relative to the activity.

If you're all interested in a particular kind of activity but only certain information was relevant for that activity, then you don't care if there are billions of data of information that are totally irrelevant and not really consistent.

A. (S. M. Deen): Only if you can assure that the classes of activity which you are separating could not then be inconsistent with the rest, and that there would never ever be a query where it's wrong. If you can you guarantee that, then fine.

Q. : That's why I was thinking of this notion, that maybe we can define something, maybe a semi-linguistic notion or maybe a relative activity where you have a core that's inaccessible relative to the language, and this inaccessible core, which can be quite large would then lead to a tremendous reduction in complexity.

Q. (W. Chu): Basically, we want to base our semantics to determine if two updates are semantically independent, then you can do that without worrying about these issues.

Meeting the Cooperative Problem Solving Challenge: A Database-Centered Approach

S. Chakravarthy[1]   S. B. Navathe[2]   K. Karlapalem[2]   A. Tanaka[3]

Computer and Information Sciences Department and
Database Systems Research and Development Center
University of Florida, Gainesville, FL 32611, USA
Email: sharma@snapper.cis.ufl.edu

Abstract

Cooperative problem solving is a complex activity requiring harmonious interaction between active agents (typically humans providing sequencing, decision making, and coordination components) and systems (typically passive - providing inferencing as well as algorithmic computation). Although each component (or the node involved in problem solving) is autonomous and is capable of sophisticated problem solving, the problem cannot be solved by any individual node and without cooperation among the nodes. This problem is currently being addressed by the research community at various levels of abstraction.

This paper concentrates on the enhancements of the functionality of a database management system required for supporting cooperative problem solving. Several problems addressed in the literature, such as automation of office environments can be viewed as a special (and perhaps a simple) case of cooperative problem solving. In our view, recent advances in database technology (viz. active and heterogeneous database management systems) and maturation of other concepts (viz. temporal and object-oriented databases) provide us with a repertoire of techniques and abstractions for formulating a viable solution to the above problem.

In this paper, we first analyze the problem of cooperative problem solving to identify key underlying characteristics. We propose a database-centered solution by combining and extending techniques and abstractions to support the characteristics identified. We describe our immediate and long-term solutions for supporting cooperative problem solving. Finally, we present an example that exemplifies our multi-staged solution.

[2]Authors' current address: College of Computing, Georgia Institute of Technology, Atlanta, GA 30332
[1]This work was partially supported by the NSF Grant IRI-9011216 and by the Florida High Technology and Industrial Council Grant UPN# 89090848
[3]Supported by the Brazilian Army and Conselho Nacional de Desenvolvimento Científico e Tecnologico

1   Characteristics of Cooperative Problem Solving

A large number of activities (including problem solving) carried out by humans requires cooperation between humans (active agents) and systems (passive agents, typically). Although, each component (or the node involved in problem solving) is autonomous and capable of sophisticated problem solving, the problem faced by the entire set of components cannot be completed without cooperation. These *cooperative activities* also involve extensive access to information repositories, computation, inferencing, and decision making. The salient characteristics of *cooperative problem solving* are: *decision making/inferencing* using a set of criteria (e.g., selecting candidates to be called for interview, selecting the computing environment for a project), *computation* using a variety of systems and tools (e.g., searching a database to select referees, computing the optimum layout of components in circuit design), and more importantly *collaboration*[4] – collective problem solving and *coordination* – to act together in a concerted way. Briefly, the main issue in collaboration is the solicitation of contributions from participating agents (as opposed to problem decomposition and *independent* evaluation) so that the problem can be solved jointly by the group where as coordination is necessary to resolving conflicts, allocate limited resources, searching in global space based on local information. Conceptually, collaboration can be viewed as planning whereas coordination corresponds to execution of a plan (either pre-defined or dynamically developed).

From the above discussion, we can infer that collaboration and coordination are two key characteristics of cooperative problem solving. In order to support cooperative problem solving, it is imperative that the underlying computing environment[5] be capable of providing support for each of the characteristics identified. Many day-to-day activities in the world fall into the above category. For example, the graduate student admission process in a university environment, typically, involves cooperation among several autonomous agents: the graduate admissions office, one or more departmental graduate offices, a graduate coordinator, and a graduate admissions committee. Perhaps diagnosis of an ailment involving multiple autonomous medical experts exemplifies the problem of cooperative problem solving and all of its facets. Finally, office automation, a specific example of cooperative problem solving, also exhibits most of the characteristics mentioned above. In order to underscore the complexity of these class of activities, it is useful to contrast them with conventional activities carried out using extant computing environments and tools. Most of the activities fall into one of the following two categories: *computation-intensive*, where there is very little interaction with the outside agent (e.g., wind-tunnel simulation, finite element analysis) and *one-on- one interaction* with an agent and the system (e.g., interactive applications).

On the other hand, a cooperative activity requires considerable collaboration as well as coordination among a large number of agents as well as systems and agents. Currently, a significant part of cooperation – both among systems, and systems and agents – is done by the (active) agents. As a consequence, agents are an integral part of the loop performing

---

[4]There is a large, separate body of work on Coordinated Distributed Problem Solving [BARR89] in Distributed Artificial Intelligence (DAI) which distinguishes distributed problem solving from multi-agent problem solving [BOND88] where the latter need to reason about the process of coordination among the agents.

[5]By underlying computing environment, we refer to the kind of support an operating systems provides for a general problem solving environment or even the support a DBMS provides for the management and manipulation of data.

required activities most of which need to be relegated to the underlying computing environment. In order to assist active agents in this process, the functionality of the underlying systems need to be augmented. Our goal is to suitably enhance the functionality of the underlying components to support the execution of cooperative activities. Our approach first identifies appropriate techniques and abstractions from several relevant technology areas and then describes how they can be adapted and/or combined synergistically to provide the required functionality in the underlying computing environment. In order to provide better support for the specification, mapping, management, and execution of cooperative activities, it is imperative to raise the level of abstraction at which cooperative activities are specified to the environment. This in turn enhances the functionality of the environment to accept, map, execute, and manage higher-level specifications.

1.1   Levels of Abstraction

Cooperative problem solving is currently being addressed by the research community at various levels of abstraction. Understanding cognitive issues of human problem solving, developing models, and building systems to support these models is the overall objective of this area of research. Nonetheless, it would still be extremely useful to develop techniques and protocols for cooperative problem solving among expert systems that are currently deployed. A large class of problems, such as autonomous navigation of a vehicle, mission planning, situation assessment, and to some extent medical diagnosis can be handled at this level of abstraction. Finally, computer-assisted (or computer-supported) human interaction can be used in automating problems that are typically handled in an office environment, assembly lines, CIM (Computer Integrated Manufacturing) where the problems are reasonably well- defined and they can be expressed as activities involving asynchronous and temporal dependencies (for example, send a message if a specified due date has been expired, change some policies regarding the admission process for some departments). Figure 1.1 shows the levels of abstraction and the increasing complexity of the problem as we go further from the center.

It is interesting to contrast the approaches taken by AI researchers and systems/database researchers for the problem under discussion. Typically AI researchers take the outside-in (or top down) approach to a given problem: addressing cognitive models of cooperation and the problem of cooperating experts before embarking on the systems support required for realizing these systems (in most of the cases, prototypes and proof-of-principle systems are built). In contrast, systems/database researchers take the inside-out (or bottom up) approach: study of the functionality necessary to support models of computation required for solving these problems. Needless to say that we are taking the latter approach in this paper.

From the systems (or the database) point of view, these levels translate to abstractions that need to be supported by the underlying system which in turn translates to the identification of appropriate functionality for each level of abstraction. As a pedagogical analogy, database researchers have developed several useful abstractions (e.g., data independence, transaction, and transparency abstractions) for raising the level at which users' interact with the system enabling them to concentrate on the application development instead of the tool.

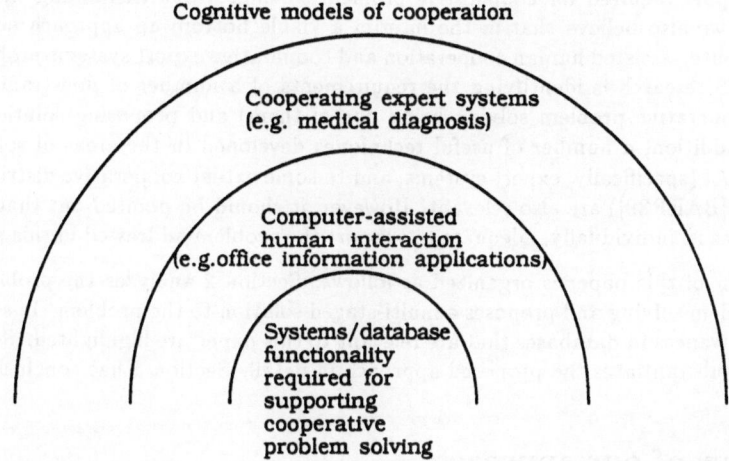

Figure 1.1 Levels of abstraction of cooperative problem solving

We believe that the database management technology can be enhanced to provide the system level support required for cooperative problem solving. Notwithstanding the top-down approach, we also believe that in the interim a viable bottom-up approach need to address the computer-assisted human cooperation and cooperative expert systems problems. Currently, DBMS research is identifying the requirements of a number of non-traditional applications (cooperative problem solving being one of them) and proposing solutions to meet them. In addition, a number of useful techniques developed in the areas of software engineering and AI (specifically, expert systems, and to some extent cooperative distributed problem solving [BARR89]) are also relevant. However, it should be pointed out that none of the technologies is, individually, adequate to support the problem addressed in this paper.

The remainder of this paper is organized as follows. Section 2 analyzes the problem of cooperative problem solving and proposes a multi-staged solution to the problem. In section 3, some recent advances in databases that are relevant to this paper are highlighted. Section 4 discusses and substantiates the proposed approach in detail. Section 5 has conclusions.

2 Overview of our approach

In this section, we provide an overview of our approach indicating: i) the relevance and usefulness of techniques culled from relevant technologies and ii) an evolutionary path leading to an integrated system for supporting cooperative problem solving.

An analysis of the characteristics of cooperative problem solving suggests the need for the following functionality in any environment supporting cooperation:

1. ability to model complex (cooperative) activity,

2. ability to support (rule based) inferencing for decision making,

3. ability to maintain historical information pertaining to an activity for: tracing its progress, querying, and inferencing,

4. ability to maintain temporal information pertaining to an activity to perform sequencing, coordination as well as inferencing (over temporal data),

5. ability to communicate asynchronously (perhaps using alerters, triggers, and other mechanisms such as mailbox) with other systems as well as agents,

6. ability to capture the capabilities of the components (heterogeneous systems and agents) as part of the data/knowledge base, and

7. ability to maintain and manage a data/knowledge base shared by the activities (in terms of consistency and being able to recover from failures).

8. ability to solve problems in parallel and build compatible solutions

Techniques for modeling cooperative activities will be developed using relevant methodologies from software engineering (e.g., modeling process) as well as active and temporal components of the data/knowledge base (item 1). Amalgamation of knowledge-representation techniques [BRAC80] into the data model of DBMSs brings with it the concomitant techniques developed for AI systems. For example, hypothetical reasoning can be used for supporting "what-if" scenarios. As another example, rule-based inferencing and explanation of conclusions arrived at can also be realized in a straightforward manner. Also, rule-based inferencing needs to be extended to include temporal data (items 2 and 4)

One of the key components of our approach is the active database abstraction which will support the coordination of activities among systems as well as systems and agents. An active database supports events (database, non-database, temporal, and composite) that can be specified on the data stored in the data/knowledge base (refer to Figure 2.2.) (item 5). Another key component of our approach is the support for maintaining both historical and time-stamp based data. These will be supported by the underlying DBMS used for the purposes of coordination (items 3, 5, 6, and 7). Loosely connected network configuration accommodates parallel problem solving and to a large extent the compatibility of interdependent solutions can be ensured using available techniques (e.g., blackboard [ENGE88] (item 8).

2.1 Multi-staged Approach to Cooperative Problem Solving

In this subsection, we first discuss the conventional approach currently being used for cooperative problem solving and its limitations. We contrast our proposed approach with the conventional approach. Finally, we provide a long-term solution which combines most of the concepts that will be developed as part of this research into an integrated solution.

Figure 2.1 indicates the current approach to cooperative problem solving. The main drawback of this approach is that the agents (usually one or more people engaged in cooperative problem solving) have to provide most of the coordination among agents as well as among systems and agents. Systems and tools are used as passive components capable only of performing computations. The onus of information propagation, reminding other systems/agents, and sequencing of activities, checking for compatibility of solutions etc, are on the agents involved in problem solving. Any system specific capability (such as e–mail, calendars etc.) is exploited in an ad hoc manner to solve the problem. The problem being solved cannot be specified to the system at a conceptual level that is complete enough to include all the coordination, sequencing, and dataflow requirements.

Our approach (Figure 2.2) is based upon the pragmatic assumption that the systems participating in a cooperative activity are autonomous and the execution of an activity can be coordinated by using a combination of database techniques developed for satisfying the requirements of non-traditional applications. An active, temporal knowledge base (ATKB) in conjunction with an active blackboard[6] is proposed as a mechanism for accomplishing cooperation among problem solving nodes (including active agents). An active blackboard provides asynchronous (through the notion of events, conditions, and actions in the form of situation-action rules [DAYA88]) mechanism for invoking and/or activating the collection of independent sources which are likely to be nodes participating in cooperative problem solving. We also envision, in our notion of an active blackboard, that both data and

---

[6]Blackboard systems provide a central data structure called a *blackboard*, which is often divided into regions or levels. A collection of independent sources called *knowledge sources* may read and write one or more levels, under the supervision of a *control system*, which may be a synchronous global scheduler, a system of concurrency locks, or a collection of integrated control-knowledge sources [HAYE85].

36

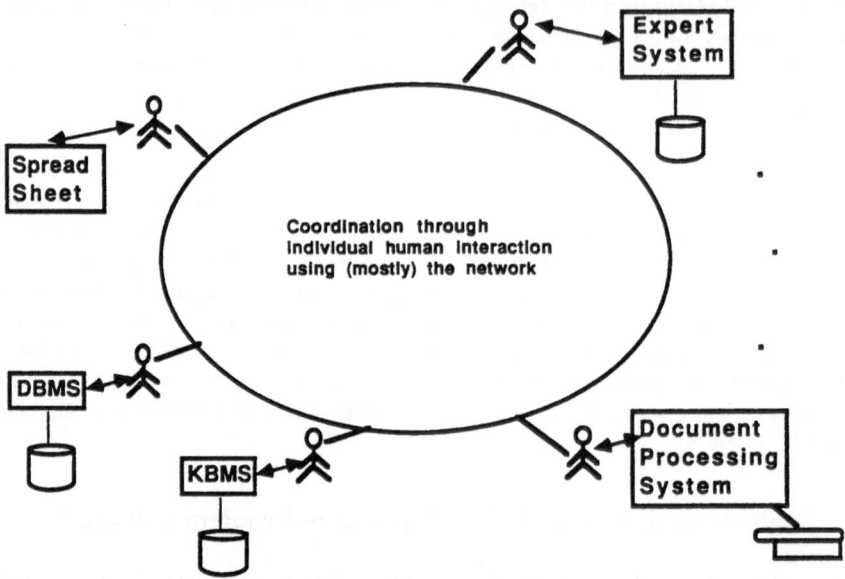

Figure 2.1 Conventional cooperative problem solving environment

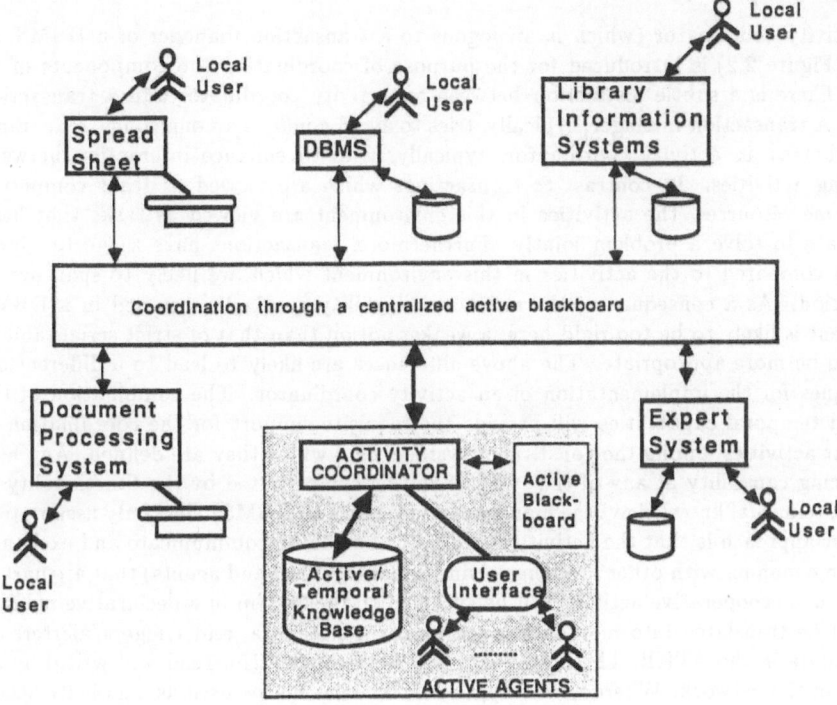

Figure 2.2 Database-supported cooperative problem solving environment

situation-action rules to be part of the shared database to which transaction oriented access and manipulation are applicable.

An activity coordinator (which is analogous to a transaction manager of a DBMS, as shown in Figure 2.2) is introduced for the purpose of coordinating the components of an activity. There is a subtle distinction between an activity coordinator and a transaction manager. A transaction manager, typically, tries to avoid *conflicts* among concurrent transactions whereas an activity coordinator, typically, tries to enhance interaction between cooperating activities. In contrast to transactions which are viewed as tasks competing for the same resources, the activities in this environment are viewed as tasks that have to cooperate to solve a problem jointly. Furthermore, transactions have a shorter duration when compared to the activities in this environment which are likely to span over a longer period. As a consequence, the strict serializability routinely assumed in a DBMS environment is likely to be too rigid here; a weaker notion than that of strict serializability is likely to be more appropriate. The above differences are likely to lead to a different set of techniques for the implementation of an activity coordinator. The combination of the active and temporal capabilities will provide the requisite support for the coordination of component activities among the constituent systems over which they are defined. Any lack of inferencing capability at any of the systems will be compensated by the functionality of the active, temporal knowledge base management system (ATKBMS). The only assumption used in our approach is that the activity coordinator be able to communicate and exchange data in some manner with other problem solving nodes (systems and agents) that are part of the network. A cooperative activity will be specified to the system in a declarative manner which will be translated into metadata, operations on metadata, and triggers/alerters on that metadata in the ATKB. The blackboard will be accessible (for read and write) by all the nodes in the network. Where necessary, the blackboard will be used as a globally accessible space for posting solutions to subproblems to have their compatibility checked. The actual execution of an activity (including coordination and sequencing) will be handled by the activity coordinator which will be responsible for information propagation, sequencing, and coordinating subactivities and atomic activities.

The essence of our approach is that the user can now specify a cooperative activity conceptually in terms of a plan (loosely, a plan can be viewed as a collection of tasks specified using a directed graph indicating precedence among tasks and temporal constraints for each task) along with the information required for coordination. The onus of its execution (optimization, management, interference with other activities) is on the activity coordinator and the ATKBMS. The activity coordinator, in conjunction with the active, temporal knowledge base and active blackboard will execute each activity (satisfying its constraints) requesting inputs from appropriate components (be it passive systems or active agents). Agents involved in the problem solving activity will play only a supervisory role in providing their inputs or decisions in contrast to the situation shown in Figure 2.2. Note that the above discussion does not assume that the problem has to be described to the system as a plan by the end user. It is very likely that there will be a high level specification language which gets translated to the input proposed above.

Figure 2.3 illustrates the next generation of cooperative problem solving environment. The previous approach essentially had one centralized activity coordinator which was responsible for coordination among all the agents. Ideally, in a distributed environment, each component need to be capable of supporting coordination which is possible only if each

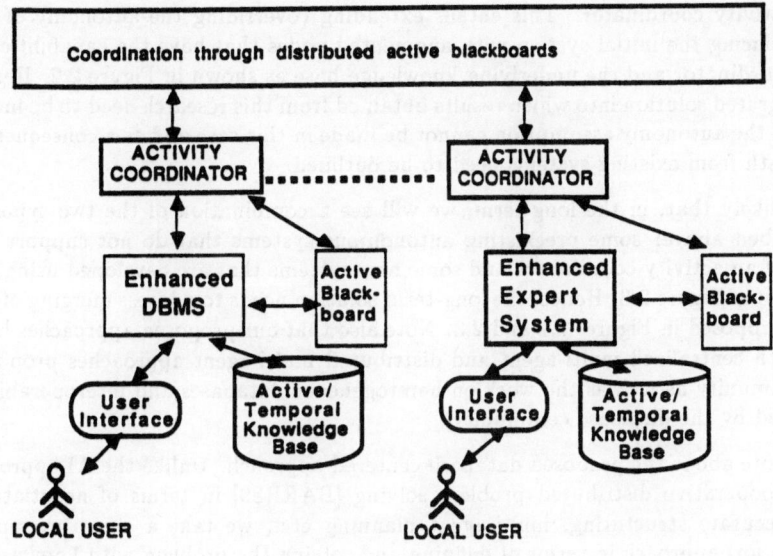

Figure 2.3   Integrated cooperative problem solving

includes an activity coordinator. This entails extending (overriding the autonomy of the system) or replacing the initial system with augmented nodes that have the capabilities of the activity coordinator and the underlying knowledge base as shown in Figure 2.2. Hence, this as an integrated solution into which results obtained from this research need to be incorporated. Also, the autonomy assumption cannot be made in this case and as a consequence, a migration path from existing systems need to be outlined.

It is more likely that, in the long-term, we will see a combination of the two types of systems described above: some preexisting autonomous systems that do not support the functionality of an activity coordinator and some new systems that are developed using the approach shown in Figure 2.3. Hence, the long-term solution needs to address merging of the architectures proposed in Figures 2.2 and 2.3. Note also that our proposed approaches have similarities with centralized multi-agent and distributed multi-agent approaches proposed by the AI community as well as the work on heterogeneous databases and interoperability issues addressed by the database community.

Finally, a note about the proposed database-centered approach. Unlike the AI approach to modeling cooperative distributed problem solving [BARR89] in terms of negotiation, functionally accurate structuring, multi-agent planning etc., we take a more pragmatic (and a bottom up) approach in terms of defining and solving the problem with known and viable DBMS functionality. The AI approach is certainly required for the complete solution of the problem whereas our approach proposes to build working systems for the subclass of problems for which solutions are either known or are likely to be obtained in the short term; the hope is that this bidirectional search will not only reduce the time taken for obtaining a complete solution to the problem but also promote cross-fertilization among AI and database researchers.

3 Relevant Technologies

Although a fair amount of research has been done in modeling and supporting office environments, recent works in active, temporal, and heterogeneous databases warrant a fresh look at the overall problem of cooperative work environments. Below we review literature in areas identified as relevant to the problem addressed in this paper.

3.1 Active Database Management

Active databases can be viewed as an abstraction for elegantly supporting a variety of database functions that were being realized using special-purpose mechanisms in conventional DBMSs. Traditionally DBMSs have been passive; that is, queries or transactions are executed only when explicitly requested.

The key advantages offered by the active database abstraction are modularity and timely response. Modularity is achieved by separating the conditions (and actions) to be evaluated from the application code as well as relieving the application programmer from having to specify the periodicity with which to check whether the conditions have become true. Timely response is obtained by virtue of the system choosing the most appropriate strategy for evaluating the conditions and further optimizing (one or more) conditions rather than the user specifying them. For example, the frequency of the polling cycle depends on various factors (such as the frequency of update, constraints about response time) and the user may not be able to always make it satisfying all the constraints. [CHAK89a] points out the usefulness of rule-based active capability for supporting a variety of DBMS functions, such as integrity and security enforcement, access control, maintenance of derived data, materialized views and snapshots, and rule-based inferencing. Other work on active databases include [CHAK89b, CHAK90, WIDO90, STON90, KOTZ88, Syba87, Inte90].

The asynchronous execution of triggers and alerters in active databases provides the basis for problem dependent asynchronous communication among the problem solving nodes. The blackboard acts as an active global scratch pad to which messages and partial solutions can be posted by any node and referred to by any other node.

3.2 Temporal Databases

Time plays a central role in cooperative work environments. For example, in the student admission process, deadlines must be observed in each term and due dates for activities involved in the process must be monitored. As another example, administrative and legal information systems must record changes in policies, procedures, and laws over a long time span and must consistently apply them to events taking place over the time span.

Recently, numerous researchers have addressed the problem of incorporating the semantics of time into information systems. Surveys appear in [BOLO82, DAYA85, SNOD86]. Most of the work reported on temporal databases extends the relational model for time support. Special time attributes are added to flat relations by [JONE80, BENZ82, CLIF83, LUM84, ARIA86, NAVA89, SNOD87], which is equivalent to time-stamping of *tuples*. Another way to classify the different proposals is by using the concepts of valid time and transaction time dimensions [SNOD85]. Valid time leads to historical databases, while transaction time leads to rollback databases. Other research in temporal databases includes [ANDE81, CAST82, GINS84, ADIB85, SHOS86, NAVA87, SARD87, SEGE88]. Little work has been done on conceptual modeling for temporal database applications barring [CHEN86, ELMA89], still restricted to the valid time dimension. In our work, we propose to provide temporal modeling at both conceptual and logical modeling level. Both valid and transaction time dimensions, as well as the mapping from the conceptual to the logical schema are important to our approach.

Combining active and temporal abstractions provides a powerful mechanism for asynchronous communication which can either be based on events corresponding to arbitrary computations or time or both.

3.3 Office Automation

The characteristics of the office information systems are similar in nature to those found in the collaborative environments. In fact, an office information system is an ideal case study to illustrate our approach.

Many conceptual modeling and design methodologies for Office Information Systems (OIS) have been proposed [SIRB81, KONS82, LOCH88, MAZE88, PERN88, PERN89].

Also, a lot of work has been done on supporting office work at progressively higher levels, by using data-based models [WHAN87], AI techniques [BARB83, CROF84, KAYE87], concurrent communication in distributed systems [AGHA87] data semantics and procedures [GIBB83], and message systems [CORT84, MAZE84, KOO88]. Recent work on computer supported cooperative work includes [GREI87, MALO87, SAMA88].

Our approach similarly explores the role of computers in managing activities performed by coordinated, and collaborative systems under various temporal and non-temporal constraints. The concept of the activity coordinator differs from that of a mediator[WIED89]. While the mediators are to contain the administrative and technical knowledge to create information needed for decision making, the activity coordinator uses the information managed by the active, temporal knowledge base to take decisions. The decisions are taken as to how and when the activity is to be executed is made by detecting events and initiating actions.

4 Details of Our Approach

In this section we elaborate on the architecture proposed in Section 2 and give a brief description of the components. The environment consists of a loosely coupled network of problem solving nodes. Duplication of functionality among the nodes is permitted. The goal is to perform a set of cooperative activities that are defined to the environment. Figure 4.1 shows the details of the approach shown in Figure 2.2. The components of the environment are a set of nodes, an activity coordinator which coordinates the set of activities, and an active, temporal knowledge base system (ATKBMS) and the corresponding knowledge base, ATKB, store information about activities used by the activity coordinator.

We briefly describe some of the concepts and the functionality of the components shown in Figure 4.1:

Nodes (Systems in the figure)

Nodes perform sub-activities (tasks) of an activity. A human can act as a node having a distinct set of roles, responsibilities, constraints, and functions. A node, in general, consists of resources (programs, accessories, peripherals, communication equipment) and information (shared data and rules, dictionary, capabilities of itself and other nodes in the network) required for solving a task. Nodes are typically static and passive and the specification of their structure and functionality does not change over long periods of time. Hence, these nodes do not evolve but they tend to be replaced. This replacement is done mostly to improve the functionality and/or the performance of the system.

Each node is autonomous and in our immediate approach may not be able to communicate *directly* with other nodes on the network. Hence they do their tasks independently or locally, with minimal knowledge about the type of processing done by other nodes. They may have very little or no knowledge of the type or functionality of processing done by the other collaborating nodes. The activity coordinator acts as the mediator for exchanging information, progress, partial solutions as well as activating and deactivating tasks at each node. As a minimum, each node is assumed to be capable of exchanging information with the activity coordinator.

Activities

Any problem to be solved cooperatively is modeled as an activity. An activity is a conceptual specification of the problem expressed in terms of capabilities present in the underlying system. An activity in general consists of a set of sub-activities, with each sub-activity being processed by one or more nodes. Sub-activities are disjoint and related, and can be classified into two sets: those which can be completely done by human nodes, and those which can be completely done by non human nodes. A sub-activity is atomic if it can be done by a single node. The activity specification is expanded until it can be expressed in terms of atomic sub- activities.

An activity is likely to be long-lived in contrast to a database transaction that, typically, has a short duration. To complete an activity, a subset of the resources of the network is required and more importantly a **collaborative schedule** that involves coordination among the nodes at either pre-specified points in time (temporal) or asynchronously (data-flow like) or a combination thereof is required. An activity, such as the process of assessing a paper for publication in a journal can be expressed as a directed graph where nodes represent receptors of data for making decisions and edges correspond to communication and flow of data and control among receptors. Although an activity may start with a preliminary topology (interconnection of nodes), the graph topology may change during execution based upon the decisions made so far and the availability of resources in the network. This aspect also differentiates a transaction from a cooperative activity.

Activity Coordinator

The activity coordinator is responsible for the execution of an activity in terms of its subactivities and orchestrating collaborative problem solving. A *conductor* paradigm perhaps best describes a centralized active coordinator. The activity coordinator has the *global understanding* of the type of processing that is supported by each of the nodes. It also knows the processing that needs of each activity in terms of subactivities and the coordination among them. It matches the requirements of subactivities with the resources available in the network. It uses the scheduler and the blackboard monitor to keep track of the progress of an activity and how various subactivities are scheduled in the network.

The functionality that is required to perform a (sub)activity (which is obtained from the resource capability information stored in the ATKB or explicitly specified by the plan) is mapped to the capabilities of the nodes and a plan is generated. This plan is the model of the interaction that is required within the nodes, within the activities, and between the activities and the nodes. This plan defines the protocol that is used by the activity coordinator in inducing the cooperation within the nodes. A high level specification of an activity whose mapping into a plan where the details of coordination are explicit should be transparent to the end-user. The coordination is carried out by means of events and condition-action rules that are supported by an active DBMS. The blackboard is specifically useful for run-time sequencing of subactivities and partial solution exchange.

Active, Temporal Knowledge Base

The specification of subactivities and their interactions determines the structure of the active, temporal database in order to support the plan for managing and executing

44

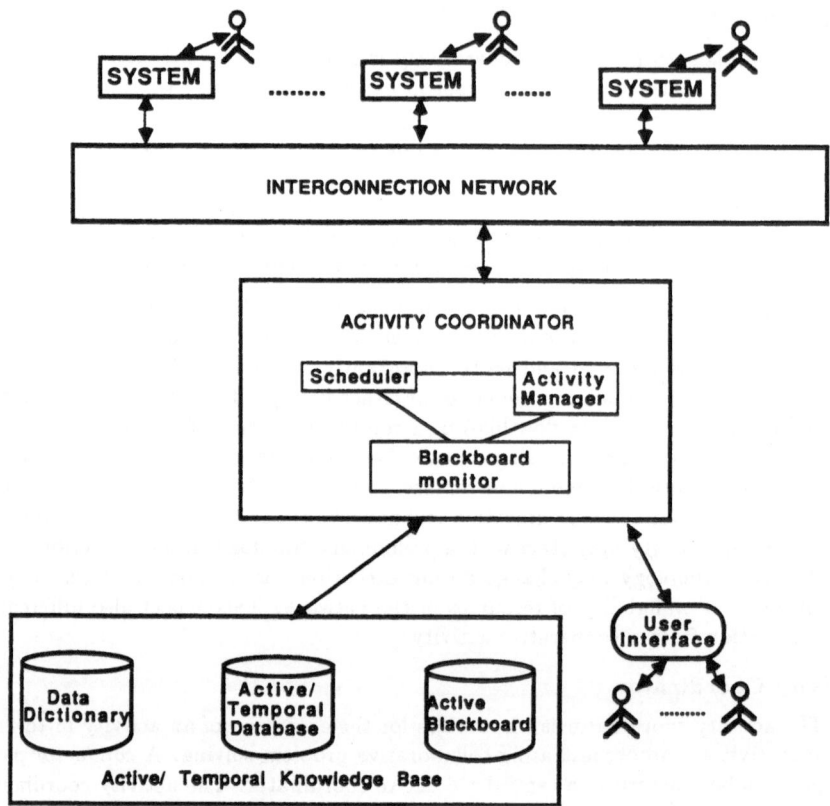

Figure 4.1 Details of the Proposed Architecture

the set of activities in the environment. An active database system supports rules that are formed by events, conditions, and actions. A condition is evaluated when the associated event happens and if the condition evaluates to true then appropriate action is taken. This simple mechanism has been shown to support a number of database functionality in an elegant way [CHAK89b]. The system is responsible for monitoring the state of the database and detecting events specified to it. An active, temporal database has the capability of monitoring temporal events (in addition to database and external events [CHAK89a]) and initiating a set of actions. The plan defines the set of situations that can arise while processing a set of activities and the set of actions that need to be taken as a result of those situations. These situations and actions are modeled in terms of the available functionality of an active, temporal database. The knowledge base is used to store the knowledge regarding the extensional and intensional data of the nodes and environment. Hence a methodology for implementing an active temporal database using design tools seems important. The role of the active and temporal database is extremely critical to cooperative problem solving. Without it, this functionality needs to be incorporated into the activity coordinator, thereby unnecessarily increasing the complexity of the activity coordinator.

Blackboard

The blackboard together with the ativity coordinator orchestrates collective problem solving of an activity. The blackboard acts as a global scratch pad in the centralized architecture and is distributed in the other case. Data used for controlling the subactivities, messages as well as partial results are posted to the blackboard. The active capability of the blackboard facilitates the coordinator to separate metadata required for coordinating an activity with other types of data (e.g., capability and resource availability at each node). Although blackboards have been extensively studied and used, monitoring what is posted to the blackboard and initiation of appropriate actions is novel to our approach. This adds asynchronous execution of sub-activities that is central to the problem being addressed.

4.1 An Example

We present a simplified example of graduate admission process in a university environment. This problem is representative of cooperative problem solving (although not computationally intensive). In this problem there are several systems (nodes) involved in collectively deciding whether an applicant should be admitted to the graduate school or not. There is the graduate admissions office which is the initial contact point which processes the application according to a set of university wide constraints; one or more departments and their graduate offices for processing applications and using departmental criteria for selecting the candidates; the graduate coordinator, and the graduate admissions committee.

Each time a new application or new documents about an existing candidate is received either by the graduate admissions office or by the department they are inserted into the database and are examined. Depending upon who receives it and the state of the file, they need to be transmitted and/or communicated to other nodes. For instance, recommendation letters are sent to the department and are held there without even knowing whether the application has been received by the admissions office. It may be useful to let the other know of the existence of these documents irrespective of the order in which they are received. If the file is still incomplete, a message requesting additional documents is sent to the candidate and a due date is established. If the list of documents is complete, a review process is initiated by the department. This includes one or more graduate coordinators and the graduate committee where the admission is sought. The status of the review is set initially to "pending" and a due date is established for the decision. Each department has its own review process in which, typically, the graduate coordinator interacts with other faculty members in order to reach a decision. When the graduate coordinator returns a decision, the status of the review is changed, and a letter is sent to the candidate informing whether the application was accepted or not. If the candidate has been accepted, a new student record is created, and the candidate record is deleted. A timeout mechanism is used as a temporal event to monitor the due dates. When the due date for additional documents expires, if the status of the documents is still incomplete, a letter is sent to the candidate informing his/her application has not been considered for the present term, and the candidate record is flagged in the database. When the due date for the graduate coordinator's decision expires, a reminder (message) is sent and a new due date is established.

This example has been overly simplified in order to bring out only important aspects of cooperative problem solving activities that were discussed in this paper. Other aspects that are important from the application viewpoint (for example, any faculty can recommend a particular candidate for admission and assistantship at any point, special cases where conditional admissions are given etc.) are ignored. This also illustrates the fact that activities may be open ended or take arbitrarily long time. Graduate admission process will continue each term and information from one or more previous terms is likely to be carried over to the current term. As a consequence, consistency, concurrency, and possibly recovery aspects need to be reevaluated in the context of cooperative problem solving.

The above scenario assumes that each node can communicate with other nodes on a network of machines (in addition to other forms of communication) and that the relevant knowledge (or rules) useful for this problem is stored in the knowledge base of the activity coordinator. We can specify this problem using the notion of activities which are decomposed into sub-activities (which make up activities) and atomic activities (activities solved either by a system or a human as an atomic task) and coordination among the subactivities. Based on the description of an activity, metadata required for the execution of that activity will be determined and triggers and alerters on metadata will be established. A node may either represent a system or computation or a role. A set of rules and triggers may also be associated with a node to perform computation and/or data/control propagation. Edges of the graph may be labeled with constraints (e.g., a limit on the number of applications for some departments). There may be some aggregation condition specified at a node when there is more than one edge incident on it (e.g., to get majority votes).

As seen by a single department, the graduate admission process constitutes only one of the activities going on within the department. Other activities such as student course drop/adds, new course introduction, introducing new research grants, scheduling visitor and meetings, ordering equipments, etc. may be concurrently in progress. The activity coordinator has to deal with the whole gamut of activities at any given point of time.

5 Conclusions

In this paper, we have analyzed the requirements of cooperative distributed problem solving problems and mapped them on to the functional as well as architectural extensions of conventional databases. We have identified the relevant technology areas, briefly described them, and have substantiated the nee for combining techniques from seemingly diverse areas. We have proposed the notion of an activity as an underlying mechanism for modeling and a plan derived from an activity as the script for executing problems that require cooperation.

We have proposed two approaches for cooperative environments – one immediate term and one long term – taking into consideration the feasibility and viability of the components involved. For one of the architectures, we have presented the functional components, interactions among the components, and interactions between the components and the rest of the system.

We have described our approach for executing an activity by means of a plan which is dynamically scheduled by the activity coordinator. We have illustrated the salient features of our approach by an example. Currently, we are developing methodologies for modeling, languages for logical specification, and algorithms for executing activities using the approach presented in this paper.

Finally, perhaps processes such as these will never get completely automated. However, real world abounds in such complex decision making scenarios. We wish to use such illustrative scenarios as targets of cooperation so as to achieve maximum functionality for supporting cooperation.

References

[ADIB85] M. E. Adiba, B. Quang, J. P. de Oliveira, "Time Concept in Generalized Databases", in ACM Annual Conference, 1985.

[ANDE81] T. L. Anderson, "The Database Semantics of Time", Ph.D. Dissertation, University of Washington, 1981.

[AGHA87] G. Agha, "Actors: A Model of Concurrent Computation in Distributed Systems", MIT Press, 1987.

[ARIA86] G. Ariav, "A Temporally Oriented Data Model", ACM Transactions on Database Systems 11, No.4, 1986.

[BARB83] G. Barber, "Supporting Organizational Problem Solving with a Workstation", ACM Transactions on Office Information Systems, 1:1, January 1983.

[BARR89] A. Barr, P. R. Cohen, E. A. Feigenbaum, The Handbook of Artificial Intelligence, vol. IV, Addison-Wesley, 1989.

[BENZ82] J. Ben-Zvi, "The Time Relational Model", Ph.D. Dissertation, UCLA, 1982.

[BOLO82] A. Bolour, et al, "The Role of Time in Information Processing: a Survey", ACM SIG-MOD Record 12, No. 3, April 1982.

[BRAC80] R. J. Brachman, "An Introduction to KL-One", in Research in Natural Language Understanding (R. J. Brachman et al, eds.), Annual Report BBN, Cambridge, Ma, 1980.

48

[BOND88] A. H. Bond, L. Gasser, Readings in Distributed Artificial Intelligence, Morgan Kaufmann Publishers, San Mateo, California, 1988.

[CAST82] I. M. V. Castilho, M. A. Casanova, A. L. Furtado, "A Temporal Framework for Databases", Proceedings 8th International Conference on Very Large Data Bases, 1982.

[CHAK89a] S. Chakravarthy, et al., "HiPAC: A Research Project in Active, Time-Constrained Database Management", Final Technical Report, XAIT-89-02, XAIT Reference Number 187, Xerox Advanced Information Technology, Cambridge, July 1989.

[CHAK89b] S. Chakravarthy, "Rule Management and Evaluation: An Active DBMS Perspective", In Special Issue of ACM Sigmod Record on Rule Management and Processing in Expert Database Systems, Vol. 18, No. 3, pp. 20-28, September 1989.

[CHAK90] S. Chakravarthy, S. Nesson, "Making An Object-Oriented DBMS Active: Design, Implementation, and Evaluation of a Prototype", Proceedings of International Conference on Extended Data Base Technology (EDBT), Venice, Italy, March 1990.

[CHEN86] P. P. S. Chen, " The Time Dimension in the Entity-Relationship Model", in IFIP Information Processing 1986, (H. J. Hugler, ed.), North-Holland, 1986.

[CLIF83] J. Clifford, D. S. Warren, "Formal Semantics for Time in Databases", ACM Transactions on Database Systems 6, No. 2, June 1983.

[CORT84] G. Cortese, and F. Sirovich, "A Daemon- based Programming System for Office Procedures", in Proceedings of the 2nd ACM-SIGOA Conference on Office Information Systems, 1984.

[DAYA85] U. Dayal, J. M. Smith, "PROBE: A Knowledge- Oriented Database Management System", Proceedings of the Islamorada Workshop on Large Scale Knowledge Base and Reasoning Systems, 1985.

[DAYA88] U. Dayal, A. Buchmann, D. McCarthy, "Rules are Objects Too: A Knowledge Model for an Active, Object-Oriented Database Management System," Proceedings 2nd International Workshop on Object-Oriented Database Systems, Bad Muenster am Stein, Ebenburg, West Germany, September 1988.

[ELMA89] R. Elmasri, G. Wuu, "A Temporal Model and Query Language for E-R Databases", Proceedings 5th International Conference on Data Engineering, 1990.

[ENGL88] R. S. Englemore, A. J. Morgan (Eds.), Blackboard Systems, Addison-Wesley, 1989.

[GIBB83] S. Gibbs, and D. Tsichritzis, "A Data Modeling Approach for Office Information Systems", ACM Transactions on Office Information Systems, 1:4, October 1983.

[GINS84] S. Ginsberg, K. Tanaka, "Computational Tuple Sequences and Object Histories", Proceedings 10th International Conference on Very Large Data Bases, 1984.

[GREI87] I. Greif, and S. Sarin, "Data Sharing in Group Work", ACM Transactions on Office Information Systems, 5:2, April 1987.

[INTE90] "InterBase DDL Reference Manual", InterBase version V3.0, InterBase Software Corporation, Bedford, MA 1990.

[HAYE85] B. Hayes-Roth, "A Blackboard Architecture for Control," Artificial Intelligence Journal, No. 26, 1985.

[JONE80] S. Jones, P. J. Mason, "Handling the Time Dimension in a Data Base", in Proceedings of the International Conference on Data Bases (S. M. Deen, P. Hammersley, eds.), July 1980.

[KAYE87] A. R. Kaye, and G. M. Karam, "Cooperating Knowledge-Based Assistants for the Office", ACM Transactions on Office Information Systems, 5:4, October 1987.

[KONS82] B. Konsynski, L. Bracker, and W. Bracker, "A Model for Specification of Office Communications", IEEE Transactions on Communications, 30:1, January 1982.

[KOO88] C. C. Koo, "A Commitment-Based Communication Model for Distributed Office Environments", in ACM Conference on Office Information Systems, 1988.

[KOTZ88] A. M. Kotz, et al., "Supporting Semantic Rules by a Generalized Event Trigger Mechanism", Proc. of Int'l Conf. on Extending Database technology, Venice, March 1988.

[LOCH88] F. H. Lochovsky et al, "OTM: Specifying Office Tasks", in ACM Conference on Office Information Systems, 1988.

[LUM84] V. Lum et al, "Designing DBMS Support for the Temporal Dimension", Proceedings ACM SIGMOD Conference on Management of Data, 1984.

[MAZE88] M. S. Mazer, "Problems in Modeling Tasks and Task Views", in ACM Conference on Office Information Systems, 1988.

[NAVA87] S. B. Navathe, R. Ahmed, "TSQL - A Language Interface for History Databases", Conference on Temporal Aspects of Information Systems, 1987.

[NAVA89] S.B. Navathe, R. Ahmed, "A Temporal Relational Model and a Query Language", Information Sciences, vol.47, no. 2, March 1989.

[PERN88] B. Pernici, "Supporting OIS Design Through Semantic Queries", in ACM Conference on Office Information Systems, 1988.

[PERN89] B. Pernici, "Objects with Roles", in Object Oriented Development, edited by D. Tsichritzis, Universite De Geneve, 1989.

[SARD87] N. L. Sarda, "Modeling of Time and History Data in Database Systems", Proceedings CIPS Congress, 1987.

[SEGE88] A. Segev, A. Shoshani, "Modeling Temporal Semantics", in Temporal Aspects of Information Systems, (B. C. Rolland, M. Leonard, eds), North-Holland, 1988.

[SHOS86] A. Shoshani, K. Kawagoe, "Temporal Data Management", Proceedings 12nd International Conference on Very Large Data Bases, 1986.

[SIRB81] M. Sirbu et al, "OAM: An Office Analysis Methodology", MIT Office Automation Group, Memo OAM-016, 1981.

[SNOD85] R. Snodgrass, I. Ahn, "A Taxonomy of Time in Databases", Proceedings ACM SIGMOD Conference on Management of Data, 1985.

[SNOD86] R. Snodgrass, "Research Concerning Time in Databases: Project Summaries", ACM SIGMOD Record 15, No. 4, December 1986.

[SNOD87] R. Snodgrass, "The Temporal Query Language, TQL", ACM Transactions on Database Systems 12, No. 2, 1987.

[STON90] M. Stonebraker et al., "On Rules, Procedures, Caching and Views in database Systems", Proc. of the ACM SIGMOD, May 1990, pp. 281-290.

[SYBA87] Sybase, Inc., "Transact-SQL User's Guide", 1987.

[WHAN87] K. Y. Whang et al, "Office By Example: An Integrated Office System and Database Manager", ACM Transactions on Office Information Systems, 5:4, October 1987.

[WIDO89] J. Widom, S. J. Finkelstein, "A Syntax and Semantics for Set-Oriented Production Rules in Relational Database Systems", IBM Research Report RJ 6880, 1989.

[WIED89] G. Wiederhold, "The Architecture of Future Information Systems", Proceedings of the International Symposium on Database Systems for Advanced Applications, 1989.

DISCUSSION

Presenter: S. Chakravarthy.

Q. (T. Brown, Brunel University) : Can I offer you one observation. You have some nice pictures where you add in the activity coordinators between the interconnecting network which can be seen as a blackboard. Can I suggest that it might be worth your looking at a book about the Cassandra architecture, where the same kind of idea is produced on a small scale by Craig. There is the central blackboard, which is the communication channel, like the network which you've got there. There is an intermediate level which is known as level controllers, and he finds that there are problems with identifying and partitioning knowledge into those level controllers, that is identifying what are going to be the level controllers and what is the scope of their work.

A. (S. Chakravarthy) : I just want to ponder that. I specifically use the word active blackboard, because blackboards are being used in AI for a long time. Essentially they are used to post information and for someone to read it, but, as far as I understand, you cannot trigger rules and guarantee transaction oriented access for things are posted on the blackboard. So what we're trying to say is that the blackboards should be active in the sense that when you post something, simultaneously somebody should be woken up to say something has happened. That I think is useful but I'm not sure whether that has been done in the literature. We certainly plan on looking at the current thinking on blackboards before proceeding with our research.

Q. (T. Brown) : I think the point I would just like to make is that you open up a number of issues which are worth reading up about.

Q. (S. Kerridge, University of Durham) : Have you any feeling on how database techniques could help with distributed AI problems like reliability? your ...?

A. (S. Chakravarthy) : Yes. A lot of these problems have been addressed in distributed databases and indeed most of the problems have been addressed. For example, techniques for eventually bringing a distributed replicated database to a consistent state in the presence of communication failures or due to partitioning of the network has been addressed. Several transaction management techniques have been developed for distributed replicated databases. So those are the major issues that have been addressed in the database literature. The main problem with, say, the communication failure is that the fragment of the database at that node will not be visible. Not only the data stored in the node (or partition), but all the activity going on in that node (or partition) will also not be visible. Since there are local activities going on when a network partitions, somebody has to worry about bringing the whole system up to date and consistent when that node (or partition) comes back on. Those are the problems that are addressing the database people. I'm not sure exactly what are the distributed AI problems or where this could be used, or whether the same problems have been addressed in this particular area.

Q. (S. M. Deen, Keele University) : In the diagram, you have got a single agent which looks after the cooperation. Where is the decentralisation?

A. (S. Chakravarthy) : Decentralisation is in the distributed architecture where each node is an agent by himself.

Q. (S. M. Deen) : So, you have many of agents?

A. (S. Chakravarthy) : Each node in the network is an agent. As a result each node should be able to communicate with one or more nodes for the purposes of coordination. And I am also assuming that somewhere, preliminary steps of coordination have already been specified as part of the problem. The support we are envisaging is going to be at the system level. If I don't know what kind of coordination is required at the problem level, it won't be possible to map them at the agent's level.

Q. (C. Kindermann, Technical University of Berlin) : I know that Chakravarthy has been related to a project on a semantic database model, Candide, which was based on a AI approach – terminological reasoning. So any relationship to the things you told us about.

A. (S. Chakravarthy) : At this point, we are exploring various alternatives for modelling the capabilities and Candide is certainly being considered as a candidate.

INTELLIGENT AGENTS IN FEDERATIVE EXPERT SYSTEMS

-

CONCEPTS AND IMPLEMENTATION

St. Kirn, G. Schlageter
University of Hagen
Department of Applied Computer Science I
P.O.B. 940
D-5800 Hagen
Federal Republic of Germany

Abstract

Today's expert systems lack possibilities to solve large, complex and heterogeneous tasks. One approach to handle these problems deals with the development of cooperating systems. Due to the major characteristics of the agents in such an environment (autonomous, decentralized, independent) we call the global system "federative expert system". Federative cooperation of intelligent systems leads to a broad range of interesting questions. Some of these are local and global architectures, assessing system's competence to solve problems, task allocation, task decomposition and synthesis of (sub-) results.

In this paper we describe a concept of federative cooperation between intelligent agents and discuss the features needed to make expert systems really competent for cooperative problem solving. One of the central questions adressed in this paper deals with the problem of how to describe and assess the competence of intelligent systems. Finally we present an implementation of a federative expert system, which solves complex and heterogenous tasks in banking.

1. INTRODUCTION

The transfer of today's AI technology from research projects to industrial use has shown a variety of problems. Some of them deal with the need of very special hard- and software-resources, some other with the acceptance of AI-systems by the end-users, but a lot of problems result from central aspects of modelling and representing knowledge. First of all, these problems occur with the design of great, complex and heterogeneous applications ([Wied 89]), because of

1. problems to administrate large knowledge bases:

*   maintenance and consistency of knowledge,
*   only one domain in a knowledge base: the number of relations between the rules in a knowledge base grows faster than the number of rules itself,
*   more than one domain in a knowledge base: relations between different domains require additional administration resources.

2. problems to use large knowledge bases:

*   performance of problem solving and
*   validation of results.

One approach to deal with these problems is the idea of cooperative problem solving. Cooperative problem solving is expected to yield the following essential advantages

*   extensibility of the overall system
*   maintenance of knowledge bases and
*   performance of problem solving.

Federative Expert Systems

Along to [Deen 88] [ScKl 88] we define a federative expert system by the characteristics of the local systems. The agents in a federative expert system

*   are autonomous,
*   do not share any resources,
*   are loosely coupled (for example via blackboard architectures or contract nets),
*   initiate cooperation only, if they identify a need for cooperative problem solving,
*   take part in a cooperation only, if they expect to be able to support the global problem solving process.

Today's research efforts in Distributed Artificial Intelligence deal mostly with those aspects which must be solved in the overall system, like inter-agent communication, cooperative problem solving among multiple experts, intelligent coordination of co-operative problem solving, etc. (see [Bond 88]).

In this paper, we describe the features needed to make problem solvers really competent for cooperative problem solving. One central question we address in the following sections is the problem of describing and assessing the competence of expert systems.

In chapter two we start with an example to give a general view of federative problem solving. This example helps to identify important properties of cooperating intelligent agents, too. Based on that, chapter three develops a general concept of local behavior during processes of federative problem solving. Then, chapter four discusses the key features of intelligent agents which take part in federative cooperation processes. Chapter 5 adresses the question of competence assessment. We propose an approach to describe and assess the problem solving competence of expert systems, based on an integration of ideas from the areas of databases and artificial intelligence. Finally, chapter six introduces an implementation of a federative expert system, implemented under Natural Expert, which solves complex problems in banking.

2. FEDERATIVE PROBLEM SOLVING: AN EXAMPLE

In this section we describe a federative expert system defined by five intelligent agents. Each of them is able to solve special problems in the area of mathematics. The local problem solving capabilities are defined as follows:

- expert system A: polynomial calculus

- expert system B: differential calculus

- expert system C: integral calculus

- expert system D: trigonometrical calculus

- expert system E: power calculus

The inter-agent communication, task description, definition and decomposition is based on a context-free grammar G defined as following:

$$G := (\{E, T, F\}, \{O, V, C\}, R, E)$$

with a rule set R:

$$E \rightarrow E{+}T \; / \; E{-}T \; / \; T \; / \; \int E \; / \; \partial E \; / \; E! \; / \; |E| \; / \; \sin E \; /$$
$$\cos E \; / \; \tan E \; / \; \cot E \; / \; \arcsin E$$
$$T \rightarrow T{*}F \; / \; T{:}F \; / \; F$$
$$F \rightarrow (E) \; / \; a \; / \; b \; / \; c \; / \; x \; / \; y \; / \; z$$

and

E: expression (and starting symbol)
T: term
F: factor
V: set of variable names, defined by $V := \{x, y, z\}$
C: set of constants, defined by $C := \{a, b, c\}$
O: set of operators, defined by

$$O := \{+, -, *, :, \int, |\;\;|, !, \partial, (,), \sin, \cos, \tan, \cot, \arcsin\},$$

The language L(G) can be used to define rather complex mathematical tasks. For example, the following term can be derived from G by simple left side derivation

$$f(x, y) := \frac{\int (1/(\cos^2(P(x)/Q(x)){-}a^2)^{0,5}) + \int(1/(a^2{-}x^2)^{0,5})}{\partial(\arcsin(Q(y)/a))} \; dx$$

This term defines a syntax graph which may serve as first possibility for task decomposition. The root of the graph defines the overall task, each sub-node represents a sub-task (Fig. 2.-1).

Now we look at the process of cooperative problem solving. Task f(x, y) may be addressed to agent A. As we see, it is not able to solve f(x, y), therefore it continues with task decomposition. The resulting subtasks may be those marked in Fig. 2.-1. Then agent A sends abstract subtask-descriptions to agents B, C, D and E. These assess their competence to solve these tasks. An essential point here is, that the agents shouldn't start local inference processes to assess their competence. Instead of this, they compare abstract descriptions of tasks with descriptions of their own (local) problem solving competence.

As a result, problem solving will continue with agents B and C. Again, each of them will reach situations, which require further cooperation. After having finished local problem solving, each agent returns its local results to the tasks manager which synthesizes the sub-results in his (local) overall result.

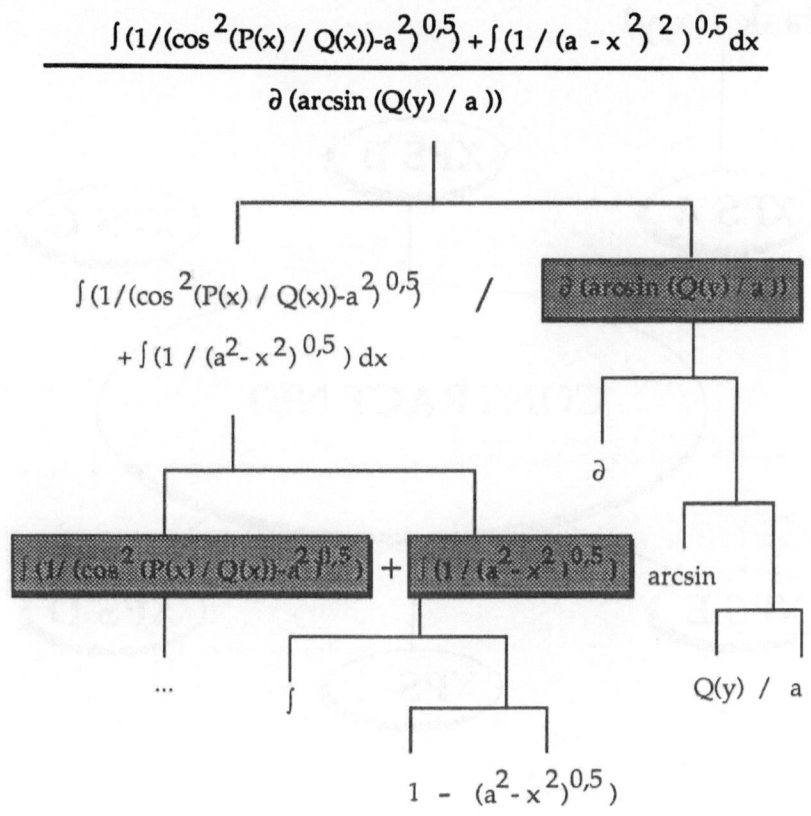

Fig. 2.-1: Syntax-based task decomposition

A general description of federative problem solving looks as follows. The first step defines, which of the agents should lead the overall problem solving activities. In the second step, this agent has to derive that degree of task decomposition, which could be usable to solve the problem. The third step deals with the allocation of sub-tasks to competent agents, which are now responsible to solve these subtasks. This process is cyclic, it continues over several levels of task decomposition and task allocation. It ends, when a subtask has been solved, or if it can't be solved definitively.

58

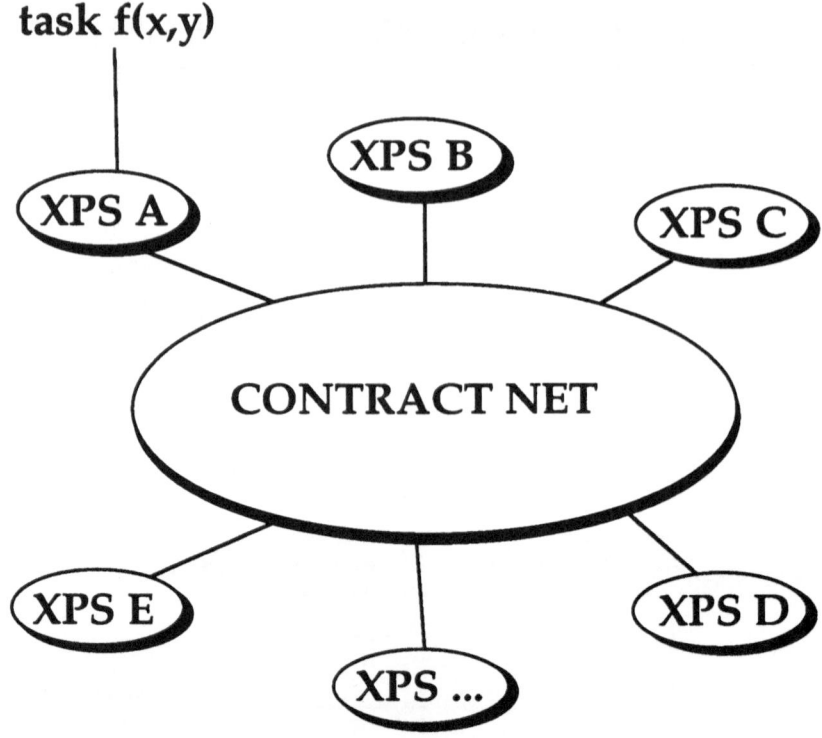

Fig. 2.-2: Dynamic cooperation in federated expert systems

What do we learn from this example?

Even without analyzing all details we see the essential characteristics of federative expert systems. First of all, the interacting agents need some common internode language. At least, this language serves as basis for inter-agent communication (in general that means communication between heterogeneous agents), task description, task decomposition and synthesis of results.

Then, task decomposition could lead to more than one possible set of subtasks, even, if there exists only one syntax graph of the task. That leads to further decentralization of the dynamic inter-agent problem solving process. That means, we have to find criteria to decide, which of them is the best one to be preferred against the others.

Thirdly, task allocation occurs which is based on negotiation between the agents. The allocation of a set of tasks to a group of intelligent agents requires some additional features of cooperating expert systems which are discussed below.

Finally, the agents must be able to synthesize sub-results to an overall result.

We see a rather interesting result in the fact, that the expert systems do not need to have any local knowledge, what problem solving capabilities are given and how they are distributed in the overall system. This feature gives a great chance to change the global configuration of the federative expert system, especially for maintenance purposes like to change problem solving capabilities of local agents dynamically, to remove old agents from or insert new agents into the federative expert system.

3. HOW AGENTS ACT IN FEDERATIVE PROBLEM SOLVING

Now we describe, how intelligent agents act in federative problem solving. The model itself provides a basis to identify those key problems, which will be discussed later in chapters 4 and 5.

The overall systems architecture and the global process of problem solving is designed as a contract net which we don't outline here (see, for example, [Smit 80], [Klet 89]). Like in Smith's contract net system we call an agent, which distributes tasks the manager of those tasks. Those agents which accept subtasks from managers are called contractors.

As we have seen, in a federative expert system every agent can get tasks, which can't be solved by itself. That means, in a first step the agent has to check, if the given job can be done locally. This is a completely new step in expert system problem solving. In some cases, this check will result in an answer, which says, that the agent can do the job definitively, or definitively not. However, in most cases there will not be a clear answer to this question. If an agent beliefs that he would be able to do the job, local inference starts. If it is not able to do the task, it will try to decompose the task to continue local problem solving. If decomposition of the task is impossible, too, the agent will return it to its manager.

Depending from the task description language, task decomposition of tasks could result in the widely known problem of information losses. That requires to identify lost information and to add them to the subtasks resulting from the decomposition. Then these subtasks are described on an abstract level to prepare the task allocation process.

The allocation of sub-tasks has to be discussed in more detail. Tasks can be allocated only, if a system knows, which agent will be able to solve this task. But in which way can an agent get this knowledge? Three basic possibilities are given:

- All agents know the global problem solving possibilities and how they are distributed over the overall system.

- Only one agent possesses this knowledge. It acts as supervisor and is responsible for global task allocation.

- None of the systems possesses such global knowledge; each agent knows only its own competence to solve tasks.

As we have shown in chapter two, federative expert systems tend to use the third alternative.

That means, in respect to task allocation we see the following central requirements of local agents. They must be able

- to estimate and communicate their own problem solving capabilities,

- given some task description to decide, if the described task could probably be solved locally,

- to decompose a task in a set of sub-tasks and

- to allocate a set of sub-tasks to a group of intelligent agents.

The process of task allocation itself is based on bilateral negotiations along the contract net protocol. In our model each agent knows, what it knows and what it is able to do. Therefore, negotiation is based on descriptions of tasks and problem solving capabilities.

Task allocation leads to further local problem solving processes, i.e., local inferences. If local inferences are terminated the system has to check if the results could be accepted. For example, PROLOG systems try to verify a given statement. PROLOG inferences continue until they find a proof. They terminate if there are no more rules to fire or if they find an error.

If in federated expert systems the situation occurs, that there are no acceptable or final results, the local system tries to continue problem solving with task decomposition, too. As a first approach, only unsolvable and undividable subtasks are delegated to other agents. I.e., a new cooperation process will be initiated.

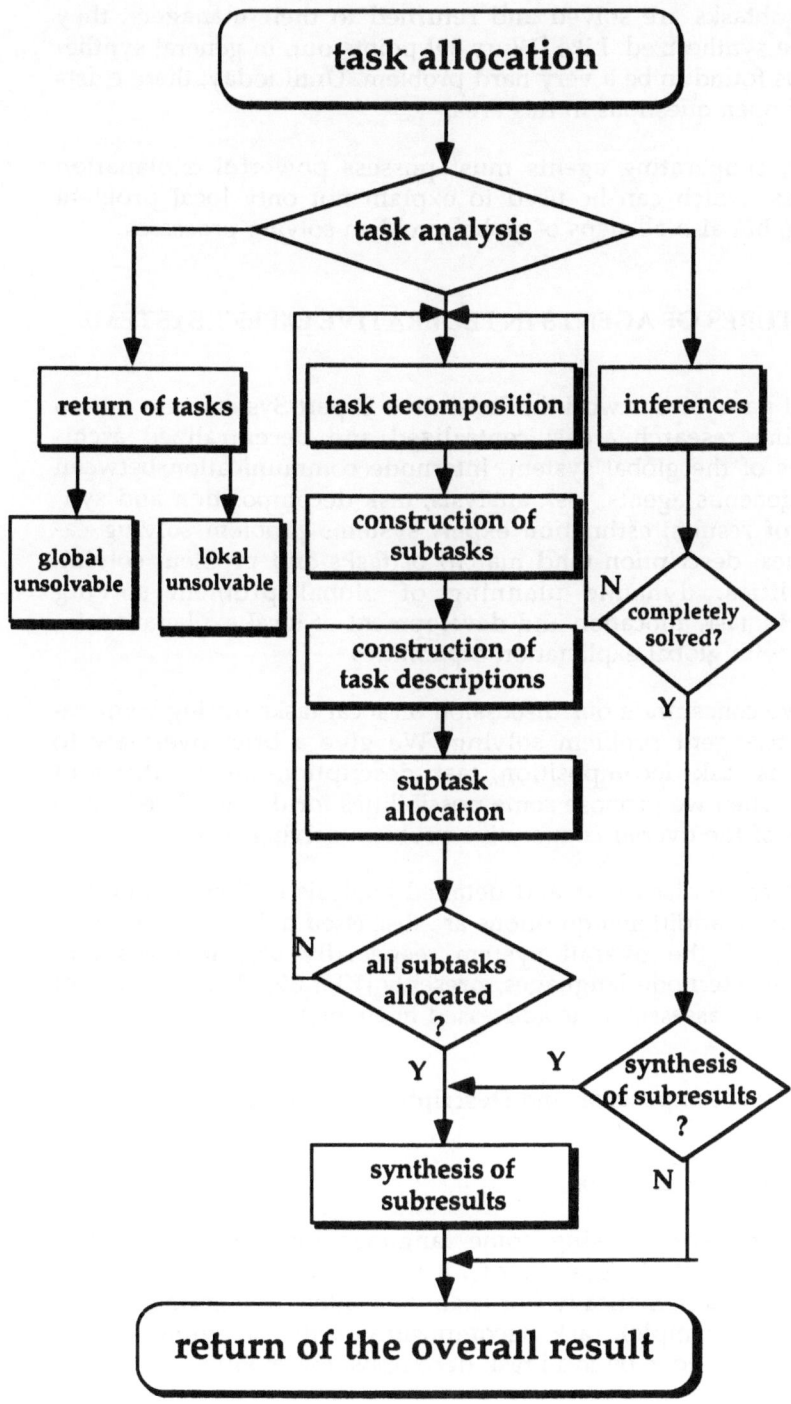

Fig. 3.-1: Local activities during federative problem solving

If all subtasks are solved and returned to their managers, they must be synthesized. Like [Wurr 89] points out, in general synthesizing is found to be a very hard problem. Until today, there exists a lot of open questions in this area.

Finally, cooperating agents must possess powerful explanation facilities, which can be used to explain not only local problem solving, but also all steps of global problem solving processes.

4. FEATURES OF AGENTS IN FEDERATIVE EXPERT SYSTEMS

Central parts of our work in Federative Expert Systems are due to following research areas: centralized and decentralized architectures of the global system, internode communication between heterogeneous agents, task analysis, task decomposition and synthesis of results, estimation expert systems problem solving capabilities, description (and match) of tasks and problem solving capabilities, dynamic planning of global problem solving activities, task allocation and development of local explanation facilities with global explanation capabilities.

Now we concentrate our discussion on local tasks during cooperative inter-agent problem solving. We give a brief overview to things as task decomposition, task description and synthesis of results. Then we propose some possibilities for decentralized, local control of the overall cooperative problem solving process.

An extensive discussion and detailed analysis of these properties and a lot of additional questions are discussed in [Kirn 91]. Central features of the overall system, especially architectures and common internode languages, presents [Klet 89]. The question of competence assessment is addressed in chapter 5.

4.1. Task Decomposition and Description, Synthesis of Results

Decomposition of Tasks

Tasks are defined using some language L(G), which itself is defined on basis of a grammar G. If we use grammars which could be analysed automatically (for example context free grammars, see the above example), task decomposition will use syntax-graphs and could be done by local task decomposition moduli.

Syntax-based task decomposition can lead to situations, which require further analysis. One example are identical sub-graphs, or sub-graphs, which are inverse to each other. The problems we address here are, in some aspects, well known from query optimization in databases.

Task Description

In federative expert systems, task descriptions must be derived from task definitions automatically. However, the development of general mechanisms for automatic deduction of abstract task descriptions still yields a wide field of difficult open questions. In a pragmatic view, however, there are some possibilities to reach first results. These possibilities depend directly on the language used to formulate tasks. From the discussions in chapter two, we could for example derive the following task descriptions

- $f(x, y)$: function, which operates on $\Re \times \Re$,

- $f(x, y)$: function, which has to solve terms like $\int E / \partial E$ ... or

- $f(x, y)$: function, which gives results in $\Re$.

Synthesis of Results

The problems to develop automatic mechanisms to solve synthesizing tasks widely depend on the language used to define tasks and results. Using context free or functional languages will help to solve these questions, while object-oriented or frame-based languages tend to complicate synthesizing problems.

In the implementation described in chapter five we use a functional language (Natural Expert Language) to represent knowledge, tasks and results, which helps to handle problems of term decomposition and synthesis.

4.2. Task Allocation

Along with [Klet 89], efficient task allocation requires solutions for two different and independent problems. First, the local agent has to find out, which set of subproblems should be allocated to other systems. This question deals with the selection of the **most appropriate task decomposition**. Second, the agent should distribute the set of selected subtasks efficiently. That means, for each subtask it should find the **most appropriate problem solver**.

Dynamic Planning of Global Problem Solving

Dynamic planning of global problem solving serves to choose the most appropriate set of subtasks from a given set of equivalent sets of subtasks. In this sense, the following sets of subtasks (from the above example) are equivalent:

Overall task

$$\{[\int(1/(\cos^2(P(x)/Q(x))-a^2)^{0,5}) + \int(1/(a^2-x^2)^{0,5})], \partial(\arcsin(Q(y)/a))]\}$$

$$\updownarrow$$

$$\{[\int(1/(\cos^2(P(x)/Q(x))-a^2)^{0,5}), \int(1/(a^2-x^2)^{0,5})], \partial(\arcsin(Q(y)/a))]\}$$

$$\updownarrow \qquad\qquad \updownarrow$$

$$\{[\int(1/(\cos^2(P(x)/Q(x))-a^2)^{0,5})], \int(1/(a^2-x^2)^{0,5})], [\partial(\arcsin(Q(y)/a))]\}$$

As we see, to answer the question which of all possible sets of subtasks would be the most appropriate one to continue problem solving must take into account the overall distribution of problem solving capabilities. In this view, syntax-based task decompositions include an important deficiency: Without additional intelligence they decompose tasks without respect to the distribution of problem solving capabilities.

In most cases the general problem of finding out all possible sets of subtasks will be found NP-hard. Therefore, we propose a heuristic mechanism to solve this question. In a first step, we decompose a given task and get some set of direct subtasks. In a second step we try to find a set of appropriate agents. Those subtasks which can't be distributed are given back to step one. This algorithm proceeds until all subtasks are distributed to other agents or some subtasks can't be decomposed further. If there is not another syntax graph to try a new way of solving the task distribution problem, the overall task can't be solved completely.

The Task Distribution Problem

Now we assume that the system gets a set of subtasks, which all could be distributed to some agents. Central function of the task distribution modul is the optimal assignment of subtasks to agents, using bilateral negotiation processes. Three different situations may occur ([SMCN 86]):

- There is no possibility to assign all tasks (for example, one agent should solve all tasks, but then it couldn't meet given time constraints).

- There is just one possibility to assign tasks to agents.

- There are more than one possibilities to assign tasks to agents.

Only the third situation defines a real optimization problem . To solve it we need mechanisms which could result in inappropriate distribution decisions. This leads to a dynamic component in task distribution, too.

5. COMPETENCE ASSESSMENT: A FIRST APPROACH

A central question in federative problem solving is, that intelligent agents must really be competent for cooperative problem solving. That means, they must be able

- to assess their own competence to solve some task T,

- to support the global problem solving process,

- to find out the most appropriate agent among a group of competent problem solvers to solve some subtask and

- to describe its own competence (without looking at any task) at different levels of abstraction.

The first approach to describe the competence of intelligent agents could be defined as case-based competence description. That means, we define predicates

- solves_task(INPUT, OUTPUT, RATING),

which establish a list of cases "INPUT" to be solved by an agent. "RATING" is a kind of quality measure to rate the "quality" of "OUTPUT" resulting from the inference process.

The second possibility to describe the competence of agents is based on their knowledge bases. [KSWu 90A] discussed first steps towards abstract descriptions of the contents of knowledge bases. Knowledge bases contain classes, frames or predicates (concepts) and instances. In a group of cooperating agents they are distributed among these systems. These considerations lead us to the following predicates:

- has_concept(C_NAME, `FRAME´ / F_NAME)
- has_instance(C_NAME, I_NAME, KEY)
- is_subset_of(C_NAME1, C_NAME2)
- identical_concepts(C_NAME1, C_NAME2)
- known_all(C_NAME).

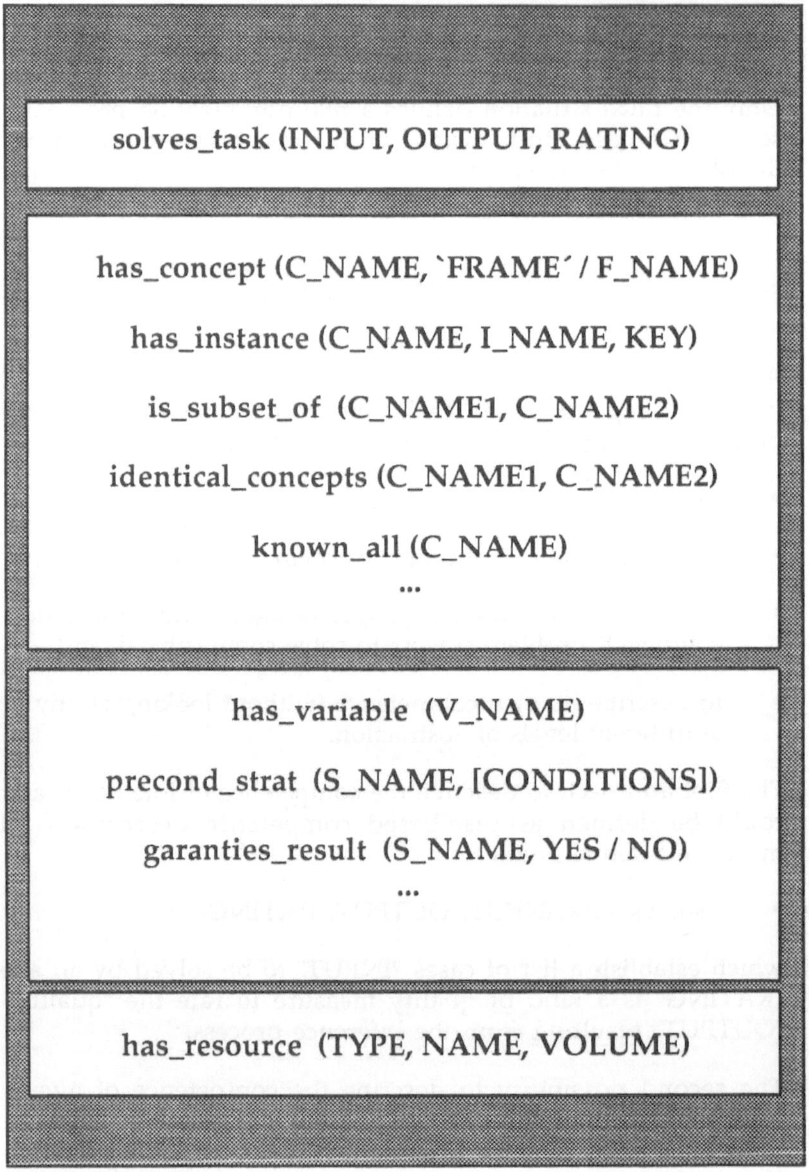

solves_task (INPUT, OUTPUT, RATING)

has_concept (C_NAME, `FRAME´ / F_NAME)

has_instance (C_NAME, I_NAME, KEY)

is_subset_of (C_NAME1, C_NAME2)

identical_concepts (C_NAME1, C_NAME2)

known_all (C_NAME)

...

has_variable (V_NAME)

precond_strat (S_NAME, [CONDITIONS])

garanties_result (S_NAME, YES / NO)

...

has_resource (TYPE, NAME, VOLUME)

Fig. 5.-1: Meta-Knowledge Base

C_NAME, F_NAME and I_NAME are the names of concepts, frames and instances. KEY defines a search key of an instance. The predicate "known_all(C_NAME)" means, that an agent possesses to the concept "C_NAME" all knowledge of the overall system.

A third approach of competence description is based on problem solving strategies. The idea is, that different types of problems may require different types of problem solving strategies. Three central problems are given:

• How could problems be classified (for example, see [Stef 82], [Clan 85], [Pupp 88])?

• How could problem solving strategies be classified?

• How could be related problems and problem solving strategies?

The last two questions are discussed in [KSWu 90A] and [Kirn 91]. In this area, the point is, what derivation strategies (for example forward and backward chaining, pattern matching) and problem solving strategies (like skeleton planning, different searching strategies) are given in an expert system and what are the problems (for example construction, simulation, diagnosis) which require just these strategies?

Today for simple cases we can show, that there exist operational relations between types of problems and problem solving strategies. Some examples are

• predicate "has_variable(V_NAME)" - to describe the list of dynamic variables needed in the case of forward chaining,
• predicate "precond_strat(S_NAME, [CONDITIONS])" and
• predicate "garanties_result(S_NAME, YES / NO)".

V_NAME and S_NAME are names of (dynamic) variables and problem solving strategies. These predicates are first steps to describe dynamic properties of expert systems. Further results still require a lot of work to be done in the area of classification of problems and problem solving strategies, a discussion, which, for example, in Germany begins to grow.

Finally, we can describe expert systems resources like main memory, graphical I/O-devices, parallel processing possibilities, real-time-features. That leads to predicate

• has_resource(TYPE, NAME, VOLUME).

68

Agent A

> father (JACK, PETER).
> grandfather (A, C) :-
>   father(A, B),
>   father(B, C).

Agent B

> father(PETER, TOM).

knowledge bases

> has_concept(FATHER).
> has_concept(GRANDFATHER).
> has_instance(JACK).
> has_instance(PETER).
> known_all(GRANDFATHER).

> has_concept(FATHER).
> has_instance(PETER).
> has_instance(TOM).

meta-knowledge bases

Distributed Tasks

-? father(JACK, PETER).
-? grandfather(JACK, TOM).
-? mother(SHEILA, JACK).

CENTRAL QUESTION

WHICH AGENT
PARTICIPATES IN PROBLEM SOLVING?

Fig. 5.-2: Using meta-knowledge bases: Example

The term VOLUME defines the quantity of a resource available, for example in case of main memory: "2 mega byte".

Fig. 5.-2 contains an example, how to use knowledge about the competence of agents.

A lot of additional topics are to be considered regarding the problems of competence assessment. Among these the (automatic) acquisition of competence knowledge, the question of local or global meta-knowledge bases, multi-user access and access rights to meta-knowledge bases, consistency between knowledge bases and meta-knowledge bases should play a major role.

6. FEDERATIVE EXPERT SYSTEM IN BANKING: AN IMPLE-MENTATION OVERVIEW

Projecting a federative expert system from existing agents is an interesting idea to couple such systems which can not or should not be integrated in one big overall stand-alone system. In such cases, following prerequisites are essential:

- there are suitable stand-alone systems,

- the domain knowledge of these agents could be combined and

- there are tasks, which are too complex to be solved only by one agent alone, but which could be solved by interacting agents possessing different problem solving capabilities.

Meanwhile, the concepts developed to make agents capable to co-operate in a rather flexible, federative manner were implemented in a banking application. In our view, banking possesses some interesting features. There are already a lot of expert systems in use (see, for example, [Ziel 89]). These systems solve tasks from different domains, which, in general are dependent upon one another and their domains often possess identical subsets of knowledge, too. Therefore, we expect interesting advantages from integrating such systems in a federative expert system.

Fig 6.-1 shows the kernel federative expert system, implemented using NATURAL EXPERT, NATURAL and ADABAS. The five agents are able to solve tasks in the following areas:

- analytical studies of balance-sheet,

- boworring power of private persons and credit decisions,

70

- capital investment,

- analysis of small and mean companies and

- analysis of investment structures.

The agents are completely autonomous. They don't share any resources. Partially, they possess common subsets of knowledge. Each agent interacts with specialized databases (companies, interest rates, rates of exchange, clients and so on). They try to solve tasks stand-alone. The system described in fig. 6.-1 already possesses a great variety of cooperation possibilities.

In the actual implementation, a local agent initializes cooperation processes, if it is not able to solve a given task alone. We have to realize, that additional motivations for inter-agent cooperations are needed and possible. Some part of the actual work is dedicated to ananlyze this question.

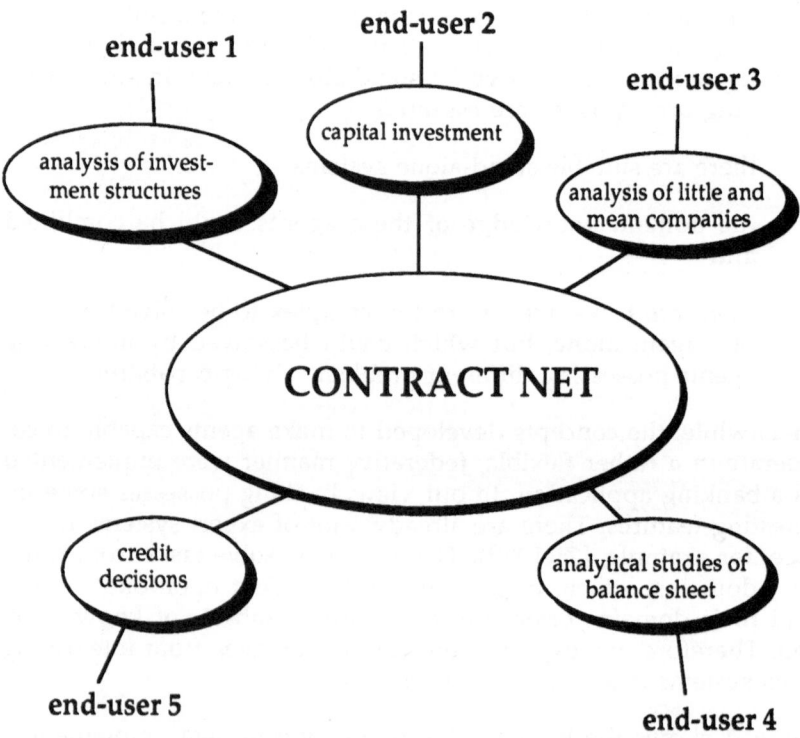

Fig 6.-1: Federative Expert System in Banking

For example we take a look at the agent which is competent for credit decisions. Maybe, the actual client is a small company with unlimited liability. That means, we have to analyse the properties of its owners, too. But also we have to look at other important things. For example, the company could possess shares of other companies, or it possesses houses or other own properties. The credit decision now may perhaps result in a need for complete capital investment reorganization. As we see, there is a strong motivation to allow flexible cooperation among the agents. In parallel that means, the agents should possess flexible possibilities to search dynamically for appropriate other agents. Now we see: The same arguments, which led to the development of expert systems now drive the design of cooperative knowledge processing from (hierarchically) distributed to more flexible concepts of cooperative problem solving.

Finally, we point out those technical properties agents must possess, if they are supposed to be integrated in a federative expert system. We concentrate the discussion on essential results, for details see [Kirn 91]. Besides the requirements of decomposing tasks and synthesize results we see the following important aspects:

1. Requirements with respect to inference engines:

- inference processes should allow full parallel knowledge processing (different tasks from different users),

- inference processes should be re-entrant in that sense, that a temporal termination with following inference continuation starting from the termination point should be possible,

- there should exist possibilities to control inferences from external processes.

2. Requirements with respect to the administration of knowledge bases:

- expert system's access to more than one knowledge base,

- multi-user-access to knowledge bases,

- administration of access-rights to knowledge bases,

- transaction concepts, concurrency control mechanisms and recovery components,

- insertion of new knowledge into knowledge bases during run-time.

Most existing expert system tools possess some of those characteristics which address the inference engine. Product studies however have shown, that the requirements to administrate knowledge bases of cooperating agents are even more critical.

7. STATUS AND FURTHER RESEARCH

The paper discusses first steps towards productive concepts for cooperative problem solving. First results of our work are given in chapter 3 to 5. Until today our work has addressed concepts and prototype implementations in the following research areas:

- contract net systems as overall architecture and cooperating concept,
- local problem solving processes with respect to cooperation,
- competence assessment,
- concepts of cooperative problem solving and
- task assignment.

Further work now deals with the following themes:

- classifying problems and expert systems to improve the possibilities to assess expert system problem solving capabilities,
- development of additional and more flexible cooperation concepts and
- improving technical instruments of knowledge base administration.

In addition, we shall integrate new expert systems of heterogeneous technology into the overall system to address questions of common internode languages and problems of translating knowledge from one representation technology to another.

8. REFERENCES

[AlOt 83]   Albert, J.; Ottmann, Th.: Automata, Languages and Machines for End-User, Mannheim, Wien Zürich 1983 (in german).

[Bond 88]   Bond, A.; Gasser, L.: Readings in Distributed Artificial Intelligence, Morgan Kaufmann Publishers, San Mateo, CA., 1988.

[Clan 85]   Clancey, W.: Heuristic Classification, AI-Journal 27, 1985, pp. 289.

[Crem 88]   Cremers, A.B.; Geisselhardt, W.: Expert Systems
               Proceedings, Symposium, Univ. of Duisburg, Fe-
               deral Republic of Germany, Feb., 18-20, 1988,
               Duisburg 1988 (in german).

[Deen 88]   Deen, S.M.: Research Issues in Federated Know-
               ledge Based Systems, British Computer Society
               Workshop Series: Research and Development in
               XPS V, Proceedings of XPS, Cambridge 1988.

[FiGa 87]   Findler, N.V.; Gao, J.: Dynamic Hierarchical Con-
               trol for Distributed Problem Solving, Data &
               Knowledge Engineering 2(1987) pp. 285-301.

[Kirn 91]   Kirn, St.: Intelligent Agents and Their Integration
               in Federative Expert Systems, FernUniversität
               Hagen, thesis, to appear, Hagen 1991 (in german).

[Klah 86]   Klahr, P.; Waterman, D.A.: Expert Systems-Tools,
               Techniques and Applications, Addison Wesley,
               Reading (Mass.) et. al., 1986.

[Klet 89]   Klett, G.: Cooperating Expert Systems with Con-
               tract Net-Architecture and Their Use in Chemical
               Applications, FernUniversität Hagen, thesis,
               Hagen 1989 (in german).

[KSWu 90A]   Kirn, St.; Schlageter, G.; Wu, X.: Meta-Knowledge
               over the Competence of Federative Expert Sy-
               stems, FernUniversität Hagen, Computer Science
               Reports No. 89, 1/1990, Hagen 1989 (in german).

[KSWu 90B]   Kirn, St.; Schlageter, G.; Wu, X.: Expert Systems
               in Federative Systems: Problem Analysis, Fern-
               Universität Hagen, Computer Science Reports
               No. 90, 2/1990 (in german).

[Pupp 88]   Puppe, F.: Introduction to Expert Systems, Berlin
               1988 (in german).

[ScKl 88]   Schlageter, G.; Klett, G.: Federative Knowledge
               Based Systems, in [Crem 88], pp. 204.

[SMCN 86]   Steeb, R.; McArthur, D.J.; Cammarata, S.; Narain,
               S.; Giarla, W.D.: Distributed Problem Solving for
               Air Fleet Control: Framework and Implementa-
               tion, in [Klah 86], pp. 391.

74

[SmDa 78]   Smith, R.G.; Davis, R.: Application of a Contract
                Net, Framework: Distributed Sensing, Proc. Arpa
                Distributed Sensing Net Symposium, Pittsburgh
                1978, pp. 12-20.

[Smit 80]   Smith, R.G.: The Contract Net Protocol: High Le-
                vel Communication and Control in a Distributed
                Problem Solver, IEEE Transactions on Compu-
                ters, Vol. C-29, No. 12, December 1980.

[Softw 90]   Software AG: Natural Expert Users Guide / Refe-
                rence Manual, Darmstadt 1990.

[Stef 82]   Stefik, M. et. al.: The Organization of Expert Sy-
                stems - A Tutorial, AI Journal 18, 1982, pp. 135,
                published in Hayes-Roth, F.; Waterman, D.; Le-
                nat, D. (eds.): Building Expert Systems, Addison-
                Wesley, 1983.

[Wied 89]   Wiederhold, G. et al.: Partitioning and Compo-
                sing of Knowledge, Stanford University, 1989.

[Wurr 89]   Wurr, P.: Model for Synthetic Tasks, Computer
                Magazin, 6-7/1989, pp. 51 (in german).

[Ziel 89]   Zielenziger, D.: Econometric Modeling For Tra-
                ders on a Budget, Global Finance, pp. 70, 1989.

DISCUSSION

Presenter: S. Kirn.

Q. (S. Sian, Imperial College, London): Sorry if I missed something, for I'm not sure what's your motivation for having a global centralised meta-knowledge base. You tell us, for example, that you had one agent knowing something about Thomas and Peter. The obvious thing to do in that case would be to ask the agent if he can talk to the grandfather. It would go as far as it can and when it can't go any further, whatever problem was remaining you would put that back onto the net, so you get some other agent to solve it. Essentially my point is that it's better for each agent to consult rather than to have a centralised notion of what every agent can do. Why have a centralised notion of capabilities, why not leave it to the agents? It's better for the agents themselves to know what their capabilities are than to have it centralised.

A. (S. Kirn): I do fully agree with you. It was not the intention of my talk to argue for centralised meta-knowledge bases. In our model local agents decide themselves whether to take part in a cooperation or not. Because of autonomy that means, they must know themselves what they are able to do and what they want to do.But now you can see possible conflicts between the particular interest of local agents and the interest of a global problem solving process. Local agent models only a small part of the overall problem solving. If you want to make this process a little bit more efficient, in some cases you could do this by using global knowledge about the competence of the agents. However, our main interest is devoted to decentralized control of global problem solving processes. Therefore, the only centralised information we would accept is a global data dictionary to exclude misunderstandings between the agents because of problems of terminology. In effect, the decision for entralised or decentralised meta-knowledge bases widely depends from a group of criteria. Among others these describe your application, the volume and complexity of the particular agents and the overall system, technical characteristics of the global problem solving processes expected and the special kind of performance problem given in your environment.

Q. (M. Boman, Stockholm University): In all distributed systems there is a problem of validation in a sense that what's represented in an agent may not be true in the universal discourse. In your system you don't separate what an agent knows and what is true, that is you have only simple models. How can you hope to define a notion of correctness in your system so that you can know what is actually a solution to the problem and what is not, since you say that you admitted your system is not complete?

A. (S. Kirn): I think that is a problem you already know from simple, stand-alone expert system. If you have only one expert system and you are the user of this expert system, then you address your question and if you have not taken the appropriate expert system, you may receive an answer which doesn't make any sense. And we do not believe that in this particular environment, we can resolve exactly this problem.

Q. (M. Boman): But I think it is possible and I would like to take issue with you on that. If you introduce say, a modal operator which can separate what is true and what is held as true by an agent, and this agent still reasons with his knowledge as if it was known, then you can advocate complete proof of the procedure for your system if it is based on a deductive database-like approach as in the example you've shown.

A. (S. Kirn) : I agree with you if in all cases this information is given, and if you could add it to the knowledge bases. But I think there exists another problem, too. If you have knowledge which is expected to be true but you use a technique to evaluate this knowledge which isn't correct for this type of knowledge - what will you do with the results now?

Q. (T. Kane, Stirling University) : It seems that this consistency problem is more difficult in distributing systems and that we've quoted your example with two agents. The second agent might know that Peter is the father of Tom from something that is grown knowledge, and your first agent might have a rule that says that Peter can't be the father of Tom because they have information that says so. So then you would have a problem you don't have a single expert system, because if those two things come together you'd never get Peter is the father of Tom. So have you got any thoughts on how you may deal with such problems?

A. (S. Kirn) : In the course of our project we address these conflicts to the user who now should decide which of the knowledge is correct. At the moment, we have no other possibilities. Maybe you could introduce modal operators, confidence factors or something like that. But if you don't have such factors I think you have only the chance to address this question to the end user.

Cooperation Framework: AI Perspectives

Diffusing Inference: An Inference Method for Distributed Problem Solving *

Yasuhiko Kitamura and Takaaki Okumoto
Faculty of Engineering
Osaka City University
JAPAN

Abstract

This paper presents the diffusing inference method, which is an inference method for distributed problem solving, and discuss its properties. Diffusing inference differs from other methods such as task -sharing and result-sharing, and is appropriate for applications that inherently require distributed search techniques. To discuss the algorithm and its properties rigorously, a formulation of distributed problem solving based on the state space graph is introduced. Local knowledge of each agent is represented as a partial graph in this formulation. Diffusing inference works as follows: an agent that received an initial state begins to search using only local knowledge for the goal state as far as it can. If it cannot achieve the goal, then it allocates the rest of the search to the other available agents and they continue to search likewise. Inference diffuses, as a result, among agents as distributed search proceeds. Furthermore, the property of completeness, i.e. the diffusing inference algorithm finds a solution and terminates whenever it is given a problem with a solution, is discussed and proved. Generally speaking, the performance of a diffusing inference system depends on the relation between its inference speed and its communication speed. Therefore a performance evaluation from this viewpoint is presented by using simulation techniques. It shows a guideline where the performance of diffusing inference by multiple agents is superior to that of a centralized search by a single agent.

1 Introduction

Distributed Problem Solving (DPS) is a subfield of artificial intelligence and distributed processing, and deals with problem solving by multiple agents or solvers that are connected by communication network. DPS has advantages such as speed-up of problem solving by parallel processing, applicability to large-scale problem solving or inherently distributed applications, reliability, extensibility and so on [2, 6, 9]. Since

---
*This research was supported in part by a Grant-in-Aid for Scientific Research of the Japanese Government under grant no. 01780051 and in part by International Information Science Foundation under grant no. 90-3-2-287. The authors would like to thank Dr. Mark Klein for reading drafts of this paper and supplying helpful comments.

each agent is usually implemented as a knowledge based system, we can say that DPS is problem solving by a network of distributed knowledge based systems.

DPS has the potential to deal with many kinds of application, which we can classify them into three categories: planning problem (factory scheduling [3] or multiple robot planning [14]), interpretation problems (sensor networks [17], image understanding [15]), and search problem (travel route finding [7], communication network configuration [5]).

R. G. Smith and R. Davis [22] classified inference methods for DPS into *task-sharing* and *result-sharing*. Task-sharing is a top-down inference method based on problem decomposition and assignment. In this method, a manager decomposes a given problem into several subproblems and assigns each of them to a worker that can solve it. Problem decomposition is important to this method, but it is often difficult to decompose a problem automatically and appropriately. Therefore most practical systems use meta-knowledge to describe how to decompose a problem [19] and/or provide conflict resolution mechanism for the case where decomposed subproblems are not independent. The Contract Net Protocol [21] is a well-known communication protocol between managers and workers used for subproblem assignment.

Result-sharing, by contrast, is a bottom-up inference method based on hypothesis generation and test. In this method problems are given to workers a priori, and each of workers generates hypotheses for its given sub-problem and sends them to its manager to synthesize a solution. If all the hypotheses generated by each agent are sent to its manager, the amount of communication will be huge and the communication channel will rapidly become saturated, so how to choose the hypotheses to send is important to this method. The Distributed Interpretation Model [17] is one representative result-sharing system.

There is, however, a third inference method: *diffusing inference*. Diffusing inference is based on distributed search. I works as follows. An agent that received an initial state searches using only local knowledge for the goal state as far as it can. If it cannot find the goal, it allocates the rest of the search to other available agents, they continue to search likewise. The inference thus diffuses among agents as the distributed search proceeds. In this method, a problem is not decomposed or assigned a priori as in task-sharing or result-sharing but is decomposed and distributed among agents as the inference proceeds.

These three inference methods: task-sharing, result-sharing, and diffusing inference have individual strong and weak points but we can say roughly that they are appropriate methods for planning problems, interpretation problems, and search problems, respectively.

In this paper, we describe the diffusing inference method and describe some of its fundamental properties. In chapter 2, to make DPS concepts and its discussion clear, we formalize problem solving based on path finding in state space graphs. Local knowledge of each agent is represented as a partial graph and it is assumed that an agent is able to search only using its local knowledge. Based on this formulation we classify DPS problems and systems.

In chapter 3, we present the diffusing inference algorithm in detail, and the following two chapters discuss its qualitative and quantitative properties. In chapter 4, as a qualitative property, we show the completeness of the diffusing inference algorithm; the algorithm always terminates with a solution whenever it is given a problem with a solution. In chapter 5, as a quantitative property, we compare DPS based on diffusing inference with centralize problem solving (CPS) where all problems are solved by a single centralized agent. The performance of DPS depends on the relation between processing speed-up by parallelism and communication delay. CPS is likely to show better performance than DPS in cases where communication delay is considerable . Therefore, we evaluate the diffusing inference method from the viewpoint by using simulation techniques. We summarize this work in chapter 6.

2 A Formulation of DPS

In this chapter, we formalize such DPS concepts as problems, solutions, agent knowledge and communities based on the state space graph, a classical formulation of problem solving [1]. We then classify problems and DPS systems according to the knowledge structure of the community.

2.1 Problems and Solutions

Problems and their solutions can be formalized as follows.

[DEFINITION1] (problems and solutions)
A *problem* p is given as 4-tuple $< S, O, s_I, G >$ where S is a non-empty set of *states*, $O(\subseteq S \times S)$ is a set of *operators*, $s_I(\in S)$ is the *initial state*, $G(\subseteq S)$ is a set of *goal states*. The tuple $< S, O >$ is called *state space graph*. When the state space graph is explicit, the problem can be described as tuple $< s_I, G >$. A *solution* is given as any path from the initial state to a goal state in the state space graph. □

We can say that non-AI problem solving is a deterministic process such that the sequence of operators is determinated for a given problem and the shape of the state space graph is like a single path from the initial state to the goal state. The problem solving process thus simply follows the sequence, and does not need to puzzle over how to select an operator. On the other hand, AI problem solving is a non- deterministic process. The process needs to select an operator from several alternatives to solve a problem and it may make mistakes. When it makes a mistake, it needs to backtrack to the point of the mistake and select some other alternatives. In some cases, we can use some heuristics to guide the selection. Therefore, AI problem solving can be formalized as a search process that seeks a solution path in a given state space graph. There are a number of search algorithms such as *breadth-first, depth-first, uniform cost method*, heuristic method like A^* *algorithm* [18] and so on. All of these methods, however, tends to face the combinatorial explosion problem. Therefore we need more processing power to deal with this problem; the DPS approach can be one remedy.

In general, a search algorithm outputs a *search tree* with the initial state s_I as the root node for a given problem. If a solution is a path through the tree, we say that the algorithm *finds a solution*. If it finds a solution for any problem with a solution, then we say the algorithm is *complete*. Breadth first and uniform cost method are examples of complete search algorithms [11].

2.2　Agents and Communities

DPS deals with problem solving by multiple agents and, in this paper, the set of agents which compose a DPS system is called a *community* . In general, the problem solving capability of each agent is partial and different from that of other agents, so we need some cooperation among agents to solve a problem. In our formulation, we present the problem solving capability of each agent as a partial state space graph, and assume that the agent can search only inside its graph. We call the partial graph the *local knowledge* of the agent.

[DEFINITION2] (knowledge)
Local knowledge of agent a is denoted by $K_a =< S_a, O_a >$. S_a is called a set of *local states* of agent a and O_a is called a set of *local operators* of agent a. Similarly, knowledge of community $K_C =< S_C, O_C >$ is defined as a sum of local knowledges as follows.

$$S_C = \bigcup_{a \in C} S_a$$

$$O_C = \bigcup_{a \in C} O_a$$

S_C and O_C are called a set of states and operators of community C respectively. □

Here we can define two concepts about the knowledge structure of community: *connectivity* and *coverage*. If a state in the knowledge of an agent is included in the knowledge of the other agent, then the state is called *connective state*. In other words, if local state s of agent a is a connective state, then there exists an agent $b(\neq a)$ with $s \in S_b$. We say agent a is connected with agent b at the connective state s.

From the relation between a problem and the knowledge of an agent or community, we can introduce the concept *coverage*.

[DEFINITION3] (coverage)
When a problem $p =< S, O, s_I, G >$ and the knowledge in agent a, $K_a =< S_a, O_a >$, are given, we say K_a *covers* problem p if $S \subseteq S_a$ and $O \subseteq O_a$. For the knowledge in a community C, the concept of coverage is defined similarly. □

With the above concepts, we can classify problems as shown in Figure 1.

Class1: Problem p is covered by K_a ($a \in C$).

Class2: Problem p is covered by K_C.

Class3: Problem p is not covered by K_C.

Problems in **Class1** are solvable by a single agent, so classical (non-distributed) problem solving is appropriate. Problems in **Class3** are not solvable by a community C since the community does not have enough knowledge to solve it. Therefore, DPS deals with problems in **Class2** or in **Class1** for the purpose of parallelism.

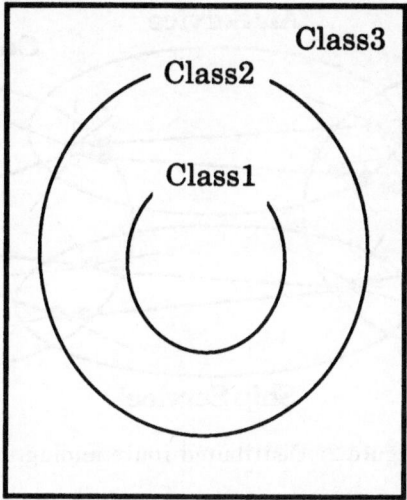

Figure 1: Classification of problems.

2.3 Knowledge Structure

Now we classify communities (DPS systems) according to their knowledge structure
[24]. When a state space graph $< S, O >$ and an agent a's knowledge $< S_a, O_a >$ are
given, if there exists a state $s \in S$ such as $O(s) = O_a(s)$ [1], then the state s is called
totally expandable by agent a. And if there exists a state $s \in S$ such as $O(s) \supseteq O_a(s)$,
then the state s is called *partially expandable* by agent a. "Totally expandable" means
state s can be expanded by a single agent and "partially expandable" means it can
be expanded only partially by a single agent.

Community C is called *totally organized system* for a given problem when any
states in its state space graph are totally expandable by any agent in the community,
and called *partially organized system* if for any state s the following conditions are
satisfied.

1. There exists a non-empty set $A_s (\subseteq C)$ of agents that can partially expand s.

2. $O(s) = \bigcup_{a \in A_s} O_a(s)$.

3. There exists no $b \in A_s$ where $O_a(s) \cap O_b(s) \neq \emptyset$. [2]

In other words, totally organized systems are communities where every agent
has the knowledge to cover a given problem. They deal with problems in **Class
1** and are characteristic of load sharing systems that promise speed-up in problem
solving and high reliability, but must consider the problems of avoiding of redundant
processing and assuring the consistency of each agent's knowledge when some of them
are revised. On the other hand, partially organized systems are communities where

---

[1]$O(s)$ is defined as $O(s) = \{s' | (s, s') \in O\}$.

[2]These definitions are modifications of Yamazaki's [24] and severer than those of his.

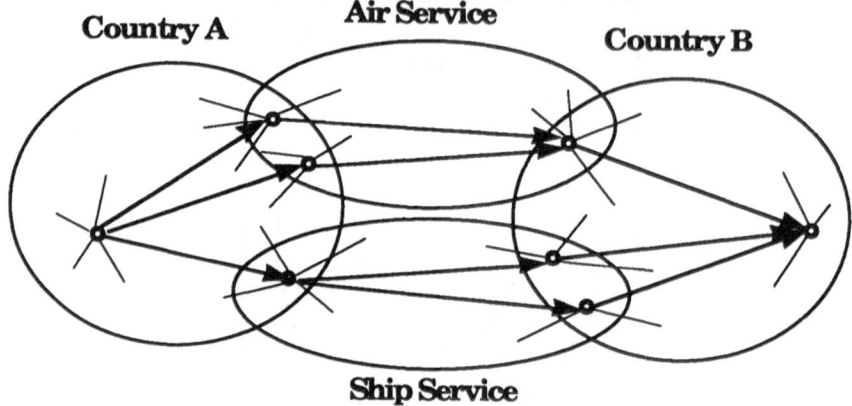

Figure 2: Distributed route finding.

each agent has different local knowledge. They deal with problems in **Class 2** and are functionally separated systems where agents are independent experts. Therefore, the system is characterized by high modularity and extensibility for system development and maintenance, and can deal with problems where frequent knowledge revision is needed. In this paper, we mentioned only two specific DPS systems, but there exist intermediate systems where the local knowledge of agents duplicates partially those of others [16].

2.4   Example

To make the above concepts clear, we use a simple example of distributed route finding (Figure 2). The problem is to find a transportation route between two places in the different countries A and B. We need much information about such things as domestic and international transportation to solve this problem. We assume there are four agents who are experts on domestic transportation in A and B, as well as international air and ship service, so we can say this community covers the problem. There is no agent that has all the required information, so this problem cannot be solved by a single agent, but can be solved by cooperation of the four agents. In the formulation presented earlier, a state stands for a place, an operator stands for a transportation, a connective state stands for an airport or a harbor, and these things make a state space graph. As agent knowledge is separated geographically (country A or B, domestic or international) and functionally (by air or by ship), this community is a partially organized system.

3   Diffusing Inference Algorithm

In this chapter, we present diffusing inference algorithm in detail.

3.1 Assumptions

Before we describe the diffusing inference algorithm, we clarify the assumptions about systems, problems, and knowledge organizations that this algorithm can be applied to.

- A diffusing inference system is a community composed of a finite number of agents. One of agents is called *root agent* a_R that acts as an interface with the user. Each agent can communicate with any other agents only by messages and we make no assumption of shared memory. No messages are lost during communication. Agent a ($\in C$) can use the following communication commands.

  - send(b,m): To send message m to agent b.
  - broadcast(m): To send message m to all the other agents. This is the equivalent to execute send(b,m) command for all $b \in C$.
  - receive(A,M): To receive a message from the other agent. A and M are variables and unified with sender's identifier and message, respectively. If there is no message comes, the agent waits until a message comes.

  An agent is in one of the following three states.

  - HALT: The state after the agent executed halt command.
  - ACTIVE: The state while the agent is executing instructions.
  - NON-ACTIVE: Otherwise. The state where the agent is waiting for a message.

- A problem can be represented as a state space graph. A feature of the state space graph representation is that we can understand the problem solving process clearly, but the number of states can be huge and it leads to combinatorial explosion. This is a research theme not only of distributed problem solving but also of general artificial intelligence. We, therefore, do not discuss any further in this paper.

- A community is a partially organized system. [3] Each agent has information about connective states, so it knows about which local state is connected to which agent. [4] This *connective knowledge* CK_a of agent a is described as $CK_a =< S_a, C >$ and $(s, b) \in CK_a$ is true when agent a and agent b are connected at connective state s.

3.2 Algorithm

The following diffusing inference algorithm is an algorithm that finds a solution of problem by cooperation of multiple agents. The initial state is given to the root agent by the user.

---

[3] When the community is not a partially organized system, we need to add a procedure that avoid redundant processing.

[4] If an agent does not have the information explicitly, it can get it by exchanging messages among agents like Contract Net Protocol [21] although the communication may become massive.

- Message

  - <search;s,r> :To request a problem $< s, G >$ and to give a subsolution r. [5] State s is called *local initial state* of the subproblem.

  - <result;r> : To notify a solution r.

  - <end> : To notify the termination of algorithm.

- Database (for each agent $a \in C$)

  - $OP_a(\subseteq S_a)$: A set of open states that are candidates to be extended.

  - $CL_a(\subseteq S_a)$: A set of closed states that have been extended.

  - $PN_a(\subseteq S_a \times S_a)$: A set of pointer between local states. $(s_i, s_j) \in PN$ means the path from s_i to s_j has been found.

- Function

  - *search_strategy* : A function to choose one open state to be extended.

- Algorithm

  <Initialize> { For root agent a_R only. }

  Step I1: send(a_I ,<search; s_I ,NIL>) for agent a_I which has initial state s_I in its local state.

  Step I2: receive(A,M). If M=<result; r >, then broadcast(<end>) and halt.

  <Main Routine> { For each agent $a \in C$. }

  Step M1: receive(A,M).

  Step M2: If M=<search; s,r >, then local_search(s,r) and go to Step M1.

  Step M3: If M=<end>, then halt.

  <Subroutine> local_search(s_{LI}, r_{LI})

  Step S0: If $s_{LI} \in CL_a$ then return.

  Step S1: Add s_{LI} in OP_a.

  Step S2: If $OP_a = \emptyset$, then return.

  Step S3: $s \leftarrow$ *search_strategy*(OP_a).

  Step S4: Add s in CL_a. Remove s from OP_a.

  Step S5: If $s \in G$, then find r that is a path from s_{LI} to s by using PN. Let r' be the concatenation of r_{LI} and r, and send(a_R,<result;r' >).

  Step S6: If $CK_a(s) \neq \emptyset$, then find r that is a path from s_{LI} to s by using PN. Let r' be the concatenation of r_{LI} and r, and send(a',<search;s,r' >) for all $a' \in CK_a(s)$.

  Step S7: For all $s' \in O_a(s)$, if $s' \notin CL_a$ then add s' in OP_a and (s,s') in PN_a.

---

[5] G is omitted.

Step S8: Go to Step S2.

□

At first, root agent a_R sends a `search` message for problem $< s_I, G >$ to the agent which has the initial state s_I in its local states. In general, an agent that receives a `search` message executes local search. In local search, the agent tries to find a goal state inside its local knowledge using the *search_strategy* function. If it reaches a connective state, it allocates the rest of the search, using a `search` message that includes the connective state and a partial solution obtained until that time, to the other agent using its connective knowledge. When it reaches a goal state, it sends a `result` message which includes a solution to the root agent. When the root agent receives a `result` message, it broadcasts the end message to all the agents to signal the termination of the algorithm.

4 Completeness of the Diffusing Inference Algorithm

In this chapter, we discuss the completeness of the diffusing inference algorithm. Classical single-agent search algorithm is complete if it finds a solution when it terminates. However, in the diffusing inference algorithm, multiple agents execute their algorithms in parallel, so we need to define the concepts of termination and completeness of algorithm in a distributed environment.

We say that the algorithm *terminates* when every agent is in HALT or NON - ACTIVE state. This means that the algorithm terminates not only when each agent is in explicit HALT state but also when in a NON-ACTIVE state where the agent cannot progress any further. [6]

Next, we define a *global search graph* as the sum of the *local search graphs*, consisting of states and paths expanded by an agent. Formally, when local search graph of agent a is represented as $T_a = < CL_a, PN_a >$, a global search graph is represented as $G_{GS} = < CL_G, PN_G >$ where $CL_G = \bigcup_{a \in C} CL_a$, $PN_G = \bigcup_{a \in C} PN_a$.

So we can define completeness of the diffusing inference algorithm as follows.

[DEFINITION] (completeness of the diffusing inference algorithm)

Given a problem with a solution, we say that a diffusing inference algorithm *finds a solution* if the solution is in its global search graph, and the algorithm is *complete* if it finds a solution whenever it terminates. □

With the above definitions, we can prove the following lemma and theory.

[LEMMA] Given a finite state space graph, the diffusing inference algorithm always terminates.

---

[6]It is possible to detect whether every agent is in NON-ACTIVE or not by attaching a procedure.
[8]

Proof: Let us assume that an agent can never be in HALT state. The state space graph is finite, so the number of local states of every agent is finite. Therefore, the OP of any agent who receives a **search** message, will be empty because of the operations CL and OP. Moreover, the number of connective states and the number of agents is finite, so the number of **search** message sent must be finite. Even though an agent can never be in a HALT state, all the **search** messages will be processed and the agent will be in NON-ACTIVE state. Therefore, the diffusing inference algorithm terminates. □

[THEORY] Given a finite state space graph, the diffusing inference algorithm is complete.

Proof: Let us assume that a solution is $(s_0, s_1, \ldots, s_n)(s_0 = s_I, s_n \in G)$. If the algorithm terminates with no solution, the solution is not a path in the global search graph. Then, in this solution path, there is a state which is not a closed state of any agents. We define the first state from s_0 as s_ι. For s_ι, one of the following conditions is satisfied.

1. $s_{\iota-1} \in S_a \wedge s_\iota \in S_a$. ($s_{\iota-1}$ and s_ι are local states in the same agent.)

2. $s_{\iota-1} \in S_a \wedge s_\iota \in S_b$ where $a \neq b$. ($s_{\iota-1}$ and s_ι are not local states in the same agent.)

Condition 1 satisfies $s_{\iota-1} \in CL_a, s_\iota \notin CL_a$ in the same agent a. Because of $s_{\iota-1} \notin G$, there is no path from $s_{\iota-1}$ to s_ι and this is a contradiction. Condition 2 satisfies $s_{\iota-1} \in CL_b$ in agent b and $s_{\iota-1} \notin CL_a$ in agent a, and $a \neq b$. In agent b, a **search** message is sent to agent a because of $s_{\iota-1} \in CL_b$ and Step S6, then there is a message that has not been processed yet by agent a. This contradicts the definition of algorithm termination.

A solution path is a path in the global search graph when the algorithm terminates. □

Now let us consider the case where the state space graph is infinite. In this case, local search in an agent may not terminate and all the other agents may be left waiting. We therefore need to deal with several local searches in an agent concurrently. This means processing several local searches by time-sharing or setting an upper bound on the number of state extension per unit time. This modification leads us to define two control levels for diffusing inference. The lower level controls state extension in local search process using the *search_strategy* function we presented, and the upper level controls local search by choosing the most promising one from multiple local searches. These things also make inference more efficient.

5　Performance Evaluation of Diffusing Inference Method

From DPS we can get the advantage of speed-up in problem solving. However, the performance of DPS may be worse than that of CPS because of communication delay;

it depends on the relation between the processing (inference) speed of agent and the communication speed among agents. Here we show a performance evaluation of DPS based on diffusing inference.

Factors that influence the performance of diffusing inference are parallelism and communication overhead. Parallelism depends on knowledge organization of agents and search strategy that agents use, and communication overhead depends on the number of connective states and performance of communication channel. It is hard to discuss the performance generally, therefore, we take a search problem on a lattice graph [20] and show the performance of diffusing inference method related to the number of agents, search strategies, and the performance of communication channel by using a simulator [13].

We use a lattice graph that has 24 × 24 states, each of them is represented as a pair of integers $(x, y)(0 \leq x, y \leq 23)$, as a state space graph. (Figure 3(a)) We use 4 communities, each of them consists of 1, 4, 9, 16 agents respectively and has a knowledge organization shown in Figure 3. Diffusing inference algorithm searches a path from the initial state $s_I = (0, 0)$ to the goal state $s_G = (23, 23)$.

We use 3 search strategies that follow the following state evaluation functions.

Strategy g: $f(s) = g(s)$

Strategy g+h: $f(s) = g(s) + h(s)$

Strategy h: $f(s) = h(s)$

When an agent expands an open state, it selects the one with the minimum value of this function. [7] $g(s)$ represents the length of the path from the initial state to the state s and $h(s)$ is a function

$$h(s) = \sqrt{(x - m)^2 + (y - n)^2}$$

where $s = (x, y)$ and $s_G = (m, n)$. The search strategy h is the strongest as its search space is smallest. On the other hand, g (breadth-first) is the weakest strategy of the three.

We assume that agents are connected by a single bus type LAN and we use a communication model of Figure 4 approximately. Messages generated by agents go into a single queue and a message comes out every D time units, that defines communication delay parameter. [8] In this model, the more messages are generated, the longer the queue becomes and the longer the communication time of message becomes.

Simulation results are shown in Table 1 when we can neglect the effect of communication delay. The performance except strategy h goes better as the number of agents increases. The speed-up of the strategy g is approximately $\sqrt{n}$ where n is the number of agents, that resembles an analytical result described in [23]. Moreover, the strategy g+h shows better performance than the strategy g. By the strategy h, agents can find a solution path without futile search. The performance is not improved by the diffusing inference. As we described in chapter 2, we can say that this is a sort of

---

[7]We use the value for the upper level control, described in chapter 4, when there are several local search processes in an agent.

[8]We assume that one open state is expanded by a single agent in one time unit.

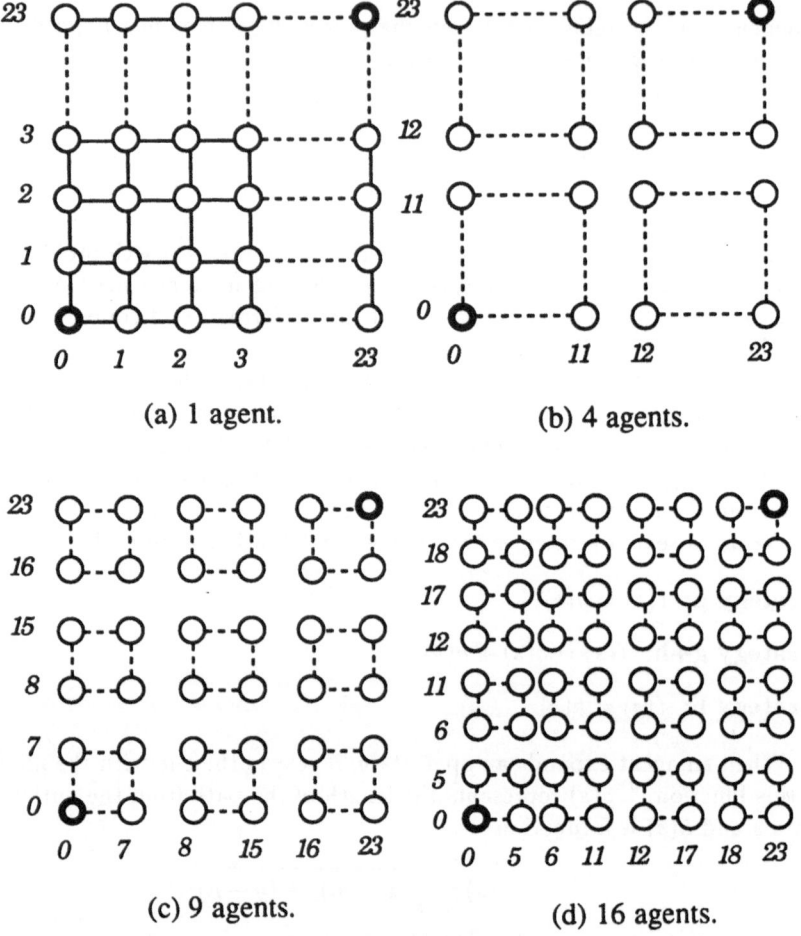

(a) 1 agent.

(b) 4 agents.

(c) 9 agents.

(d) 16 agents.

Figure 3: Knowledge organizations.

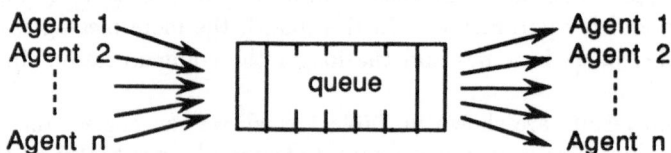

Figure 4: Communication queue.

Table 1: Simulation results without communication delay (total search time and its speed-up)

Num. of agents	Search Strategy		
	g	g+h	h
1	576 (1.00)	576 (1.00)	47 (1.00)
4	289 (1.99)	274 (2.10)	47 (1.00)
9	194 (2.96)	175 (3.29)	47 (1.00)
16	147 (3.91)	131 (4.39)	47 (1.00)

non-AI problem solving since the search strategy is strong enough and the problem solving process can be represented as a procedure. On the other hand, the strategies g and g+h are so weak and so partial that the diffusing inference method works well.

When we consider the effect of communication delay, apparently the longer the communication delay is, the lower the performance is. (Figure 5) The influence becomes outstanding as the number of agents increases. When the communication delay becomes a certain amount, a community that consists of fewer agents shows better performance. This is because messages are accumulated in the communication queue and they hinder the message passing that is requisite for finding the solution path. One approach to improve the performance is to apply a priority communication [12]. If we can exchange messages according to its importance such as the value of state evaluation function, not dealing with them equivalently, we would have the better performance.

6 Conclusion

In this paper, we described diffusing inference and its properties. To make the discussion clear, we formalized DPS rigorously and classified problems and systems accordingly. We then presented a detailed algorithm and discussed its completeness as well as its performance. The results obtained here are fundamental and need more experiments and considerations for practical use.

The most important thing is to improve performance. Just as search strategies and heuristics are important for classical search technique, they affect the performance of diffusing inference as shown in chapter 5. In DPS, not only the amount of calculation but also the amount of communication is critical. To make diffusing inference show better performance, we need more insights into not only on local pruning inside agents but also into global pruning (e.g. the decision about to which agent an agent should send a search message). We then need two kinds of heuristics; one for local pruning of calculation and the other for global pruning of communication.

For building a practical system, the evaluation of performance is important. One way to do this is theoretical evaluation that uses measures like computation complexity and message complexity used in the field of distributed algorithm [4, 10], but such models of an agent are too abstract for the evaluation of the diffusing inference algorithm and need further study.

There has been little work for automated problem decomposition in DPS although

92

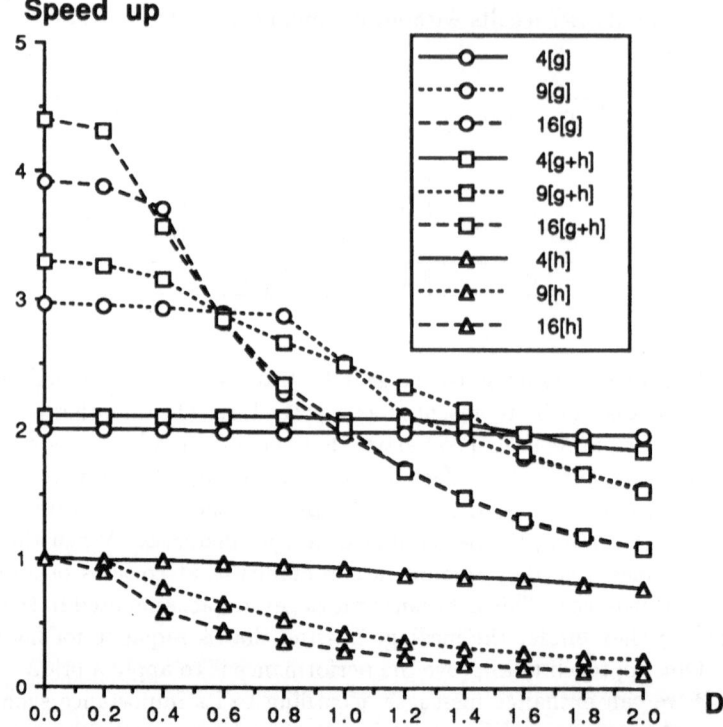

Figure 5: Simulation results.

it is an important function for DPS system [2]. The diffusing inference method inherently contains a function of problem decomposition and it can be a step and worth what we continue to study.

References

[1] Ranan B. Banerji. *Artficial intelligence: a theoretical approach.* Elsevier North Holland, Inc., 1980.

[2] Alan H. Bond and Les Gasser. An analysis of problems and research in dai. In Alan H. Bond and Les Gasser, editors, *Readings in Distributed Artificial Intelligence*, Morgan Kaufman Publishers, Inc., San Mateo, California, 1988.

[3] David A. Bourne and Mark S. Fox. Autonomous manufacturing: automating the job-shop. *IEEE Computer*, 76–86, September 1984.

[4] To-Yat Cheung. Graph traversal techniques and the maximum flow problem in distributed computation. *IEEE Transactions on Software Enginerring*, SE-9(4):504–512, July 1983.

[5] Susan E. Conry, Robert A. Meyer, and Victor R. Lesser. Multistage negotiation in distributed planning. In Alan H. Bond and Les Gasser, editors, *Readings in Distributed Artificial Intelligence*, Morgan Kaufman Publishers, Inc., San Mateo, California, 1988.

[6] Keith S. Decker. Distributed problem solving techniques: a survey. *IEEE Transactions on Systems, Man, and Cybernetics*, SMC-17(5):729–740, September/October 1987.

[7] S. M. Deen. Cooperating agents - a database perspective. In *Draft Proceedings International Working Conference on Cooperating Knowledge Based Systems*, pages 39–45, October 1990.

[8] Edsger W. Dijkstra and C. S. Scholten. Termination detection for diffusing computations. *Information Processing Letters*, 11(1):1–4, August 1980.

[9] Edmund H. Durfee, Victor R. Lesser, and Daniel D. Corkill. Trends in cooperative distributed problem solving. *IEEE Transactions on Knowledge and Data Engineering*, 1(1):63–83, March 1989.

[10] Ken-ichi Hagihara. Distributed algorithms. *Journal of Japanese Society for Artificial Intelligence (in Japanese)*, 5(4):430–440, July 1990.

[11] E. Horowitz and S. Sahni. *Fundamentals of Computer Algorithms.* Computer Science Press, 1987.

[12] Yasuhiko Kitamura, Hitoshi Ogawa, and Tadahiro Kitahashi. A communication method for problem distribution in distributed problem solving. *IEICE Transactions (in Japanese)*, J71-D(2):439–447, 1988.

[13] Yasuhiko Kitamura and Takaaki Okumoto. A brief survey of distributed problem solving simulator: DPSS. In *40th National Convention Record of Information Processing Society of Japan (in Japanese)*, pages 198–199, 1990.

[14] Kurt Konolige and Nils J. Nilsson. Multiple-agent planning systems. In *Proceedings of 1980 Conference of the American Association for Artificial Intelligence*, pages 138–142, 1980.

[15] D. M. Lane and A. G. McFadzean. Co-operative issues in a multi-agent vision system. In *Draft Proceedings International Working Conference on Cooperating Knowledge Based Systems*, pages 5–7, October 1990.

[16] Victor R. Lesser and Daniel D. Corkill. The distributed vehicle monitoring testbed: a tool for investigating distributed problem solving networks. *The AI Magazine*, 15–33, Fall 1983.

[17] Victor R. Lesser and Lee D. Erman. Distributed interpretation: a model and experiment. *IEEE Transactions on Computers*, C-29(12):1144–1163, December 1980.

[18] Nils J. Nilsson. *Problem Solving Methods in Artificial Intelligence*. McGraw-Hill, New York, 1971.

[19] H. Van Dyke Parunak. Manufacturing experience with the contract net. In Michael N. Huhns, editor, *Distributed Artificial Intelligence*, pages 285–310, Morgan Kaufman Publishers, Inc., Los Altos, California, 1987.

[20] Judea Pearl. *Heuristics*. Addison-Wesley, 1984.

[21] Reid G. Smith. The contract net protocol: high-level communication and control in a distributed problem solver. *IEEE Transactions on Computers*, C-29(12):1104–1113, December 1980.

[22] Reid G. Smith and Randall Davis. Framework for cooperation in distributed problem solving. *IEEE Transactions on System, Man, and Cybernetics*, SMC-11(1):61–70, January 1981.

[23] Kumiko Wada and Nobuyuki Ichiyoshi. *A Distributed Shortest Path Algorithm and Its Mapping on the Multi-PSI*. Technical Report 79–11, IPSJ Computer Architecture SIG, 1989.

[24] Haruaki Yamazaki. A system for distributed database with deductive search mechanism: SD^3 and its protocol. *Transaction of Information Processing Society of Japan (in Japanese)*, 26(2):288–295, March 1985.

ARCHON: A COOPERATION FRAMEWORK FOR INDUSTRIAL PROCESS CONTROL

C.Roda, N.R.Jennings, E.H.Mamdani [1]
QMW University of London,
Dept. Elect. Engineering
Mile End Road,
London E1 4NS,
UK

Email: C_Roda@eurokom.ie
          N_Jennings@eurokom.ie
          A_Mamdani@eurokom.ie

Abstract

This paper describes some of the issues involved in developing a cooperation framework for industrial process control. The underlying domain characteristics of heterogeneity and pre-existing problem solvers are explained and their impact on the cooperation framework design are outlined. Problems which arise when trying to coordinate multiple problem solvers are described and then attention is focused on the concept of loosely coupling and how this affects urgency (task and message scheduling in a cooperative environment).

Keywords: Cooperation Framework, Heterogeneous Agents, Loose Coupling, Autonomy, Industrial Process Control.

(1) This paper reflects the effort of the whole ARCHON consortium. The partners are: Krupp Atlas Elektronik, JRC Ispra, Framentec, QMW, IRIDIA, Iberduero, Labein, ERDC, Amber, Technical University of Athens, University of Amsterdam, Volmac, CERN and University of Porto.

1 INTRODUCTION

Examination of the Distributed AI (DAI) literature [Bon88, Gas89, Huh88] reveals that a significant proportion of existing (mainly prototypical) cooperative systems have been purpose-built to solve particular problems using techniques which are not easily generalisable (e.g. Air Traffic Control [Cam83], Vehicle Monitoring [Dur88] and speech recognition [Erm75]). However the ARCHON[2] project aims to be less related to one specific domain, providing a cooperation framework suitable for the spectrum of problems which can be grouped together under the loose heading of industrial process control. Another distinguishing characteristic is that ARCHON aims to develop real-size industrial applications, rather than being limited to small-scale, simplified scenarios.

There are several characteristics of the industrial process control domain which impact upon the framework's design. Firstly, there is a substantial amount of existing domain-level[3] software, meaning that pre-existing systems as well as problem solvers specifically built with this cooperation framework must be capable of being incorporated.

It is possible to view the construction of a multi-agent community from two perspectives: either as a top-down process aiming to create "a team of cooperating agents that act together to solve a single task" [Dec87] or as a bottom-up process aiming to construct an environment in which agents who justify their own existence[4] [Mul89] can cooperate. ARCHON is considering issues related to both of these approaches; however because of space limitations this paper concentrates on the bottom-up perspective. This approach is important because of the desire to incorporate existing software and also because the chosen applications do not solve one single task which can be easily decomposed. In order for agents to justify their own existence they need to be capable of a significant amount of computation (coarse granularity [Sri87]) - this complexity justifies the sophistication of the cooperation framework. It would be inefficient to construct such a framework for simple problem solvers because an overly large proportion of its activity would be spent in coordination rather than actual problem solving.

---

2 ARCHON stands for "Architecture for Cooperative Heterogeneous On-line systems" and is an ongoing ESPRIT II project P2256.
3 In electricity management applications, for instance, domain level systems include diagnosis expert systems, databases containing network topology and conventional software for computing the effects of various loading policies.
4 Contrast this with the elementary problem solvers present in the neural network paradigm [McC86] or blackboard knowledge sources [Hay83, Erm75] which are rendered useless when removed from the community.

The second domain characteristic is that of heterogeneity; most work presently documented deals with homogeneous agents. However in industrial process control this is not a realistic assumption. Typical domain level systems which need to be considered include: expert systems, planners, databases and conventional numerical software. This means the framework must provide appropriate facilities to support a multitude of levels and styles of interaction.

The design goals (increased reliability and enhanced problem solving capabilities in this case) are another influence on system architecture. These aims lead to two forms of distribution - namely physical distribution and decentralisation. Reliability criteria imply the need for **physical distribution** of agents; having the community distributed over several machines means that failure of a single component is less significant. Reliability also implies that the system should have **decentralised** problem solving - hence the community is organised as a group of problem solvers. Characteristics of groups include a limited number of members (few agents in the community) and the absence of an explicit control hierarchy [Fox81]. Control hierarchies are also ruled out because they do not exhibit graceful degradation of performance.

Decentralization and the group organisational strategy implies that individual agents have a limited view of the overall problem (**bounded rationality** [Sim57]) and that coordinated behaviour is hard to guarantee [Dav83]. Therefore mechanisms must exist within the framework for coordinating community activity, these should ensure that:

- Misleading and distracting hypotheses are not spread

- Multiple agents do not compete for or try to access resources simultaneously

- Agents do not undo the results of another

- Actions are not carried out redundantly

In the remainder of the paper communication as a support mechanism for coordination and two aspects of coordination itself (urgency and uncertainty) are analyzed. The structures described assume that each agent has a model of other "interesting" community members (**acquaintances**), such models are discussed in the next section.

2 AGENT MODELLING

It is now well established (in DAI, psychology and sociology) that sophisticated cooperation requires agents to be able to reflect about their role and also that of others within the community. However, one of the many open issues in DAI is the type of knowledge (about the domain, the self and of others) which needs to be maintained and the associated processing which is necessary to support complex social interactions. As yet no consensus has emerged; however by examining existing systems (such as MACE [Gas88] and CooperA [Avo89]) several strands of commonality appear [adapted from Bra89 and Wer89]:

- **Domain Knowledge**: facts and relationships which hold about the environment in which the multi-agent community exists.

- **State information**: indicates the approximate state of processing of other community members.

- **Capability knowledge**: stable information about other community members (eg capabilities and areas of expertise).

- **Intentional knowledge**: what an agent intends to do - usually described in terms of plans.

- **Evaluative knowledge**: meta-knowledge which permits agents to distinguish between agents which offer similar services. It may include a competence rating for skills, a measure of reliability attached to information coming from a particular agent or a measure of punctuality in a time-critical environment.

It is envisaged that the above types of information will also be embodied in our agents models. However this area is still dominated by ad hoc approaches and ongoing work within the project aims to formalise the types of knowledge required to support different modes of cooperative interaction (eg task-sharing, result sharing [Smi81] and coordinating joint actions).

3 THE COMMUNICATION PLATFORM

The aim of the ARCHON Communication Platform is to support distribution at both a physical and a conceptual level. At the physical level, distribution is supported by providing mechanisms for information exchange amongst agents resident on different machines. At the conceptual level, distribution is supported by a set of functions which allow acquaintances to establish meaningful dialogues facilitating decentralized problem solving.

A physical communication service is necessary for any community composed of agents resident on different physical media. However this is not the case for conceptual distribution support; since communication strategies are normally incorporated in the control mechanism of each agent, conceptual communication platforms are not always explicit. ARCHON allows the multi-agent system builder to use conceptual communication functions (e.g. "send this message to all agents which are interested in it") as well as physical communication functions (e.g. classical send and receive). In ARCHON both platforms are based on a message exchange paradigm; shared memory systems were considered less robust for the target environment.

The physical communication platform is based on the OSI standard. The session layer service as defined in the CCITT recommendation X.200 has been extended to support the types of communication required for cooperation. It assumes the existence of a communication mediator which acts as a "Conference Co-ordinator". This structure allows point-to-point, point-to-multipoint and broadcast communication as well as providing storage and retrieval of messages and transparent synchronization.

The conceptual communication platform adds one level of abstraction to the physical communication platform, providing: intelligent addressing, filtering and scheduling.

Intelligent addressing allows agents to send messages to "relevant" acquaintances. For example if information has been generated by agent A1, it may want to send it to all agents which are interested in it. Intelligent addressing mechanisms are based on parameters which specify how to decide the relevance of a message to an acquaintance, and on a description of its knowledge and goals (information embodied in the acquaintance's models).

Filtering means that agents only receive relevant messages - "intelligent addressing" can be seen as filtering out-going messages. An agent can use filtering to receive messages only from certain acquaintances or about certain subjects, for instance.

Scheduling mechanisms in the conceptual communication platform, allow agents to receive messages in a specified order. The order being defined on the basis of message type (e.g. messages carrying an answer to a previous question, messages carrying information spontaneously supplied by other agents or messages carrying requests from other agents) or on the basis of an abstract description of the message's content.

The need for message abstracts representing domain knowledge occurs in the three types of conceptual communication described. Both filtering (in/out) and scheduling may need such domain knowledge. An example of the use of this knowledge is the Time-Out service which enables communication to be aborted when a message becomes obsolete.

In general the evaluation of the timeliness [Dur88] of a message is strictly related to its meaning in the domain of the application.

4 COORDINATING ACTIVITY

This section describes the mechanisms and problems associated with one aspect of the design of a cooperative framework - namely coordination. The issues of urgency (intelligent task and message scheduling) and uncertainty (both domain and organisational level) are highlighted as being crucial for coordinating group problem solving.
When designing multi-agent systems in a top-down manner, problem decomposition and allocation of tasks to appropriate agents is one of the primary considerations[5]. However with a bottom-up approach these issues may not be as relevant. For example, if goal G can only be achieved by a single agent then task allocation is trivial. However if multiple agents can achieve G then task allocation becomes more complex and necessitates reasoning about acquaintances[6].

With the bottom-up perspective, coordinating activity within the community becomes the major issue. If agents merely pursue their own goals then overall community performance is likely to degenerate. One aspect of coordination involves reasoning about the beliefs, desires and intentions of acquaintances - to ensure that agents do not undo or hinder work of others (eg one robot continually moving a block onto the floor and another continuously placing it back in its original position)

4.1 Urgency

In the course of our research we observed that a clarification of the "coupling level" concept was necessary in order to define priorities amongst (evaluate the urgency of) agents' activities in an intelligent and beneficial manner. This section describes how an individual agent's activity is affected by the scheduling of activities of others.

Agents' interrelations can be observed at both static and dynamic levels. Static relations are due to the software

5 Much of this work is termed "Distributed Problem Solving" and considers how the work of solving a particular problem can be divided among a number of modules that cooperate [Gas89].
6 If multiple agents can achieve goal G and they all use the same methods and resources, then selection of the agent to achieve G can only be based on state and intentional knowledge. However if the achievement of G differs in some respect, then knowledge about the differences can also be used to make the decision (evaluative knowledge).

design and hardware configuration, dynamic ones to the problems to be solved and the strategies used to achieve their solution. The concept of coupling to describe static relations has been extensively studied in the field of software engineering and computer architectures. Multiprocessor architectures, for example, are classified as tightly coupled if there is complete connectivity between the processors and memory. In software engineering, coupling refers to the number of data interfaces between two higher-level processes, as represented by the number of data flows that connect them and the volume and type of data transferred. Coupling is therefore a measure of the degree to which software modules are interrelated - a concept which has been extensively studied and which has resulted in various levels of coupling being identified [Ste74]. Both the aforementioned definitions of coupling apply to the domain level. We believe that a definition of activity relationships at the cooperation level is required and that it will be a useful metric that can be used to influence and evaluate behaviour in a multi-agent community.

In DAI applications many references are made to "loosely coupled" entities but all proposed definitions are limited to intuitive descriptions. The most precise explanation is due to Smith and Davis: "Loose coupled means that individual KS's spend most of their time in computation rather then communication" [Smi80, Dav83]. This sentence implies a definition of coupling level as:

$$\frac{\text{communication time}}{\text{computing time} + \text{communication time}} \qquad (1)$$

Firstly it is necessary to clarify at which level of description of the system we are defining the coupling concept. Definition (1) is still strictly dependent upon the chosen hardware platform and the software design. It depends upon the computing power of the machine used and the type of connections exiting between agents. Moreover it gives rise to the anomaly that agents which are able to cooperate without communication are not coupled at all (following Stevens' terminology they are independent).

We aim to provide a measure that describes the extent to which agents' activities are interrelated. In what follows no assumptions are made about the communication media nor about the means by which agents get to know other agents' needs and capabilities - they may have this knowledge and cooperate without communication or they may dynamically inform each other. In the latter case, the level of coupling may be increased because of delays in the activity of communication[7].

---

7 note that communication is just seen as any other agent's activity

From our preliminary study of coupling and autonomy, we have concluded that they respectively give a quantitative and a qualitative description of the agents' activity. We say that an agent is tightly coupled to another (set of) agent(s) if it spends the majority of its time waiting for information / resources / activities which other agents control. Therefore the level of coupling measures the percentage of time spent by an agent waiting for some event controlled by another agent to happen. We substitute definition (1) with the following:

$$\text{coupling}(A) = \frac{\text{time A spends waiting}}{\text{time A spends waiting + A's computing time}}$$

Where the "waiting time" is the time the agent has spent waiting for other agents results or activities and "computing time" is the time spent processing. We define

$$\text{total time (A)} = \text{time A spends waiting + A's computing time}$$

Communication may be exploited to supply agents with information which allows them to minimize waiting times. Note that the level of coupling of an agent may be measured with respect to the whole community or to a single acquaintance. For example the level of coupling of agent A with agent B is given by:

$$\text{coupling}(A,B) = \frac{\text{time spent by A waiting for B's activity/results}}{\text{total time (A)}}$$

Obviously Coupling(A,B) is not necessarily equal to Coupling(B,A), but the following relations do hold:

$$\text{Coupling}(A_1, A_2 \text{ \& } A_3) = \text{Coupling}(A_1,A_2) + \text{Coupling}(A_1,A_3)$$

$$\text{Coupling}(A_1) = \text{Coupling}(A_1, A_2 \text{ \& } A_3 \text{ \& } \dots \text{ \& } A_n)$$
where n = number of agents in the community

This definition of coupling is not static, it depends upon the particular problem being solved, the strategies used to solve the problem and the knowledge that agents have of each other.

Given the above definitions, autonomy may be defined by looking at the activities an agent can accomplish between waiting times. If this activity can be seen as "complete" (e.g. it solves a subgoal), then the agent is autonomous. Whilst the coupling level measures the "quantity" of activity an agent is able to perform independently from its acquaintances, the autonomy level describes the "quality" of this activity. We will concentrate on the former measure which can be specified in a domain independent manner, i.e. agent A is loosely coupled to the community if generally, less then a predefined percentage of its time is spent waiting for other agents' activities.

The treatment of urgency (task and message scheduling in a cooperative environment) is seen as a means by which agents can be kept loosely coupled. Dependencies between agents' activities must be recognized and dynamically reduced by a selective choice between different forms of eager or lazy evaluation. It is recognised that the coupling level in multi-agent systems is strongly related to the design of the domain level systems[8]. However, assuming a domain level design which permits decoupling to some extent, dynamic management of dependencies can improve the evaluation of urgency in task/message scheduling.

The following examples should clarify the aforementioned concepts.

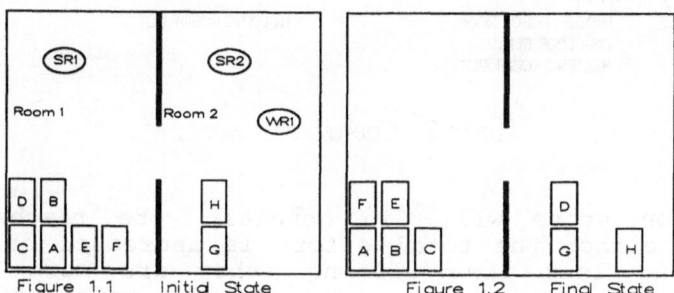

Figure 1.1   Initial State   Figure 1.2   Final State

Figure 1.1 describes the initial state in a domain in which three robots operate. Stationary Robots SR1 and SR2 are able to *stack* and *unstack* blocks in their room. Walking Robot WR1 is able to *take* blocks from the floor of one room to the floor of another one. Whilst *stack* and *unstack* operators are atomic, *take* is achieved via the execution of three actions, namely *pick-up*, *goto* and *put-down*. Figure 1.2 describes the final state the agents want to achieve (goal-state) and figure 2 gives a STRIP-like [Fik71] description of the operators used.

Graph 1 (at end) shows three possible activity sequences for the agents. All three are solutions in that they allow a transaction from the initial state to the final state. To analyse community performance three metrics are used:
- TIME necessary to complete the goal
- TOTAL EFFORT: total number of atomic actions executed by the agents
- COUPLING LEVEL

8 This means that a system which is <u>statically</u> tightly coupled may not become loosely coupled in the dynamic definition. For instance, loose coupling is often not achievable when each agent has different capabilities and all the capabilities are necessary to solve the problem.

STACK(ROBOT,BLKx,BLKy,ROOM)

PRE	INROOM ROBOT ROOM	CLEAR BLKx	ON-FLOOR BLKY
	INROOM BLKx ROOM	CLEAR BLKy	
	INROOM BLKy ROOM	ON-FLOOR BLKx	
ADD-POST·	ON BLKx BLKy ROOM		
DEL-POST.	CLEAR BLKy	ON-FLOOR BLKx	

PICK-UP(ROBOT,BLKx,ROOM)

PRE.	INROOM ROBOT ROOM	CLEAR BLKx
	INROOM BLKx ROOM	ON-FLOOR BLKx
ADD-POST:	HOLDING ROBOT BLKx	
DEL-POST·	ON-FLOOR BLKx	

UNSTACK(ROBOT,BLKx,BLKy,ROOM)

PRE.	INROOM ROBOT ROOM	INROOM BLKx ROOM
	ON BLKx BLKy	
ADD-POST·	CLEAR BLKy	ON-FLOOR BLKx
DEL-POST·	ON BLKx BLKy	

GOTO(ROBOT,ROOMx,ROOMy)

PRE·	INROOM ROBOT ROOMx
ADD-POST:	INROOM ROBOT ROOMy
DEL-POST·	INROOM ROBOT ROOMx

PUT-DOWN(ROBOT,BLK,ROOM)

PRE:	INROOM ROBOT ROOM	HOLDING ROBOT BLK
ADD-POST:	ON-FLOOR BLK	
DEL-POST:	HOLDING ROBOT BLK	

Figure 2   Operators

The solution state will, in general, be reached more quickly if either the total effort is increased or if the agents spend less time waiting (they are more loosely coupled). Figure 3 gives the value of time, total effort and coupling level for each of the three solutions. It can be seen that appropriate scheduling mechanisms may improve both the execution time and the coupling level whilst leaving the total effort unchanged.

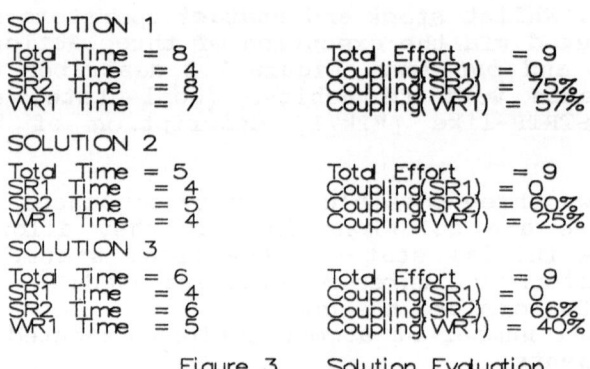

SOLUTION 1

Total Time = 8			Total Effort	= 9
SR1 Time	= 4		Coupling(SR1)	= 0
SR2 Time	= 8		Coupling(SR2)	= 75%
WR1 Time	= 7		Coupling(WR1)	= 57%

SOLUTION 2

Total Time = 5			Total Effort	= 9
SR1 Time	= 4		Coupling(SR1)	= 0
SR2 Time	= 5		Coupling(SR2)	= 60%
WR1 Time	= 4		Coupling(WR1)	= 25%

SOLUTION 3

Total Time = 6			Total Effort	= 9
SR1 Time	= 4		Coupling(SR1)	= 0
SR2 Time	= 6		Coupling(SR2)	= 66%
WR1 Time	= 5		Coupling(WR1)	= 40%

Figure 3   Solution Evaluation

In the solution described in graph 1.2, SR1 starts by unstacking block D enabling WR1 to take it in room2 and, as a consequence, SR2 has a lower waiting time. To choose the

correct action SR1 must know that the execution of
UNSTACK(SR1,D,C,ROOM1) leads to ON-FLOOR(D) which is the
precondition for WR1 to execute PICK-UP(WR1,D,ROOM1). This
information may be contained in SR1's model of WR1. If SR1
does not have this knowledge then the situation of graph 1.1
may occur. If SR1 sees that WR1 will want to PICK-UP D then
the optimum may be achieved as described in graph 1.2. Graph
1.3 shows the situation in which SR1 is only able to
recognise that WR1 requires D ON-FLOOR when WR1 explicitly
starts waiting for the state ON-FLOOR(D). Further options
may also be considered, e.g. WR1 may itself explicitly
require that SR1 *unstack* D.

This scenario represents a typical bottom-up domain - SR1,
SR2 and WR1 are preexisting agents which justify their own
existence and have fixed capabilities. Task allocation is
trivial (each sub-goal can only be solved by a single agent)
and coordination is the major issue. Each agent, solving its
own sub-goals, must reason about the consequences that its
actions have on other agents' activities. In particular this
section has described how appropriate scheduling of actions
may improve the overall result.

If considered at a certain level of abstraction, this
process may appear to bear similarities to critical path
analysis. However because planning and execution are
interleaved (meaning that the complete solution path is not
available for analysis until the end of the interaction)
critical path analysis may not be flexible enough to be
applicable.

4.2 Uncertainty

Uncertainty in a multi-agent community can be an inherent
property of the domain, implying agents must be able to
exchange and manage it even in presence of heterogeneity.
Another source of uncertainty is caused by the interaction
amongst agents (organizational uncertainty).

The first uncertainty problem is related to heterogeneous
representations of ignorance/fuzziness at the domain level.
Since domain level problem solvers may have been designed as
systems in their own right, they may also have completely
different semantics. Therefore uncertainty may be due to
different "points of view" or to different methodologies
used to integrate uncertain information in the reasoning
system. Consider the sentence:

"it will be cold with probability .75"

Suppose agent1 wishes to exchange this information with
agent2. Also assume both agents measure the truth of their
sentences and inferences using probabilistic methods. Even
in this seemingly homogeneous situation, differing semantic

interpretations may ensue. Firstly, agents may use different scales for measuring their probabilities: agent1 uses 0-1 and agent2 0-10. Secondly, the temperature values associated with "cold" may differ: agent1 may consider "cold" to range from -1 to 15°C agent2 from -5 to 7°C. If the two agents use different methods to represent and manage uncertain information (e.g. one uses Bayesian and the other credibility functions) the problem of consistent semantic interpretation becomes even more complex. One approach currently being investigated is to decouple uncertainty treatment and reasoning techniques - the interested reader is referred to [Saf90].

Uncertainty due to interaction may occur even when the application domain is completely well specified and all information is certain. A first type of interaction-related uncertainty is due to communication failures or delays. For instance agent1 may have requested information from agent2 and even received an acknowledgement saying it will be supplied. However, agent1 is still faced with the following uncertainties:

- it cannot be certain the information will be received because the communication channel may go out of service

- it cannot be certain to the correct information will be received because of transmission errors

- it cannot be certain about the time when the information will be received because of transmission delays

Halpern and Moses show that not only is common knowledge not attainable in systems where communication is not guaranteed, it is also not attainable in systems where communication is guaranteed, as long as there is some uncertainty in message delivery time [Hal86].

A second type of interaction-related uncertainty is concerned with acquaintance reliability e.g. agent1 may believe that information supplied by agent2 is not completely certain. A third type of uncertainty is due to the fact that each agent cannot be sure about when and if an acquaintance will undertaken a required activity.

Durfee et al. [Dur85] note that it is possible to reduce interaction related uncertainty by appropriate exchange of information. For example information about uncertainty of knowledge can be used to synthesize results or allocate tasks [Dav83, Smi81, Dur88].

We are currently investigating these issues and believe that the agent modelling and the associated reasoning proposed in this paper will provide an appropriate platform to address these topics.

5 CONCLUSIONS

Some of the issues related to the construction of a cooperation framework suitable for industrial process control applications have been described. This paper concentrates on a bottom-up design approach; meaning that whilst subjects such as problem decomposition become less central in this perspective, others such as communication, urgency and uncertainty become correspondingly more complex and vital.

The need for explicit knowledge about other agents has been explained along with a tentative categorisation of this knowledge. The decoupling of communication into a physical and a conceptual service has also been dealt with.

We have explained why coordination becomes a major issues in a decentralized multi-agent system composed of pre-existing agents and two aspects of coordination have been stressed: urgency and uncertainty management. Definitions of coupling level and autonomy have been postulated with the aim of showing how appropriate scheduling may lead to more loosely coupled systems. Finally problems related to uncertainty management in an environment of heterogeneous agents have been highlighted.

Whilst this paper does not aim to give complete solutions to the problems presented, we believe it contains useful insights into some of the main issues involved in building a cooperation framework from a bottom-up perspective.

REFERENCES

[Avo89]   Avouris,N.M., Liedekerke,M.H.V. & Sommaruga,L., (1989), **"Evaluating the CooperA Experiment"**, Proc. DAI Workshop, pp 351-266.

[Bon88]   Bond,A.H. & Gasser,L., (1988), **"Readings in Distributed Artificial Intelligence"**, Morgan Kaufmann.

[Bra89]   Brandau,R. & Weihmayer,R., (1989), **"Heterogeneous Multiagent Cooperative Problem Solving in a Telecommunication Network Domain"**, Proc DAI Workshop, pp 41-57.

[Cam83]   Cammarata,S., McArthur,D. & Steeb,R., (1983), **"Strategies of Cooperation in Distributed Problem Solving"**, IJCAI, pp 767-770.

[Dav83]   Davis,R. & Smith,R.G., (1983), **"Negotiation as a Metaphor for Distributed Problem Solving"**, Artificial Intelligence, 20, pp 63-109.

[Dec87]   Decker,K.S., (1987), **"Distributed Problem Solving Techniques: A Survey"**, IEEE SMC, 17, 5, pp 729-740.

[Dur88]   Durfee,E.H.,   Lesser,V.R.   &   Corkill,D.D.,   (1988),
            "Cooperation through Communication in a Distributed Problem
            Solving Network", in [Huh88], pp 29-59.
[Dur85]   Durfee,E.H., Lesser,V.R. & Corkill,D.D., (1985), "Coherent
            cooperation among communicating problem solvers". Proc DAI
            Workshop, pp. 231-276.
[Erm75]   Erman   L.D.   &   Lesser   V.R.,   (1975)   "A   Multi-Level
            Organization for Problem Solving using Many Diverse
            Cooperating Sources of Knowledge", IJCAI.
[Fik71]   Fikes R.E. & Nilsson N.J.,(1971) "STRIPS: A New Approach to
            the Application of Theorem Proving to Problem Solving".
            Artificial Intelligence 2, pp.189-208
[Fox81]   Fox M.S.,(1981)   "An Organization View of Distributed
            Systems". IEEE SMC,11,1.
[Gas89]   Gasser,L. & Huhns,M.N., (1989), "Distributed Artificial
            Intelligence Volume II", Pitman Publishing.
[Gas88]   Gasser,L., Braganza,C. & Herman,N., (1988), "MACE: A
            Flexible Testbed for Distributed AI Research", in [Huh88],
            pp 119-153.
[Hal86]   Halpern,J.Y., (1986), "Theoretical Aspects of Reasoning
            About Knowledge" Proc. of the 1986 Conference, Morgan
            Kaufmann.
[Hay83]   Hayes-Roth B., (1983) "The Blackboard Architecture: a
            General Framework for Problem Solving ?", Stanford Heuristic
            Programming Project, HPP-83-30
[Huh88]   Huhns,M.N., (1988), "Distributed Artificial Intelligence",
            Pitman Publishing.
[McC86]   McClelland,J.L.   &   Rumelhart,D.E.,   (1986),   "Parallel
            Distributed Processing", MIT Press.
[Mul89]   Muller,J. & Demazeau,Y., (1989), "Decentralized Artificial
            Intelligence", Proc. of First European Workshop on Modelling
            an Autonomous Agent in a Multi-Agent World.
[Saf90]   Saffiotti,A., (1990), "A Hybrid Framework for Representing
            Uncertain Knowledge", AAAI, pp 653-658.
[Sim57]   Simon, H.A., (1957) "Models of Man" Wiley
[Smi81]   Smith,R.G. & Davis,R., (1981), "Framework for Cooperation in
            Distributed Problem Solving", IEEE SMC, 11, 1, pp 61-70.
[Smi80]   Smith,R.D. (1980) "The contract net protocol: high level
            communication and control in a distributed problem solver"
            in [Bon88].
[Sri87]   Sridharan,N.S., (1987), "1986 Workshop on Distributed AI",
            AI Magazine, Fall 1987, pp. 75-85.
[Ste74]   Stevens,W. Myers,G. Constantine,L. (1974) "Structured
            Design". IBM System Journal, 13(2), pp. 115-139.
[Wer89]   Werner,E., (1989), "Cooperating Agents: A Unified Theory and
            Social Structure", in [Gas89] pp 3-36.

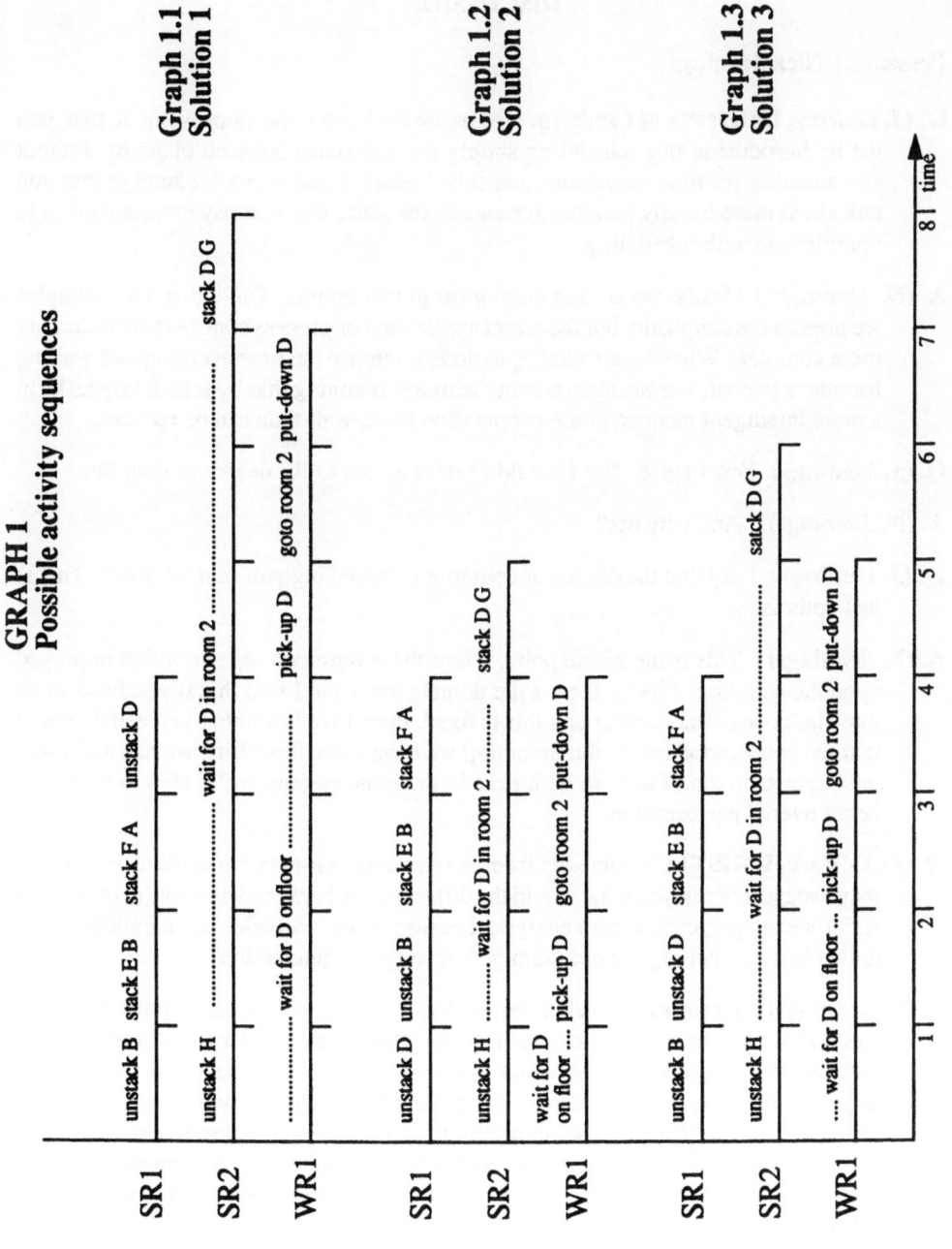

GRAPH 1
Possible activity sequences

Graph 1.1
Solution 1

SR1 unstack B stack E B stack F A unstack D
SR2 unstack H .... wait for D in room 2 .... stack D G
WR1 .... wait for D onfloor .... wait for D pick-up D goto room 2 put-down D

Graph 1.2
Solution 2

SR1 unstack D unstack B stack E B stack F A
SR2 unstack H .... wait for D in room 2 .... stack D G
WR1 wait for D on floor .... pick-up D goto room 2 put-down D

Graph 1.3
Solution 3

SR1 unstack B unstack D stack E B stack F A
SR2 unstack H .... wait for D in room 2 .... satck D G
WR1 .... wait for D on floor ... pick-up D goto room 2 put-down D

1   2   3   4   5   6   7   8 time

DISCUSSION

Presenter: Nick Jennings.

Q. (J. Lenting, University of Limberg, Netherlands): Isn't the improvement that you get by introducing this scheduling simply the difference between planning without any attention for time constraints and scheduling? I find it is a bit strange that you talk about more loosely coupled systems in the sense that you pay more attention to optimisation with scheduling.

A. (N. Jennings): Firstly, we are not aiming for global optima. Obviously the examples we present are simplistic, but the target application of process control is considerably more complex. What we are aiming to do is minimise the time agents spend waiting for others to complete problem solving activity, assuming that by scheduling tasks in a more intelligent manner, at the cooperation level, wait time can be reduced.

Q. (J. Lenting): Yes, I agree. But I wouldn't refer to that as the degree of coupling.

A. (N. Jennings): And why not?

Q. (J. Lenting): I say that the degree of coupling is something you start out from. This is just optimising.

A. (N. Jennings): This is the whole point. I said there were two aspects which impinged upon the coupling. Firstly, there's the domain level and I said that if you need to do three tasks one after another and this is fixed, then there is nothing you can do about it at the cooperation level. But assuming we have some flexibility, we can add some intelligence on top of this; so with exactly the same system, we're able to achieve a better overall performance.

Q. (G. O'Hare, UMIST): If someone from the audience was to be particularly simplistic, may I suggest or ask you what would the difference be between what you're proposing and, for example, critical path analysis, because strong analogies and parallels can be drawn between getting the optimum path through the interaction?

A. (N. Jennings): At a certain level of abstraction, you may view what we have presented and techniques such as critical path analysis as being similar. However critical path analysis requires that the whole solution path be available when the analysis is performed. In process control environments such paths will typically not be available a priori. Therefore we concentrate on improving the system's performance characteristics in a dynamic manner as the solution unfolds. This improvement is typically performed also by means of local optima as a complete global picture is often not available.

Q. (P. Bobbie, University of West Florida): If you have more than one agent that can satisfy the subtask, which one would you use?

A. (N. Jennings): What we've tried to define are the types of information which may be taken into consideration during the cooperation process, in general. With regard to task allocation in particular, it is possible to combine it in various ways, by means of some form of utility function, in order to decide which agent should undertake the particular task. However at any particular instance not all the information may be available and so the decision will have to be made on that subset which is. The single most important piece of information is the fact that an agent is capable of carrying out a particular task. In addition to this if other types of information are available then they may be used to enhance the decision process. If you have some knowledge of the state of the agents, that one agent is busier than another for example, then you may be inclined to choose the less busy one, given no further information. If you have evaluative information about the task; which one is faster, which one is more reliable and so on, then you'd use this type of information. If you have intentional information, such as I know an agent intends to perform a task which doesn't require too much of a deviation to incorporate what I want, then this can also be used. And so the type and availability of this information, defines how the decision is made. However it is important that the time spent reasoning about this process is proportional to the task's importance and the gain which can be achieved by such reasoning. So even if all the information is available you might decide just to use a subset of it if you required the task to be completed rapidly or that is relatively unimportant or most of them will complete it to about the same standard.

Q. (P. Bobbie) : Would you consider having more than one strategy to satisfy the same problem?

A. (N. Jennings) : It again depends on the systems that are put into the multi-agent community. We have applications in which the task of fault diagnosis can be carried out by more than one agent using different knowledge and different reasoning paradigms. They diagnose exactly the same fault, but one can do it in a very fast manner and gives a less accurate result whereas the other performs a more rigorous analysis but takes a correspondingly longer time. Therefore depending on the context in which the information is to be used and on the availability of various alarm types, different strategies may be used.

Q. (S. Sian, Imperial College, London) : I think I disagree with your notion of coupling. An intuitive notion of coupling is more of reliance. So if something is more closely coupled it's more that this agent, agent A, is more reliant on agent B, rather than a notion of how long it has to wait for agent B to complete its task before it can carry on. But I think you have one measure of a coupling then you optimise your plan to ensure that you minimise the time that one agent waits for another.

A. (N. Jennings) : Yes, this is exactly what we said.

Q. (S. Sian) : I don't think you're lowering the coupling by reducing the time that an agent waits. I think coupling is a pre-notion, two agents have a level of coupling between them which is a measure of how reliant one agent is from a different agent.

A. (N. Jennings) : As we said, there are two levels at which coupling can be observed. At the domain level and at the cooperation level. At the domain level the coupling level is pre-determined; however what we are interested in is limiting the effects of coupling at the cooperation level. In order to think about cooperation level coupling we assume that there is sufficient flexibility and redundancy in the domain level coupling.

Q. (S. Sian): You optimise the solution rather than reduce the coupling?

A. (N. Jennings): We do not reduce the domain level coupling as it is inherent in the problem. We're trying to manage the message and task scheduling in an intelligent way at the cooperation level in order to reduce the amount of time spent waiting.

Q. (K. Sundermeyer, Daimler-Benz AG.): On one of your transparencies showing the different types of knowledge, you used a sort of a code with desires, beliefs and so forth, does it mean that you have some logic or some syntax for desires, intentions, beliefs and so forth?

A. (N. Jennings): What was presented was just a standard belief representation. What we'd like to try and do, is to formalise the types of knowledge you need in different situations. Obviously you need some formalism to be able to do this, and so this is a start point.

Collaboration of Knowledge Bases via Knowledge Based Coordination

Donald D. Steiner [1]
Siemens AG
steiner@dfki.uni-kl.de

Dirk E. Mahling [1]
DFKI, Univ. of Massachusetts
mahling@dfki.uni-kl.de

Hans Haugeneder [2]
Siemens AG
haugeneder@dfki.uni-sb.de

Abstract

To take advantage of the growing number of databases and knowledge bases, we present a system that allows for cooperation among spatially distributed agents. Cooperation is supported by providing a uniform agent model and a framework for instantiating various cooperation strategies. The knowledge base functionality forms an agent's body, while the cooperation functionality is achieved via the agent's head, which is a highly specialized coordination and communication expert system. The power of the cooperation arises from the ability to combine highly specialized knowledge bases and powerful reasoning engines to "expert system task forces". These task forces are created only for the duration of a certain project and modify themselves as the need arises. This flexibility brings the benefits of coordination technology from the area of computer supported cooperative work to distributed knowledge bases. We demonstrate these ideas using the domain of linguistic knowledge representation.

1 Introduction

As the tasks in our society grow in complexity, ways must be found to aid in the solution of problems in work and private life. Knowledge bases were developed to make a first step towards the solution of this problem. As is apparent now, isolated knowledge bases can cope with the demands of real world applications only in very special cases. It is therefore necessary to pool the knowledge resources available for a problem at hand. This means allowing knowledge bases to cooperate with each other and also to cooperate with humans. An example of such a situation is a knowledge base which needs to process knowledge beyond its capabilities and therefore must access another knowledge source. The major problem facing us then,

---

[1] DFKI, Postfach 2080, D-6750 Kaiserslautern, Germany
[2] DFKI, Stuhlsatzenhausweg 3, D-6600 Saarbrücken 11, Germany

is to allow independent, knowledge based agents (humans or AI systems) to coordinate their efforts. We present a model of cooperating agents, which works effectively for supporting cooperation among knowledge based systems. We view *cooperation* among agents as a two-step process. In order to effectively *collaborate* (work together in order to to solve a task), agents must first *coordinate* their task solving approach. This need not necessarily be done by all agents together (resulting in the cooperative task of deciding on the correct coordination), but may be handled by specialized coordination agents. Cooperation involves many iterations of coordination/collaboration. In this paper we discuss the efforts of Project KIK [1] concerning the cooperation among knowledge bases taking both steps into account. We also take advantage of the fact that knowledge bases can exist independently from inference engines.

Project KIK brings Distributed Artificial Intelligence, Socio-Cognitive Engineering, Telecommunication, and Interface Design together in an attempt to provide integrated solutions to collaboration problems. Viewing human and machine agents as partners in communication, cooperation, problem solving, and task execution extends the conventional CSCW paradigm to Human-Computer Cooperative Work (HCCW).

The combination of rapid advances in CSCW, Socio-Cognitive Engineering, and DAI, as well as in network and communication technology, have the synergetic potential to design systems allowing for novel scenarios which substantially exceed the performance of current cooperation systems. We are developing a design paradigm for cooperative systems that starts by mapping the social, cognitive, and functional territory [Mah90]. This mapping process includes traditional task and goal analysis, ethnographic methods, and other behavioral and analytical techniques. After the mapping survey of users, tasks, goals, requirements, etc. has reached a stable level, the formation of a model can start. For this purpose, existing models and theories in the scientific body of knowledge that can be used to embed, explain, or predict findings from the mapping process are indexed. Facts and observations that can not be covered in this way, possibly lead to additional theoretical research. Eventually a model will be synthesized that integrates data from the mapping process, existing models and theories, which are applicable, and sub models from additional research. Based on this synthesized model, implications can be drawn on how to design or modify the collaboration among human and machine agents. Rapid prototyping in conjunction with user-centered design and user participation is used to build initial versions of a solution to work and cooperation problems. These solutions are iteratively refined, until operational usability goals are reached [WBH87].

The goal of the TEAMWARE subproject of KIK is the specification and design of an architecture for a wide class of cooperation systems. In order to support the logical aspects of distribution and cooperation in such systems we are building the extended multi-agent framework MECCA (Multi-Agent Environment for Constructing Cooperative Applications). This framework, based on the general agent model, will be used as the underlying architecture for constructing CSCW applications.

In this paper, we describe the particularly important roles that knowledge bases play in the CSCW effort. We further present a general model of agents in distributed

---

[1] Project KIK is a collaborative effort between the German Research Center for Artificial Intelligence (DFKI) and Siemens AG; the acronym KIK arises from the german abbreviations for *Künstliche Intelligenz (KI)*, meaning AI, and *Kommunikation*, meaning communications.

systems and demonstrate how this model will support the incorporation of knowledge bases into CSCW systems. We end with a particularly relevant CSCW application, namely that of constructing large knowledge based systems in a team.

Much of the research done in CSCW has focused on providing low-level support for communication between agents. It is our hypothesis that, in order to provide effective support and coordination, the system must contain a model of the overall environment and of the agents. The particular approach to knowledge based support that we are proposing emphasizes the use of knowledge bases, plans, and agent models. A plan-based approach has significant advantages in making knowledge based support feasible in environments which are dynamic and inherently open-ended.

2 Agent Model

In this section we describe a general model of an agent which was developed in order to support the wide variety of agents, communication structures, and cooperation structures required by the CSCW and DAI scenarios. The two major roles of such an agent are:

1. Execution of assigned tasks bringing the group closer to the top-level goal;

2. Participation in the cooperation process.

Execution refers to the agent's individual task functionality for performing subtasks in the application domain; the complexity of the individual skills of various agents may differ drastically (from, say, printing a document to highly sophisticated knowledge based deduction).

Participation refers to the agent's capability for performing cooperation tasks. The central issue from a cooperative point of view is the additional amount of processing an agent must perform in addition to subtask execution in the application domain. This additional behavior of agents is based upon knowledge which explicitly represents the underlying cooperation model. This will generally involve interacting with other agents requesting information, giving information etc.

Further, in order to cooperate effectively, an agent must be able to communicate with other agents in the system (i.e. send and receive messages to and from other agents) and to react appropriately upon receipt of a message (i.e. based upon the content of the message perform some task).

2.1 General Agents

An agent can be decomposed into the following parts [SMH90]: the functional, task-solving component *agent body*, the cooperative superstrate *agent head*, the communication functionality *mouth*, and the physical connections to other agents via the communication channels.

The body of an agent constitutes its internal problem-solving expertise and provides the basic functionality of the agent: that portion which the agent can do independent of cooperation and on its own. An agent body can be a piece of hardware (e.g. sensor or robot) or software (e.g. financial advisor package) or humans with their respective skills. An agent body can be pre-existing hardware or software. It may be independent of any multi-agent system, as a stand-alone application, or participate in different systems. Once created, an agent is expected to follow the general rules of that multi-agent environment until released. Reusability and duplication of bodies of machine agents is generally possible. The head of an agent is that portion which allows the agent to participate in the cooperation process. For machine agents, it is generally a software system with several components. For human agents it will be comprised of the human's own knowledge and an intelligent user interface between the human and the other agents.

In order for an agent to contribute to the overall problem solving process in a goal oriented fashion it must have knowledge about:

- its own facilities and capabilities

- facilities and capabilities of other agents (potentially incomplete)

- inter-agent communication facilities

- the current task

Thus the head can be seen as a mediator between the agent's individual functionality and the overall problem solving context. Further, in order for the agent to actively cooperate with other agents, it must have knowledge about the relevant aspects of cooperation such as:

- its own cooperation role(s)

- cooperation roles of agents, with which it is cooperating (this may not be all agents in the c-world)

- globally available cooperation strategies, from which it can choose to implement new cooperation structures

- current cooperation structures it is involved in.

Knowledge of an agent may be determined upon startup of the system (such as a database) or may be acquired dynamically, by transfer between agents in the course of problem solving.

An agent's knowledge can thus be divided into two parts: that which allows it to define its own behavior, at a meta-level, and that used to solve problems or execute tasks [Mah90]. The agent should be able to express meta-knowledge, i.e. a set of knowledge about other knowledge. Meta-knowledge of capabilities, status and behavior of other agents is referred to as *epistemic knowledge*. *Autoepistemic knowledge* pertains to knowledge about an agent's own capabilities. These two types of knowledge make it possible to deal with interaction among agents. In the course of receiving messages, an agent may use its autoepistemic knowledge concerning its capabilities to retrieve information or to accept messages it is interested in, while in sending, its epistemic knowledge allows it to choose the appropriate addressees.

Epistemic knowledge can take the form of acquaintances which concern beliefs about interests (goals, plans, etc.) and the capabilities of other agents.

Though application independent cooperation functions are desirable, the requirements will also be driven by the concrete application needs. Thus we will allow for customized tailoring of these features according to the goal and purpose of each individual application. Of further interest is the interface between an agent's head and its body. If the body is an advanced system, the interface will have to be very broad, allowing for the many capabilities of the body. On the other hand, if a body is simple, the interface will be correspondingly less complicated.

In order to communicate with other agents, an agent needs to have access to appropriate telecommunications channels and network information about the agents, such as their various addresses. The mouth is that portion of the head which fulfills this communication functionality. So the mouth of an agent would basically process a message from the head, find out which address to deliver it to and send the message. It would also receive messages from other agents and send them to the head for further processing. Thus, the mouth represents the interface from the agent to the cooperation world. The mouth also has the responsibility of receiving messages from other agents and passing them on for further processing to the head.

2.2 Knowledge Bases and Inference Engines as Agents

This general agent model enables existing or new knowledge bases to communicate with other agents, such as human users, reasoning engines, or other knowledge bases. This ability is achieved by providing the knowledge base body with a head and a mouth. The head consists of a cooperation knowledge base and other coordination modules, while the mouth serves as the actual communication device. Inference and deduction engines, which usually form the reasoning module in knowledge based expert systems, can be extended similarly. The body functionality of these agents is, of course, different from the knowledge bases. Conventional expert systems consist of a knowledge base and a reasoning engine, either deductive or inference, in one system.

3 Expert System Ad-Hocracies

With cooperating knowledge bases and modularized expert systems, we have the opportunity to configure expert systems for very specific purposes as the need arises and to quickly reconfigure them for the next task. Coordination technology, enabling human task forces and ad-hocracies, thereby breaking up rigid organizational structures and allowing flexible responses to changes in complex environments, can be expanded to the realm of machine agents.

The most basic case is to link a particular knowledge base to a specified reasoning engine. These two agents thereby form a conventional expert system for the time of their cooperation. Important issues in this case are the compatibility of system formalism and the question of initiative for finding a partner. This scenario can be extended to a reasoning engine cooperating with several knowledge bases to solve a certain problem. Questions of compatibility between knowledge base formalisms and aliasing problems arise here. The most sophisticated case would be the cooperation between several reasoning engines, where each engine draws on one or more knowledge bases. Conflict resolution between contradicting findings of the engines are just one of the many issues in this scenario. The fourth general scenario, many reasoning engines cooperating with a single knowledge base, is not too different from the two previous scenarios. The issues concerned with these scenarios will be discussed in the following subsections.

3.1   Matching Reasoning Engine and Knowledge Base

Traditionally, expert systems consist of a reasoning engine and a knowledge base [Buch83, Nil80]. The reasoning engine is usually tuned to the types of problems the expert system is expected to solve, eg., deduction, induction, means-end analysis, etc. The knowledge base is viewed as a module that carries the static domain expertise. By changing the current knowledge base in an expert system, problems of the same type, eg., fault diagnosis, but in a different domain should be approachable. In a system of cooperating knowledge bases and reasoning engines, where every knowledge base could possibly be connected with any one of the reasoning engines, the conventional expert system paradigm presents the base case and is achieved by connecting a knowledge base and a reasoning engine over a certain period of time.

This most basic case of cooperation between a knowledge base and a reasoning engine can be initiated in many ways. A human user browsing a number of knowledge bases and deciding to use an appropriate knowledge base to work on a certain problem can leave the initiative with the knowledge base. In this case, a reasoning engine needs to be found that is compatible with the knowledge base formalism and that does the type of reasoning the user desires, e.g., medical analysis, mechanical configuration, etc. If, for example, the user wants to diagnose a liver disease and has already decided on a particular knowledge base, containing information on such diseases, an engine must be found that is capable of doing medical diagnosis.

On the other hand, the user could have started from the reasoning engine side, rather than from the knowledge base side. The user has decided on a certain reasoning engine, or class of reasoning engines, by browsing the system or by a focused search. By first deciding on the type of reasoning engine desired, the initiative for finding the cooperation partner to form a complete expert system would be shifted to the engine. The two cases (knowledge base first, engine first) are symmetric, as far as the communication between the heads of the agents (the knowledge base and the reasoning engine) is concerned. The agent that was initially selected has to find a compatible partner. The third case, where the user selects both agents and directs them to cooperate with each other is very similar to the conventional expert system view and does not present many cooperation problems.

To help an agent (knowledge base or reasoning engine) find the partner that is needed to successfully solve the user's problem, knowledge about the agent's own abilities and needs is used, as well as knowledge about other agents in the world that can possibly cooperate with oneself and the description of the task to be solved. The single most important factor lies in the compatibility of formalisms, though current research is trying to solve the problem of compatibility between different knowledge representation schemas [Kirn90]. Histories of previous, successful cooperations and general match-making strategies give the agent looking for a partner a wide variety of cooperation possibilities. If the agent knows about matching partners, requests are send out to these partners. If more than one partner respond, the initiating agent applies conflict resolution strategies to choose the best partner. Factors in such strategies are the degree of match for the problem at hand, the time/load constraints of the partner, the cost of communication, and other less important factors. If neither of the addressed partners replies, the initiating agent puts an advertisement for a job to be done on the net. This gives all agents in the system the chance to participate in the particular task. It also presents a chance for the agents to learn about new agents that joined the system and were not part of their initial, local knowledge about the system. Agents receiving an advertisement decide on the basis of the workload and appropriateness whether to respond or not. The initiating agent will apply the same conflict resolution strategies as above in the case of many responses. The worst case consists of no agent responding at all. The human user must then be informed that the problem is currently not solvable. A special case consists of an agent promising to cooperate in the future but being unable to do so immediately because of other duties. In this case the human user can be informed and decide whether to wait or to cancel the query. When two machine agents have agreed to cooperate, they have to define the terms of this cooperation. Time limits, security issues, etc. must be specified. This can take the form of inter-machine negotiation. The result is an apparently conventional, but highly specialized expert system, which will exist only temporarily.

3.2 Beyond Dyadic Cooperation

Although creating highly specialized expert systems on a demand basis is already a large benefit of cooperating knowledge bases, the true power of such systems arises when more than two agents join forces. This is the case when a reasoning engine consults several knowledge bases, rather than merely one, or when several engines work on the same problem. These benefits do not come for free though. Problems, such as concurrent processes, contradicting derivations, and inconsistent knowledge bases, are just a few of the large set of issues to be regarded. Obviously, we can not provide solutions to all these problems, but we can sketch the way such systems could be build and how separate solutions to the above problems could be integrated.

The most pressing problems from the cooperation point of view are those of co-operation strategies. *Cooperation* can be decomposed into a planning component and an execution component. We ascribe the term *coordination* to the joint solving of the problems and planning of action, while joint execution of these plans is labeled *collaboration*. Cooperation strategies can be instantiated idiosyncratically in both realms. In general, we can find two extremes on the spectrum of cooperation strategies: master-slave-cooperation and democratic-participation. A large number of other strategies, such as mutual-observation or consider-leader-proposal-first, lie between these two extremes.

3.2.1   One Reasoning Engine with Several Knowledge Bases

An expert system can boost its power by certain orders of magnitude if the reasoning engine in the system can draw on a larger amount of knowledge. More knowledge means more ways to solve a problem or achieve a goal for the system, or being able to tackle problems that were previously unconquerable. The approaches taken to supply an expert system with a more complete domain model, range all the way to machine learning and expertise transfer. By allowing knowledge bases and reasoning engines to cooperate freely, we open a simple alternative to the above strategies. Instead of linking one reasoning engine with just one knowledge base, many knowledge bases can be made available to the reasoning engine.

The way this cooperation can be brought about is similar to the case where a reasoning engine is actively searching or generally advertising for a knowledge base. When the reasoning engine receives offers from a number of compatible knowledge bases, it can choose among a number of cooperation strategies. Given that the knowledge bases are willing, the reasoning engine can assume a coordinator role and assign passive roles to the knowledge bases, meaning that the knowledge bases will only provide information when queried for by the reasoning engine. A more relaxed scheme allows the knowledge bases to communicate among each other and to detect contradictions before the reasoning engine can reach faulty conclusions.

The advantages for a reasoning engine of having available multiple knowledge bases arises mostly from the fact that knowledge bases can complement each other and that the engine can verify a derivation in several ways. Knowledge that might be missing in one knowledge base can possibly be found in another one. A "knowledge gap" can therefore be bridged by switching to another knowledge base until work with the first one can safely be resumed. This process of employing several knowledge bases to bridge knowledge gaps is not necessarily restricted to two knowledge bases but is easily applied a number of knowledge bases. The second advantage, multiple derivations, also arises from the fact that more knowledge is available to the reasoning engine. A derivation that was justified only marginally by facts in one knowledge base can gain in plausibility when facts in other knowledge base support the same derivation. This helps in the decision among alternatives and adds to the credibility of the overall system.

Again, these advantages are bought at a cost. While additional knowledge can help to bridge the knowledge gap and lead to additional support for certain derivations, it can also lead to contradictive derivations and aliasing problems. The same propositions might be called by different names in the participating knowledge bases. Thus a fact that can actually help to bridge the knowledge gap, would not be recognized. Cooperation in this case means constructing aliases tables from dictionary knowledge bases. Another class of problems arise, when the same label of a proposition carries different meanings for the participating knowledge bases. The proposition **breaks** could be used transitive and intransitive, as in *John breaks the glass* or as in *the glass breaks*, which have clearly different meanings. This case is harder to resolve than the previous one of merely aliasing via a translation table. In the case of different meanings (proposition overloading), the instances of overloading have first to be recognized and recorded. Then measures can be taken to either rename proposition when used by the reasoning engine, or to decide to stop using one of the knowledge bases involved. Problems can also arise, when different knowledge bases allow the engine to reach contradicting conclusions. Knowledge base "A" might for instance allow the conclusion of "X", while knowledge base "B" supports "not X". Conflict resolution strategies and negotiation policies have to help the reasoning engine to deal with these matters.

3.2.2 Several Engines with Several Knowledge Bases

The most complicated case of cooperating knowledge based systems consists of several reasoning engines cooperating with one or more knowledge bases, forming a distributed hybrid expert system with a large variety of reasoning methods, parallelism, and an extensive domain model. The advantages of such a system are obvious. Alternative solutions to the same problem, shared work load, and highly efficient means end analysis are just a few. These advantages, however, still have a certain price: contradictions, inconsistencies, access rights, and contingencies, to name just a few.

For the moment, we will consider only the coordination problems of such agents. First the question of initiative has to be addressed. As in the cases above, a human user could order one or more agents from the knowledge base and reasoning engine domain to work together and, if necessary, look for partners. This leaves us in the general case with a set of knowledge bases and reasoning engines, which still need to involve other agents to solve the task given by the user. We can view the following coordination process as a set of rounds which never produces a stable solution. First the agents look for the partners needed by themselves. After the agents have independently found partners, they have to determine the compatibility of all agents involved. This leads to certain partners leaving the group and a tighter set of "partner requirements" being developed. After a number of such rounds, the groups grows more stable and compatible, and certain partners might be able to start solving parts of the task given.

Another possibility is to have a central agent, which serves as a register for available knowledge bases and reasoning engines. An agent, requiring a partner to solve a task issues a request concerning the problem at hand to the register. Based upon its knowledge as to the capabilities of the various other agents in the system, it could match one or more partners to the original requesting agent. An extended role of this register agent would be actual coordination of the agents, specifying who should do which task and recognizing plan overlaps [Stu85].

4 Constructing Linguistic Knowledge Bases: A Case Study in Cooperative Knowledge Base Development

Linguistic knowledge bases (LingKBs) such as grammars, lexicons and domain models are playing the central role in the development and application of natural language systems. Due to the complexity of the task it is generally not feasible for a single person to construct the set of LingKBs necessary for a typical application, as machine translation systems, language dialogue systems, general purpose natural language interface components or text understanding components. Development is most often accomplished by a group of linguistic knowledge engineers. In the simplest case such a team works together at the same time on one physical linguistic workbench (LingWB). This, however, is a severe restriction which does not take into account the practical needs that show up in the development process of large coverage linguistic knowledge sources with the aid of a LingWB. In a more realistic situation the members of the team may be far apart, both spatially and temporally, and must deal with different portions and different versions of the KBs, residing possibly on different machines. The members of the team also have to ensure that their input into or modification of the single knowledge chunks (as e.g. lexical items) are valid and consistent with respect to the other entries, and that the knowledge chunks are consistent with other knowledge sources (as the syntactic grammar or the semantic rules) of the system.

Although these problems exhibit some similarity to those encountered in developing large software systems and databases, they are much more relevant in the area of knowledge bases such as LingKBs. These knowledge bases are not as modularly designed and the process for developing them is usually not as rigidly structured as is the case in standard software systems and standard software development methodologies. This is basically due to the quantitative and qualitative complexity of the linguistic knowledge to be encoded as well as to the lack of a standardized formal knowledge engineering methodology.

In the following analysis we will concentrate on a specific linguistic knowledge source, namely the lexicon.[2] Thereby we do not make any specific assumptions regarding either specific theoretical foundations for encoding lexical information or any application issues. The central assumption underlying our approach is to consider the lexicon, which is *the* central knowledge source that is needed for many demanding applications in natural language processing, as a highly structured extensionally large knowledge base that supplies relevant linguistic knowledge at various levels (such as phonology, morphology, syntax, semantics, and conceptual models).

This assumption is also supported by the increasing role in the grammatical description of natural language that is attributed to the lexicon by various linguistic theories (cf. [Uszk86]). Furthermore we assume that the current state of the art of lexical theory and knowledge representation formalisms does not supply us with a sufficiently powerful and static theoretical framework for encoding *all* of the relevant lexical information.[3] Thus, systems supporting the development of large polytheoretical lexical knowledge bases (LexKB), lexical workbenches (LexWB), have to cope with the following inherent features:

- very large amounts of knowledge

- a complex internal structure and high interdependence of the knowledge chunks

---

[2]A more comprehensive discussion of this area can be found in [Haug90].

[3]This is not intended to neglect the substantial progress that has been achieved in the area of linguistic knowledge representation especially in those approaches based on lexicon-centered declarative representation formalisms at the level of syntactic and semantic description. It rather expresses the fact that no fully satisfactory and stable formalism(s) is available at the moment, if one takes into account the totality of necessary linguistic knowledge.

- a certain amount of dynamics in the underlying theoretical and representational framework

These characteristics lead to the following three requirements of a distributed multi-person lexical development environment:

Collaborative task granularity The size of the lexicon and the diversity of the knowledge that has to be encoded in a lexicon requires a large number of members (people and machine subsystems) in a lexical team.

Flexible cooperation structures Highly diverse interaction styles and a large variety of cooperative activities has to be provided among the individual (especially the human) members of the lexical team.

Human-computer cooperation facilities Certain subtasks that are performed by machine subsystems; they have to be integrated in the cooperation process smoothly and effectively.

Before proceeding with the cooperation aspects of LexWBs we shall outline what we envisage to be the necessary ingredients of a functionally comprehensive single person version of such a workbench. An ideal LexWB would provide, at the least, the following tools supporting the corresponding necessary operational facilities:

Tools for knowledge specification: creation, addition and modification of lexical entries, grammar specifications etc.

Version management facilities: handling of logically and physically distributed lexica, merging of various lexica, consolidation of authorized versions, creation of application-specific sublexica

Lexical checkers and debuggers: checkers for syntactic inconsistencies, components for maintaining operational consistency i.e. applying lexical information to sample data under different computational viewpoints such as parsers, generators, classifier-like operators, components for interactive debugging of lexical entries

Lexical knowledge acquisition tools: semi-automatic extraction of linguistic knowledge from standard machine-readable lexical sources, induction of linguistic knowledge from text, interactive template-based editors and example-based lexical acquisition tools

Manipulation facilities for representation formalisms: specification of new expressive constructs and modification of existing coding/representation conventions

Formalism mappers: components for transforming polytheoretically represented linguistic information into specific theoretical frameworks and formalisms

The pure accumulation of all these functionalities, however, does not offer anything that contributes to the problems that occur, if more than one person uses such a LexWB over a longer period of time with the goal of specifying a common lexical knowledge base. Thus, certain support facilities need to be available, allowing for cooperative development of LexKBs.

In order to make a genuinely cooperative multi-person LexWB out of such a set of tools, i.e. to transform a LexWB into a lexical workshop ([Wahl89]), additional functionality has to be provided with respect to the following two different aspects:

1. Each of the single tools has to be augmented by facilities for their effective multi-person use in a cooperative context; examples for these types of tools in the area of LexWB are shared lexicon editors with simultaneous multi-person usability or distributed grammar debuggers.

2. Beyond this type of upgrading of the individual tool's operational facilities their effective use in a cooperative context must be supported i.e. these tools must be integrated in a distributed cooperative work environment.
   In order to achieve this a global architecture has to be supplied, that integrates these tools in a fashion that is powerful enough to support their collaborative use; this basically means that an explicit representation of the cooperative processes underlying various collaborative activities that arise in practical development of large coverage LexKBs.

The following examples may suffice to give an illustration of these activities. They exemplify typical activity and coordination sequences of quite differing granularity involving various subsets of the overall team, the support of which is critical for the work progress. These include cooperative processes like:

- negotiating coding conventions,

- performing face-to-face debugging

- notifying responsible team members

- establishing and maintaining subgroups of knowledge enterers with a specific task responsibility

- performing regular checks on operational consistency

- handling of task-oriented, controlled distribution lists

Summing up the preceding analyses the scenario under investigation can be characterized by the following features:

Distribution Collaboration among the members of a team has to take into account distribution along the dimensions of locality, time, and competence:

   Space The team members work at different places.

Time The team members work during different, possibly non-overlapping intervals of time.

Competence In general the competence with respect to the relevant LexKB is spread across the whole team.

Responsibility The responsibility for various aspects of the development process is distributed over different members or subsets of members of the team.

Redundancy The various partners' competence may be overlapping and even competing; this leads to increased requirements concerning the modeling of the overall cooperation process.

Heterogeneity A team may have a wide variety of members, ranging from simple components like printers via complex software systems such as consistency checkers to humans, which have drastically varying functionalities and cooperative capabilities.

Dynamism The cooperation roles of the individual members of a team are not totally predetermined on the basis of a rigid organizational structure or standardized work procedures; rather they can be adopted dynamically during the work process, depending on the technical competence of the collaborators and the structure of the collaborative task.

Thus, it seems clear that the development of large coverage linguistic knowledge bases will be significantly enhanced by an integrated environment that offers flexible support for the interperson/machine cooperation processes of the type described. And although we have focused our considerations on the development of the lexicon in computational linguistics this is just an example of a much wider class of such distributed collaborative work processes of that type namely the multi-person specification, maintenance and debugging of large knowledge bases.

A short final sketch of how a typical activity sequence that occurs in the development process of knowledge bases by a man-machine team can be modeled on the basis of MECCA may demonstrate the usefulness of the approach described. Thus, in the LexWB scenario, a typical agent would be a consistency checker of lexical knowledge distributed across various lexical entries, extended by a cooperative superstrate. This agent automatically searches for inconsistencies in the lexical knowledge base by performing tests at regular intervals, triggered by incremental saves or initiated by user interaction. Upon encountering an inconsistency between two entries of the knowledge base, encoded by different members of the team, the head of the checker is able to determine from the head of the lexicon server agent, who was potentially responsible for the inconsistency and would notify the relevant subteam. Note that this is not necessarily a function of the consistency checker itself, rather of its head. If the team members responsible for the inconsistency need to confer directly with each other, their corresponding heads establish an appropriate communication link and initiate a specific work procedure involving the relevant members of the team. This may additionally lead to the need of transferring information between them, such as graphical representation of the problem at hand as provided by a debugging tool which may in turn be an independent agent, cooperating with the responsible team members in order to resolve inconsistencies or initiate further actions.

5   Summary and Future Research

We presented an agent model and a number of cooperation strategies that enable knowledge bases and reasoning engines to form highly specialized expert systems. The benefits of cooperation techniques and technologies from the are of human cooperation are transplanted fruitfully to the area of cooperating machine agents. We are currently implementing this agent model and are starting to formalize cooperation strategies on the basis of coordination science. In order that the Knowledge Bases and Reasoning Engines involved in the cooperation process be as heterogeneous as possible, it is desirable to have a formal knowledge representation language (FRL) to be used as a default for communication. Each knowledge base/Reasoning Engine would be able to translate the FRL into its own internal representation language. Agents with the same internal representation language could then use that for more direct communication, involving less overhead. Several efforts are being made to establish a FRL [BCM90, MCC90], whether suitable translation engines can be developed remains to be seen.

6   Acknowledgments

We would like to thank Dieter Scheidhauer, Astrid Scheller-Houy and Andreas Lux of the KIK Project for contributing ideas in this paper regarding the agent model. We would also like to thank Wolfgang Wahlster of the University of the Saarland for discussions leading to the linguistic knowledge base example.

References

[Buch83] B. G. Buchanan, et. al., "Constructing an expert system," In *Building Expert Systems*, F. Hayes-Roth, D. A. Waterman, and D. B. Lenat (Eds.), Addison-Wesley, Reading, Massachusetts, 1983, pp. 126-167.

[BCM90] N. Bhandaru, W. B. Croft, and D. E. Mahling, "A Task-Centered Theory of Cooperative Work," Technical Report 90-25, COINS, University of Massachusetts, Amherst, MA, March 1990.

[Calz84] N. Calzolari, "Detecting Patterns in a Lexical Database," In *Proceedings of the 10th International Conference on Computational Linguistics*, Stanford, CA, 1984, pp. 170-173.

[Gass88] L. Gasser, C. Braganza, and N. Herman. "Implementing Distributed AI Systems Using MACE," In *Readings in Distributed Artificial Intelligence*, Alan Bond and Les Gasser (Eds.), San Mateo, CA, 1988, pp. 445-450.

[Grf88]   Irene Greif (Ed.): *Computer-Supported Cooperative Work: A Book of Readings*, San Mateo, CA, 1988.

[Haug90]   Hans Haugeneder and Donald Steiner, "Towards a Distributed Multi-Person Lexical Environment," In *Lexikon und Lexikographie*, B. Rieger and B. Schaeder (Eds.), Hildesheim, 1990.

[Kirn90]   S. Kirn and G. Schlageter, "Intelligent Agents in Federated Expert Systems: Concepts and Implementation," In *Proceedings of CKBS 1990*.

[Mah90]   D. E. Mahling, *A Visual Language for Knowledge Acquisition, Display and Animation by Domain Experts and Novices*, PhD thesis, University of Massachusetts, February 1990.

[MCC90]   D. E. Mahling, B. G. Coury, and W. B. Croft, "User models in cooperative task-oriented environments," In *Proceedings of the 23rd Hawaii International Conference on Systems Science*, IEEE, 1990.

[Nil80]   N. J. Nilsson, *Principles of Artificial Intelligence*, Morgan Kaufmann, Los Altos, 1980.

[SMH90]   Donald Steiner, Dirk Mahling, and Hans Haugeneder, "Human Computer Cooperative Work," In *Proceedings of the 10th International Workshop on Distributed Artificial Intelligence*, MCC Technical Report Number ACT-AI-355-90, MCC, Austin, TX, 1990.

[Stu85]   Christopher Stuart, "An implementation of a multi-agent plan synchronizer," In *Proceedings of IJCAI 1985*, 1985, pp. 1031-1033.

[Uszk86]   Hans Uszkoreit, "Syntaktische und semantische Generalisierungen im strukturierten Lexikon," In *GWAI-86 und 2. Österreichische Artificial-Intelligence-Tagung*, Claus-Rainer Rollinger and Werner Horn (Eds.), Berlin, 1986, pp. 78-100.

[Wahl89]   Wolfgang Wahlster, "Linguistische Werkbänke: KI Software für Linguisten," Talk given at Sektion Computerlinguistik der DGfS, November 1989.

[WBH87]   J. Whiteside, J. Benett, and K. Holtblatt, "Usability engineering: Our experience and evolution," In *Handbook of human-computer interaction*, M. Helander (Ed.), North-Holland Press, 1987.

[Wilk88]   Yorik Wilks, et. al., "Machine Tractable Dictionaries as Tools and Resources for Natural Language Processing," In *Proceedings of the 12th International Conference on Computational Linguistics*, Budapest, 1988, pp. 750-755.

[Zern85]   Uri Zernik and Michael G. Dyer, "Towards a Self-Extending Lexicon," In *Proceedings of the 23rd Annual Meeting of ACL*, Chicago, IL, 1985, pp. 284-292.

DISCUSSION

Presenter: Donald Steiner.

Q. (N. Mitchison, ISPRA) : The head/body relationship seems to me a very interesting one. You mention that you wanted at some time in the future to be able to incorporate any body straight away into an existing system. That seems an excellent objective. Have you made any progress yet in thinking about how a head-builder copes with the problem, "Here's a new body, I must construct a head which, among other things, has to know quite a lot about what this body can or cannot do in order to function properly with it."?

A. (D. Steiner) : This whole area of epistemic and auto-epistemic knowledge is a big research area on its own. Basically, the answer is we've been looking at it. In one sense the head is a user of the body. If the body is, for example, a software program, when the human sits there and types in input and receives output and passes it on, the head is basically a computer user of the body. So the basic interface to the body is nothing more than what you actually expect as far as input and output from the body. Just based upon that the head cannot know exactly what the body is capable of doing, so where you have bodies you will have to work on how do you represent this meta-level reasoning and put that into the head.

No progress yet as it were, but interested.

Q. (M. Huhns, MCC) : Along those same lines, I'd like to suggest that Mark Klein has identified some domain-independent cooperation knowledge, knowledge for resolving conflicts amongst agents and for enabling cooperation and this is domain-independent. You might try to take advantage of this as part of this head that you're trying to implement.

A. (D. Steiner) : Our goals within the project are actually not to implement all portions of the head, that would be too much. Rather what we really are looking for and one of the major reasons why I'm here, is to identify other people and other works that have been going into work on these portions.

Q. (D. Cockburn, ERDC) : Can the heads be written in different programming languages or have you chosen just one language?

A. (D. Steiner) : It's my actual personal opinion that the head itself will be written in a lot of different languages. Some representation for the cooperation strategies and the planning portion of the head will actually probably get written in a different language than the internal interface, this neck portion connecting to the body. So the head will actually be in a sense a big cooperative agent in its own right. One thing I did want to mention, the head does not necessarily have to have all of this knowledge, doesn't have to know about all the variety of cooperation strategies in the world and so on. One thing is necessary is that it has sufficient knowledge to be able to reason about such things, and if it does not have all of the knowledge, for example if the head doesn't have a very good planner, it can always find another agent whose body is exactly that of the functionality, or provides the functionality that the head would like to have, such as a planner or a contradiction resolution system. So, if a head can't form the best of plans itself, it should have the capability, there should be the option there to call up a planner as an agent and say, "I have this overall planning scenario with these agents and these tasks and sub-tasks and so on. What is the best plan?"

Knowledge Revision

DISTRIBUTED TRUTH MAINTENANCE

Michael N. Huhns and David M. Bridgeland
Microelectronics and Computer Technology Corporation
Artificial Intelligence Laboratory
3500 West Balcones Center Drive
Austin, TX, U.S.A.   78759-6509

Abstract

In this paper we define the concept of logical consistency of belief among a group of computational agents that are able to reason nonmonotonically. We then provide an algorithm for truth maintenance that guarantees local consistency for each agent and global consistency for data shared by the agents. Furthermore, we show the algorithm to be complete, in the sense that if a consistent state exists, the algorithm will either find it or report failure. The algorithm has been implemented in the *RAD* distributed expert system shell.

1   Introduction

Two trends have recently become apparent out of the widespread use of knowledge-based systems: 1) systems are being developed for larger and more complicated domains, and 2) there are attempts to use several small systems in concert when their application domains overlap. Both of these trends argue for knowledge-based systems to be developed in a distributed fashion, where modules are constructed to interact productively. The individual modules then are characteristic of intelligent agents. The interconnected agents can cooperate in solving problems, share expertise, work in parallel on common problems, be developed modularly, be fault tolerant through redundancy, represent multiple viewpoints and the knowledge of multiple experts, and be reusable. Additional motivations are presented in [Huhns 1987] and [Gasser and Huhns 1989]. But in order for these agents to coordinate their activities and cooperate in solving mutual problems, it is essential that they be able to communicate with each other. Further, in order for them to interact intelligently and efficiently, we believe that the agents must be able to assess and maintain the integrity of the communicated information, as well as of their own knowledge.

2   Knowledge Base Integrity

There are many desirable properties for the knowledge base of an expert system or agent, such as completeness, conciseness, accuracy, and efficiency. For an agent that can reason nonmonotonically, there are additional properties used to describe the *integrity* of the agent's knowledge base: stability, well-foundedness, and logical consistency. A *stable* state of a knowledge base is one in which 1) each knowledge base element that has a valid justification is believed, and 2) each knowledge base element that lacks a valid justification is disbelieved. A *well-founded* knowledge base permits no set of its beliefs to be mutually dependent. A *logically-consistent* knowledge base is one that is stable at the time that consistency is determined and in which no logical contradiction exists. Depending on how beliefs, justifications, and data are represented, a consistent knowledge base may be one in which no datum is both believed and disbelieved (or neither), or in which no datum and its negation are both believed. These concepts are often extended to include other types of contradictions.

In addition, any algorithm that attempts to maintain well-founded stable states of a knowledge base, such as one of the many algorithms for truth maintenance [Doyle 1979, de Kleer 1986, Martins and Shapiro 1988, McAllester 1980, Russinoff 1985], should be *complete*, in the sense that if a well-founded stable state exists, the algorithm will either find it or report failure. In general, we desire each agent in a multiagent environment to have a complete algorithm for maintaining the integrity of its own knowledge base.

However, the above definitions of properties for a single knowledge base are insufficient to characterize the multiple knowledge bases in such a multiagent environment. When agents that are nonmonotonic reasoners exchange beliefs and then make inferences based on the exchanged beliefs, then new concepts of knowledge-base integrity are needed. In addition, the relevant concept of global truth maintenance becomes especially problematic if agents must compute their beliefs locally, based on beliefs communicated and justified externally. The next sections extend the above definitions to the multiagent case.

2.1   The JTMS

We presume that each agent has a problem-solving component, separate from its knowledge base, that makes inferences and supplies the results to the knowledge base. Our discussion applies to the set of beliefs that are held and maintained in this knowledge base. In particular, we focus on the systems for maintaining beliefs known as truth-maintenance systems (TMS) [Doyle 1979].

TMSs are a common way to achieve knowledge base integrity in a single agent system, because they deal with the frame problem, they deal with atomicity, and they lead to efficient search. Furthermore, the justification networks they create can be used for nonmonotonic reasoning, problem-solving explanations to a user, explanation-based learning, and multiagent negotiation. Our research is based on a justification-based TMS, in which every datum has a set of justifications and an associated status of IN (believed) or OUT (disbelieved).

In the example considered below, an initial state of a distributed knowledge base is given and presumed consistent. Our goal is to construct a consistent extension of this state or determine that no such extension exists. The distributed TMS (DTMS) algorithm presented for this task is most often invoked to restore consistency when a consistent state is disrupted by altering the justification for a datum.

2.2   Consistent Beliefs among Agents

Consider a network of many agents, each with a partially-independent system of beliefs. The agents interact by exchanging data, either unsolicited or in response to a query. Each agent has two kinds of data in its knowledge base:

Shared Data Beliefs that the agent has shared with another agent sometime in the past.

Private Data Beliefs that the agent has never shared with another agent.

A private datum might become a shared datum by being told to another agent, or by being the answer to some other agent's query. Once shared with other agents, a datum can never again be private. Each shared datum is shared by a subset of the agents in the network—precisely those that have either sent or received assertions about the datum.

We extend the concept of knowledge-base consistency stated above by defining four degrees of consistency and well-foundedness that are possible in a multiagent system.

Inconsistency: one or more agents are individually inconsistent, i.e., at least one agent has a private datum without a valid justification and labeled IN, or a private datum with a valid justification and labeled OUT.

Local Consistency: each agent is locally consistent, i.e., no private OUT datum has a valid justification, and each private IN datum has a valid justification. However, there may be global inconsistency among agents: there may be a shared datum that one agent believes to be IN and another believes to be OUT.

Local-and-Shared Consistency: each agent is locally consistent and groups of agents are mutually consistent about any data they all share, i.e., each shared datum is either IN in all the agents that share it or OUT in those agents. There is, however, no global consistency.

Global Consistency: the agents are both individually and mutually consistent, i.e., their beliefs could be merged into one large knowledge base without the status of any datum necessarily changing.

In the absence of interagent communication, and presuming the local environment of each agent is consistent, then Local Consistency should hold. The introduction of interagent communication, however, tends to drive the system towards Inconsistency, because the agents might receive data that conflict with their current beliefs. The mechanism for truth maintenance we describe below enables each agent then to strive for Local-and-Shared Consistency. The presumption here is that the shared data are the most important, because they affect the problem solving of another agent, and so special effort should be made to maintain their consistency.

Although our goal is to maintain Local-and-Shared Consistency, we at times allow the system to fall short of this goal in order to permit agents to have different viewpoints. In this case, one agent may hold a belief that is known to be contrary to the belief of a second agent. The agents do not attempt to resolve this dispute if resolution would result in their being individually inconsistent. A consequence of this is that these agents should then not believe any data originating from each other, unless that agent can prove that its belief for that data is independent of the disputed data.

Ill-Foundedness: one or more agents have beliefs that are internally ill-founded.

Local Well-Foundedness: each agent has beliefs that are internally well-founded; however, one or more agents may have shared data that are IN but have no valid justifications in any agent.

Local-and-Shared Well-Foundedness: each agent has beliefs that are internally well-founded, and every IN shared datum has a valid justification in some agent; however, there may be ill-founded circularities of beliefs among groups of agents.

Global Well-Foundedness: every datum has a globally valid justification and no set of data, whether local to an agent or distributed among a group of agents, is mutually dependent.

3   A Multiagent TMS

In the classical TMS, a datum can be either IN or OUT. For the DTMS, we refine the IN status to two new statuses: INTERNAL and EXTERNAL. An INTERNAL datum is one that is believed to be true, and that has a valid justification. An EXTERNAL datum is believed to be true, but need not have a valid justification. Intuitively, the justification of an EXTERNAL datum is "so-and-so told me." Hence, only a shared datum can be EXTERNAL. For Local-and-Shared Well-Foundedness, a shared datum must be INTERNAL to at least one of the agents that shares it and either INTERNAL or EXTERNAL to the rest of the agents.

The only justification-based TMS labeling algorithm known to be complete [Russinoff 1985] takes a generate and test approach, first unlabeling a collection of data, then attempting to relabel that collection. On failure to relabel, a superset of the last unlabeled collection is unlabeled. We take a similar approach in the DTMS. Since new data in one agent can change not only the status of that agent's beliefs, but also that of other agents, our unlabeling and subsequent labeling will sometimes involve multiple agents.

The support status of a shared datum is jointly maintained by several agents. Hence, a single agent is generally not free to change the status of a shared datum on its own accord. It must coordinate with the other agents so that they are all consistent on the status of the datum. Central to the DTMS then is the single agent operation of **label-wrt**. **label-wrt** is a variation of classical TMS labeling in which the statuses of some data—though unlabeled—are fixed by external requirements.

More precisely, **label-wrt** is given a network of data. Some of the data have statuses of IN, OUT, INTERNAL, or EXTERNAL. Other data are unlabeled. For each shared datum, there is a *desired* label of either OUT, INTERNAL, or EXTERNAL. **label-wrt** either finds a consistent well-founded labeling of the network that satisfies the shared data requirements, or it reports failure. Space prohibits a presentation of an algorithm to implement **label-wrt**. Our approach is a variation of Russinoff's well-founded and complete labeling algorithm [Russinoff 1985].

3.1 Algorithm Schema

The DTMS is a double generate and test. Relabeling is invoked by the addition or removal of a justification. When invoked, the DTMS does the following three things:

1. Unlabel some data, including the newly justified datum and presumably its consequences. This unlabeled data set might be confined to a single agent or it might span several agents. If a shared datum is unlabeled in some agent, it must be unlabeled in all the agents that share it.

2. Choose labels for all the unlabeled shared data, as defined above.

3. Label each of the affected agents with respect to the requirements imposed by the shared data, invoking **label-wrt** as described above. If any of the affected agents fails to label, then backtrack. Either choose different labels for the shared data (step 2), or unlabel a different set of data (step 1).

This schema will be refined later, but some nice properties emerge at this abstract level:

- Any labeling found by the DTMS will have Local-and-Shared Consistency and Well-Foundedness.

- If the two generate steps are exhaustive, the DTMS is complete: it will find a labeling should one exist.

Note that these properties are true both of the DTMS algorithm described in this paper, and any other algorithm that conforms to this schema.

3.2 Unlabeling

When the DTMS algorithm is invoked, it starts by unlabeling a collection of data. This collection may be confined to a single agent or it may span many agents. However, it must meet the following constraints:

1. It must include the datum that originally acquired the new justification.

2. A shared datum that is unlabeled in one agent must be unlabeled in all the agents that share it.

3. On failure to label the collection, it must generate a new collection of unlabeled data. To guarantee completeness, the generation must be exhaustive: it must eventually generate a collection sufficiently large that failure to label it means the whole network cannot be labeled.

Using only these constraints, unlabeling is underconstrained: many algorithms satisfy. For example, on any status change one could unlabel all data in all agents. This global unlabeling satisfies all the constraints and is also quite simple, but also is too inefficient for practical use. The global unlabeling does reveal two DTMS principles that motivate the more complex algorithm presented later:

Principle 1 *Belief changes should be resolved with as few agents as possible.*

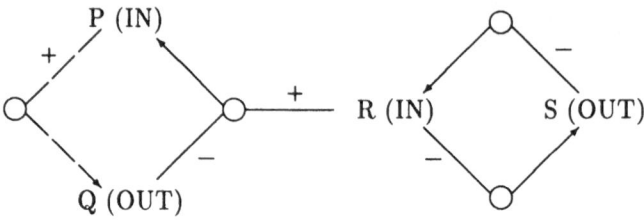

Figure 1: Relabeling upstream data to resolve an odd loop

Principle 2 *Belief changes should be resolved by changing as few beliefs as possible.*

Most belief changes can be resolved by changing things only "downstream" of the new justification, i.e., those data that directly or indirectly depend on the datum newly justified. It is sometimes necessary to move "upstream" as well, and relabel data that directly or indirectly support the status of the newly justified datum. Consider the knowledge base for a single agent shown in Figure 1 [Russinoff 1985]. Here, datum Q acquires the new justification shown in dotted lines. If only P and Q are reassigned, the system is forced to report an unsatisfiable circularity. In order to restore stability, the status of the data upstream from P must be changed: if the system makes S OUT and R IN, both P and Q can be OUT.

Principle 3 *Belief changes should be resolved downstream if possible; upstream relabeling should be minimized.*

The above principles motivate the algorithm **unlabel**. It attempts to minimize both the involvement of other agents and the unlabeling of upstream data, but prefers the former to the latter. **Unlabel** is invoked on a list containing either the newly justified datum, when **unlabel** is first invoked, or the unlabeled data that could not be labeled on a previous invocation. **Unlabel** attempts to find yet to be unlabeled private data downstream of those already labeled. If there are none, it looks for shared data downstream, unlabeling those in all the agents that share them, and also unlabeling private data downstream of the shared data. Finally, if there are no shared data downstream that are yet to be unlabeled, it unlabels data just upstream of all the downstream data, and all private data downstream of that. If there is nothing yet to be unlabeled upstream, **unlabel** fails and, in fact, the data admit no Local-and-Shared Consistent and Well-Founded labeling.

Consider the DTMS network in Figure 2. There are two agents, Agent 1 and Agent 2, and they share the datum T. As in Figure 1, the initial labeling shown in the diagram is perturbed by the addition of the new dotted justification. Agent 1 initially unlabels just the changed datum and private data downstream, P and Q, but there is no consistent relabeling. Hence, Agent 1 unlabels all shared data downstream of P and Q, and all private data downstream from there: P, Q, both Ts, and U. Again labeling fails. Since there is no further shared data downstream, Agent 1 and Agent 2 unlabel upstream and privately downstream from there: P, Q, Ts, U, R, and S. Now labeling succeeds (with S and U IN and everything else OUT). Had labeling failed, **Unlabel** would not be able to unlabel more data, and would report that the network is inconsistent.

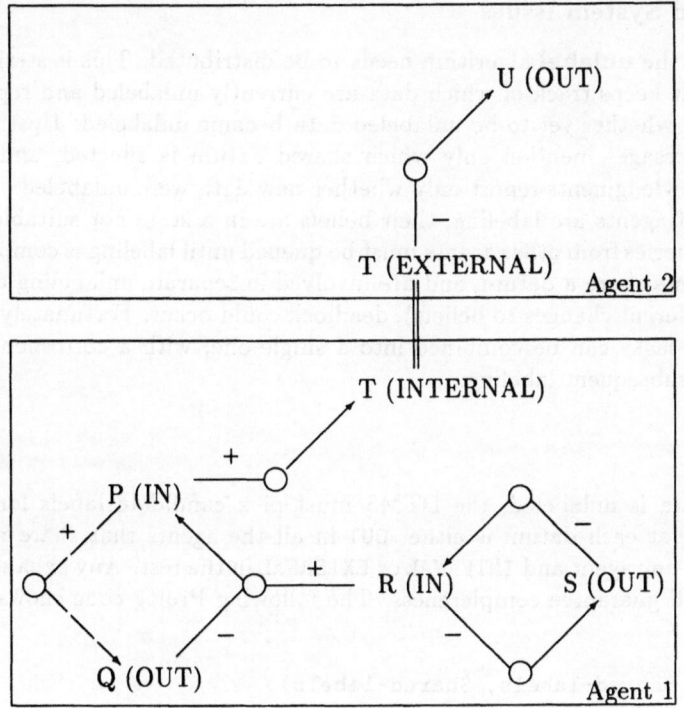

Figure 2: A DTMS network before relabeling

3.2.1 Distributed System Issues

To be implemented, the **unlabel** algorithm needs to be distributed. This is straight-forward if each agent keeps track of which data are currently unlabeled and reports to other agents only whether yet to be unlabeled data became unlabeled. Upstream and downstream messages mention only which shared datum is affected, and the corresponding acknowledgments report only whether new data were unlabeled.

When a group of agents are labeling, their beliefs are in a state not suitable for reasoning. Hence, queries from other agents must be queued until labeling is complete. However, if two agents share a datum, and are involved in separate unlabeling tasks (i.e., initiated by different changes to beliefs), deadlock could occur. Fortunately, the separate unlabeling tasks can be combined into a single one, with a corresponding combination of the subsequent labeling.

3.3 Labeling

Once an area of data is unlabeled, the DTMS must pick candidate labels for the shared data, such that each datum is either OUT in all the agents that share it, or INTERNAL in at least one agent and INTERNAL or EXTERNAL in the rest. Any exhaustive means of picking will guarantee completeness. The following Prolog code shows one means:

```
label-shared([], Shared-labels, Shared-labels).

label-shared([Agent|Agents], So-far, Final) <--
   label-one-shared(Agent, So-far, New),
   label-shared(Agents, New, Final).
```

label-shared relates its first argument—a list of agents—and its third argument—a list of shared data and their labels. The second argument is used to pass commitments about labels for shared data to recursive calls to **label-shared**. The relation calls **label-one-shared**, attempting to assign labels to a single agent that are consistent with those already assigned to others. If it finds such an assignment, it recursively attempts to find labels for the other agents. On failure, it backtracks and looks for alternatives to the previous single-agent labeling.

This algorithm could be implemented on a fully connected multiagent system by making each agent responsible for generating labels that are consistent with others already generated, as in **label-one-shared**, and implementing the recursive nature of **label-shared** with a message passed depth-first from agent to agent. This message needs to contain a list of agents already visited, so that none are revisited, and a list of the already labeled shared data. Also, before an agent passes a message to another, it needs to record its state for future backtracking. The shared-data labeling fits into the larger labeling process as follows:

```
label(Agents) <--
   label-shared(Agents, [], Shared),
   label-private(Agents, Shared).

label-private([],Shared).
```

```
label-private([Agent|Agents],Shared) <--
  local-shared(Agent, Shared, Local-Shared),
  label-wrt(Agent, Local-Shared),
  label-private(Agents, Shared).
```

The private labeling follows the shared data labeling. The private data are labeled one agent at a time. First the relation **local-Shared** extracts the shared labels relevant to a single agent from the list of all the shared labels. Then **label-wrt** attempts to label the private data consistently with the shared data. Any failure to label causes backtracking. This algorithm will find a Local-and-Shared Consistent and Well-Founded labeling of an unlabeled area in a collection of agents.

Unfortunately, this algorithm has poor computational performance. If there is no consistent labeling of the agents, the DTMS will generate all shared data labelings and attempt to label each privately. The performance can be improved by interleaving the labeling of the shared data and the private data. Failure in a single agent to find a private labeling consistent with the labels of the shared data will then cause earlier backtracking:

```
label(Agents) <-- label-internal(Agents, []).

label-internal([], Shared).

label-internal([Agent|Agents], So-far) <--
  label-one-shared(Agent, So-far, New),
  local-shared(Agent, New, Local-shared),
  label-wrt(Agent, Local-shared),
  label-internal(Agents, New).
```

Label-internal could be implemented by a message passed depth-first from agent to agent. This message needs to contain a list of the agents visited so far, and a record of the labels given so far to the shared data.

Consider again Figure 2. R, S, P, Q, U, and both Ts have now been unlabeled. Agent 1 chooses labels for T and attempts to label his private data in a consistent manner. If Agent 1 chooses INTERNAL as T's label, he finds there is no labeling of his private data to make T internally justified. A next attempt with EXTERNAL is consistent (with S IN and everything else OUT), and Agent 1 passes his label of T to Agent 2. Agent 2 must then label T INTERNAL, but finds there is no way to label U. Agent 2 then backtracks and Agent 1 tries a final attempt to label T, this time as OUT. This succeeds with S IN and everything else OUT, and Agent 2 can also label T OUT by labeling U IN.

3.4   Optimizations

This DTMS algorithm admits several local optimizations:

1. An agent can forego the labeling of its unlabeled shared data by **label-one-shared** and instead label everything that is unlabeled with **label-wrt**. This requires a more sophisticated **label-wrt** that can generate INTERNAL and EXTERNAL labels for the shared data, as well as IN and OUT labels for the private data.

142

2. An agent can keep a record of label attempts, caching for each combination of shared data labels whether it succeeded or failed to find a private labeling. A call to **label-wrt** will first consult the cache, thus avoiding redundant work. Ordering the shared data and then indexing the combinations in a discrimination net seems to be a good implementation for this cache.

3. In the above algorithm, only one agent is active at a time. However, there is something productive that the other agents can do: fill in their label caches by attempting to find private labelings for shared data combinations not yet examined. In fact, this effort could be guided by other agents. If agent 1 shares data with agents 2, 3, and 4, when agent 1 passes a label-internal message to agent 2, it could advise agents 3 and 4 about its decisions on the labels of shared data. Then other agents could work only on that portion of their caches that are consistent with agent 1's decision.

4 Discussion

There have been many other attempts to develop systems of cooperating agents or knowledge sources. Early attempts, based on the blackboard model, involved agents with independent knowledge bases. The independence was achieved by restricting agent interactions to modifications of a global data structure—a blackboard—and by minimizing overlap in the agents' knowledge. Later systems allowed richer agent interactions and overlapping knowledge, but the agents were required to have consistent knowledge and to reason monotonically. This led to representational problems, because different experts in the same domain often have different perspectives and *conflicting* knowledge, making it difficult to construct a coherent problem-solving system for that domain. Earlier solutions were to allow inconsistent knowledge bases; this enabled the conflicting knowledge to be represented, but it did not confront the problem of how to resolve the conflicts.

Other researchers have explored negotiation as a means to mediate among conflicting agents. These systems have involved either monotonic reasoners, such as [Sycara 1989], or nonmonotonic, but memoryless, reasoners, such as [Zlotkin and Rosenschein 1989], i.e., reasoners that simply discard old solutions and re-solve in the face of conflicts.

Another approach is to consider the research efforts in multiple-context truth-maintenance systems [de Kleer 1986, Martins and Shapiro 1988] from a distributed viewpoint. These systems manipulate belief spaces, or contexts, in order to remove inconsistent ones. One might imagine each belief space represented by a different agent, who then maintains it. However, in this model, the belief spaces themselves do not interact and, in fact, the belief revision system treats each space separately.

A notable exception to this is the work of [Mason and Johnson 1989], who developed a distributed assumption-based TMS. In this system, agents interact by exchanging data, with their associated assumption sets, and NOGOODS, i.e., bad assumption sets. The agents maintain separate belief spaces and may disagree about an exchanged datum. The agents therefore have Local-and-Shared Well-Foundedness, but only Local Consistency.

The system we presented herein, although an improvement in that it achieves Local-and-Shared Consistency, nevertheless suffers from several deficiencies:

- First, by not supporting some form of explicit negation or reasons for disbelief in a datum, the system allows an agent with less information to dominate an agent with more. For example, if two agents each have an identical justification for belief in a shared datum, and one agent learns a fact that invalidates its justification, the other agent's still-valid justification will be sufficient for both to continue believing in the datum.

- Second, our algorithm can involve significant computational overhead if the agents have shared a large amount of data, if the data have many connections to the rest of the agents' belief networks, and if the status of their beliefs changes frequently.

- Third, we believe unsatisfiable circularities are more likely in a distributed system.

We are currently investigating the likelihood and severity of these deficiencies in real-world application domains. We are also developing a mechanism for negotiation that uses the beliefs supplied by our DTMS.

The above algorithm has been implemented in the *RAD* distributed expert system shell, which includes a framework within which computational agents can be integrated. RAD is a first step toward cooperative distributed problem solving among multiple agents. It provides the low-level communication and reasoning primitives necessary for beneficial agent interactions, but it does not yet guarantee successful and efficient cooperation. The next steps will require increased intelligence and capabilities for each agent, resulting in more sophisticated agent interactions occurring at a higher level.

References

[de Kleer 1986] Johan de Kleer, "An Assumption-Based TMS, Extending the ATMS, and Problem Solving with the ATMS," *Artificial Intelligence*, vol. 28, no. 2, March 1986, pp. 127–224.

[Doyle 1979] Jon Doyle, "A Truth Maintenance System," *Artificial Intelligence*, vol. 12, no. 3, 1979, pp. 231–272.

[Gasser and Huhns 1989] Les Gasser and Michael N. Huhns, eds., *Distributed Artificial Intelligence, Volume II*, Pitman Publishing, London, 1989.

[Huhns 1987] Michael N. Huhns, ed., *Distributed Artificial Intelligence*, Pitman Publishing, London, 1987.

[Martins and Shapiro 1988] Joao P. Martins and Stuart C. Shapiro, "A Model for Belief Revision," *Artificial Intelligence*, vol. 35, no. 1, May 1988, pp. 25–79.

[Mason and Johnson 1989] Cindy L. Mason and R. R. Johnson, "DATMS: A Framework for Distributed Assumption Based Reasoning," in [Gasser and Huhns 1989], pp. 293–317.

144

[McAllester 1980] David A. McAllester, "An Outlook on Truth Maintenance," AI Memo No. 551, Artificial Intelligence Laboratory, MIT, Cambridge, MA, August 1980.

[Russinoff 1985] David M. Russinoff, "An Algorithm for Truth Maintenance," MCC Technical Report No. ACA-AI-062-85, Microelectronics and Computer Technology Corporation, Austin, TX, April 1985.

[Sycara 1989] Katia P. Sycara, "Multiagent Compromise via Negotiation," in [Gasser and Huhns 1989], pp. 119–137.

[Zlotkin and Rosenschein 1989] Gilad Zlotkin and Jeffrey S. Rosenschein, "Negotiation and Task Sharing Among Autonomous Agents in Cooperative Domains," *Proceedings IJCAI-89*, Detroit, MI, August 1989, pp. 912–917.

DISCUSSION

Presenter: Michael Huhns.

Q. (N. Jennings, Queen Mary and Westfield College, London) : Can you explain how
   an agent can draw a conclusion based on facts from two other agents if these facts
   are inconsistent with each other?

A. (M. Huhns) : If one agent, for example, believes some fact and another agent does not
   believe that fact and each of these agents has a valid reason for its beliefs and their
   disagreement cannot be resolved (that is, there is no consistent labeling of these facts),
   then what happens is the agents agree to disagree. In order to maintain consistency,
   the agents each regard the fact as a local datum and they can hold separate beliefs
   about it. Now at this point a third agent can then learn something from each of these
   two agents that is based on this inconsistent data and can draw a conclusion that could
   not be justified globally if all this information was in the same large knowledge base.
   There is simply no way we know of to get around this without trying to put all the
   knowledge into one large knowledge base, and that's basically infeasible. Of course,
   humans don't resolve things like this either. Two people can tell you something and
   you can draw a conclusion based on that, but then they could each be basing what
   they tell you on some inconsistent fact. If they do not resolve this, then you are
   believing something that really has no sound basis.

Q. (L. Gasser, University of Southern California) : I'd like to ask Mike about whether
   he has any sense of the limitations of the system or a future policy for development?

A. (M. Huhns) : Well, one limitation is the computational complexity. We have not used
   the DTMS for any large system yet and so we don't have a feel for how expensive
   it is to do the labeling when many agents are involved, each with a large knowledge
   base. We don't know at this point how often large amounts of global relabeling might
   be needed. It is our intuition that this is not likely to happen, because in a single
   agent it is rare, indeed it is potentially impossible, for the entire knowledge base to
   get relabeled every time a new fact is added. In our experience, those relabellings
   that occur usually involve a small part of the knowledge base. We expect this will
   be true for more agents but we don't know that for a fact so we are investigating it
   now. At this point we are concentrating on developing new applications. Real world
   experience with this system is needed to find its limitations.

Q. (S. M. Deen, University of Keele) : If I may ask Mike a database question: What
   happens if, during the process of changing the belief system, a query arrives and
   is answered? That is, you are in the middle of updating your system with the new
   belief, when the query arrived. Do you lock the whole system before answering the
   query, or do you allow the query to proceed without locking, in which case you have
   an inconsistency problem?

A. (M. Huhns) : At this point we lock the whole system. This is certainly a problem that
   the database community has addressed and we have not. I'm not aware of any work
   in distributed AI that is looking at problems of this type. This is definitely, from the
   DAI standpoint, a good research area and an area where much can be learned from
   the database community.

Q.(S. M. Deen) : If you lock the whole system, it is going to be expensive in terms of both time and computational cost. I presume that you also keep a version number, so that if something has been done with the past beliefs you can give an explanation, even though the past belief isn't there in the current version any more. Also, is it at all feasible to reduce the computational time by broadcasting the change in belief to everybody, so that if any of their beliefs is based on that belief they can then automatically be updated in parallel?

A. (M. Huhns) : Broadcasting is possible, except that the agent often does not know what the belief should be in order to broadcast it. So it is not so much announcing that a change in belief has occurred, as that a new status is being sought. This has to be communicated to the other agents, but our incremental communication should be sufficient; we hope that it will involve as few agents as possible, so other agents can go on with their problem solving. Moreover, that's what we expect will happen. Now, in terms of maintaining a version or history with this system, it is somewhat different than a DBMS in that data does not go away in a truth maintenance system. When you change something, such as someone's age from 35 to 36, 35 doesn't disappear to be replaced by 36, 35 is still there but the system's belief in someone's age being 35 is now out and its belief in their age being 36 is now in. If it later learns that its new information about the change in age was wrong, then the age being 36 goes out and the previous belief comes back in. This is the way that rollbacks occur in a system that has a truth maintenance system.

Q. (S. M. Deen) : Why cannot each agent keep a history of the basis of its beliefs, so that if a new announcement is made it could check against the history and then it could find out whether it has used that source of information?

A. (M. Huhns) : Certainly agents can maintain this history; in fact, they maintain all the beliefs they have ever had. Another characteristic of a truth maintenance system is that there is no convenient way for it to forget, so it grows monotonically. But there is a potential for some circularity of beliefs and inconsistency, so that although we could maintain a consistent set of beliefs, we might not be able to maintain a well-founded set of beliefs. So our DTMS algorithm guarantees this well-foundedness as well.

Q. (W. Chu, UCLA) : I have some comments on Professor Deen's question. I feel that from the database point of view, in the past we have been regulating and locking everything and when the system gets large we really want to relax those assumptions to make them weaker, so that a lot more things can go on in parallel. So we should allow data to be processed with inconsistency in there, provided we have some handle on it, and I think this should be applied to knowledge as well. I think the basic idea along that line is traditional semantics: if you know the semantics of the transaction, there are certain things that can go on in parallel without having any conflict. For example, withdraw many and deposit many are quite different; for deposits you can do things in parallel without too much of a conflict, but for withdrawals you have to be more careful. Also, the amount of withdrawal makes a difference. I think, likewise, that knowledge maintenance should be treated similarly. If you lock everything up, it would be very inefficient. Instead, you categorise. I think, because knowledge and semantics are so closely related, you have a better way of handling it from that point of view.

A. (M. Huhns) : Yes, using the semantics of the data in this way is a very good suggestion for improving the efficiency of consistency maintenance.

Cooperative interaction as strategic belief revision*

Julia Rose Galliers
University of Cambridge Computer Laboratory
Cambridge CB2 3QG, ENGLAND

Abstract

Choice in belief revision is presented as a fundamental aspect of rational interaction with the world. Communication as a type of rational interaction with a world comprised of other agents, is a development of this. Since worlds comprising other agents are open or uncertain, communicated information cannot be assumed as reliable and/or fully informed. Agents must decide *whether* as well as how to revise their views on recognition of another's intention that they do so.

This autonomy over changes to cognitive states during communication determines the nature of cooperative interaction. There is no need for special axioms dictating 'helpfulness' and imposing cooperation as benevolence, for example. All that is needed is a strategic approach to communication in which cooperative dialogue is both determined by and determines the belief revisions between autonomous agents. A computational model on this basis is currently being developed at Cambridge University Computer Laboratory. The benefit for a multi-agent environment, of action being thus jointly determined via cooperative interaction as a series of negotiated belief revisions, is that the action is then coherent with all that is believed yet *distributed* between the individual agents. Action is adaptive and flexible to the entire context.

1 Introduction

The aim is firstly to present a theory of choice or preference in belief revision as a fundamental property of rational agenthood, extensible to multi-agent contexts. It is then claimed that cooperative interaction emerges naturally from this understanding, without recourse to imposed behaviours such as 'helpfulness' or 'sincerity'.

Agents designed to be autonomously in control of their own mental states generate cooperative *and* adaptive behaviour. Flexibility and

---

*Research supported by a SERC postdoctoral IT fellowship.

adaptation is crucial to successful modelling of multi-agent contexts as open systems in which the context is constantly changing and no one agent can be in possession of complete information at all times. Previous cooperative frameworks incorporate a cooperative rationality with inbuilt 'helpfulness', in which requests are positively received and attended to, unless contradictory to some pre-existing goal. This assumes any request to be appropriate to the entire context, which in turn assumes the requesting agent as reliably and fully informed. In contrast, a general framework of autonomous belief revision and strategic utterance planning is suggested. Cooperative interaction results naturally from this, without imposed behaviours and with the positive role of conflicts and their resolution properly acknowledged (Galliers, 1989, 1990b). Cooperative dialogue is modelled according to such a framework as a series of negotiated belief revisions to mutual satisfaction.

This paper elaborates and explicates the above theoretical stance which forms the basis for a computational model of dialogue currently being developed at Cambridge University Computer Laboratory (Galliers, 1990a). The application domain is library search. Section 2 describes the nature and theoretical background of autonomous belief revision (ABR) and its current implementation status as a component of the dialogue model. Section 3 describes ABR's role in strategic utterance planning.

2 Autonomous belief revision as the basis of cooperative interaction

Many researchers in AI are concerned with the design of automated systems which can plan and execute actions. These actions should be appropriate to the goals of the system, and its context or environment. In this sense they are rational behaviours. They are determined according to the constraints imposed by the system's cognitive architecture (Rosenschein, 1988) comprising three related and dependent components of perception, belief and desire, and action. And in the sense of being determined thus, and by past and present experience of the world as opposed to inflexible, imposed assumptions of the designer (Russell, 1989), a system can be autonomous. Being an autonomous, rational agent then is about having a basis upon which to reason about relations and behaviour appropriate to self and the world. And that world includes other agents, who similarly reason in order to act autonomously and rationally.

Primary in this reasoning are representations; beliefs or cognitive states generated through perception and inference, and related to desires and action according to the rules of rationality encoded into the system. But these cognitive states are inevitably constantly changing. The world is dynamic. Expansion and contraction of a belief set occurs as new data is perceived or inferred, and old data is lost over time or in the light of new evidence. Often expansion and contraction occur together. This is belief revision (Gärdenfors, 1988, 1989); changing one's cognitive state.

But new data or evidence may be accomodated into a belief set in alternative ways, and all of these maintain consistency. This is known as the 'multiple extensions' problem. For example:

$$(a) P \vee Q \quad (b) R \supset Q \quad (c) P \vee R$$

$$\text{new evidence:} \neg P \wedge \neg Q$$

Incorporating the new evidence results in two logically equivalent extensions. These are (b) and the new evidence, or (c) and the new evidence, because (a) is inconsistent with the new evidence, and *either* (b) *or* (c) are consistent with it, but not both (Rescher, 1964). Alternatively again, the new evidence can be rejected if it is not assumed as 'truth' in which case the third possible extension is (a), (b) and (c). Some basis for prioritising or ordering alternative combinations of belief is necessary to resolve such situations; principles of *preference* embodied within the rules of rational belief change.

New data or evidence can be perceived directly from the world, or it can be communicated via another agent. An utterance is a perceived event that conveys an intention; the communicating agent's intention that the attending agent recognise an intention for a particular *change* in the attendee's cognitive states. This last phrase may be more traditionally presented as the intention to *induce* a particular belief or goal. The point being made is that it is not so much the individual belief or goal that is of interest. Agents always have some existing mental state. Any change in the environment, including the recognition of a communicative intention via an utterance, *changes* that entire mental state. *Communication is an incidence of revision.* Communicating agents plan to revise other's belief states, and recognise each other's plans as such. Communication is therefore subject to theories of belief revision (briefly described in section 2.1). Basic principles of choice or preference in belief revision between competing, alternative states are an important part of the belief revision theory.

Principles of choice in revision are in fact especially pertinent in communication. This is because communication is a special case of belief revision. As well as the perceived change that the communicating agent has a communicative intention, the latter intention also has *content*. The content relates to yet *another* cognitive state change; specifically that the receiving agent adopt a particular belief or goal. It is this secondary aspect which is the focus of interest here, and which inevitably involves choice. The reason is as follows:

Multi-agent contexts are 'open' environments (Hewitt, 1986). Amongst other things, this means that the flow of information is such that no one agent can *know* everything about its environment. Such a state of affairs would not even be desirable as there would be unnecessary bottlenecks of information processing (Hewitt, 1986, Gasser, 1989, Galliers, 1990b). Therefore it is incorrect to assume that the content of any utterance is necessarily accurate. This means that on recognition of x's intention that y change her cognitive state to incorporate a belief that p for example, y incorporates the belief of x's intention as assumed 'truth' (using the terms above), because it is perceived and hence self-evident. *But*, given the open and distributed nature of multi-agent environments, y cannot assume the 'truth' of p, and hence its appropriateness for adoption.

ABR is the principled basis upon which y can make the choice. It is a fundamental basis of preference between competing alternative cognitive states, generalising to any such context, such as the further use of competing inferences for example from conflicting default rules. It is described in detail below. But the payoff in the communication context is not merely generality. These principles as the basic elements of interactive rationality, remove the need for separate explicit statements or assumptions about cooperation and sincerity. The accepted basis upon which one belief set is preferable to another, for example in cases of contradiction yet logical equivalence as in the Rescher example cited above, are equally applied in a context of contradiction arising as a consequence of an utterance. There is no need for separate axioms describing helpful agents as those that always adopt other's recognised goals, for example to believe p, unless they conflict with one in existence, such as already believing not$p$ (Cohen and Levesque, 1987, Perrault, 1987). There is no need to dictate either adoption or persistence, or to treat contradictions in any way as a special case. A basic system of preference is laid down and understood, general enough to encompass change of beliefs as expansion, contraction or revision wherever in the world the new evidence comes from. What is being considered is: Which is the more coherent state given an existing cognitive state and this (these) potential change(s)? It is knowledge of this basic principle of rationality which determines the revisions planned to other's belief states in communication, and the cooperative nature of the interaction. This is described further in section 3.

2.1 Preference and belief revision

There are currently two competing theories of rational belief change, either of which could offer a basis within which an ordering or system of priorities for revision can be accomodated. They are *foundation theory* and *coherence theory*.

Foundation theory considers new beliefs are only to be added on the basis of other justified beliefs, and beliefs no longer justified are abandoned. An example of this approach in practice is the truth (reason) maintenance system of Doyle (1979) and de Kleer (1986). Foundation theory takes its name from the emphasis on justification for belief, which obviously is not infinite. Where it ends up is in beliefs which are justified by themselves, and which then justify or are *foundational* to others. These are self-evident beliefs or *assumptions*, for example an observation.

Coherence theory on the other hand, represents a conservatism whereby justification is only a requisite condition of believing if there is a special reason to doubt a belief. If there is such a challenge, the guiding principles are those of *minimal change* and *maximal coherence*. In other words, changes are allowed, but only to the extent that they yield sufficient increases in coherence. Coherent beliefs are mutually supporting. *p* can be justified because it coheres with *q* and *q* be justified because it coheres with *p*. The nature of this mutual support or coherence ideally, is *intelligibility*, in particular intelligible deductive and non-deductive explanation of why or how it is that something is the case. For example, if one believes *p*, *q* and *r*, but also *r because p* and *q*. The 'because' can be deductive in *p* and *q* implying *r*, or it could be statistical as in *p* and *q* generally implies *r*' if other things are equal', or it could be based in commonsense psychology (Harman, 1986).

Within either theory, the determination of *preferred* cognitive states, can be done in various ways. Individual beliefs can be ascribed a probability to determine maximally preferred sets. Such an approach considers beliefs as variably certain. It is more common in AI however, to treat beliefs as equally certain; believed or not believed. Certain beliefs can then be distinguished on a basis of variable *corrigibility* or openness to disbelief (Levi, 1984). For example, *p* is believed more strongly than *q* if it would be harder to stop believing *p* than to stop believing *q* (Harman, 1986). For Gärdenfors(1988) this relative ease of disbelief is related to a belief's utility in inquiry and deliberation. He offers an ordering of epistemic *entrenchment* stated in terms of the logical relations which exist between pairs of propositions in alternative belief sets. Doyle combines notions of utility with probabilities, which grounds his preference relation in economic decision theory (Doyle, 1988, 1990).

In Galliers and Reichgelt (1991), we present a general logical framework for theories of ABR which supports both coherence and foundation theories of belief revision. Various ordering relations for preferred revisions are compared within the framework, such as those of Gärdenfors (1988, 1989) Nebel (1989) and Doyle (1990). A new coherence-style ordering is presented as particularly suited to ABR for communication and cooperative dialogue modelling. This is *increased coherence* or *mc*. A description follows in the next section.

2.2 Autonomous belief revision

An agent is assumed to have a finite set of beliefs K, which is consistent but not necessarily closed under deduction. The framework postulates two operations on belief sets, addition and deletion. The addition of a proposition ϕ to K, $K^a \phi$, is then defined as:

$$K^a \phi = \{K' \mid K' \subseteq K \cup \{\phi\} \text{ and } cons(K') \text{ and } K' \vdash \phi\} \cup \{K\}$$

where $cons(K)$ intuitively means "K is consistent" and can be defined as "there is a ψ such that $K \not\vdash \psi$". Thus, the addition operator defines a set of possible revised belief sets. Note that, because $K \in K^a\phi$, $K' \in K^a\phi$ does not always imply that $K' \vdash \phi$. After all, we are interested in autonomous belief revision in which an agent may decide to ignore a new piece of evidence. Also, the members of $K^a\phi$ are not necessarily maximal subsets of K. The only restriction that we have is that, if one decides not to engage in belief revision, nothing changes.

The deletion of a proposition ϕ from a belief set K, $K^d\phi$, can be defined in a similar vein as:

$$K^d\phi = \{K' \mid K' \subseteq K \text{ and } cons(K') \text{ and } K' \nvdash \phi\} \cup \{K\}$$

Our addition and deletion operators define a set of potential new belief sets.

In order to decide which belief set will actually be adopted as preferred, the logic requires an ordering relation between belief sets. Increased or more-coherence mc orders logically consistent sets according to maximal derivability of core beliefs. This is based on the intuition that an agent has a number of central beliefs and that any piece of evidence that increases the agent's confidence in the central beliefs will be adopted. We say that a proposition ϕ increases the coherence of K with respect to some goal ψ if adding ϕ to K would generate a new proof of ψ. In order to establish whether this is the case, we first remove ψ from K, after which we add ϕ to each resulting belief set. The aim is to establish whether ψ can then be proved in at least one of the resulting belief sets. Thus, we define $mc(K, \psi, \phi)$ (ϕ increases the coherence of K with respect to ψ) as

$$mc(K, \psi, phi) \text{ iff there is a } K' \in (K^d\psi)^a\phi, K' \vdash \psi$$

We can then start preferring belief sets that have an increased coherence with respect to some goal ψ. Thus, we define the ordering $\leq_\psi$ as

$$K' \leq_\psi K \text{ iff for all } \phi, \text{ if } mc(K', \psi, \phi) \text{ then } mc(K, \psi, \phi)$$

We can then define a strict ordering in the normal way as $K' <_\psi K$ iff $K' \leq_\psi K$ and $K \nleq_\psi K'$.

The above describes a more-coherent belief base relative to some goal, as the harder to disbelieve because there are more justifications, more proofs of that goal. For example, r and q are believed as self-evident assumptions. In addition r can be justified by believing p in conjunction with q. p is the new evidence. If p were incorporated into the belief set, r's existence would then be additionally justified. Without p, r is still believed, but the cognitive state with p is the more coherent with respect to r. The latter is harder to disbelieve because disbelief involves believing either r and p false, or r and q false, or r and $p \wedge q$ false. Without p there is only r to be disbelieved.

The more-coherent set does not have to be one including the new evidence. Each potential state is compared equally and autonomously. For example, maybe $p \leftrightarrow \neg s$ is also believed, with $s \wedge q$ additionally

154

justifying r. Again, p is the new evidence. Which is the more coherent state: the one with p or the one with s? According to the above, in fact these are *both* preferred or more-coherent states. We suggest a heuristic, guiding means of discrimination between such cases. The heuristic relates to the source or *endorsement* of assumptions, making statements about their relative reliability and hence informational value (Galliers, 1990).

2.2.1 Endorsements

Assumptions are a foundational notion. They are a set of self-evident beliefs which found or justify all other beliefs. Our model of ABR is a coherence model, but one which incorporates an element of foundationalism in the existence of ground level assumptions. These are *endorsed* with non-numeric indicators of source information (Cohen, 1985).

Endorsements approximate with respect to issues such as relative informational value and explanatory power. The intuition is that there are general rules related to the sources of information which are relevant when considering how relatively 'hard' that information is then to give up. For example, whether they came from a reliable source such as directly from sensory apparatus, or alternatively, indirectly via another agent, or if they were assumed on the basis of generalised knowledge in the absence of anything more specific, and so on. Other works concentrating on the role of the source of evidence when reasoning in situations of uncertainty are Thost (1989) and Garigliano (1988).

Each founding assumption is endorsed as:

1. *communicated*, either *first-hand* (sensory information) or *second-hand* (via another agent or text). These assumptions are also very roughly graded as 'pos' if they are communicated with conviction or from a very reliable source, or 'neg' if they are communicated from a spurious source or without conviction: [1c-pos], [1c-neg], [2c-pos] or [2c-neg].

2. *given*, either as *specific* information widely believed and without any particular source, for example 'James Dean was a film star', or as *default* generalities similarly widely believed. For example, 'birds fly'. Alternatively, given assumptions may be *values* denoting a notion of goodness which may be linked with desires. Values can also be 'pos' or 'neg' as a rough grading scheme between those more persistent in being considered a 'very good thing' and those just considered 'a good thing'. These are obviously subjective to the individual being modelled, although generally accepted (culturally held) values such as it being good to have money or to be conscientious or trustworthy can be incorporated as defaults. The possibilities are: [spec], [def], [value-pos] or [value-neg].

3. *hypothetical*, with no evidence at all other than as a possible grounding for a belief under consideration [hypoth].

Combinations of endorsed assumptions underlying competing revisions are compared using a set of very simple guiding heuristics (Galliers, 1990a):

1. Belief states founded upon first-hand evidence are harder to disbelieve than those founded on any other combination of assumptions. (This does not take the possibility of faulty sensors into account).

2. The more positive communicated assumptions or specific assumptions, that ground a belief state, the harder the process of disbelief, regardless of the number of 'neg' or default or value assumptions.

3. Combinations of 'neg' endorsed assumptions and defaults can be relatively ranked, and values can enhance these. Believing it would be good to believe something does additionally endorse its belief. However, values are only compared when in conjunction with other endorsements. For example, however much it may be believed that it is good to win the pools, this can only endorse and make more persistent the belief state in which I believe I have won the pools if I have some other even vague, evidence for this. The ranking orders [1c-neg] as relatively more persistent than either [2c-neg] or [def] which are equivalent. These all supercede [value-pos] which offers slightly more persistence support than [value-neg].

We have a preliminary implementation of ABR as a belief revision mechanism which incorporates ordering on a three tiered basis, and in which the three-tiered determination of *how* to revise is also a model of *whether* to revise, because the preferred state may be the one in which there is no change.

The first tier of ordering results in a set of possible revisions in which the alternative belief sets are logically consistent and comprise only self-evident assumptions and beliefs derived from these (as in foundational belief revision systems such as an ATMS (de Kleer, 1986). Disbelief is propagated backwards to founding assumptions so that removed beliefs cannot be immediately rederived. Choices of assumptions to remove occur according to the same principles of ABR. Disbelief propagation does not occur forwards however, to other beliefs justified by the removed belief(s). Unjustified beliefs become new assumptions, but obviously not well endorsed ones.

The second tier of ordering is *mc*; only those sets which also support the derivation of core beliefs are retained. And finally, the third level ensures that of these sets, the preferred alternative is well grounded in terms of its self-evident assumptions; the preferred belief set(s) are the best endorsed.

3   ABR for strategic utterance planning

Revision of another's cognitive state was suggested in section 2 as the motivating force for communicative behaviour. But if there are no specialised rules dictating what is a cooperative response, the success of an utterance is not guaranteed. Autonomous agents may or may not comply with the recognised intended effects of an utterance on their cognitive states. It is the above principles of choice or autonomous, rational belief change which must be addressed. Communicative action is planned not only purposively, but *strategically* (Galliers, 1988,1989).

Strategic interaction acknowledges all participants as sharing control over the effects of a communication. The aim in utterance planning, is to determine one's own actions according to one's own goals and the context. *But*, this context includes the other agent and her autonomy over presumed existing mental states. Strategic action is that which maximises one's own outcome (Schelling, 1960); maximising one's own outcome in a situation of shared control, is a matter of it being maximal for the other party(s) also. *Strategic planning to achieve a desired change in another's belief states is therefore a matter of setting the goal state based upon a prediction of the context of that other agent, such that the general rules of rational autonomous belief revision would then dictate the desired change anyway.*

Predictions about another agent's beliefs and endorsed assumptions, and their roles in determining potentially increased coherence, determine intended revisions in strategically motivated utterances. It is the theory of ABR that must be taken into account as the basis for addition of conveyed propositions. As part of a plan comprising x having a goal for y to believe p for example, x makes a prediction re the preference of y's alternatives on recognising x's intention that y adopt p. In nearly all existing cooperative dialogue planning literature, x's plan would include not a prediction, but a simplifying assumption that y will adopt x's recognised intended belief state unless there is a contradiction with existing belief, because y is defined to be 'cooperative' in this way. In this strategic model however, if x believes y to posess the belief states given in the example of section 2.2. for example, x would predict via ABR that y could *either* choose to retain the cognitive state where $p \leftrightarrow \neg s$ is believed but together with s, *or* to revise such that s is disbelieved and p adopted. It may be that y does autonomously prefer to adopt p; this is more coherent for y. But it may be that there is information which y has and that x does not have, which makes s more coherent for y. In this case, y is apparently uncooperative; y does not adopt x's recognised intended belief. However, if the overall context is one in which the participants are conversing in order to achieve some mutually satisfactory state, for example an agreed description or solution to a problem for which each may have differing expertise, then such an eventuality motivates further strategic planning. Either x must provide more information to make p more coherent to y, or else y should provide x with the information which may make s more coherent to x, thus leading to x abandoning the goal for y to adopt p.

Dialogue on such a strategic basis is adaptive *and* cooperative. There is a defined basis upon which the distributed belief state across both agents can change and develop. Both agents are attempting to revise the belief states of the other in the light of what is coherent with what they currently believe. If either is unsuccessful, then the effect of continued communication with further well-endorsed information, may be that the initial intended change is no longer desired. And so, the dialogue as a series of mutual revisions, ensures coherence widely within the joint space of all that is believed between communicating agents, without any one agent having to believe it all and dominate the control of adaptive responses. And the self-motivated conflicts which get resolved in the process, crucially achieve cooperation.

This theory is currently being applied in ESRC/MRC/SERC Cognitive Science/HCI Initiative Project ID: 90/CS42, under the joint direction of myself and Dr. Karen Spark Jones. The context is the interaction between a library user and a librarian. It is hoped to generate successively more complex versions of an 'automatic librarian' to establish this theory of cooperative dialogue as better than those currently proffered, and lay a foundation for an eventual real automated library interface. The study context was chosen as one in which neither participant in the dialogues is dominant in terms of knowledge. The librarian knows more about the library system and the user knows more about themselves and their overall objective, but only together can they achieve the knowledge required for appropriate problem description and document retrieval.

4 Conclusions

Distribution of information in open, multi-agent environments, is the background within which choice in belief revision as a fundamental property of agenthood, is particularly relevant to communication as a special case of belief revision. Strategically rational interaction is determined according to an understanding of the nature of this autonomous belief revision. Cooperative dialogue as a series of strategically determined and mutually accepted revisions, ensures action that is then coherent and adaptive to the multi-agent context as a whole.

To summarise the main points:

- An agent always has a cognitive state. Perceiving and inferring new beliefs changes this state by expansion, contraction and revision. There are principles which determine how this takes place; principles of rational belief change. For incidences of competing, logically equivalent alternatives, these include principles relating to *preference* of cognitive states.

- Communication is a special case of belief change which involves other agents. Agents plan to revise, and perceive (recognise) other's plans as such.

- An utterer's intention is perceived change yet it also has content; the intended change or effect on the recipient's belief state. Because of the distributed nature of knowledge in open, multi-agent systems, the content of communicated intentions are not assumed as necessarily well-informed.

- Agents are autonomous. They determine their own cognitive states according to the principles of rational belief change. There are no special axioms dictating helpfulness and promoting cooperation when in a multi-agent context.

- Multi-agent communication is therefore strategically driven. Plans to effect changes to another's cognitive state can only be successful if they take into account the principles whereby rational and autonomous agents change their beliefs. Maximising one's own outcome with respect to another agent is dependent upon them maximising theirs.

- Cooperative behaviour can emerge from general principles of rational belief change and agent autonomy.

- Cooperative dialogue as a series of mutual revisions, ensures coherence widely within the joint space of all that is believed yet distributed between communicating agents. It is adaptive and flexible, where designer-imposed cooperation as benevolence is not.

5 Acknowledgements

Thanks to Han Reichgelt and Steven Reece.

References

[1] Cohen P.R. Heuristic Reasoning about Uncertainty: an Artificial Intelligence Approach, Pitman, Boston, 1985.

[2] Cohen, P. and Levesque H. Rational Interaction as the basis for Communication. Technical report No. 89, Centre for the Study of Language and Information, Stanford University, California, U.S.A., 1987.

[3] De Kleer J. An Assumption-based TMS. Artificial Intelligence Vol 28 No. 2 pp127-162,1986

[4] Doyle J. AI and Rational Self Government. TR. CMU-CS-88-124, Carnegie-Mellon University, U.S.A.

[5] Doyle J. Rational Belief Revision. Preliminary Report. 1990.

[6] Galliers, J.R. and Reichgelt, H. A Framework for Autonomous Belief Revision. University of Cambridge Computer Laboratory, Working paper, 1991.

[7] Galliers J.R. Belief Revision and a Theory of Communication. Cambridge University Computer Lab. Tech Report No. 193. 1990a

[8] Galliers J.R. The Positive Role of Conflict in Cooperative Systems. In Demazeau Y. and Muller J-P. (eds) '89 Decentralized Artificial Intelligence, Elsevier, Amsterdam, 1990b

[9] Galliers, J.R. A Theoretical Framework for Computer Models of Cooperative Dialogue, Acknowledging Multi-Agent Conflict. PhD thesis. Cambridge University Computer Lab. Tech Report No. 172, and HCRL, Open University Tech Report No. 51, 1989.

[10] Galliers, J.R. A Strategic Framework for Multi-Agent Cooperative Dialogue. Proceedings of the Eighth European Conference on Artificial Intelligence, Munich, pp 415-420, August, 1988.

[11] Gärdenfors P. Knowledge in Flux: Modeling the Dynamics of Epistemic States. MIT Press, 1988.

[12] Gärdenfors P. The Dynamics of Belief Systems: Foundations vs Coherence Theories. To appear in Revue Internationale de Philosophie, 1989.

[13] Garigliano R., Bokma A. and Long D. A Model for Learning by Source Control. In Uncertainty and Intelligent Systems, 2nd Int. Conf. on Information Processing and Management of Uncertainty in Knowledge-Based Systems. Italy. Springer-Verlag. 1988.

[14] Gasser L. et al. Representing and Using Organizational Knowledge in Distributed AI Systems. In eds: Gasser and Huhns. DAI Volume 2. Pitman, London, 1989.

[15] Harman G. Change in View - Principles in Reasoning. Bradford Book, MIT Press, Camb., Mass. 1986

[16] Hewitt, K. Offices are Open Systems. ACM Transactions on Office Information Systems, 4(3) pp 271-287, 1986.

[17] Levi I. Truth, Fallibility and the Growth of Knowledge. in Decisions and Revisions, Cambridge University Press, 1984.

[18] Nebel, B. A Knowledge level analysis of belief revision. In R. Brachman, H. Levesque & R. Reiter (eds) Proceedings of the first international conference on Principles of Knowledge Representation and Reasoning, San Mateo, CA: Morgan Kaufmann, 1989.

[19] Perrault, C.R. An application of Default logic to Speech Act Theory. Report No. CSLI 87-90, CLSI, SRI International, California, U.S.A., 1987.

[20] Rao A.S. Dynamics of Belief Systems: A Philosophical, Logical and AI Perspective. TR No.2. Australian, Artificial Intelligence Institute, Victoria, Australia. 1989.

[21] Rosenschein, S. A Cognitive Architecture for Rational Agents. SRI Report, 1988

[22] Russell S.J. Execution Architectures and Compilation. IJCAI '89, Detroit, U.S.A. 1989.

[23] Schelling. T.C. The Strategy of Conflict. Harvard University Press, Camb., Mass. 1960

[24] Thagard P. Explanatory Coherence. Behavioural and Brain Sciences Vol. 12 No. 3. 1989.

[25] Thost M. Generating facts from Opinions with Information Source Models. in Proceedings of IJCAI '89, Detroit, U.S.A. 1989.

DISCUSSION

Presenter: J. Galliers

Q. (F. Farhoodi, Logica, Cambridge) : I'm interested to know how you would deal with the situation where an individual is acting according to some procedures which are designed by the organisation in which the agent exists. So, when it comes to communication on a particular issue, it's also these procedures that dictate to the agent what he's supposed to be doing. Would you include the procedures in this model of the agent's, if you like, rationality, or would they be external to it?

A. (J. Galliers) : If they are absolutely unchangeable, then they are the beliefs that that agent holds, that he/she/it can't deviate from and therefore any information that comes in has to be rational in the sense of being coherent with these. If it's not then it's rejected.

Q. (T. Boyle, Manchester Polytechnic) : At the start of your talk you said that agents had joint goals. I didn't see where that came into the talk at all?

A. (J. Galliers) : This is always difficult because when you say joint goal often people think of something very specific. All I meant is literally at the level of two agents. If there wasn't some overall goal that they'd be coordinating or communicating then they would walk away from each other. It's simply at that level, that there is some aim for some state of cooperation where there will be agreement on something.

Q. (E. Werner, University of Hamburg) : A comment and a question. I like the direction your work's going because in my work on communication it's one of the things that I consider and I think the direction you're going is the best way to deal also with these, what I call, pragmatic operators. The question is what if you have imperfect information, both strategic and state information?

A. (J. Galliers) : What do you mean by imperfect?

Q. (E. Werner) : If the agent doesn't have complete information about the world, doesn't have complete information about what the other agents are going to do? Also, what if the agent has a lot of very small non- interesting beliefs so that the sheer quantity will give you incorrect coherence results? Do you have some nice evaluation? Is that what you mean by preference, that you can affect some kind of evaluation beliefs based in the terms of agent interests and those interests then determine events?

A. (J. Galliers) : I'll deal with the second one first. That is an interesting point and it's a problem. I have to limit the belief sets because size actually becomes practically impossible, I meant to mention that but I didn't. Practically using reason maintenance systems is hell, because give it any reasonable belief set and it just explodes. This is a problem and I had to make assumptions that the beliefs I'm using are all of interest but this is something I hope to get to grips with on the new research project when we get going on it. It's to try to be able to withdraw a subset of relevant beliefs and have a good principled basis for calling them relevant. In fact having lots of extra beliefs around doesn't mess up the endorsement business. If you are looking at two alternative belief sets, let's say you were only looking at two, any irrelevant extraneous beliefs would be in both so they just cancel each other out.

What was your first question, imperfect information?

Q. (E. Werner): You say the agents are in states of uncertainty so in that sense the agent has very little information about what the other agent actually believes. So say I'm in a strategic position where one persuades another person, and I have some kind of particular linguistic strategy on a use for that end, to minimise the other person's gains and maximise my own by using some sort of game theoretic thinking. Then the existence of strategies will depend on the pattern of information I have about the other agents beliefs.

A. (J. Galliers): That's fine. The assumption is that you don't have an empty head. There would be generalities, or default assumptions in there, about how people behave when I say things to them, I might get it wrong but I have general assumptions I can use if I need to. And, in the system there would be the same kinds of default assumptions about how other nodes or other agents are likely to respond, what they are likely to believe. The only thing that's important about this is, not about getting down to the right set of responses, it might in fact be wrong, all it is is a guide, it's a half logical and half heuristic system to home in on what might be the preferred beliefs set.

Q. (S. Sian, Imperial College, London): I don't see the relative importance of endorsements as compared to normal change. Do I understand correctly that the first criteria is minimal change? Then if you can't resolve it, then you plan endorsements? Is that true?

A. (J. Galliers): Yes.

Q. (S. Sian): That means that in these situations, sometimes a strong endorsement can mean that you would accept a greater change?

A. (J. Galliers): That's right. We're working on it.

Q. (J. Lenting, University of Limberg): Your autonomous approach doesn't always agree with real-life. In life you do not tackle the problem of an organisation in which the people are perfectly satisfied with their functioning but the management isn't. Coherence is defined in terms of more or less local satisfaction with functioning and not as the global functioning of the system. I think, ultimately, what you need when designing cooperative systems is an assurance that it will function alright globally viewed from an external viewpoint. Do you have any ideas how this can be incorporated?

A. (J. Galliers): It's not something I've thought about a lot because I've been trying to do it where each agent is completely equal, there is not hierarchy. I think if you wanted to incorporate a hierarchy, I don't see why it isn't feasible.

Q. (J. Lenting): Sorry, I don't want to impose a hierarchy, I just want to be able to design a measure for a global functioning of the system and then ensure in one way or another that this measure is achieved.

A. (J. Galliers) : That's not something I've addressed. I'm sure I need to but it's not something I have as yet. You mentioned it, didn't you, in your talk in summing up yesterday? We keep talking about global coherence, but what is it we're actually looking at?

The Role Of Cooperation in Multi-Agent Learning

Sati S. Sian

Department of Computing

Imperial College

180 Queen's Gate, London SW7 2BZ

sss@doc.ic.ac.uk

ABSTRACT

We are currently investigating the problem of dynamic adaptation in systems consisting of multiple intelligent agents. An essential characteristic of these systems is that the salient knowledge for learning is distributed amongst the agents. As in human communities, effective learning therefore requires cooperation amongst the constituent members. In this paper we detail the role of cooperation in such learning systems and the problems introduced by it. These ideas have been used in **MALE** (Multi-Agent Learning Environment) from which an illustrative example is shown.

1. INTRODUCTION

The study of systems consisting of multiple intelligent agents is receiving increasing attention in the AI community. Under the umbrella of Distributed Artificial Intelligence (DAI) much effort has been focused on issues such as multi-agent planning and organisational control [Bond88][Huhns87]. Until recently however the question of adaptation in such systems was not studied [Gasser89]. The MINDS system [Huhns87] for intelligent document retrieval took the first step in giving its individual agents learning abilities. The learning of user access preferences in this system however was an activity local to an agent requiring no interaction with the other agents. A more cooperative approach based on genetic transformation and an extension of the Contract Net Protocol has been reported in [Shaw89]. In their system an agent that successfully bids for a task is accorded a reward which positively affects its ability to bid for future tasks. Agents not successful in bidding eventually die out. Crossover and mutation operators are used to generate new agents which inherit the abilities of the successful agents. The problem with such a scheme however is that it is only useful when agent abilities are of the form which allows arbitrary combination and for which an encoding of these abilities suitable for genetic algorithms can be found.

We are concerned with adaptation in multi-agent domains where the agents are persistent objects and in which the agents are actively learning from their experiences. In this paper we concentrate on an analysis of the role of cooperation in relation to the problem of learning. The issues involved are similar to the analysis of cooperation in problem solving. Specifically we want to address the following:

- Why do we need to cooperate? What problems does individual learning not address?

- When or at what level do we cooperate? Can we do with simply collecting the information from all the agents at a central point?

- How do we cooperate?

This analysis forms the basis for our model for multi-agent learning. We briefly describe this model and show how we can use it to address some of the issues outlined previously. MALE is an implementation of this model and has been used to evaluate it. Some results from this study are presented.

2   THE ROLE OF COOPERATION

2.1   The Motivation

To adapt successfully to its conditions, a system needs to learn from previous situations and apply the learnt knowledge to subsequent situations. This problem within a single agent has been extensively studied by the Machine Learning community [Michalski86][Kodratoff87] and the various empirical systems have led to theoretical results as to when useful learning is possible [Valiant89]. A number of learning strategies are now recognised such as; *inductive* learning where the object is to generalise from specific instances to more general hypotheses that explain all of the positive instances and none of the negative ones; *deductive* learning [Mitchell86] in which a deductive proof is generalised to create a more useful description of a concept; and *analogical* learning [Carbonell83] in which similarities in problem situations are used to re-use previous solutions. In general, the quality of the learnt knowledge is dependant both on the quality and the extent of the source data.

An essential attribute in all distributed systems is that knowledge is spread out amongst the constituent parts. In a system consisting of multiple expert systems, for example, each agent is encapsulating a specific piece of knowledge and the total expertise of the system results from a combination of these sub-systems. For an agent in such a system, trying to use conventional methods for learning poses two main problems; lack of completeness and lack of quantity.

- *Lack of completeness*: In multi-agent domains, an agent's operating context is dependant on the actions and knowledge of the other agents. Such dependence may be explicit as for example in Distributed Problem Solving systems in which a large problem is split into smaller partially linked sub-problems or it may be implicit as for example in systems consisting of autonomous agents who have interacting goals. Such dependencies are significant for the agent when it is trying to learn about the problem in which it is involved. However information regarding these dependencies is not global. The agent's learning information is therefore incomplete and effective individual learning not possible.

  Consider for example multiple agents involved in the design of a car. Each agent is responsible for a particular part of the car such as the body shell, the interiors or the engine. Each agent may locally learn what is good and bad in its own sub-section but to learn how to make a good car requires cooperative learning. The inter-dependencies between the parts means that the best car is not made simply of the best sub-parts. A very powerful engine, for example, requires a stronger and therefore heavier body shell and the best interiors raise cost reducing the potential market for the car.

  In general the problem of incompleteness in an agent's learning knowledge will occur in all situations where it's choices are dependant on the choices of others and the details of such dependencies are not known globally.

- *Lack of quantity* : Distribution also implies that where agents are learning from a similar environment, a large amount of data that is potentially useful to any particular agent is held by the other agents. The quantity of data available to an agent is important in learning since the agent's confidence in a particular hypothesis is dependant on the number of instances consistent with the hypothesis. As this data is spread out amongst the other agents, any particular agent's confidence in its learnt information is not as great as it could be. On the other hand other agents may hold data that argues against a hypothesis. The non-availability of this may mean that an agent is using an incorrect hypothesis that could be avoided.

By introducing cooperative learning, we are aiming to make more effective learning possible by overcoming incompleteness in source knowledge where it exists and amalgamating experience where it is distributed.

2.2   Problem Structure and its Affect

The role of cooperation when learning is dependant on the agent structure and problem composition (or decomposition) of the system. We have identified three different forms:

• *Homogeneous composition* : This is the case where the agents have equivalent sub-problems. An example of this is the Air-Traffic Control System [Cammarata85] in which the global problem of air-traffic management consists of each agent (an aeroplane in this case) having the equivalent sub-problem of planning a collision free route from its source to its destination.

Agents in homogeneous systems *can* learn at the individual level. However since the other agents are also learning in the same problem domain much of what one agent learns can be used to reinforce or refute the other agents' learnt knowledge. Cooperative learning here, though not mandatory, gives the agents significant temporal advantages. Agents may be able to learn about situations in which they themselves have too little experience to formulate generalisations but about which the others agents have already received much more information.

• *Heterogeneous composition* : Systems of this form consist of distinct sub-problems, the solutions from which are integrated to form the global solution. An example would be Distributed Manufacturing (e.g [Parunaik87]) in which individual agents are responsible for the different components that make up a particular item. The completion attributes of an item (quality, speed, final location e.t.c) will depend on all the sub-parts. Therefore an agent trying to improve its contribution will in many cases have to take into account the work of the other agents. Cooperation is therefore mandatory to achieve successful learning.

• *Multifarious composition* : Between the above two extremes are systems in which the sub-problems have both distinct and shared attributes. An example would be a distributed commodities trading system in which individual agents are responsible for different commodities. Each agent has specific expertise with regard to its commodity and yet shares with the other agents the knowledge common across commodities. Cooperation for learning may be necessary in cases where the commodities are linked

168

and useful for reinforcement or refutation where generalised knowledge about commodities has been learnt.

2.3 Levels at which to cooperate

Intelligent agents will operate at a number of levels when carrying out tasks. Consider Figure 1 which shows one possible way of looking at the levels within an agent and the external attributes necessary in a multi-agent scenario.

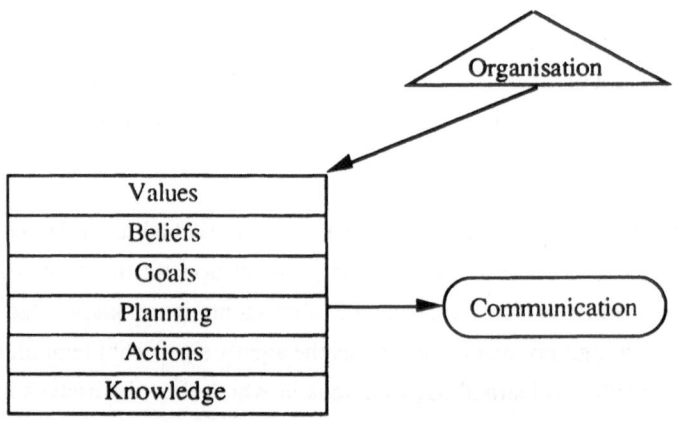

Figure 1: Levels within an agent

Cooperation for problem-solving may occur at any of these levels although modifications in the meta-level notions of *values* and *beliefs* tend to be local decisions on the part of an agent. For the purposes of learning *knowledge, action, planning* and *goals* are more relevant.

Cooperative learning at the knowledge level would require the exchange of knowledge held by the agents. This itself may consist of sub-levels. The very simplest cooperation would be an exchange of facts. Above this the agents may cooperate in the inductive learning of rules based on these facts. At the next level, given histories of plans and the actions generated by these plans, agents may cooperatively try to find generalised descriptions of the sort of actions that result in successful execution of given sorts of plans. Cooperative learning of the plans themselves may involve determining strategies for successful planning for given goals based on past experiences.

Similarly attributes necessitated by a multi-agent scenario namely organisation and communication are themselves amenable to dynamic learning. As shown in [Fox81] organisational structure has important consequences for the efficiency of a multi-agent system. Learning generalised descriptions of organisational forms that succeed for given problems would give these agents significant advantages. The same situation also applies to communication. Where agents have flexibility in deciding what form of communication to use, past experiences of the results of using given communication forms can be used to influence subsequent communication.

In general therefore, the learning processes are relatively immune to what is being learnt. The important factor is that we have an effective representation of the information that we are trying to learn. An additional point to note with these levels is that the higher up the hierarchy we consider cooperative learning the greater the sophistication of what is learnt and the lesser the volume of interaction. If we view the role of cooperative learning as the means to fill in gaps in an agent's knowledge, then the higher up the levels we go the smaller but more specialised these gaps become. The filling of these gaps is more difficult but more economic.

2.4 Means of cooperative learning

The question now arises as to how the agents can cooperate in the process of finding a consistent hypothesis. Since cooperation is to be based on communication of information, the two extremes of possibilities are *total* communication and *no* communication. The first involves the agents communicating all the data they have which is obviously prohibitive in terms of volume of data. The optimised version of this where agents send all their data to one special agent and let it do the learning using standard single agent methods is also not practical as in most systems the volume of data is likely to be too great to be handled by one agent. In addition such a centralised solution retracts from a level of agent autonomy (reducing the role of the agents to simple information gatherers) and suffers from all the problems of centralised systems (e.g failure protection and lack of resilience).

The other extreme of no communication, although shown as a possible means of simple cooperation [Rosenschein86], is inappropriate for learning where we have assumed benevolence on the part of the participating agents and the existence of some communication mechanism. In such situations communication gives a much more efficient cooperation scheme.

We have to find a place between these extremes in which we use a high enough level of communication so as to minimise the volume while ensuring that such abstraction does not make certain forms of learning impossible. A look at learning in human groups is instructive as to how multi-agent learning may occur. The general learning process in peer groups consists of individual agents using their own experiences to learn locally as a precursor to cooperation. At the cooperative stage, agents can put forward their learnt knowledge for consideration by other agents and at the same time evaluate other agents suggestions using their own local experiences. This is an iterative process where modifications to original hypotheses will result from the interaction and where the eventual goal is to arrive at a version that has the most support. However the problem with trying to adopt this approach in an automated system is that in human groups the sophistication of the agents involved and power of the language common to them allows this process to be arbitrarily complex. We will restrict ourselves to using a simplified model of this process.

2.5 Forms of Learning

As we mentioned earlier, work in machine learning has identified different strategies for learning. Given a cooperative scheme of the kind described in the previous section we can see how each of these strategies could be applied in a multi-agent scenario.

Inductive learning with multiple agents is ideally suited to the above form of cooperation. Learning in individual agents would involve local induction based on data available to each agent. The results from this would form the basis for the proposals and other agents could then use their results to modify these proposals so as to make them consistent with their data. The net result of this process would be to arrive at an inductive hypothesis that is consistent with all the data held by the agents in the system.

In deductive learning we have to start by constructing a proof of why an instance is an example of a concept using the domain knowledge available. In the presence of multiple agents where domain knowledge may be partitioned this may involve *distributed inference* ([Kitamura90] suggest one possible way of doing this). Agents would cooperate both in the formation of this proof and the subsequent step of generalising it into a more useful form.

A form of learning that would translate well from the single to the multi-agent scenario is analogical learning. The essential process of recognising similarity between two situations at some abstract level and then transforming previous solutions based on the reversal of the abstraction process works just as well intra-agent as it does inter-agent. However a general scheme for such a process in even the single agent case is not yet well understood. Much of the current work relies heavily on specific representation of the problems and domain specific attributes and knowledge.

2.6   Issues

We will restrict our attention to inductive learning in cooperative systems. Given that we wish to use a *consensus* model for such learning based on the type of peer group learning described above with agents proposing, evaluating and agreeing on proposals, we can examine briefly the issues that will be involved:

- *Communication* : To be able to cooperate, the agents will need a common communication language with agreed semantics to talk about proposals from the participating agents. This language has to allow the agents to express the range of possible responses to a given proposal. In addition there has to be an underlying protocol for the use of this language which structures the interaction between the agents.

- *Forming alternative views* : Each agent will have constructed a higher level generalised view of the experiences or other data available to it. In a multi-agent environment it is likely that different agents will form different views of the same information. So a difference in such higher level constructs may in fact simply be due to an alternative view of the same information rather than a genuine difference. Therefore, to be able to effectively evaluate other agents' proposals, each agent must be able to construct or possibly even retain alternative views for the same information.

- *Reaching consensus* : In cases when the participating agents are unable to agree on one form of a proposal, we have to try and select one of the possible candidates as the most reasonable one. The basis for this selection is to find that which has the most collective support. To do this each agent has to be able to give a measure of how confident it is in its opinion about any proposal. The function to get this measure must be consistent across agents to allow any sensible combination of these values. The selection of a proposal can then be based on a total confidence value resulting from an integration of the individual values.

- *Knowledge integration* : The nature of adaptation by learning is that knowledge is continuously changing. This means that each agent must face the problem of knowledge revision in the light of newly learnt knowledge. In addition, within consensus based activity they are always cases when complete unanimity is not achievable and therefore acceptance of views that are not consistent with the agents individual experiences may be necessary.

2.7 Summary

The ability to adapt by learning is a necessary attribute of persistent intelligent agents. In multi-agent systems cooperative learning is necessary in some cases and highly beneficial in most cases. Different forms of multi-agent systems will benefits in different ways. Such cooperation is possible at the various levels that these agents operate and a mechanism based on individual learning followed by interaction to arrive at a consensus provides one possible means for such cooperative learning.

3 A MODEL FOR COOPERATIVE LEARNING

The analysis above provides the basis for our model for cooperative learning. In this section we will give a brief overview of the model (references are given in the text to more detailed descriptions). In our model we have adopted a consensus based approach modelled on group learning with the following simplifications:

1) We have assumed 'truthful' agents in that agents opinions are a true reflection of their information.
2) We use a fixed communication language whose semantics are common across agents.
3) The value function V which the agents use to express confidence in their opinion is consistent across agents. Therefore, everything else being the same, the value that one agent will give to its opinion based on n supporting instances will be the same as any other agent.
4) We assume that a proposal that has the most support is more likely to be correct and all agents accept this proposal without further justification.

Our model consists of three primary components: **individual learning agents**, an **interaction board**, and an **interaction language & protocol** (see Figure 2).

- *Learning Agents* : Each agent in the system is an active learning agent and consists of a *non-monotonic knowledge base*, an *experience store* and a *learning component*. The learning component contains an incremental learning algorithm that uses the contents of the experience store to construct a generalisation hierarchy that contains multiple generalisations which cover recent experiences [Sian91a]. Accumulation of sufficient supporting instances (a configurable parameter) for a generalisation means that it can be nominated as a candidate for consideration by the other agents.

- *Interaction Board* : This is a multi-leveled structure based on a blackboard. However items on the board are not tasks but hypotheses and the interaction with this board is asynchronous with no explicit scheduling. Peer agents are connected to a single level with successively higher agents (e.g. managers) connected to higher levels.

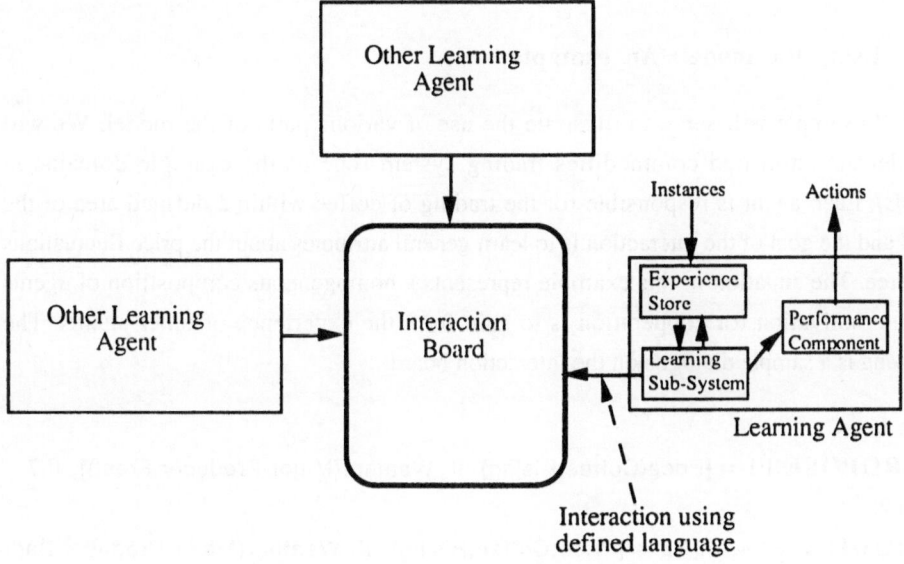

Figure 2: Components of the Model

- *Interaction Language* : We have defined the following set of operators connected with hypotheses that give the agents the ability to introduce, remove and modify hypotheses on the interaction board:

  - Introduction/Removal :
    PROPOSE(H,C), WITHDRAW(H)
  - Evaluation :
    CONFIRM(H,C), DISAGREE(H,C),
    NOOPINION(H), MODIFY(H,H',C,S)
  - Status modifiers :
    ACCEPT(H), AGREED(H,C)

where H is a hypothesis and C is the agent's level of confidence in the utterance.

The agents use these operators to introduce new hypotheses that are suggested by their learning algorithm. The other agents evaluate these proposals relative to their own experiences and use the evaluation operators to return a response. Each proposal and its associated responses have confidence values attached to indicate the agent's level of confidence which in turn reflects the amount of experience that gave rise to that response. The protocol includes an **COMB()** function [Sian91b] that determines the net support value of a hypothesis based on the responses received from the participating agents. The hypothesis with the highest support value is the one accepted by the agents.

3.1 Using the model: An example

A small example will serve to illustrate the use of various parts of the model. We will consider an automated commodities trading system (one of the example domains in MALE). Each agent is responsible for the trading of coffee within a defined area of the world and the goal of the interaction is to learn general attributes about the price fluctuations of coffee. The situation in this example represents a homogeneous composition of agents and the motivation for cooperation is to gain from the experience of other agents. The following is a sample dialogue on the interaction board:

Agent 1:

PROPOSE P1 = [Price(Coffee,Rising) if Weather(Major-Producer,Frost)], 0.7

Agent 2:

MODIFY P1 with P2 = [Price(Coffee,Rising) if Weather(Major-Producer,Bad-Weather)], 0.5,1

Agent 3:

MODIFY P1 & P2 with P3 = [Price(Coffee,Rising) if Weather(Major-Producer,Bad-Weather) & AdverselyAffects(Bad-Weather,Coffee)],0.8,0.9

Agent 1:

{*COMB(P1) = 0.85*}, **CONFIRM** P3 0.7

Agent 2:

{*COMB(P2) = 0.77*}, **CONFIRM** P3 0.5

Agent 3:

{*COMB(P3) = 0.985*}, **AGREED** P3 0.985

Agent 1:

WITHDRAW P1, **ACCEPT** P3

Agent 2:

WITHDRAW P2, **ACCEPT** P3

Agent 1 initiates the interaction with its proposal. The number at the end indicates the agent's confidence in its proposal. 'Pn' is the identifier for the proposals. The other agents respond after evaluating the proposal. Agent 2 modifies Agent 1's proposal by generalising the attribute 'Frost' to the more general 'Bad-Weather' since it has evidence for drought causing the same result. However Agent 3 has experience of some sorts of Bad-Weather (for example floods) having no effect on the price of coffee. The hypothesis P2 is therefore too general and Agent 3 uses its knowledge to find a relation that distinguishes between these weather types with regard to coffee and thus provide the required specialisation. This P3 is consistent with the experiences of both Agent 1 and 2 and they are able to CONFIRM. P3 therefore receives the highest COMB() value (0.985) and as a result is accepted while the other proposals are WITHDRAWN.

For the sake of brevity we have excluded details in this example of the source data available to the agents from which these responses arise. However, the example illustrates how the interaction language in combination with local learning can be used to get consensus based cooperative learning. The advantages to the group are obvious. Agent 1 has gained a more generalised hypothesis than could be justified from its own data. Agent 2 has had its hypothesis specialised because Agent 3 had some refuting evidence that Agent 2 had not experienced. Agent 3 has increased its confidence in its hypothesis since the others have instances that are covered by it. In this case, the net result is the same as if one agent had had all the data. Such amalgamation of experience was precisely the goal.

3.2   An implementation : MALE

MALE (Multi-Agent Learning Environment) is an implementation of the above model in PROLOG. We have used this in a commodities trading domain with a number of agents engaged in trying to construct general causal relations for price fluctuations of these commodities. In particular we have conducted experiments which compare multi-agent learning using this model with first a non-learning version of the same system and secondly the same system but with the agents only learning locally with no cooperation. The results from these experiments show that a multi-agent system with any form of learning, individual or cooperative, performs better than one without. In addition, for a given number of instances, the predictive power of the agents is much greater in the multi-agent cooperative learning case than in the individual learning case. The penalty to pay for this is that is such a system is slower than the other two as it has the overhead of cooperation. In addition the gains become less pronounced if the spread of source data is biased towards one or two agents [Sian91a]. We are now evaluating the model using the soya bean data from AQ15 [Riene87].

4.   CONCLUSION

Given the need for adaptation in all intelligent systems, our main aim in this paper has been to analyse the role of cooperation when learning. We have shown that in heterogeneous

176

multi-agent systems effective adaptation in not possible without cooperation. Additionally, in homogeneous systems where agents share experiences about the same problem, a cooperative learning framework gives the agents access to the processed results of others experiences.

Using simple aspects of human cooperative learning as the basis we have briefly described a model for such learning in multi-agent systems. An implementation of the model has allowed us to evaluate its merits in sample domains and demonstrate the effectiveness of cooperative learning as compared to no learning or individual learning.

REFERENCES

[Bond88] - A. Bond, *Chapters 1-5*, in Readings in Distributed AI, A. Bond & L. Gasser (Eds.), p67-99, Morgan Kaufmann, San Mateo, 1988.

[Cammarata83] - S. Cammarata, D. McArthur & R. Steeb, *Strategies of Cooperation in Distributed Problem Solving*, in Proceedings of IJCAI-83, p767-770, University of Amerhurst, August 1983.

[Carbonell 83] - J. Carbonell, *Learning by Analogy*, in R. Michalski, J. Carbonell & T. Mitchell (Eds.), Machine Learning: An AI Approach, Morgan Kaufmann, San Mateo, 1983.

[Gasser89] - L. Gasser & M. Huhns, *Chapter 1*, in Distributed AI Vol 2, L. Gasser & M. Huhns (Eds.), p5-20, Pitman, London, 1989.

[Huhns87] - M. Huhns, *Introduction*, in Distributed AI, M. Huhns Ed.), p5-12, Pitman, London, 1987.

[Kitamura90] - Y. Kitamura & T. Okumoto, *Diffusing Inference: An Inference Method for Distributed Problem Solving and its Property*, in this volume.

[Kodratoff88] - Y. Kodratoff, *Introduction to Machine Learning*, Pitman, London, 1988.

[Michalski83] - R. Michalski, *Overview of Machine Learning*, in R. Michalski, J. Carbonell & T. Mitchell (Eds.), Machine Learning: An AI Approach, p3-25, Morgan Kaufmann, San Mateo, 1983.

[Mitchell86] - T. Mitchell, R. Keller & S. Kedar-Cabelli, *Explanation-Based Generalisation: An Unifying View*, Machine Learning, Vol 1(2), April 1986.

[Parunaik87] - H. Parunaik, *Manufacturing Experience with the Contract Net*, in Distributed AI, M. Huhns (Ed.), p285-310, Pitman, London 1987.

[Riene87] - R. Riene & R. Michalski, *Incremental Learning of Concept Descriptions*, in Machine Intelligence Vol 11, J. Hayes, D. Michie & J. Richards (Eds.), p263-288, Morgan Kaufmann, San Mateo, 1987.

[Rosenschein86] - J. Rosenschein, M. Ginsberg & M. Genesreth, *Cooperation without Communication*, in Proceedings of AAAI-86, p51-57, May 1986.

[Shaw89] - M. Shaw & A. Whinston, *Learning and Adaptation in Distributed AI*, in Distributed AI Vol 2, L. Gasser & M. Huhns (Eds.), p413-429, Pitman, London, 1989.

[Sian90] - S. Sian, *Adaptation Based on Cooperative Learning in Multi-Agent Systems*, in Proceedings of MAAMAW '90, St. Quentin-en-Yvelines, France, August 1990. Also in Decentralized AI Vol 2, Y. Demazeau & J-P. Muller (Eds.), Elsevier Science Pub. B.V, 1991.

[Sian91a] - S. Sian, *Extending Learning to Multiple Agents: Issues and a Model for Multi-Agent Machine Learning*, in Proceedings of Fifth ESWL 1991, Y. Kodratoff (Ed.), Lecture Notes in AI Series, Springer-Verlag Pub., 1991.

[Sian91b] - S. Sian, *Learning in Distributed AI Systems*, PhD. Thesis, Department of Computing, Imperial College, University of London (forthcoming).

[Valiant84] - L. Valiant, *A Theory of the Learnable*, Communications of the ACM, Vol 27(11), November 1984.

DISCUSSION

Presenter: S. Sian.

Q. (R. Zanconato, Cambridge Consultants Ltd.) : Do you feel it's safe to retract a more specific rule to replace it with basically a more general rule? Or do you think it's possible to have a role for a more specific rule, particularly if the belief of the more specific rule is higher and the inferences that you can make are better by using the more specific than of the more general rule?

A. (S. Sian) : It is well known that any generalised rule produced by induction is potentially false. However one has to balance this against the fact that the generalised rule can deal with a lot more cases than the more specific version. The agents will therefore always try and use the maximally specific generalisation [Michalski 83] that correctly covers the instances available to them. Note however that if a more specific rule has greater support/belief value then it is accepted in preference to a less supported general rule. Generalised rules only increase the number of inferences that you can make from them rather then reduce them.

Q. (R. Zanconato, Cambridge Consultants Ltd.) : The other question was, have you thought about incorporating something like a truth maintenance system into your system, so when the rules are retracted then the associations made by those rules previously are also retracted?

A. (S. Sian) : Yes. The last thing that an agent does with a rule once it has been accepted, is to integrate it into its own knowledge base. This is where the belief revision part comes in. We have tried to use an approach based on belief times but that isn't the main emphasis of the work here.

Q. (P. Bobbie, University of West Florida) : I have a question about your confidence level. You say they are not probabilistic, or they are not associated with any distribution function?

A. (S. Sian) : The COMB() function is very much empirically motivated; our primary justification is that it tends to work in the environment we are using. But the function lacks a firm theoretical foundation. The problem as I have indicated is due to the fact that the values that the agents give to a proposal are not probabilities. This is easily shown by noting that when an agent gives a confidence value x to a hypothesis H one cannot conclude, as would be required by probability theory, that it would give the value 1-x to NOT H. The values are more a level of belief that the agent has based on the instances that it has encountered. Similar problems have been encountered in work such as MYCIN. We are not aware of any theoretical work that deals adequately with these values, so I think it's actually an open problem at the moment, how to combine what essentially are levels of belief rather than distinct probabilities of something occurring.

Promising areas for working include Shafer-Dempster Theory and fuzzy sets, but even these actually assume that you have complete sets, which in this case means complete sets of possible hypotheses, which in a practical domain like this it's not possible to construct.

Q. (T. Kane, Stirling University): I sympathise very much with what you're trying to do, and I think it's very important to do this in distributed AI, but I'd like you to try to think what you mean by belief. If you're going to combine something, and you don't know what it is, with a mechanism, and you don't know how it works, then you're going to produce a system that's not going to have much use really. First of all, if you don't know what your belief is then where did the number come from? Second, if you don't have a clear semantics for your COMB() function, what were you doing with this thing you don't know anything about in the first place? Things like Mycin and fuzzy logic are actually quite poor. I would suggest you look at probability theories because there's a lot you can do with Bayesian networks.

A. (S. Sian): As I said, I think we are fortunate in this particular domain in that those values actually have meaning because they are based on a number of instances on which that hypothesis is formed. But then, it still is a problem using probabilities, because these things aren't probabilities and it's difficult to assign probabilities to these things.

Q. (T. Kane, Stirling University): That's what I mean. I think that's an idea for you to research because they haven't really done it very well in expert systems. I think if you had meaning for your number which isn't heuristic, if you have some meaning for your evaluation function which is non- heuristic, then you can say you have something new.

[Author's Later Note: We have more recent work described in [Sian91b] in which we have axiomatically defined the combination function and formally derived the function from this definition.]

Q. (M. Shaw, University of Illinois): Any machine learning program basically has two steps that are essential. One is transformation to a new description. My interpretation of this in your work is that the transformation in your system is done by knowledge sharing between the multiple agents. Then you try to evaluate the knowledge of each agent and identify the better one and then the better one would be used by the group of agents. Is that the only transformation in your system in the context of learning?

A. (S. Sian): Each agent does its own learning during which it employs the full range of transformations that are available in the machine learning wherever it does generalisation or specialisation. So it will do as much single agent learning that it can do. And then on the board itself, once you have the co-operation, there you still have the process applied which does specialisation or generalisation, so there's induction going on the board itself, but based on instances that the agents have themselves.

Q. (M. Shaw, University of Illinois): So in your example of the three agents, the three production rules you show are actually result of their own individual learning?

A. (S. Sian): Absolutely. Those are the results of their local learning and they're trying to solicit help from the other agents for better learning.

Q. (M. Shaw, University of Illinois): So, perhaps they have a different set of training examples. Because of that they have different learning?

A. (S. Sian) : Exactly. They're in their own part of the world. One might be dealing with coffee trading in South America, one might be doing it in Africa, for example. They're part of a company that does multi- trading all over the world. Each of them is receiving their own instances, but they're all dealing with coffee trading so there must be some similarities. So there's a possibility for learning.

Q. (M. Shaw, University of Illinois) : If that is the case, you may want to take advantage of individual learning results. Otherwise they redundantly solve the same problem based on their own observations and then you identify it as solution. Would that be a possibility?

A. (S. Sian) : Yes, but the confidence in a 'solution' that is confirmed by the other agents is obviously greater.

Q. (T. Brown, Brunel University) : I'm going to engage in a bit of cooperative communication and propose a hypothesis that in fact there's a fourth piece of further work that you could engage in,that is to look at the role of intentionality. The reason I bring this up is because some time in the past I did a management training course which was given by psychologists who looked at interaction of people in committee meetings. Some of the operators that you mention in your language are very close to some of the terminology that's used in the interaction process analysis which is what they determine. For example, the whole role of the course was to tell you how to take over a committee meeting and they gave various techniques for doing it, I don't intend to use them here, but one of the ones was, if somebody has made a proposal, you build on it, modify it in your terms, modify that proposal; that gives the original proposer a nice warm feeling. So, in fact, you can use that not to alienate somebody but to get what you want by building on their proposal. So it suggests to me that there are certain rules about interaction process analysis, about behaviour of human agents, and then there might be some similar sort of rules in agents about their intentionality that's worth researching.

A. (S. Sian) : We haven't really looked at the whole area of intentionality. We assume benevolence on the part of the participating agents. We only get together and learn from each other rather than actually try and have a notion that one agent wants to get across what it believes really must be the truth. In our case the agents are very willing to accept the proposals of other agents if they have a higher confidence factor.

Conflict Resolution Strategies

Conflict Resolution Strategies for Cooperating Expert Agents

Susan Lander, Victor R. Lesser and Margaret E. Connell

Department of Computer and Information Science
University of Massachusetts
Amherst, MA 01003

Abstract

Problem-solving approaches which incorporate specialized cooperating expert agents seem intuitively appropriate for many complex problems. However, integrating diverse expertise requires that the experts have some mechanism for dealing with conflicts that occur during problem-solving. We describe the Cooperating Experts Framework (CEF), a framework developed to support cooperative problem-solving among sets of knowledge-based systems with limited information about each other's local states. The systems solve subproblems relevant to their specific expertise and integrate their efforts using conflict resolution strategies that are appropriate to the problem solving context. In choosing a strategy CEF makes tradeoffs between the potential quality of a solution, the amount of processing required to apply a strategy, and the effect of local changes on the global solution. We also describe TEAM, a system implemented in the CEF framework, that designs steam condensers.

1 Agents Interacting as Cooperating Experts

Many complex problem-solving tasks are intuitively amenable to the cooperating expert approach in which multiple specialized agents work together to generate solutions. Examples of the integration of expertise through cooperation are seen in human problem-solving tasks such as design, research, business management, and human relations. The realization of this approach as a computational model, however, requires a framework within which agents can share information and resolve conflicts that arise during problem solving. In this paper we describe the Cooperating Experts Framework (CEF) that supports cooperative problem-solving among sets of knowledge-based systems, and TEAM, a system for steam condenser design that is built in CEF.

Examples of the integration of expertise through cooperation are seen in human problem-solving tasks such as design, research, business management, and human

This research was supported by DARPA under Contract # N00014-89-J-1877 and by a University Research Initiative Grant, Contract # N00014-86-K-0764.

relations. To motivate the Cooperating Experts approach, consider a team of human experts working in an office who are given the task of choosing a telephone company. The team consists of a manager and an accountant. They have the shared goal of selecting an appropriate system for their office, but each individual would like to insure that her own priorities receive top consideration. Unfortunately, many of the individuals' local goals and priorities are conflicting from a global viewpoint. For example, the accountant would like to try Cost-Company, a company with excellent long-distance rates, to save money. The manager is concerned about the quality of service and would rather choose Qual-Company, a company with a known high level of quality. How can the agents come to a decision when there are no global criteria for evaluation?

In this situation, it is very difficult to judge which solution is the "correct" solution since it depends on the criteria used to decide. In truth, there is no right or wrong answer: the company may need the level of service provided by Qual-Company, but it may also need to save on costs through Cost-Company. The agents must reconcile their differences and reach a decision, taking into account both viewpoints. Since solution correctness is an elusive concept, the experts strive for balance. A solution which is acceptable to all experts, though possibly not ideal for any one, is the best that can be hoped for.

One of the motivating factors in the Cooperating Experts approach is the need to find a solution when there is no strong global model of correctness or optimality. This occurs when global evaluation criteria are absent, when global evaluation criteria are too expensive to compute, or when a global evaluation is some combination of a set of locally computed evaluations [11]. The latter case occurs when the problem is decomposed in such a way that each agent has enough expertise to evaluate some part of the solution, but not all of it. To compute a comprehensive evaluation, a "super agent" would be required, yet it is not always desirable or even possible to build systems with this all-encompassing outlook.

Continuing the example above, let us say that it is company policy to always choose the least expensive alternative when faced with an ambiguous choice. The company therefore does impose a global evaluation function which can be used to guide the decision. However, the manager has worked out a scenario in which Qual-Company is actually less expensive than Cost-Company because salesmen have fewer delays in placing calls, there are fewer communication errors when transmitting data, and, in general, the phone service is faster and more reliable. This theory could be tested by setting up experiments comparing phone service and productivity over some time period. However, the type of savings being talked about is not enough to justify the cost of evaluation: a global evaluation exists but it is too costly to compute.

Again, the agents must come to terms without any absolute notion of truth: it simply is not clear which is the "right" solution. There are several ways of reaching agreement on a solution however; for example, they can look for other alternatives (is there a MidQualMidCost-Company somewhere?), they can try to convince each other, or they can look at solutions to similar conflicts that occured in the past. In the end some solution must be agreed upon whether or not that solution is guaranteed to be optimal with respect to the company's policy.

Conflict inevitably occurs when multiple intelligent agents must cooperate. It can occur due to incorrect or incomplete local knowledge, different goals, priorities and solution evaluation criteria, and resource contention. It should be viewed as a positive part of the problem-solving process. The resolution of conflict involves information exchange among participants and this communication provides improved robustness, breadth, and balance in the integrated solution.

There are various methods that have been used in the past to manage conflict. A common practice in building systems with diverse heuristic knowledge is to avoid potential conflict situations through analysis and consistency checking of knowledge at development time. This is difficult and costly in any case, but as the amount and diversity of information increases, this approach becomes decreasingly viable.

Traditional blackboard systems provide an early model of multiple specialists working together [3]. Cooperation among the specialists occurs implicitly through the incremental extension of globally available hypotheses. Conflicts are not resolved explicitly—instead competing hypotheses coexist and vie for processing resources to improve their believability.

Human negotiation and creative problem-solving models [10, 4, 2] offer insight into possible strategies for conflict resolution and for the use of conflict as a platform for creativity. However they can't be directly applied to computational models because they contend with human motivational factors that aren't present in machine agents and that greatly influence the process.

Sycara [13] presents a negotiation model which applies case-based and utility reasoning methods to conflicts. Klein [5] has developed a hierarchy of conflict types and resolution strategies in which conflicts are categorized and mapped to specific resolutions by a global controller. In these systems, conflict resolution is not sensitive to the problem-solving context. In CEF, conflict resolution techniques are chosen based on characteristics of the problem-solving state such as the flexibility of a particular agent, and the amount of effort that has been expended on a particular solution to date.

In this paper, we give an overview of the Cooperating Experts Framework and an application program, TEAM, developed within the framework. Section 2 describes the problem domain of TEAM, Section 3 discusses conflict resolution strategies and heuristics, and Section 4 gives a summary of the project.

1.1 The Cooperating Experts Framework

CEF agents are complete knowledge-based systems with their own internal agendas, knowledge bases, solution generation procedures, evaluation criteria, constraints, and goals. Within the agents, evaluation criteria, constraints, and goals must be explicitly represented since they are communicated to other systems as part of the conflict resolution process. Agents keep local histories of their actions and decisions to enable the revision of solutions in response to conflict situations. Local processing results are not accessible to other agents unless they are explicitly shared. If an agent's internal language is not the shared language, translation procedures must be provided for shared information. Because the agents are self-contained and heterogeneous systems, it is not possible to have strong predictive models of other experts' behavior. However, information about non-local constraints and goals is collected during problem-solving.

We envision a "warehouse" of expert agents where each agent represents a body of knowledge without regard to the particular problem at hand. Given a specific task,

186

a customized agent set can be created. Different sets of agents can handle different problems or fit different levels of resource availability. Agents can be varied according to expertise, desired inferencing techniques, or based on the amount of computational overhead that can be supported. The integration of independent agents in this manner is a powerful and viable problem-solving paradigm. However, the interactions among agents become very sophisticated and require a great deal of domain-independent control and cooperation expertise.

Along with the agent set, CEF contains centralized structures and procedures that facilitate communication. These structures are implemented on top of a generic blackboard framework, GBB [1]. The domain-independent framework control shell integrates agent execution with execution of framework knowledge sources (FKSs) for performing high-level tasks on the GLBB objects. The general architecture is shown in Figure 1. Any information placed on the global blackboards (GLBB) must

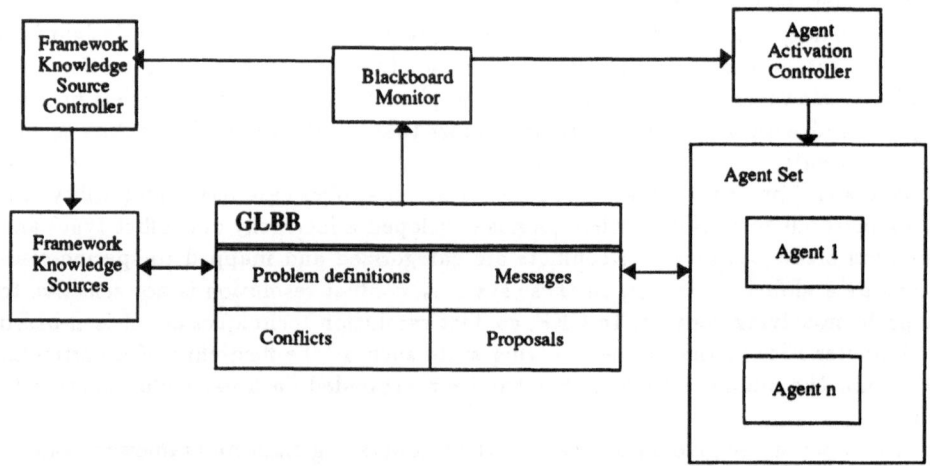

Figure 1: The CEF Architecture

be represented in a common language shared by all agents. The language is defined using the object definition capabilities of GBB. There are both domain-independent and application-specific objects and blackboard structures. The domain-independent structures are supplied by the framework; examples are conflict and message objects and message and proposal blackboards. Application knowledge is contained in the domain-specific objects and blackboard spaces: in the steam condenser design domain described below, examples include pump, heat exchanger, and motor objects and blackboard spaces. The global blackboards for the steam condenser domain are shown in Figure 2. Although CEF is implemented on top of a blackboard framework, the sophistication of the agents and the agents' explicit conflict resolution expertise results in very different flavor of cooperation and control and allows solutions to be found despite inherent inconsistency among the agents.

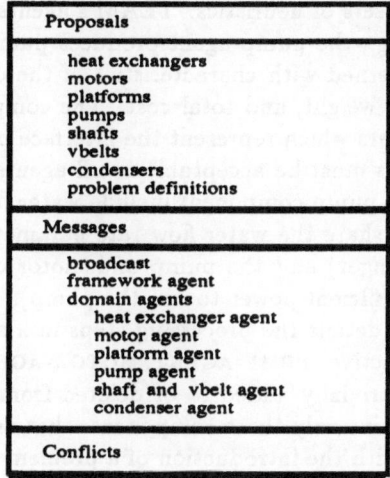

Figure 2: Global Blackboards (GLBB) in TEAM

2 The Problem Domain

CEF is being used as the basis for a system that does parametric design of steam condensers, TEAM. In parametric design, the general form of the artifact being designed is known, but the designer must find values for variable parameters of the artifact. The domain knowledge used by TEAM was initially designed and implemented by Meunier [9] for another system that used an iterative redesign algorithm. Much of the domain-level code from that system is intact in TEAM, although we have a different problem-solving methodology.

Figure 3 shows the general form of a steam condenser, comprising a pump, heat

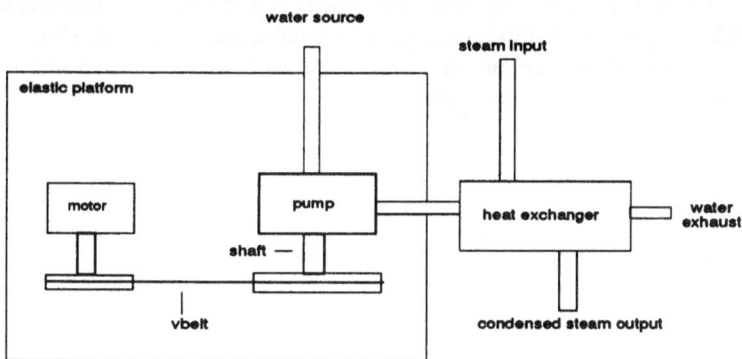

Figure 3: A Steam Condenser

exchanger, motor, platform, shaft and v-belt. CEF agents produce *proposals* which represent solutions to subproblems. In TEAM, a proposal is either a component for a condenser or a complete condenser. Each component is designed by an agent with expert knowledge and problem-solving methods that can include anything from numerical optimization to sets of heuristics. TEAM's agents correspond to the components of a condenser, e.g., the pump agent produces pump components. There is also an agent that is concerned with characteristics of the complete condenser such as natural frequency, total weight, and total cost. The components are independent except for shared parameters which represent the interface points of the design. The values for these parameters must be acceptable to all agents that use them. For example, the parameters of a pump component include water flow rate and power. The pump and heat exchanger share the water flow rate parameter (water flows between the pump and heat exchanger) and the pump and motor components share power (the motor must deliver sufficient power to run the pump).

The following example details the processing steps in a sample TEAM execution in which three agents are active: PUMP-AGENT, MOTOR-AGENT, and HEATX-AGENT. Agents in TEAM can be trivially added to or deleted from the active set although the completed design contains only those components that are represented by agents. TEAM processing starts with the introduction of a problem definition to the system. The problem definition defines a set of constraints that must be fulfilled in the completed design. These user-defined constraints are non-negotiable, although the agents can report back to the user if the constraints are causing poor designs. A typical problem definition is shown below:

```
Problem_definition_1
    Platform-side-length 120
    Maximum-platform-deflection .01
    Required-capacity 100
```

The constraints imposed by this problem definition will be incorporated by all agents as inflexible local constraints: $platform\_side\_length = 120$, $maximum\_platform\_deflection = .01$, and $required\_capacity = 100$. The problem definition is placed on TEAM's global blackboard (GLBB) which is accessible by all expert agents and by the set of framework knowledge sources that do high level operations on GLBB objects.

The new problem definition stimulates the creation of an initial condenser proposal with unspecified components by the condenser agent. A simplified version of the proposal is shown below; many of the attributes are not shown because they aren't relevant to the current problem.

```
Condenser_1:
    active_agents                   (condenser-agent)
    platform_side_length            120
    maximum_platform_deflection     .01
    required_capacity               100
    water_flow_rate                 nil
    required_power                  nil
    head                            nil
    total_cost                      nil
    total_weight                    nil
    natural_frequency               nil
    pump                            nil
    motor                           nil
    heat_exchanger                  nil
```

This proposal is posted to GLBB, in turn triggering the execution of agents that can supply component proposals. Any agents that have work to do (whether pending or in reaction to new objects on GLBB), will execute during each processing cycle. In this case, the pump, heat exchanger, and motor agents will begin local processing based on the new problem definition.

All agents in a CEF set must be able to create new proposals, either using default assumptions about shared parameter values and constraints or using actual values supplied by other agents. In response to the problem definition, each triggered agent performs a *create-proposal* task incorporating the values supplied by the problem definition and using default assumptions for all other attributes. The capability of using default assumptions for non-specified attributes allows the agents to execute immediately rather than waiting for those values to be supplied externally. The agents can therefore avoid the problems associated with sequential execution—basically, the problem of doing a depth-first search when each agent only has access to its own search space. In a sequential model, constraints on the search process may not be introduced until after a significant amount of work has been done by previously executing agents to ensure acceptability of their own work.

In this example, attribute values for most of the components are virtually unconstrained on this point in processing. The agents take advantage of this opportunity to propose their "best" solutions; that is, solutions that best fulfill their local evaluation criteria. Unfortunately, the agents are often at odds. For example, PUMP-AGENT generates pump proposals by matching constraints on parameter values to pump models in a catalog, and choosing the cheapest and lightest pump model that satisfies those constraints. In general, the cheapest and lightest pumps have low values for water flow rate and delivered head. HEATX-AGENT, on the other hand, uses a more customized design process and tends to favor high values for head (water flow rate is relatively unconstrained).

Continuing with our example, the agents' newly-generated component proposals are placed on GLBB. The pump proposed by PUMP-AGENT is shown below. Again, we have simplified the proposal to include only relevant attributes:

```
Pump_1:
    parameter_names          (water_flow_rate, head,
                                required_power)
    model                    model4_imp1
    required_capacity        100
    water_flow_rate          40
    head                     12.38
    required_power           7.06
    cost                     103.63
    weight                   33.23
    local_evaluations        (pump_agent excellent)
```

Each of the other agents similarly produces an independent component proposal that best fulfills its local constraints. These initial proposals usually have high ratings from the initiating agent since they are relatively unconstrained. Agents evaluate their own proposals and any external proposals that have shared parameters. TEAM agents use five ratings, ranging from *infeasible* to *excellent*. Local evaluation criteria measure the feasibility of a particular value or set of values given the evaluating agent's constraints and local knowledge. For example, if HEATX-AGENT proposes a heat exchanger with a water flow rate of 500 gallons per minute and the pump agent knows that the highest water flow rate it can deliver with any pump is 415 gpm, an inflexible constraint of the pump agent is violated by the heat exchanger proposal under evaluation. An agent may also have *preferences* that are violated by a proposed value. For example, the pump agent might have a pump model that can deliver 500 gpm, but that model is expensive and not within the preferred set of less expensive models.

During the evaluation process, a local history of the interaction is built that includes the proposal evaluated, the agents involved, constraints and preferences that have been violated, and the ratings on potential local solutions. This history will be expanded to track the development of particular paths through local search as processing continues.

Continuing with our example, after the proposed components are placed on GLBB, framework knowledge sources link the proposed components to their triggering condenser proposal as shown below.

```
Condenser_1:
    active_agents                    (condenser-agent, pump-agent,
                                      heatx-agent, motor-agent)
    platform_side_length             120
    maximum_platform_deflection      .01
    required_capacity                100
    water_flow_rate                  ((pump-agent 40)(heatx-agent 400))
    required_power                   ((pump-agent 4)(motor-agent 1))
    head                             ((pump-agent 12.38)(heatx-agent 810))
    total_cost                       nil
    total_weight                     nil
    natural_frequency                nil
    pump                             pump_1
    motor                            motor_1
    heat_exchanger                   heat_exchanger_1
```

Their compatibility is checked by doing a syntactic analysis of the parameter names and values. When conflicts are found, an FKS does a cursory analysis of the conflict at the global level. This analysis includes the agents and parameters involved in the conflict and the depth of the solution path. This information is stored in a conflict representation object that is placed on GLBB. Each of the involved agents is notified of the conflict situation and uses the conflict analysis, other globally available information such as the proposal units, and local information about its own problem-solving resources and constraints to decide what action to take.

3   Conflict Resolution

We have specified a set of strategies which can be used to resolve conflicts. The choice of strategy, given a particular conflict situation, is itself a knowledge-based problem. Information which can be applied to this choice includes available problem-solving resources, the amount of effort that has already been expended in producing a solution, the solution's rating, an estimate of the amount of processing required to generate a new solution or to repair the current one, the dependency structure of related proposals, the importance of a particular component to the global solution, the number and type of conflicting parameters, the severity of the conflict, and the flexibility of agents involved in the conflict. Some strategies are more computationally expensive than others, some are inexpensive but less likely to produce promising proposals. Some can be used to "fix" existing solutions that seem promising, others can be used to jump into a significantly different part of the search space.

3.1   Identifying an Appropriate Strategy for a Conflict

We identify some problem characteristics which are useful in determining a conflict resolution strategy. A description of the strategies is deferred to the following section.

- Other equally good proposals exist or can be generated inexpensively. Not much effort has been expended in developing the current proposal. Try *Generate Random Alternatives*. This approach doesn't require any analysis of the problem. For example, scheduling a meeting: "Can't make it Monday morning? How about Tuesday afternoon."

- The proposal under consideration is close to being acceptable to all the agents involved. There are a small number of dimensions in conflict and the dimension type is numeric or there is a known ordering on potential values. None of the agents are tightly constrained on the variables in question. The problematic constraints are not highly dependent. Try *Compromise*.

- Same conditions as for *Compromise*, except that one or more of the agents is too inflexible, has a strong belief in the problematic values, or has some constraints which must be addressed. Try *Generate Constrained Alternatives*, exchanging constraints in order to bring the viewpoints closer together.

- There are a large number of conflicting parameters or there are no existing proposals which are close to being acceptable to all agents (the conflict is severe) or the constraints in conflict have many dependencies. Try *Generate Goal Alternatives*.

- There are multiple conflicting parameters and the dependencies among them are not well-understood. Improving one parameter value may cause the proposal as a whole to have a lower rating. Try *Case-Based Parameter Set Retrieval* to find a set of changes that can be applied to improve the complete proposal.

- None of the other methods have resulted in acceptable solutions or it is believed that the problem is overconstrained. Try *Revise and Merge Goals*. This is the most computationally expensive strategy.

3.2 Conflict Resolution Strategies

In this section, we describe some of the strategies that can be used to resolve conflicts that occur.

- *Generate Random Alternatives*: In some types of problem-solving, multiple solutions exist and can be generated with little extra computational overhead. For example, in a typical blackboard system, multiple solutions exist at any given time. A highly rated one is chosen as "the answer" but there may be others that are rated equally or just slightly lower.

- *Compromise*: Find an intermediate proposal that is within the acceptable range of all agents using variable value relaxations. This strategy is the typical compromise that is used in buy/sell or other numeric transactions. Numerical optimizations or techniques based on the type of dimension can result in quick and fair results.

- *Generate Constrained Alternatives*: Generate new alternatives based on constraints that are received from an inflexible agent or based on some other agent's partial solution.

- *Generate Goal Alternatives*: The original proposals are abandoned. Alternate proposals are generated by looking for alternate goal expansions. If necessary, some goals can be relaxed or relinquished. This can lead to substantially different proposals being generated at the level in which the conflict occurred. This strategy is useful for changing the focus of the system from a plateau to a new area of the search space.

- *Case-Based Parameter Set Retrieval*: Find a previous solution that succeeded in resolving a conflict involving a similar set of parameters. Make the set of changes rather than isolated modifications. This approach minimizes oscillation that occurs in the overall proposal rating when dependencies among parameter values are not well-understood.

- *Revise and Merge Goals*: Prioritize goals and relinquish unimportant subgoals. Build a new mutually-defined goal structure that incorporates the most important goals of all agents involved in the conflict. Generate a solution guided by the new structure. This approach is computationally expensive and will only be used in situations where no other technique seems promising, the system cannot produce a feasible design, or where an innovative proposal is explicitly requested by the user. It is hoped that the mutual goal structure will cause a jump into a new area of the search space which would not be explored during the normal course of problem-solving.

Conflict resolution protocols are realized as formal dialogues with specific actions that can be taken at each processing step [12, 6]. All agents know the protocols and can formulate the messages required for their role in a particular conflict situation. For example, an agent that is beginning a new *Respond to Conflict Task* first analyzes the conflict from its own point of view and suggests a particular resolution method and possibly a set of resolution values. It sends this message to all other agents involved in the conflict. It then waits for confirmation from those agents. The other agents must respond to the message, either that they accept the resolution method, they accept the suggested resolution, or that they are proposing a different solution or method. The method is sometimes changed because another agent has a local view which makes the suggested method inappropriate. For example, the originating agent may suggest using *compromise* but the receiving agent is too inflexible. The receiving agent might then suggest *generate constrained alternatives* and send its inflexible constraints to the originating agent. Sometimes the method is acceptable, but a different solution is suggested. The originating agent cannot consider the conflict resolved until all participating agents have confirmed that a suggested solution is acceptable to them.

The conflict resolution strategies fall into two major classes: those that are used to redirect the local search of an individual agent and those that are used to mutually negotiate new values. In the examples below, we illustrate the use of two of the strategies, *generate constrained alternatives* and *compromise*, as representative of the two classes. Constrained alternative proposal generation is the creation of an alternative proposal by an individual agent, incorporating information gathered from other agents such as values for shared attributes. Compromise, on the other hand, requires the coordinated effort of multiple agents [5, 8, 7, 10, 14] to define the set of mutual constraints and preferences on conflicting attributes and, using that set, determine a fair value for the attributes. The agents may have to relax preferences to find a solution. This differs slightly from the common use of compromise as it describes human interactions. There, the conflict participants are more selfishly motivated and an agent never divulges her "bottom line" constraints. CEF agents are primarily interested in getting the best global solution possible rather than the best local solution. They are therefore willing to share their constraints and preferences. Once the bottom line information is known, a solution can often be computed directly without iteration.

The combination of these methodologies is a requirement for effective multi-agent, cooperative problem-solving. However, it is often very difficult to decide which is appropriate in a given situation. *Generate constrained alternatives* is a directed local search method that can result in high-quality, non-conflicting solutions. When the problem is overconstrained though, individual local search can't lead to a satisfactory solution because none exists. *Compromise* is a multiple-agent search method that includes constraint or goal relaxation methods to directly resolve overconstrained situations. In this section, we show examples of the two methods and discuss the control issues involved in using them.

When is it appropriate to generate alternative random or constrained proposals? It is usually appropriate in early stages of problem-solving when it is useful to explore multiple potential solution paths. It is also useful when problem-solving has stalled, and new ideas are needed. However when there are inconsistencies or conflicting knowledge among agents, indiscriminate proposal generation will lead to massive and unproductive shallow explorations of different areas of the search space.

When is compromise appropriate then? When effort has been expended in gathering and evaluating potential solution paths, it becomes necessary at some point to commit to a particular path, even though there may be obvious conflicts that will need to be addressed. Compromise is the tool for reconciling the inconsistencies among agents and exploring a particular path in depth.

We illustrate the two strategies discussed above in the context of a two-agent TEAM execution, using the same problem definition and initial proposals generated by PUMP-AGENT and HEATX-AGENT as those in Section 2. Relevant information from the component proposals of PUMP-AGENT and HEATX-AGENT are shown below:

```
Pump_1                          Heat_exchanger_1
   Water-flow-rate 40              Water-flow-rate 400
   Head 12.38                      Head 810
   Local evaluations:              Local evaluations:
      (pump-agent excellent)          (heatx-agent excellent)
```

PUMP-AGENT and HEATX-AGENT share the parameters *water-flow-rate* (in gallons per minute) and *head* (in feet). These agents are peers in the sense that there isn't any inherent ordering on the priority of the components they represent. Therefore conflicts must be resolved through mutual agreement rather than through priority protocols. Given these initial proposals, there are two possible actions for each agent at this time. One action is to further explore both of the suggested solutions through the *generate constrained alternatives* strategy, e.g., the PUMP-AGENT could use the heat exchanger proposal as an anchor point for generating a new pump proposal and vice versa. The values of shared parameters in the existing proposal serve to constrain the generation of the new proposal. The relevant attribute values of the constrained alternative proposals are shown below, along with the agents' evaluations of these proposals.

```
    Condenser_2                        Condenser_3
       Water-flow-rate 400                Water-flow-rate 40
       Head 810                           Head 12.38
       Local evaluations:                 Local evaluations:
          (pump-agent infeasible)            (pump-agent excellent)
          (heatx-agent excellent)            (heatx-agent good)
```

PUMP-AGENT finds Condenser_2 infeasible because it has no pump model in its catalog of potential models that can support both a water flow rate of 400 and a head of 810. However, Condenser_3 is deemed reasonable by HEATX-AGENT and PUMP-AGENT (which initiated the proposal) rates it as excellent. These ratings are sufficient to consider the proposal acceptable. Acceptability is determined by calculating the average of local evaluations and applying thresholds to both the average evaluation and the minimum evaluation.

In contrast to the constrained proposal generation shown above, a second possible action would be to try to merge the proposals directly through compromise. All agents know the negotiation protocols and can formulate the messages required for their role in a particular conflict situation. An agent starts the negotiation dialogue by sending a message to other participating agents that it would like to compromise a specified set of proposals. It includes a possible set of compromise values and any explicit constraints or preferences it has on the conflicting parameters. Other agents check the suggested values and either accept them or respond with a new set of suggested values and any additional constraints. Currently, our algorithm for determining suggested values is to calculate average values and adjust them according to relevant constraints if necessary. This process may require multiple iterations if all the relevant calculations can't be explicitly represented by shareable constraints.

In this example, after several iterations that involve adjusting the *head* value from an initial compromise suggestion of 411 due to a dependency between the values of *head* and *water flow rate* in PUMP-AGENT, the following acceptable solution is found:

```
    Compromise_1
       Water-flow-rate 220
       Head 327.67
       heatx-agent constraints:
          Preference:  head > 250
       pump-agent constraints:
          Constraint:  (water-flow-rate <= 415)
       Local evaluations:  ((heatx-agent good) (pump-agent fair))
```

In the first example, Condenser_3, comprising the initial heat-exchanger proposal and a constrained alternative pump proposal, is acceptable and highly-rated by both participating agents. In the second example, Compromise_1, a mutually developed compromise solution, is acceptable but not as highly rated by either agent. Constrained proposal generation did better by not committing too early to a particular path. This happened because the problem was not overconstrained and there was no need to negotiate the relaxation of constraints and preferences.

In most realistic problems, there is no guarantee that a solution exists that is not over-constrained. Even when there is one, the resources that can be devoted to finding it may be limited. After some amount of individual search, it becomes reasonable to assume that either a mutually satisfactory solution doesn't exist or that it will be too expensive to find. At this point, compromise can be used to resolve the inconsistencies that are causing the individual searches to fail.

To illustrate this, we show a problem that is overconstrained. No solution can be found without one or both agents relaxing preferences on attribute values. In this example, PUMP-AGENT and MOTOR-AGENT are active. They share *horsepower*, the power delivered by the motor to the pump. Each pump requires a certain minimum horsepower calculated from the pump model, head, and water flow rate. Each motor model can deliver a fixed maximum horsepower. The motor agent has a preference constraint on horsepower that is calculated from the set of motor models: (*horsepower* < 5). This value comes from computing cost and weight of available models and generating a preferred set. The pump agent similarly has a preference set of pump models. Because the horsepower required by the pump is a calculated rather than fixed value, the preference is expressed in terms of pump models. The pump agent also has a preference constraint on water-flow-rate, that is based on restrictions from information from the heat exchanger agent, (*water-flow-rate* > 200). The initial proposals generated by PUMP-AGENT and MOTOR-AGENT and their evaluations based on internal preference constraints are shown below:

```
Pump_1                          Motor_2
    Water-flow-rate 220             Horsepower 1
    Horsepower 17.09
    Evaluations:                    Evaluations:
        (pump-agent fair)               (pump-agent infeasible)
        (motor-agent poor)              (motor-agent excellent)
```

A compromise is generated:

```
Compromise_2
    Water-flow-rate 170
    Horsepower 8.17
    motor-agent constraints:
        Preference:  horsepower <= 5.0
    pump-agent constraints:
        Preference:  (water-flow-rate >= 200)
    Evaluations:  ((motor-agent fair) (pump-agent fair))
```

by relaxing the preferences of both agents, resulting in an acceptable compromise. In this problem, no acceptable solution would be reached through constrained alternative proposal generation, because none exists. However, because exhaustive local search is rarely possible, the decision to move to compromise must be heuristically motivated.

In this problem, multiple alternative proposals (not shown here) are generated without improving the initial proposal evaluations.

4 Summary and Status of the CEF Project

We have developed a framework for cooperating knowledge-based systems that includes conflict resolution as an integral part of the problem-solving process. The framework comprises a unifying structure for communication and a set of independent agents with the requisite capabilities. We have defined a rich set of methods for negotiation and control of the problem-solving process that effectively exploits the diversity of expertise in the agent set. Our ultimate goal is to develop an architecture to support the "warehouse" vision of problem-independent expert agents.

In support of that goal, TEAM is partially implemented in the CEF framework. The final version of TEAM will have six agents: pump, heat exchanger, motor, platform, shaft and v-belt, and condenser. Each of these will be implemented as an independent system. Three of the agents are substantially implemented (pump, heat exchanger, and motor) and we are experimenting with conflict resolution concurrently with the implementation of the other agents. Each agent makes independent scheduling decisions for all tasks, including conflict resolution. We are investigating various scheduling strategies, conflict resolution strategies, and choice heuristics.

References

[1] Daniel D. Corkill, Kevin Q. Gallagher, and Kelly E. Murray. GBB: A generic blackboard development system. In *Proceedings of the National Conference on Artificial Intelligence*, pages 1008–1014, Philadelphia, Pennsylvania, August 1986.

[2] Edward de Bono. *Lateral Thinking for Management, A handbook of creativity*. American Management Association, 1971.

[3] Lee D. Erman, Frederick Hayes-Roth, Victor R. Lesser, and D. Raj Reddy. The Hearsay-II speech-understanding system: Integrating knowledge to resolve uncertainty. *Computing Surveys*, 12(2):213–253, June 1980.

[4] R. Fisher and W. Ury. *Getting to Yes: Negotiating Agreement without Giving In*. Houghton Mifflin, 1981.

[5] Mark Klein. Supporting conflict resolution in cooperative design systems. In *Proceedings of the 10th Workshop on Distributed Artificial Intelligence*, Bandera, Texas, October 1990.

[6] Thomas Kreifelts and Frank V. Martial. A negotiation framework for autonomous agents. In *Proceedings of the Second European Workshop on Modeling Autonomous Agents and Multi Agent Worlds*, Paris, France, August 1990.

[7] B. Laasri, H. Laasri, and V.R. Lesser. Negotiation and its role in cooperative distributed problem solving. In *Proceedings of the 10th International Workshop on Distributed Artificial Intelligence*, Bandera, Texas, 1990.

198

[8] Susan Lander and Victor R. Lesser. The use of problem solving context in choosing conflict resolution strategies for cooperating expert agents. In *Proceedings of the International Working Conference on Cooperating Knowledge Based Systems*, University of Keele, England, October 1990.

[9] Kenneth L. Meunier. *Iterative Respecification: A Computational Model for Automating Parametric Mechanical System Design*. PhD thesis, University of Massachusetts, Amherst, Massachusetts 01003, February 1988.

[10] Dean G. Pruitt. *Negotiation Behavior*. Academic Press, 1981.

[11] Arvind Sathi, Thomas E. Morton, and Steven F. Roth. Callisto: An intelligent project management system. *AI Magazine*, 7(5):34–52, Winter 1986.

[12] John R. Searle. *Speech Acts: An Essay in the Philosophy of Language*. Cambridge University Press, 1970.

[13] Katia P. Sycara. Negotiation in design. In *Proceedings of the MIT-JSME Workshop on Cooperative Product Development*, Massachusetts Institute of Technology, Cambridge, MA, November 1989.

[14] Katia Sycara-Cyranski. Arguments of persuasion in labour mediation. In *Proceedings of the Ninth International Joint Conference on Artificial Intelligence*, pages 294–296, Los Angeles, California, 1985.

DISCUSSION

Presenter: S. Lander.

Q. (J. Lenting, University of Limberg): I would like to know, do you measure progress, and if so, how?

A. (S. Lander): Do we measure progress in finding a solution?

Q. (J. Lenting): In the architecture, in the quality of the architecture?

A. (S. Lander): You mean in the quality of the solutions that are being developed? Okay. We do. Our evaluation criteria are based on local evaluations by the agents and in order for a solution to be acceptable we have a function which is a combination of the agents' evaluations. That is subject to change right now, we're experimenting with it a little bit. But the types of things that we do are to have a threshold on the lowest evaluation that we can accept. For example, if an agent rated a proposal as poor we might have a threshold set at fair so that would automatically disqualify that solution in the current form. It might be that the average of all the evaluations has to be fair. So we combine some set of thresholds on how low you can go and then we have a function that combines the evaluations. Also, we have an average and we have to reach that average. So we are definitely not looking for optimality of solutions, we're looking for acceptability of solutions.

Q. (J. Lenting): Yes, but is this so difficult for this system? I can't imagine that for this schema it's so difficult to come up with a global criteria?

A. (S. Lander): That's true. It's possible that with schema, if we worked at it we could probably come up with some global evaluation. The reason that we chose this domain in spite of that is that when you start looking at domains where you really can't come up with a global evaluation they're very complex and it's hard. We don't have a hundred man-years to put into this project. However, I don't think that detracts from it being a reasonable domain because it does have the other qualities. Maybe the one quality that's lacking is that you probably could come up with some global evaluation function if you worked at it hard enough.

Q. (J. Lenting): I must say that I doubt whether there are problems where you can't at all come up with an evaluation function?

A. (S. Lander): There are certainly problems where there is no right answer. You can imagine human situations where agents have different criteria for judging. I can give you the example where you have two people who are working together, an accountant and an office manager. They have to pick a phone company. One of them, the accountant really wants the cheapest phone company. The office manager really wants the best quality phone company they can get, in terms of speed of connection and that kind of thing. There's no right answer, unless you impose a God figure. How do you have a global evaluation function? There really isn't one, there's only these two disparate views of what is the proper answer.

Q. (J. Lenting): Okay, there isn't a specific one, but it's very easy to choose one. I mean that's what's normally done.

A. (S. Lander) : Well, that's true if there is some authority figure who can pick. But if there is no authority figure then these two agents have to work it out for themselves.

Q. (G. O'Hare, UMIST) : My mind at the moment is awash with analogies and comparisons. For example your point that you made earlier on that you didn't want to predict the types of conflict that may take place because in so doing, and in trying to take early preventative measures, you can make the system brittle. I've got a lot of feeling for that viewpoint and I sympathise greatly. However, there seems to be certain similarities, deadlock, for example, which is a specific instantiation of a type of conflict. In the software engineering arena there are approaches too for deadlock detection which is what your system is advocating, the detection of conflict. But there are other situations where there are attempts for deadlock avoidance. So to my mind, it seems that perhaps you need a combination of both and perhaps there might be specific classes of well defined types of conflict for which you could, in early stages, prevent them occurring. For example, a little work at an early stage might prevent two agents getting into situations of intransigence and a lot of subsequent work.

A. (S. Lander) : I totally agree with you. I'm not going to build that into my system because that's not really my focus, but if we're talking about building the ultimate system I agree with you. I think that's right and both things should be taken into account and it would certainly be valuable to do that, but I'm not doing it.

A Computational Model for Conflict Resolution in Cooperative Design Systems[*]

Dr. Mark Klein
Advanced Research Lab
Hitachi Ltd
Hatoyama, Saitama 350-03, Japan
mklein@harl.hitachi.co.jp

Prof. Arthur B. Baskin
Dept. of Veterinary Biosciences
University of Illinois
1408 W. University
Urbana, IL 61801
baskin@gaea.cs.uiuc.edu

Abstract

Design of complex modern-day artifacts can be modelled as the cooperative activity of groups of design agents, each with their own areas of expertise. The interaction of such agents inevitably involves conflict. This paper presents a computational model for the resolution of such conflicts based on studies of human cooperative design. This model is based centrally on the insights that general *conflict resolution expertise* exists separately from domain-level design expertise, and that this expertise can be instantiated in the context of particular conflicts into specific advice for resolving those conflicts. Conflict resolution expertise consists of a taxonomy of design conflict classes in addition to associated general advice suitable for resolving conflicts in these classes. The abstract nature of conflict resolution expertise makes it applicable to a wide variety of design domains. This paper describes this conflict resolution model and provides examples of its operation from an implemented cooperative design system for local area network design that uses machine-based design agents.

---

[*] The invaluable assistance of Profs. Stephen C-Y. Lu and R.E. Stepp at the University of Illinois, as well as Drs. Motoda, Kawaguchi, Yoshida and Suwa at the Hitachi Advanced Research Lab is gratefully acknowledged.

1. The Challenge: Conflict Resolution in Cooperative Design

Design has increasingly become a cooperative endeavor carried out by multiple agents with diverse kinds of expertise. For example, the design of a car may require experts on design for function, ease of manufacturability, safety regulations, available means for shipping vehicles, potential markets, and so on. The development of tools and underlying theories for supporting cooperative design has lagged, however, behind the growing needs implied by this evolution.

A critical component of a model of cooperative design is a theory of how conflicts among the different design agents can be resolved. Different agents will often have different notions concerning what kind of design is best. One design agent may specify that a given part have a given shape to maximize strength, while another may prefer a different shape that simplifies the operations needed to produce the part. In general, when different agents give incompatible specifications for a given design component, or one agent has a negative critique of specifications asserted by another agent, we can say that a conflict has occurred.

While conflict-free cooperation among multiple sources of expertise has been well-studied, cooperation where conflict can occur is less well-understood. Existing approaches to conflict resolution in knowledge-based systems suffer from the fundamental limitation that the conflict resolution (CR) expertise is represented and reasoned with, if at all, using "second-class" (poorly expressive or inferentially weak) formalisms.

This work presents an implemented computational model for conflict resolution in cooperative design that is based on studies of human group problem solving. In this model, "first-class" formalisms are used to represent conflict resolution expertise applicable to a wide variety of design domains. This expertise is instantiated in the context of a particular conflict, via interaction with domain-specific expertise, to produce suggestions for resolving that conflict.

Developing a comprehensive theory of conflict resolution is clearly an extremely ambitious task. Our current work focuses on an important subset of this problem:

- Competition vs Cooperation: In competitive conflict situations each party has solely their own benefit in mind and has no interest in achieving a globally optimal situation if such a solution provides them no added personal benefit. In cooperative situations, the parties are united by the superordinate goal of achieving a globally optimal solution, which often requires sacrificing personal benefit in the interest of increased global benefit. These different conflict situations are associated with widely differing conflict resolution strategies (e.g. bluffing vs. compromise). Our model is oriented towards cooperative conflict resolution, since that is most appropriate for cooperative design where the shared goal of producing the best possible product exists.

- Domain Level vs Control Level Conflicts: Domain-level conflicts concern conflicting recommendations about the actual form of the design, while control-level conflicts concern conflicting recommendations about the direction the design process should take in trying to create a design. While conflict resolution at the control level is clearly important, there does not seem to be a good theory of control even for individual agents. It thus appears premature to try to develop a theory for resolving control level conflicts among multiple agents.

The remainder of this paper is organized as follows. Existing work on conflict resolution is critically reviewed, and our own model, which we believe avoids important limitations in existing work, is presented. Examples of the operation of cooperative design system we implemented that detects and resolves conflicts are then presented. This paper concludes with a discussion of the important lessons we have learned so far, and considers avenues for future research.

2. Contributions and Limitations of Existing Research

The work on conflict resolution comes from AI and related fields as well as the social sciences. For a comprehensive review, see [Klein-90a]. A large body of work is devoted to *analyzing* human conflict resolution behavior [Pruitt-81, Coombs-88, Axelrod-84, Fisher-81, Feldman-85]. This work highlights the importance of conflict in group interactions, but provides few prescriptions for how conflict resolution can be facilitated. In addition, much of this work focuses on issues specific to the psychology of human participants, rather than on the general nature of conflict resolution.

There is in addition some work on *supporting* human conflict resolution [Johansen-79, Sarin-85, Pferd-79, Stefik-81, Chang-87, Hale-87, Loy-87, Carey-88, Fedrizzi-88, Matwin-89]. This includes research on group consensus building and group decision support systems, or GDSSs. This work focuses, however, on competitive conflicts and/or limits itself to structuring interactions among group members, rather than applying conflict resolution expertise to help resolve the conflicts. The conflict resolution expertise is thus still expected to reside in the human participants.

To find work on *computational models* that actually encode and use conflict resolution expertise, we need to turn to AI and related fields such as single-agent planning/design as well as concurrent engineering. The relevant literature can be grouped into three categories according to the extent to which conflict resolution expertise is given "first-class" status, i.e., is represented and reasoned with explicitly using formalisms as robust as those used for other kinds of expertise:

- Development-Time Conflict Resolution: Systems of this type require that potential conflicts be "compiled" out of them by virtue of exhaustive discussions when they are developed [Bezem-87, Nguyen-85, Suwa-82, Trice-89, Reboh-83]. The conflict resolution knowledge utilized by the domain experts is then implicit in the individual conflict resolution decisions made during development. This approach has a number of serious disadvantages. For example, it is very time-consuming to change or add to the existing design agents. In addition, this approach makes the unrealistic assumption that *human* design agents in a cooperative design system will never make assertions that conflict with those made by other agents.

- Knowledge-Poor Run-Time Conflict Resolution: Many of the disadvantages of development-time conflict resolution approaches can be avoided by allowing conflicts to be asserted by the design agents as the system runs, and then resolved by some kind of conflict resolution component. Some examples include approaches using backtracking [Sussman-77, Sussman-80], numerically-weighted constraint relaxation [Fox-84, Descotte-85] and pieces of specific conflict resolution advice [Brown-85, Marcus-87]. Such approaches harness little conflict resolution expertise, however, and use restrictive formalisms to represent it.

- General Conflict Resolution: Work in this class come closest to providing conflict resolution expertise with first-class status. It includes implemented systems such as HACKER [Sussman-73], and BARGAINER [Goldstein-75], as well as proposals for systems [Hewitt-86, Wilensky-83, Lander-88]. None of this work, however, constitutes a comprehensive theory of conflict resolution. Little conflict resolution knowledge applicable to cooperative conflict situations is described, and/or the attempt is made to express this heuristic expertise inappropriately as deductive knowledge. In addition, either few commitments are made concerning how conflict resolution strategies should be represented or reasoned with, or the commitments made are idiosyncratic to a "toy" domain with limited extensibility. Finally, none of these approaches take into account issues particular to distributed contexts (e.g. the need for a shared inter-agent communication language).

In general, work on conflict resolution has evolved towards making this expertise more explicit and using it to support cooperative problem solving. Up until now, however, no implemented system that achieves these goals has been developed.

3. The Conflict Resolution Model

Our own work has involved designing and implementing a cooperative design system that provides first-class status for conflict resolution expertise. The theory underlying this work is based on insights derived from studies of human cooperative design in two different domains: Solar Home design [Klein-90b] and Local Area Network (LAN) design [Klein-90a]. In these studies the interactions among human design experts were analyzed with particular focus on how these experts identify and resolve conflicts among themselves. These studies showed that conflict identification and resolution represents an ubiquitous part of the cooperative design process, and that the expertise used by the designers for resolving specific conflicts can be isolated and generalized to produce domain-independent expertise suitable for a wide range of conflicts. In the sections below we consider first just what is meant by the notion of conflict resolution as a separate kind of problem solving expertise. An implemented computational model that makes effective use of this kind of expertise is then described. Finally, we discuss how the CR expertise crucial for the operation of our model can be acquired, as well as its completeness and generality evaluated and improved.

3.1. Conflict Resolution: A Distinct Kind of Problem Solving Expertise

The fundamental tenet underlying this work is that general conflict resolution expertise can and should be treated as a separate category of problem solving expertise for it to be used effectively. We can understand what this means by analogy to the treatment of control knowledge in knowledge-based systems (Figure 1). Early knowledge-based system shells such as OPS5 provide a structure for expressing facts and if-then rules, as well as some simple built-in syntactic criteria for deciding what rules run first out of the set of potentially applicable rules. Any useful domain-specific control expertise has to be compiled into the rules themselves. As a result, many rules are complicated by preconditions and actions used to express control expertise.

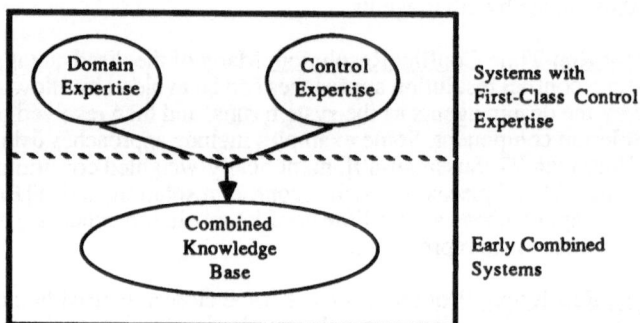

Figure 1: Treatment of Control Expertise in Knowledge-Based Systems

In knowledge bases of this sort, relatively simple bodies of domain expertise and control expertise are combined, via a "cross-product"-like process, to produce a more complicated combined body of expertise where neither of the precursors are available in their original form. Since such knowledge bases no longer make explicit the domain/control distinction present in the original expertise, they are difficult for domain experts to express, understand and modify.

More recently, knowledge-based systems are making it possible to express domain and control expertise separately, so that each kind of expertise is available in its original, more succinct form. In addition to being more understandable, having control expertise represented explicitly makes it much easier to reason with, for example to decide which kind of control scheme is appropriate for a given situation, or to understand why a given control choice was made. Allowing us to represent and reason with control expertise in this way gives it a status equivalent to that previously accorded only to domain knowledge; in other words, it gives control expertise *first-class* status. Doing so has resulted in increases in the flexibility and generality of knowledge-based systems.

The same argument can be made for conflict resolution expertise. Almost all knowledge-based systems currently mix different bodies of domain expertise along with conflict resolution expertise into a single knowledge base, resulting in the same sorts of problems that result from mixing domain and control expertise (reduced understandability, flexibility, and so on) (Figure 2).

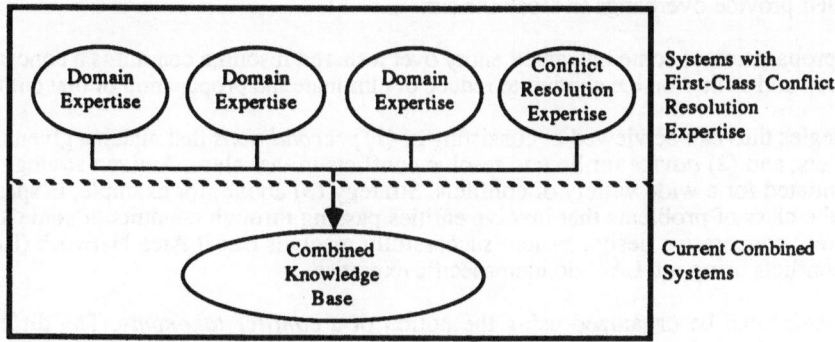

Figure 2: Treatment of CR Expertise in Knowledge-Based Systems

Giving CR expertise distinct first-class status allows us to capture succinctly useful general conflict resolution principles, and also allows bodies of domain-level design expertise to be represented in "pure" form without having to anticipate potential conflicts with each other. This leads to an increase in the flexibility and generality of multiple-expertise knowledge-based systems.

The aim of this work can thus be viewed as an attempt to further the evolution of computer-based systems towards distinct handling of distinct forms of knowledge. Conventional programming languages distinguish only data and procedures. Traditional expert systems are (beginning to) treat control expertise as a distinct form of expertise. The work described herein attempts to take this one step beyond traditional expert systems by treating conflict resolution expertise as a separate category, thus giving it first-class status as well.

Given that it is useful to acquire and represent conflict resolution expertise separately, what is the nature of this expertise? Because conflict is common, people have accumulated through experience a large collection of strategies, both specific and general, for resolving conflicts in ways that are as satisfying as possible for all the parties involved. Consider the following examples:

1) Jan and Mark are cooking dinner. Jan wants to add some hot spices to the meal, but Mark would prefer not to. They decide to cook the meal without the spices, and allow Jan to add them to her own portion after serving, even though this means the spices have less chance to cook into the meal.

2) Bob and Mike are designing a home. Mike would like large windows on the south-facing front facade of the house because of their aesthetic effect. Bob is concerned that the summer-time insolation through these windows will lead to excessive cooling costs. They decide to add an overhang over the windows to provide shade for the high summer sun.

3) Jeff and Arthur are designing a Local Area Network (LAN) for some clients. Arthur suggests a simple design that involves a single LAN trunk interconnecting all the workstations and servers at the site. Jeff is concerned that a single failure at any point

along the trunk will cause the entire site to cease functioning. They decide to add several repeaters to the trunk to prevent the propagation of failure from one LAN trunk segment to another.

The conflict resolution instances given above can be thought of as instances of the following conflict resolution strategies:

1) **If** two plans for achieving two different agents' goals conflict
   Then find an alternate way of achieving one goal that does not conflict with the other agent's plan for achieving its goal

2) **If** excessive summer insolation through south-facing windows is a concern
   Then provide overhangs to block the sun

3) **If** propagation of some unwanted entity over a shared resource conduit is a concern
   Then add a filter on the conduit to reduce or eliminate the propagation of that entity

CR strategies thus can be viewed as consisting of (1) *preconditions* that match a given class of conflicts, and (2) *advice* for how to resolve conflicts in that class. A given strategy can be instantiated for a wide variety of conflicts. Strategy (3) above, for example, is specific only to the class of problems that involve entities passing through conduits of some kind. Our current cooperative design system successfully resolves Local Area Network (LAN) design conflicts using *no* LAN-domain specific expertise.

CR strategies can be organized using the notion of a *conflict taxonomy*. The different classes of conflicts form an abstraction taxonomy that includes very general classes of conflict near the top, and more specific classes near the bottom. CR strategies high in the taxonomy apply to a wide range of conflicts, while those lower down have narrower coverage. A CR strategy can be viewed as consisting of a pointer from a conflict class to advice for resolving conflicts subsumed by that class, where the CR strategy preconditions give the class's defining characteristics. Several pieces of advice can be associated with any given class. The CR strategies described above, for example, can be organized into the following conflict taxonomy fragment (Figure 3):

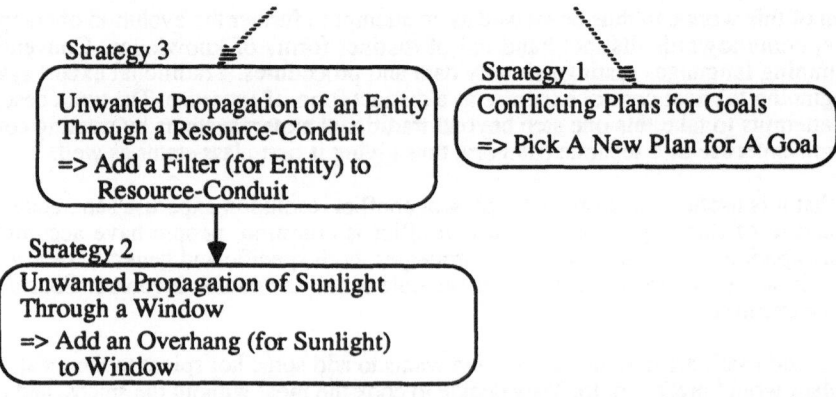

Figure 3: Fragment of Conflict Taxonomy

CR expertise exhibits an *applicability vs efficiency* tradeoff. Very general strategies that apply to a wide variety of situations can often be instantiated many different ways, only some of which are apt to result in satisfactory conflict resolutions. More specific strategies have narrower coverage, but may lead to a satisfactory solution sooner. For example, strategy (3) applies to a wide variety of conflicts including those represented by strategy (2). However, this strategy does not supply any constraint on the *kind* of filter best-suited to the situation described. As a result, this strategy might have to be instantiated with a number of different filters (e.g. window shades, shade trees, and so on for the excessive insolation conflict) until a satisfactory resolution is produced. Strategy (2), by contrast, applies to a much smaller range of conflicts but provides a specific suggestion concerning what kind of sun-filtering device to use, thus reducing the number of possibilities that need to be considered and increasing the efficiency of the strategy.

CR expertise is *heuristic* in nature since it deals with the interaction of internally consistent but mutually inconsistent domain theories in different design agents [Hewitt-86]. When we choose a particular strategy for a conflict, then, we are in effect making the *hypothesis* that the conflict is one that can be addressed by the given piece of advice, and must be able to respond appropriately if the advice fails.

In addition to a set of CR strategies, CR expertise also includes *control* knowledge for determining which of a potentially large set of applicable CR strategies should be tried first for a particular conflict. Like CR strategies themselves, this kind of expertise has proven to be specific at most to classes of problem domains.

3.2. The Computational Model

In this section we describe our computational model for harnessing conflict resolution expertise. Since CR expertise is functionally distinct from domain-level design expertise, agents in a cooperative design system can be viewed as being made up of a *design* component that can update and critique designs, as well as a *conflict resolution* component that resolves design agent conflicts (i.e. when two design agents produce incompatible specifications on a design component, or one agent is dissatisfied with specifications produced by another agent) (Figure 4).

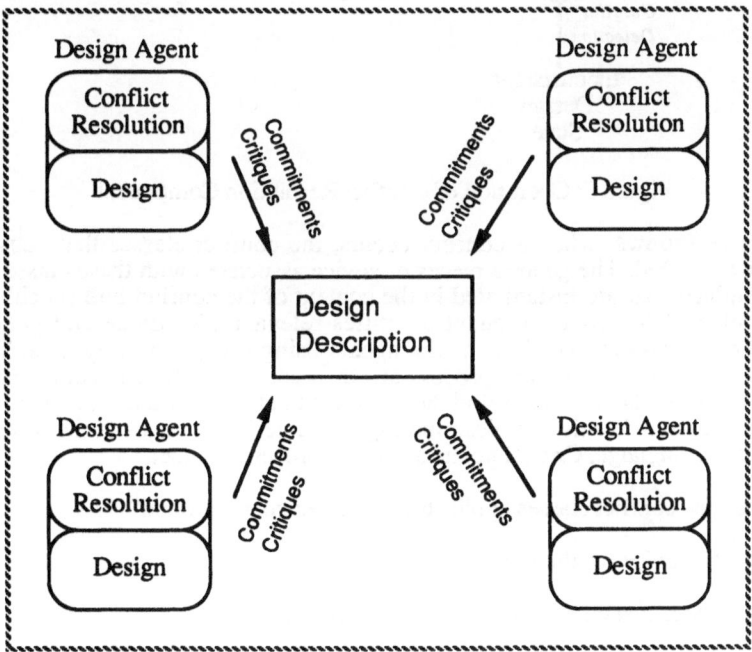

Figure 4: Components of a Cooperative Design System

The conflict resolution component of all design agents are identical; this component is replicated among the design agents to avoid limiting design agent autonomy by maintaining a single distinguished conflict resolution agent. Though they are functionally distinct, combining the design and conflict resolution components into a single design agent is straightforward, as we shall see, due to the clean interface between these two entities.

The CR component finds resolutions for conflicts using a meta-planning framework [Wilensky-83] (Figure 5). An inconsistent design state manifests as a design conflict when detected by the conflict-detection mechanism (this can be done in a domain-independent manner by looking for unsatisfiable constraints on design features; see [Klein-90a]). The conflict is mapped to the goal of resolving the conflict, and from there to a set of alternative specific CR plans for achieving that goal.

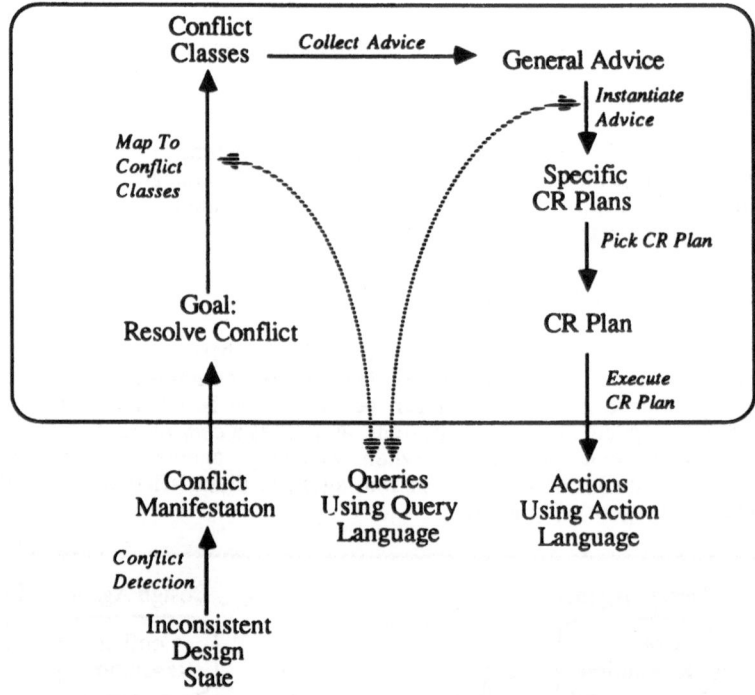

Figure 5: Operation of Conflict Resolution Component

This works as follows: when a conflict occurs, the conflict classes that subsume this conflict are identified. The general pieces of advice associated with these classes are then used as templates that are instantiated in the context of the conflict into specific conflict resolution plans. The CR component identifies relevant CR advice and generates its instantiations by asking questions of the agents using the *query language*. The plans accumulated by the instantiation process are then sorted by the CR component, using domain-independent heuristics, to find the one most likely to succeed. The top plan is then executed; the actions in this plan describe suggested design changes to the design agents using the *action language*. Critical points about this process include:

- How are the conflict classes applicable to a given conflict found?

- How is the advice for these classes collected?

- How is advice instantiated into specific CR plans?

- How are the best plans chosen by the CR component?

- How are these plans executed?

- What happens if these plans fail?

These points will be considered in the following paragraphs.

Finding Conflict Classes: Classes in the conflict class taxonomy have abstract defining characteristics described in terms of the design commitments underlying a conflict as well as the reasons behind these commitments. For example, the preconditions for the "unwanted propagation" class include "The conflict involves a critique of a component", "The component critiqued is a kind of resource conduit" and "The critique concerns unwanted propagation of some entity along that conduit". The preconditions for the "poor plan choice" class include "The conflict is supported by a plan", "The plan is supported by a goal" and "There are untried alternate plans available for that goal." These preconditions are expressed using a set of primitive question types that together constitute the *query language* used by the CR component.

The design agents are responsible for producing specific responses to these abstract questions. For example, a design agent in a cooperative LAN design system should know that a LAN trunk is a kind of resource conduit. The CR component has, in general, an "abstract vocabulary" of abstract design entities (e.g. goal, plan, constraint, resource, conduit, storage-container) that the design agents should recognize. The current implementation does this using ISA hierarchies.

Finding the conflict classes for a conflict thus involves determining which conflict classes have their preconditions satisfied by the conflict at hand. It is usually difficult to determine the cause for a conflict without having a complete model of the expertise in all the design agents involved in the conflict. As a result, the defining characteristics of a conflict class often have to be operationalised as a weaker set of conditions. For example, the "poor plan choice" class should only be triggered when the conflict is due to picking the wrong plan from a set of alternatives. To determine this one would of course have to try all plan alternatives first, which may be computationally prohibitive. The conflict class's preconditions instead are operationalised by simply checking for a goal with untried alternative plans.

Collecting the CR Advice: Every conflict class has one or more associated abstract pieces of advice for resolving conflicts in that class. The conflict resolution advice applicable to a conflict are found by simply collecting together all the pieces of advice associated with all the conflict classes that match a conflict into a set.

Instantiating the CR Advice: These pieces of advice, once collected, need to be instantiated into specific CR plans suitable for the current conflict. CR advice includes a number of "slots" that have to be filled with context-specific values in order to be executable. The CR component ask questions of the design agents, using the above-mentioned query language, to provide the values for these slots.

For example, imagine we have a conflict matched by the "poor plan choice" conflict class. The associated advice ("backtrack to another plan") can be instantiated by finding a goal supporting the conflict as well as the untried plans for the goal. The advice is instantiated into one CR plan for every untried plan for the goal. Advice is often instantiated into more than one plan.

Selecting Conflict Resolution Plans: Once a set of candidate CR plans for resolving a conflict is identified, the CR component needs to determine which ones should be tried first. The final decision concerning which resulting design is best is left, of course, to the design agents, since they are expert at evaluating design alternatives. The CR component can, however, use domain-independent heuristics to suggest first the CR plans more likely to succeed. Some examples of such heuristics include "choose the most specific plan available" (to use the knowledge most closely suited to this particular conflict) and "choose the plan that makes the smallest changes to the design" (to avoid undesirable side-effects).

CR Plan Execution: When conflict resolution plans are executed, suggestions are made to the design agents using statements from the *action language*. There are four kinds of statements:

- Use More Careful Model: A commitment based on a "shallow" model is re-considered using a more "careful" version of the model.

- <u>Modify Value:</u> A goal or design feature constraint is changed to some new value.

- <u>Pick Plan for Goal:</u> A previously untried plan is picked for a goal.

- <u>Add Detail:</u> Some new detail (i.e. a patch of some kind) is added to the design.

The action language described has proven adequate for describing all the conflict resolution strategies considered so far in our work.

<u>When CR Plans Fail:</u> Since conflict resolution expertise is heuristic in nature, a given conflict resolution plan CR plan may not work at all, or produce "secondary" conflicts as a result of trying to resolve the initial conflict. As a result, it may take several CR suggestions in a row to completely resolve a particular conflict.

Conflicts resulting from suggestions of the CR component are treated the same as conflicts due to design agents actions. In such situations the CR component finds itself involved in the rationale for the conflict, will ask questions of itself using the query language, and may even give conflict resolution suggestions to itself using the action language. The CR component thus uses a single uniform mechanism for dealing with all types of conflicts.

This conflict resolution process can be described using Clancey's heuristic classification model [Clancey-84] (Figure 6). This model views classification as heuristic matching between abstracted data describing a problem and one or more abstract solutions in a pre-enumerated solution taxonomy, followed by refinement of abstract solutions into specific ones.

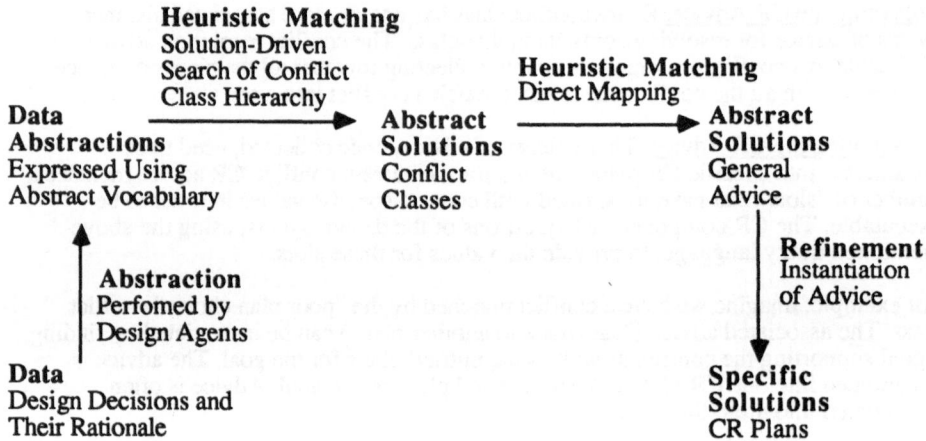

Figure 6: Conflict Resolution as Heuristic Classification

The data is the design decisions and rationale supporting a conflict. Abstraction is performed by the design agents when they answer abstract query language questions. The heuristic matching step is performed by searching the conflict class taxonomy in a solution-driven manner (i.e. by successive discrimination from general to specific classes). The conflict classes are then mapped in a second heuristic matching step (direct mapping in this case) to general pieces of advice, which are refined to specific suggested solutions (CR plans) for a conflict. Heuristics guide the refinement process, in effect, to produce first suggestions that are more likely to work.

3.3. Acquiring Conflict Resolution Expertise

Conflict resolution expertise can be acquired by generalization from examples of specific conflict resolutions, or by directly eliciting general strategies from domain experts. It can be changed or added to at any time, allowing the conflict resolution behavior of the system to be changed easily. A discussion of how a conflict class taxonomy is developed is given in [Klein-90a].

An important issue is the completeness and generality of this knowledge. In order to understand this issue better we need to distinguish between the different abstract types of problem solving (Figure 7):

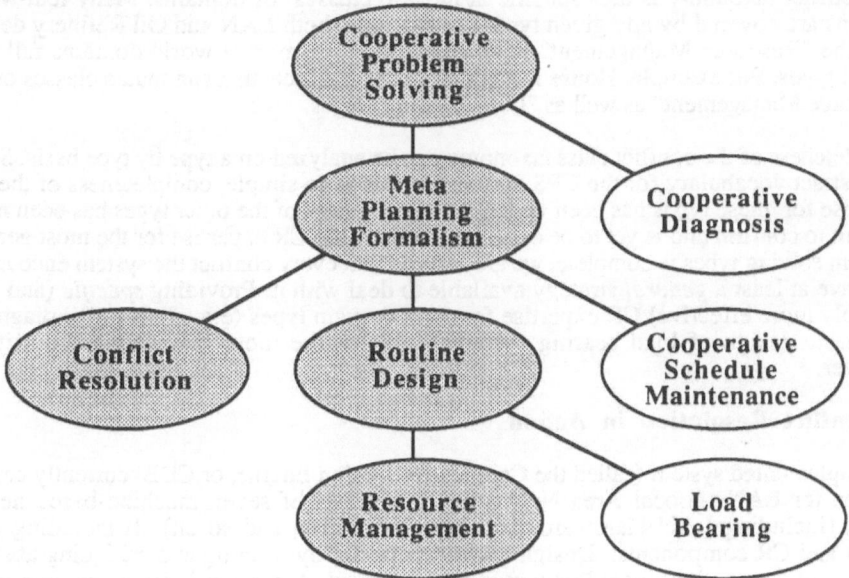

Figure 7: Types of Problem Solving

Types lower in the hierarchy are specializations of their parent types. Every type has a different abstract vocabulary (set of terms for describing objects in its domain) as well as different characteristic classes of conflict and associated conflict resolution strategies. The current implementation has conflict resolution expertise for the five types of problem solving shaded in the figure above:

- Cooperative Problem Solving (CPS): Problem solving where multiple agents are working together to solve a problem, and each agent uses a possibly shallow model to inform its choice of commitments. The abstract vocabulary includes "agent" and "model". An example CR strategy for this type is "IF an agent used a shallow model to produce a conflicting design statement, THEN ask the agent to try again using a less shallow model".

- Meta-Planning Formalism (MPF): Agents use a least-commitment meta-planning formalism [Wilensky-83] to produce commitments. The abstract vocabulary includes "constraint", "plan" and "goal". Example: "IF a conflict involves a relaxable constraint, THEN try relaxing that constraint".

- Routine Design (RD): Agents work by configuring and connecting known components. The abstract vocabulary includes "component", "component feature" and "component database". Example: "IF the conflict is caused by being unable to find an existing component in the components database for a given set of relaxable design constraints, THEN relax the constraints such that a matching component can be found."

- Resource Management (RM): The design agents are designing a system to manage resources. The abstract vocabulary includes "storage container", "conduit", "consumer" and "filter". Example: "IF the conflict is due to unwanted propagation of some entity along a conduit, THEN add a filter for that entity to the conduit".

- Conflict Resolution (CR): Problem solving where resolutions for conflicts are found. The abstract vocabulary includes "conflict". The CR component uses this expertise to handle conflicts resulting from its own actions. Example: "IF a conflict is caused by a CR strategy, THEN try running a different CR strategy for the original conflict".

The conflict taxonomy is thus specific at most to *classes* of domains. Many real-world domains are covered by any given type. For example, both LAN and Oil Refinery design fit in the "Resource Management" type. In addition, many real world domains fall into several types. For example, House Design produces conflicts that can match classes of the "Resource Management" as well as "Load Bearing" types.

Completeness of the conflict class taxonomy can be analyzed on a type by type basis. Since the abstract vocabulary for the CPS and MPF types is so simple, completeness of the CR expertise for these types has been verified. Completeness of the other types has been more difficult to confirm and is yet to be established. Since the CR expertise for the most general problem solving types is complete, we are assured that every conflict the system encounters will have at least a *general* strategy available to deal with it. Providing *specific* (and thus probably more effective) CR expertise for other domain types (e.g. cooperative diagnosis or routine design of load bearing systems) will require more knowledge acquisition, however.

4. Conflict Resolution in Action

Our implemented system (called the Cooperative Design Engine, or CDE) currently creates designs for LANs (Local Area Networks). It consists of seven machine-based design agents (including LAN Hardware, Security, Reliability, and so on) all including both design and CR components. Design agents cooperate by refining and critiquing abstract component descriptions stored on a central blackboard. A domain-independent constraint propagation mechanism detects conflicts by looking for unsatisfiable constraints on a given component feature. Design agents are implemented as rule-based expert systems. The CR component includes a conflict class taxonomy with a total of 115 conflict classes, with 13, 14, 58 and 30 classes of the CPS, MPF, RD and RM types, respectively.

Let us consider a pair of examples of conflict resolution performed by our system while designing a LAN. In this scenario, the system has refined the LAN design description into, among other things, a trunk for carrying data traffic. The next step is for the Hardware agent to try to determine a physical topology for the trunk. It does so by asking other agents for the preferred trunk media and protocol, and then searching its components database for a physical topology that supports these preferences. For this case, the Vendor agent prefers the token-ring protocol and thin baseband coax media. The Hardware agent, however, finds no existing LAN technology that satisfies these constraints, and accordingly returns an unsatisfiable constraint on the topology, which is recognized as a conflict by the conflict detection machinery. The conflict in this case is between a Vendor agent that wants a particular set of design features, and a Hardware agent that wants to create viable designs but cannot.

The Hardware agent's CR component now tries to find one or more CR plans that can potentially resolve this conflict. It begins by looking for classes in the conflict taxonomy which subsume it. One of the classes in the taxonomy has defining conditions we can paraphrase as follows:

> "A design agent is unable to find a component in a components database that satisfies some set of constraints because the constraints were too rigid."

As noted above, a conflict class's preconditions are actually expressed as a set of query language questions. The CR component asks these questions of the design agents to check if the CR class preconditions are satisfied, and the agents respond, typically providing context-specific information. A trace of the resultant dialogue is given below; items in italic font represent abstract vocabulary items used by the CR component, and items in bold represent context-specific values returned by the design agents:

CR Component	Design Component
What *facts* support **Conflict1?**	Assertion1: The Physical-Topology of LAN-Trunk-1 is nil
Physical-Topology isa *component*?	Yes
What *rule* created **Assertion1?**	Plan1
Plan1 isa *database-search-plan*?	Yes
What are the *input-constraints* to **Plan1?**	Assertion2: The Media of LAN-Trunk-1 is thin-baseband-coax Assertion3: The Protocol of LAN-Trunk-1 is Token-Ring
Is **Assertion1** relaxable?	Yes
Is **Assertion2** relaxable?	Yes

As a result of this dialogue, the CR component finds that conflict class indeed subsumes the conflict, and also learns the identities of the constraints, component and database search plan involved in the conflict. After exhaustive consideration of the entire conflict class taxonomy, several subsuming conflict classes may be identified in this way.

The next step is to collect the general advice associated with these classes. While several such pieces of advice would in general be returned, let us consider only the piece of advice associated with the class described above:

> "Change the input constraints to the database search plan so that a component can be retrieved from the components database, and re-run the plan."

This piece of general advice needs to be instantiated into one or more specific suggestions, by filling in context-specific slots, before it can be executed. This process takes place via another query-language dialogue, as follows:

CR Component	Design Component
What changes to the *input-constraints* will allow **Plan1** to return a viable value for the **Physical-Topology** of **LAN-Trunk-1?**	Change Assertion2 to Ethernet OR Change Assertion2 to STARLAN Assertion3 to Phone-Line

Using this information, the CR component can instantiate its general advice into the following CR plans, expressed using the action language described above:

> CR Plan1: Modify **Assertion2** to **Ethernet** AND rerun **Plan1**.

> CR Plan2: Modify **Assertion2** to **STARLAN** AND modify **Assertion3** to **Phone-Line** AND rerun **Plan1**.

The CR component then has to decide which CR plan to actually execute. Based on the heuristic "prefer simpler CR plans", CR Plan1 is chosen. Let us imagine that Assertion2 can be changed as requested. After rerunning Plan1 with the changed input constraints, the "Bus" topology is successfully selected for LAN-Trunk-1. LAN-Trunk-1 is then refined by the Hardware agent into a bus with two terminators (one at each end). This particular refinement represents the simplest way a bus topology can be refined (i.e. there are no filters on the trunk); simple designs are preferred by default by the Hardware agent.

This topology, however, is critiqued by the Reliability agent. This agent prefers to keep the reliability of the LAN trunk high, but when a failure occurs anywhere on a filter-less bus-type trunk, this failure propagates throughout the whole trunk. This low reliability assessment conflicts with the goal of maintaining high reliability, and thus a conflict is asserted.

The Reliability agent's CR component is activated. In this case, the CR component finds the following conflict class subsumes the conflict:

"There is a resource conduit that suffers from the propagation of some unwanted entity"

The associated advice is:

"Add a filter for that unwanted entity to the resource conduit"

The dialogue with the design agents for this case proceeds as follows:

CR Component	Design Component
What *facts* support **Conflict2**?	Goal1: The Reliability of LAN-Trunk-1 is High Assertion4: The Reliability of LAN-Trunk-1 is Low
LAN-Trunk-1 isa *resource-conduit*?	Yes
What *facts* support **Assertion4**?	Assertion5: The Failure-Propagation of LAN-Trunk-1 is High
Failure-Propagation isa *unwanted-feature-propagation*?	Yes
Is there a *filter* suitable for stopping **Failure-Propagation** on **LAN-Trunk-1**?	Yes - an Ethernet Repeater

The first four exchanges verify that the conflict class subsumes the conflict, and the last one provides the domain-specific information needed to instantiate the advice associated with that class, producing the following CR plan:

CR Plan3: Add an **ethernet-repeater** to **LAN-Trunk-1**.

This CR plan, when executed, generates a goal to add an ethernet repeater to the LAN trunk. The trunk is now refined into a pair of trunk segments with an ethernet repeater between them. The Reliability agent is satisfied, and this phase of the design thus terminates successfully.

As we can see, our model of conflict resolution works via interactions between general conflict resolution expertise and domain-specific design expertise. General advice is identified and then instantiated through this interaction into plans suitable for a specific conflict in a given domain. This division of labour allows a relatively compact corpus of CR expertise to be applied to a wide variety of design conflicts.

5. Conclusion

This paper presents an approach to conflict resolution in cooperative design that avoids many of the limitations of previous work in this area. Previous work has not, for the most part, supported run-time conflict resolution. Those approaches that have attempted to do so can be distinguished according to the kind of conflict resolution expertise they express, as well as by the power of the representational and inferential formalisms they use to do so (Figure 8).

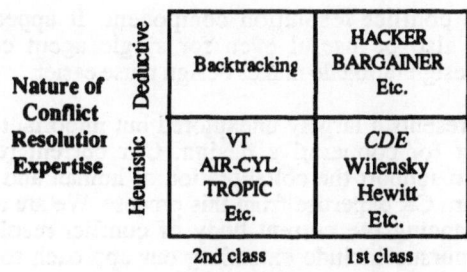

Figure 8: Work on Run-Time Conflict Resolution

Many approaches (such as backtracking systems, VT, AIR-CYL and so on) use only second class formalisms for representing and reasoning with CR expertise, resulting in serious deficits in their conflict resolution abilities. Other approaches (such as HACKER and BARGAINER) have given conflict resolution expertise first-class status, but have attempted to encode deductive strategies, i.e. strategies guaranteed to work based on complete understanding of the problem. This approach is fundamentally flawed because most CR expertise is by nature heuristic. Some existing proposals for run-time conflict resolutions (e.g. by Hewitt or Wilensky) do not suffer from these limitations, but make very few commitments concerning how such an approach could actually be realized. CDE is the only system that embodies a detailed computational model of knowledge-intensive run-time conflict resolution as well as a sizable collection of conflict resolution expertise. Further, CDE is one of the few systems explicitly aimed at the kind of distributed problem solving context involved in cooperative design.

The conflict resolution model incorporated in CDE *subsumes*, in fact, previous work on conflict resolution in cooperative design. The techniques used in systems like AIR-CYL, HACKER or VT are embodied as one or more CR strategies in CDE's conflict resolution taxonomy.

Our work has led to a number of useful insights into conflict resolution in cooperative design:

- General CR Expertise Exists: General conflict resolution represents an important category of knowledge in cooperative design, distinct from domain expertise. We were able to collect a body of such expertise from a number of different domains.

- CR Expertise Can Be Harnessed: A computational model that can harness this expertise can be developed. Such a model is incorporated in the CDE cooperative design system.

- CR Expertise is Heuristic: CR expertise appears to be largely heuristic and thus fallible. The ability to deal with failed CR suggestions is thus critical.

- CR Expertise Can Be Acquired: CR expertise can be acquired readily from human experts. The experience of collecting this expertise has led to a number of insights into how this process can be structured more effectively and possibly even automated.

- CR Expertise Completeness Can Be Approached: Techniques for helping to evaluate and improve the completeness of a given body of conflict resolution expertise have been uncovered by our work and have been applied successfully.

- Design Agent Models Face New Challenges: This work's focus on conflict resolution in cooperative design has revealed new challenges for design agent models, including providing design agents with greater self-awareness (i.e. the ability to represent richer design rationale), and greater self-modifiability (i.e. the ability to change the design produced in response to suggestions), so they can better respond to the queries and suggestions of the conflict resolution component. It appears that meeting such challenges should also be useful even for single agent contexts; for example, maintaining a rich design rationale makes design reuse easier.

Conflict resolution represents a largely unexplored but important next step in providing truly effective support for cooperative design. Our current research is focused on expanding our model to support the collaboration of human and machine-based design agents, as well as to learn CR expertise from this process. We are also constantly engaged in evaluating and enhancing the current body of conflict resolution expertise. Other directions we plan to pursue include extending our approach to other design domains (including planning, the design of *temporal* artifacts) and exploring the use of analogy and learning to enhance the coverage and effectiveness of existing conflict classes.

6. References

[Axelrod-84] Axelrod, R. *The Evolution Of Cooperation,* Basic Books, Inc. (1984).

[Bezem-87] Bezem, M. Consistency Of Rule-Based Expert Systems. Tech. Report Centre for Mathematics and Computer Science, July 1987.

[Brown-85] Brown, D.C. *Failure Handling In A Design Expert System,* Butterworth and Co. (November 1985).

[Carey-88] Carey, J.M., Olson, D.L., and Paradice, D. Icrss: Interactive Conflict Resolution Support System For Inter-Group Situations. *Proc 22nd Annual Hawaii International Conference on System Sciences 3*(1988) Pps. 512-516.

[Chang-87] Chang, E. *Participant Systems For Cooperative Work,* Morgan-Kaufman (1987) Pps. 311-339.

[Clancey-84] Clancey, W.J. Classification Problem Solving. *AAAI* (1984) Pps. 49-55.

[Coombs-88] Coombs, C.H. and Avrunin, G.S. *The Structure of Conflict,* Lawrence Erlbaum Associates (1988).

[Descotte-85] Descotte, Y. and Latombe, J.C. Making Compromises Among Antagonist Constraints In A Planner. *Artificial Intelligence 27*(1985) Pps. 183-217.

[Fedrizzi-88] Fedrizzi, M., Kacpryzk, J., and Zadrozny, S. *An Interactive Multi-User Decision Support System For Consensus Reacing Process Using Fuzzy Logic With Linguistic Quantifiers,* Elsevier Science Publishers, Vol. 4 (1988) Pps. 313-327.

[Feldman-85] Feldman, D. A Taxonomy Of Intergroup Conflict Resolution Strategies. *The 1985 Annual Conference on Developing Human Resources* (1985).

[Fisher-81] Fisher, R. and Ury, W. *Getting to Yes: Negotiating Agreement Without Giving In,* Houghtin Mifflin (1981).

[Fox-84] Fox, M.S. and Smith, S.F. Isis - A Knowledge-Based System For Factory Scheduling. *Expert Systems* (July 1984).

[Goldstein-75] Goldstein, I.P. Bargaining Between Goals. Tech. Report Massachusetts Institute of Technology Artificial Intelligence Laboratory, 1975.

[Hale-87] Hale, H. and Haseman, H. EECS: A Prototype Distributed Executive Communication and Support System. *Proceedings of the Twentieth Hawaii International Conference on System Sciences 1*(1987) Pps. 557-565.

[Hewitt-86] Hewitt, C. Offices Are Open Systems. *ACM Transactions on Office Information Systems 4,* 3 (July 1986) Pps. 271-287.

[Johansen-79] Johansen, J., Vallee, V., and Springer, S. *Electronic Meetings: Technical Alternatives and Social Choices,* Addison-Wesley (1979).

[Klein-90a] Klein, M. *Conflict Resolution in Cooperative Design*, Ph.D. dissertation, University of Illinois at Urbana-Champaign, January 1990.

[Klein-90b] Klein, M. and Lu, S.C.Y. Conflict Resolution in Cooperative Design. *International Journal for Artificial Intelligence in Engineering* (1990).

[Lander-88] Lander, S. and Lesser, V.R. Negotiation To Resolve Conflicts Among Design Experts. Tech. Report Dept of Computer and Information Science, August 1988.

[Loy-87] Loy, L., Pracht, P., and Courtney, C. Effects of a Graphical Problem Solving Aid on Small Group Decision Making. *Proc 20th Hawaii International Conference on System Sciences 1*(1987) Pps. 566-574.

[Marcus-87] Marcus, S., Stout, J., and McDermott, J. VT: An Expert Elevator Designer. *Artificial Intelligence Magazine 8*, 4 (Winter 1987) Pps. 39-58.

[Matwin-89] Matwin, S., Szpakowicz, S., Koperczak, Z., Kersten, G., and Michalowski, W. Negoplan: An Expert System Shell For Negotiation Support. Tech. Report University of Ottawa, February 1989.

[Nguyen-85] Nguyen, T.A., Perkins, W.A., Laffey, T.J., and Pecora, D. Checking An Expert Sytems Knowledge Base For Consistency And Completeness. *Proc IJCAI-85* (1985) Pps. 375-378.

[Pferd-79] Pferd, P. and Peralta, P. Interactive Graphics Teleconferencing. *IEEE Computer* (November 1979).

[Pruitt-81] Pruitt, D.G. *Negotiation Behavior,* Academic Pres (1981).

[Reboh-83] Reboh, R. Extracting Useful Advice From Conflicting Expertise. *Proceedings of the International Joint Conference on Artificial Intelligence 1*(1983) Pps. 145-150.

[Sarin-85] Sarin, G. Computer-Based Real-Time Conferencing Systems. *IEEE Computer* (October 1985).

[Stefik-81] Stefik, M.J. Planning With Constraints (Molgen: Part 1 & 2). *Artificial Intelligence 16*, 2 (1981) Pps. 111-170.

[Sussman-73] Sussman, G.J. A Computational Model Of Skill Acquistion. Tech. Report PhD Thesis. AI Lab, MIT, 1973., 1973.

[Sussman-77] Sussman, G. Electrical Design - A Problem For Ai Research. *Proceedings of the International Joint Conference on Artificial Intelligence* (August 1977) Pps. 894-900.

[Sussman-80] Sussman, G.J. and Steele, G.L. Constraints - A Language For Expressing Almost-Hierachical Descriptions. *Artificial Intelligence 14*(1980) Pps. 1-40.

[Suwa-82] Suwa, M., Scott, A.C., and Shortliffe, E.H. An Approach To Verifying Completeness And Consistency In A Rule-Based Expert System. *AAAI* (1982).

[Trice-89] Trice, A. and Davis, R. Consensus Knowledge Acquisition. Tech. Report Information Technologies Group, MIT School of Management, April 1989.

[Wilensky-83] Wilensky, R. *Planning And Understanding,* Addison-Wesley (1983).

DISCUSSION

Presenter: M. Klein.

Q. : I have a question about another kind of conflict that might occur at a meta-level in your framework. I didn't see it in your paper, but you may have dealt with it in another way. Namely, a conflict like deadlock. It seems there could be circularities of conflicts which might only be addressable with a higher level view?

A. (M. Klein) : Yes, I alluded to that just briefly in passing. That's manifested by the system being stalled, by the design state progress being stalled. We arbitrarily define that as a conflict. It is essentially a kind of conflict where you don't really know where to point the finger precisely and so the search for a classification for that conflict traverses a bigger percentage of the conflict hierarchy. But we do deal with that and, in fact, the stalled database search is a simple instance of a circularity. The circularity is entirely in one agent in that example but the system works the same way whether the circularity involves several agents or just the one that was asserting the two things that are mutually exclusive.

Q. : Does it ever happen that there is a circular conflict in the conflict resolution process?

A. (M. Klein) : Circularity in the conflict resolution process is avoided because the conflict resolution agent does not ignore prior activity when putting forward a strategy. So if you come back with essentially the same conflict then the conflict resolution agent knows what strategies it has tried already and will preclude a circularity that way. When a circularity is detected the conflict resolution agent thus abandons the whole circle and goes up a level. That's when we get to the fairly general strategies at the root of the conflict tree.

Q. (F. Farhoodi, Logica, Cambridge) : When you are referring to the process of interaction between the conflict resolution expert and the other agents you didn't explicitly mention the word negotiation. You use a dialogue, which can just actually have to do with information, whereas in the concluding part of your remarks you mentioned negotiation. Does this system explicitly support negotiation for conflict resolution or not?

A. (M. Klein) : No. It is properly just a dialogue and in that sense is in counterpoint to what we heard in an earlier session which would properly be called negotiation. We believe that we have teased out domain independent conflict resolution expertise. This is more likely to give good structure to the negotiation process than just leaving participants on their own. So we therefore give primacy to the conflict resolution agent and it actually makes the decision about what strategy to use.

Q. (F. Farhoodi) : Doesn't that limit the capability of the system? In many situations, for example in air traffic control or management, it is very important for the agents to be able to negotiate amongst themselves, especially where a lot of automation is allowed. By delegating all these tasks to one central agent, (a) could create this bottleneck situation, (b) would not really leave you much scope for dealing with more complex types of conflict.

A. (M. Klein) : The short answer to that question, and it doesn't do full justice to the question, is that we have provision for in effect replicating the conflict resolution agent as an adjunct to each design agent. So what was centralised comes to work by interaction among multiple instantiations of conflict resolution agents, each of which carries on a dialogue with its associated design agent. This avoids the problems with the single centralized conflict resolution agent that you mentioned.

Multi-agent Development Model

Modeling Concurrency in Rule-Based Development Environments

Naser S. Barghouti and Gail E. Kaiser

Department of Computer Science, Columbia University
New York, NY 10027

Abstract

We investigate the problem of cooperation among multiple agents in a class of knowledge-based systems called rule-based development environments (RB-DEs). RBDEs use knowledge about the specific development process of a software project in order to provide automated assistance to developers working on the project. The knowledge is in the form of rules, where each rule models a development activity. The rules operate on the project components which are abstracted as attributed objects and stored in a database. Each user command corresponds to a rule, which is fired when the user requests the command. The activity encapsulated in the rule might introduce changes in the database that satisfy the condition of one or more other rules, causing the firing of these rules. The database is thus treated as the working memory of the rule system. When multiple developers request commands concurrently, the rule chains initiated by their commands access the same database concurrently, with the potential of conflicting access. We investigate the nature of these conflicts and how to detect them. We outline an approach for using knowledge about the project in order to resolve the conflicts without obstructing cooperation among the users. The full paper appears in *IEEE Expert*, December 1990.

1 Introduction and Motivation

Rule-based development environments (RBDEs) use knowledge about the specific development process of a software project in order to provide automated assistance to developers working on the project. The knowledge is provided in the form of an object-oriented data model and a rule-based model of the project's development process. The data model defines the organization and structure of project components and the process model defines each development activity in terms of a rule that manipulates the components. The data model and the rules are loaded into the RBDE which then tailors its behavior accordingly. The tailored RBDE presents the users (the developers of the project) with commands that correspond to the loaded rules.

The users request commands which the RBDE executes by firing the corresponding rules. RBDEs assist in automating the development process by applying forward and backward chaining on the rules in order to automatically perform some of the chores that developers would otherwise do manually. Chaining is initiated when the rules corresponding to user commands introduce changes in the database, which is treated as the working memory of the rule system. The RBDE model has become popular [Per89], and a number of environments based on it have been proposed and constructed (e.g., [CLF88, MR88, HL88]).

However, existing RBDEs do not scale up to real software development projects involving teams of cooperating developers. These developers share expertise, knowledge and data to perform development tasks that require their concerted efforts. In order to effectively assist in the development of real projects, RBDEs must support cooperation among the developers while maintaining the consistency of the project's database. *Cooperation* among these developers requires that they (and the rule chains initiated by their commands) be allowed to concurrently access the project database. This is analogous to having multiple rule chains access the same working memory in an expert system. Unfortunately, the current expert system paradigm, on which RBDEs are based, lacks appropriate synchronization mechanisms through which multiple *agents* can concurrently access the working memory without rendering the data in it inconsistent. We use the term *agent* to refer to both human developers and rules that are fired on their behalf.

There has previously been some successful research on cooperation among multiple expert systems, each with its own rules and *separate* working memory — typically with communication through a blackboard architecture [Nii86]. But there has been little consideration of the problem of *synchronizing* the simultaneous access of multiple rule chains to the contents of the same shared working memory while multiple human users are also updating the working memory. Sharing of the working memory, which represents the project database, is necessary for cooperation among the members of a large software project.

The problem of concurrent rule executions on a shared working memory has been addressed previously in the context of speeding up the execution of production systems through the use of parallelism [Gup86]. We address a different problem that appears superficially similar. In multi-user RBDEs, parallelism is *intrinsic* and not a technique used for improving the performance of the expert system. Multiple users request commands concurrently. Each of these commands causes one or more rules to fire. Unlike in production systems where only one rule is fired out of the set of matched rules, all of the rule chains must be fired concurrently in order to execute the user commands. The concurrent rule chains access the same database to read and write the objects representing project components. The concurrent accesses may cause conflicts. These conflicts cannot be avoided by firing only one rule at a time because this would force the users whose commands correspond to the delayed rules to wait an arbitrarily long time before their commands are executed. In addition, cooperation among users might necessitate that the execution of their commands (including the rule chains that are initiated by these commands) be interleaved.

In this paper we explore the problem of synchronization in multi-agent RBDEs. We outline a solution that divides the problem into two components: (1) how to detect potential conflicts between the concurrent activities of developers; and (2) how to use

```
rule:

  condition

  { activity }

  effect1; effect2; . . .
```

Figure 1: A Generic Rule in the RBDE Model

knowledge about the development process and user tasks to resolve these conflicts. Our solution exploits recent advances in extended transaction models [BK91], which provide clues as to how to support cooperation while guaranteeing the consistency of data. We believe that our approach to solving these problems can be generalized to other classes of expert systems. This research was motivated by our previous work on a single-user RBDE called MARVEL [KFP88, KBFS88, KBS90].

We first describe the rule execution model in RBDEs and explain why the peculiarities of modeling software development require divergence from the conventional rule execution model in production systems. We then describe the synchronization problem introduced by supporting multiple users in the same RBDE. We introduce our approach to solving the multi-agent problem: we sketch how we detect conflicts, and how a rule-based specification of the project's consistency requirements is used to resolve conflicts between concurrent rule chains without obstructing cooperation among human developers.

2 The RBDE Model

RBDEs provide assistance during the development of a software project by automatically firing rules that manipulate project components, each of which is abstracted as an object and stored in a database. The rules encapsulate software development activities (for instance editing, compilation, debugging, etc.), which are performed using conventional software development tools outside the RBDE (e.g., the editors, compilers, debuggers, etc.). By *encapsulating* an activity in a rule, we mean that the rule specifies the condition that must be satisfied in order for the tool that performs the development activity to be invoked on the specified objects, and the effects of invoking the tool on the objects. Since the development of different projects often requires different sets of tools, and since each project has its own restrictions on how these tools must be used, the rules must be made explicit and provided to the RBDE rather than built into its interpreter. We envision that a project administrator writes the development rules of the project and loads them into the RBDE.

The users of an RBDE do not have to be aware of the existence of rules. They simply request commands, each of which either corresponds to a rule or is built into the environment (e.g., commands to add and delete objects). If the command

```
build[?p:PROGRAM]:

    # if all the libraries belonging to the project (instance of the
    # PROJECT class) that contains the program have been archived,
    # and if all the C files (instances of the class CFILE)
    # that are components of the program have been successfully
    # analyzed and compiled, then the program can be built by calling
    # the BUILD tool.  Depending on the result of the tool, update the
    # status attribute of the program to be either Built or NotBuilt.

    (and (forall PROJECT ?P suchthat (member [?P.programs ?p]))
         (forall LIB ?l suchthat (member [?P.libraries ?l]))
         (forall CFILE ?c suchthat (member [?p.cfiles ?c])))
    :
    (and (?c.analyze_status = Analyzed)
         (?c.compile_status = Compiled)
         (?l.archive_status = Archived))

    { BUILD build_program ?p }     # this is the activity of the rule

    (?p.build_status = Built);     # postcondition in case of success
    (?p.build_status = NotBuilt);  # postcondition in case of failure
```

Figure 2: Example of a Marvel Rule

corresponds to a rule that causes a chain of other rules to be invoked (explained shortly), the user sees only the results of the chain of activities that the RBDE is automatically performing on his or her behalf. As shown in figure 1, each rule has a condition that must be satisfied before the second part, the development activity the rule encapsulates, is executed. The condition is essentially a query (i.e., read operation) on the status of objects in the database.

Due to the lack of knowledge about the internals of the tools invoked and the human decisions that will be made during the activity (e.g., for interactive tools like editors), the activity is modeled as a "black box" whose inputs and possible outputs are known. But in order to determine which of several possible outputs it will produce, the black box must be executed. The third part of each rule is a set of mutually exclusive effects, each of which changes (i.e., writes) the status of objects in the database. The results of the rule's activity determine which effect to assert. Thus, the rules employed in the RBDE model differ from those in most other expert systems in that (1) they are made up of three parts rather than a condition/action pair; and (2) the rule's "action" might be external to the rule system (in the case of tool invocation). An example rule understood by our MARVEL system is shown in figure 2. We have intentionally chosen simple rules because we are mainly concerned with how the rules interact through their conditions and effects, and the examples demonstrate that aspect.

2.1 Rule Execution Model

We assume a model in which rules define opportunities for automation, and both forward and backward chaining are supported. This model is implemented in several RBDEs including MARVEL. The main aspect that distinguishes this model from chaining models used in conventional AI systems is the fact that rules may invoke external tools, whose effects can not be determined before the tool invocation terminates. A tool might also perform some actions that are irreversible as a side effect of running the tool. This fact, which is a requirement of the domain, manifests itself in two ways: (1) the tools operate on the file system outside the project database, and whatever these tools change while they are running cannot be monitored by the RBDE, which only has control over changes done to the project database; and (2) the existence of multiple mutually exclusive effects of a rule. Because of these two aspects, the nature of both forward and backward chaining in the RBDE model is different from other rule-based systems.

If the effect of a rule changes the database in such a way that the conditions of other rules become satisfied, all of those rules are fired automatically. These rules are considered implications of the original rule. This kind of forward chaining is similar to what is implemented in OPS5 production systems, except that all the rules whose conditions become satisfied are invoked rather than just one chosen by a conflict resolution strategy. This is necessary because the reason for firing these rules in the first place is to automatically carry out as many activities as possible. Thus, it would not make much sense for the RBDE to arbitrarily choose just one rule to fire rather than attempting to automatically carry out as many rules as it can in order to achieve maximum automation.

If the condition of the original rule matching the user command is not satisfied, backward chaining is performed to attempt to *make* it satisfied. Although this sounds similar to backward chaining in theorem provers, constraint systems and some production systems, there are two differences. First, unlike these systems, backward chaining in RBDEs is not used to *verify* that a condition is satisfied; the rules invoked during a backward chain might actually modify objects (change facts) in the database (working memory) that satisfy the original condition which was false before the backward chain. For example, say that there are two rules, `edit` and `reserve`, which apply to source files. The condition of `edit` specifies that a file cannot be edited unless it has been reserved. The effect of `reserve` specifies that if the reserve tool can be run successfully on a file, the file is marked as reserved. Say that a user, Bob, requests a command to edit a file, `f1`, which has not been reserved. The RBDE attempts to fire `edit` to execute the user's command, but finds that its condition is not satisfied. The RBDE applies backward chaining, firing `reserve` on `f1`, which makes `f1` become reserved, satisfying the condition of `edit`. Only then does the RBDE fire `edit`.

The second difference between our model and more traditional rule execution models is that rules fired in a backward chaining cycle may have invoked external tools, whose actions cannot be reversed if the chaining fails. This is a direct implication of not being able to monitor the changes that an external tool caused on the file system, and thus not being able to fully undo them. To illustrate, suppose that rule `r1` invokes a mail tool that sends a message to the manager of a project, and has two effects `e1` and `e2`; rule `r2` has a condition `c1`, which can be satisfied if `e1` is asserted. Assume that a developer requests a command that corresponds to r2, which can not be immediately executed because its condition c1 is not satisfied. In order to try to satisfy this condition, the RBDE might automatically invoke r1. However, it cannot be determined a priori whether invoking r1 will satisfy the condition of r2 because it might be the case that the second effect e2 is the one that will be asserted rather than e1. In this case, if there is not another rule with an effect that satisfies c1, the backward chaining fails and the rule r2 can not be executed. The mail tool, however, would have already been invoked when r1 was fired, sending a message to the manager. This can not be undone. In most other rule-based systems the effects of a failed backward chaining cycle can be reversed.

2.2 Multi-Agent RBDEs

Most existing RBDEs are single-agent in the sense that they allow only one activity to be performed at any one time on any one database. Some RBDEs require one developer to lock the whole project database, while other RBDEs allow multiple developers to access different copies of the whole database concurrently, forcing them to merge their changes manually later. Merging changes is often a cumbersome task, and is sometimes not possible if the changes conflict with each other. Single-agent RBDEs perform the activities on the project database (i.e., any single and consistent copy) in a strict serial order. They do not execute activities in the background while the developer executes a foreground activity. This is important in the software development domain because each activity might take an arbitrarily long period of time; forcing the user to wait while his command is being executed decreases his productivity. In addition, single-agent RBDEs do not allow two developers to access the same copy of an object in the database, thus preventing cooperation.

When multiple developers cooperate on a project within an RBDE, they share a common database that contains all the components of the project. Each developer starts a *session* in order to complete his or her assignment; the sessions of multiple developers may execute concurrently and the developers may concurrently request operations that access objects in the shared project database. This presents several new technical challenges, one of which is the interaction among concurrent chains of rules. This interaction can introduce *conflicts* that violate the consistency of the objects they access. A conflict occurs when the condition of a rule, r1, that has already been executed in a rule chain, c1, is negated by the effects of another rule, r2, in a concurrent rule chain, c2. All the rules that were fired after r1 in the chain c1 are invalidated because of this negation since the reason for firing them (i.e., the successful firing of r1) has now been reversed. This can happen only if two rule chains access the same objects concurrently.

There is a need to synchronize concurrent operations if they change the same object, or objects that are semantically dependent on each other. Synchronization in an RBDE involves not only the human developers but also the rules that automatically perform operations on their behalf, since those rules also access the shared database. What is missing in existing RBDEs is the ability to synchronize concurrent accesses by multiple agents to the shared database while still providing an environment that supports cooperation.

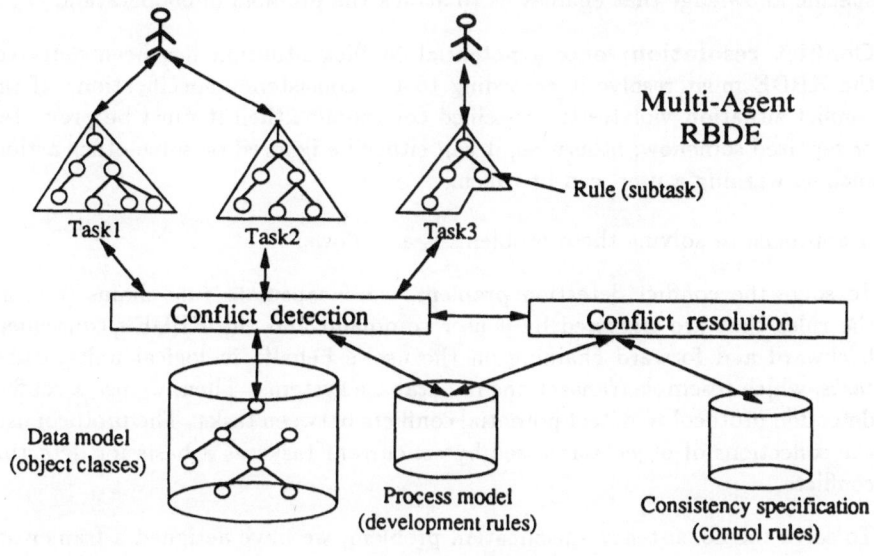

Figure 3: The Multi-Agent Problem in RBDEs

3 Overview of our Approach

The overall behavior of cooperating developers in an RBDE can be modeled as concurrent requests by users to execute commands, each of which might cause the firing of a backward rule chain and a forward rule chain; these rule chains then execute concurrently, performing operations on objects in the shared project database. The trivial solution of simply serializing chaining cycles is not satisfactory, since the activities that are automatically invoked might take an arbitrary amount of time and it would not be possible to cooperate by sharing knowledge during the chaining. What is needed is a concurrency control mechanism that allows cooperation among multiple agents. This cooperation is *synergistic* in the sense that the total effect of the cooperation among the developers cannot be achieved by isolating them, i.e., forcing them to take turns in developing common parts of the project. The developers need to exchange knowledge while their work is in progress.

We divide the synchronization problem into three subproblems, which are depicted in figure 3.

- **Conflict detection**: before firing a rule within an in-progress rule chain, the RBDE must decide whether or not the rule could cause access conflicts with any other rule that has already been fired in a concurrent chain. If it does, a potential conflict is detected and must be resolved before evaluating the rule's condition and invoking it's activity.

- **Consistency specification**: the kind of consistency that must be maintained in the database of the particular project, which might be different for different projects. This specification, together with the rules, represent the domain-specific knowledge that enables us to attack the problem of cooperation.

- **Conflict resolution**: once a potential conflict situation has been detected, the RBDE must resolve it according to the consistency specification. If the conflict situation violates the specified consistency, then it must be prevented or repaired somehow; otherwise, it can either be ignored or some other action, such as warning a user, can be taken.

Our approach to solving these problems is as follows:

1. To solve the conflict detection problem, we encapsulate rule chains (i.e., all the rules that are triggered by a user command and the RBDE's consequent backward and forward chaining on the user's behalf) in logical units, called *tasks*, which resemble transactions in database systems. Then, we use a conflict detection protocol to detect potential conflicts between tasks. The protocol uses the collections of objects accessed by concurrent tasks as a basis for detecting conflicts.

2. To solve the consistency specification problem, we have designed a framework in which it is possible to: (1) define conflict situations using our concept of troupes of rules (defined shortly); and (2) prescribe how the conflict situation should be resolved.

3. To resolve a detected conflict, we have developed a synchronization mechanism that uses the consistency framework to achieve a reasonable compromise between two conflicting goals:

   (a) Maximize concurrent access by multiple agents to the shared project database, and thus maximize the number of operations that can proceed concurrently. This has the effect of decreasing the environment's response time to user commands, and thus improves the overall productivity of the team of cooperating developers.

   (b) Maintain the project database in a consistent state as specified in the consistency framework, thus eliminating the time wasted on repairing inconsistent data manually, and thereby facilitating the successful completion of the software project.

4   Detecting Concurrency Conflicts

We explain the conflict detection problem by means of an example. Suppose that Bob and Mary want to test module ModA by running a test suite, S. ModA consists of two procedures, p1 and p2. When Bob and Mary request commands concurrently, Bob's command might trigger a chain of rules, one or more of which might conflict with some of the rules in the in-progress chain that Mary's command has triggered.

Suppose that Bob requests a command `test modA` (corresponding to the test rule shown in figure 4) at time `t1`, which triggers the forward chaining cycle shown in figure 5. Mary requests a command `test p1` (corresponding to the second test rule

```
test [?mod : MODULE; ?test : TEST]:

    # We can test a module only after all of its component
    # procedures have been tested.  'Run' is the name of the
    # tool that executes the test bound to the variable
    # ?test on the module bound to ?mod. If the module
    # passes the test, set its test-status attribute to
    # 'tested'; otherwise, to 'failed'.

    (forall PROCEDURE ?p suchthat (member [?mod.procs ?p])
    : (?p.test-status = tested))
      { TESTER run ?test ?mod }
    (?mod.test-status = tested);
    (?mod.test-status = failed);

test [?proc: PROCEDURE; ?test : TEST]:

    # A procedure can be tested only if it is available;
    # i.e., it is not reserved for editing by any user.

    : (?proc.availability = available)
      { TESTER run ?test ?proc }
    (?proc.test-status = tested);
    (?proc.test-status = failed);

edit [?proc : PROCEDURE; ?user : USER]:

    # We can edit a procedure only if it has been reserved by
    # the same user who initiated the edit rule.

    : (and (?proc.availability = reserved)
           (?proc.reserver = ?user))
      { EDITOR edit ?proc }
    (?proc.status = changed);

reserve [?obj : OBJECT; ?user : USER]:

    # A user can reserve an object if it is available in the
    # sense that no other user has reserved it.

    : (?obj.availability = available)
      { RCS reserve ?obj ?user }
    (and (?obj.availability = reserved)
         (?obj.reserver = ?user));
```

Figure 4: Example Rules Based on Marvel Notation

232

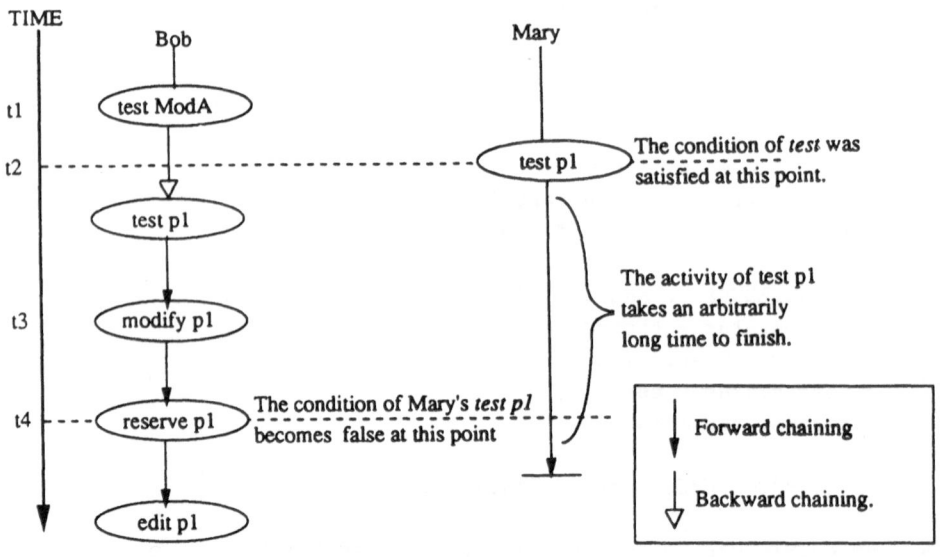

TIME

t1

t2   The condition of *test* was satisfied at this point.

The activity of test p1 takes an arbitrarily long time to finish.

t3

t4   The condition of Mary's *test p1* becomes false at this point

Forward chaining

Backward chaining.

Figure 5: Example of the Conflict Detection Problem

in figure 4) at time t2. The condition of the rule is satisfied at that time, causing the activity of the rule to be invoked. Meanwhile, Bob discovers that p1 has a bug so he issues the command `modify p1` at time t3, which triggers a backward chain to `reserve p1` before calling the editor on p1. The sequence of activities depicted in figure 5 causes a conflict because the effects of the **reserve** rule in Bob's chain will negate the condition of Mary's **test** rule, already in-progress. This causes Mary's test to be invalid since the procedure she is testing is about to be modified by Bob.

To detect conflicts similar to the one presented above, each chaining cycle triggered in response to a developer's command is encapsulated in a *task*. Each rule in the task is a *subtask* of the task representing the whole chain. A potential conflict between concurrent tasks occurs when the firing of a rule (subtask) within one of the tasks violates the serializable execution of the in-progress tasks. An execution is said to be serializable if an equivalent serial execution can be found. This concept of serializability is the correctness criterion used to maintain consistency in database systems.

The conflict detection mechanism detects a violation of serializability by using a *nested incremental locking* (NIL) protocol based on the standard two-phase locking (2PL) protocol used in most traditional DBMSs [EGLT76]. 2PL divides each transaction into two phases, a growing phase, in which locks on objects are acquired, and a shrinking phase, in which locks are released. The shrinking phase begins with the first release of a lock, and during that phase the transaction can not acquire any new locks or reacquire old locks that have been released. 2PL ensures that only serializable schedules of transactions are allowed.

Like 2PL, NIL associates two locks with every object in the database, a read lock and a write lock. These locks are internal to the conflict detection mechanism and invisible to developers and the rest of the system. When initiating a rule and before evaluating the condition of the rule, read locks must be acquired by the task containing the rule on all the objects accessed in the condition, and write locks on all the objects accessed in its effects (these are added to the set of locks previously acquired, hence the protocol is *incremental*). A conflict is detected when a rule attempts to set a read or write lock when another rule already holds a write lock on the same object; multiple rules can simultaneously hold the read lock in any case, but multiple rules can simultaneously hold the write lock only if this is permitted by the conflict resolution mechanism, described later.

The objects accessed by the condition of a rule are determined by the logical clause of the condition. This clause describes a set of objects that possess a certain property. An example of such a clause is the set of all objects that are both instances of the PROCEDURE class and contained in module ModA. This clause is used in the test rule of figure 4. The effects of a rule only write the values of the attributes of objects passed to the rule as actual parameters.

Like 2PL, NIL requires that all tasks be *well-formed* in order to test for serializability: (1) they do not relock objects that have been locked earlier in the task, and (2) they are divided into a growing phase, in which locks are only acquired and a shrinking phase, in which locks are only released. During the shrinking phase, a task is prohibited from acquiring locks. This is done by acquiring locks as the rule chain grows, and not releasing any locks until the chain terminates.

If a rule attempts to acquire a lock that has already been acquired by a rule that is a subtask of another task, this is a *conflict*. The rule does not wait for a lock when there is a conflict, as might be done in a conventional database management system. Instead, the conflict resolution mechanism is invoked. Thus there is no possibility of deadlock, where one task would be waiting for another task to release a lock while this other task is waiting for the first task to release another lock.

In the example of figure 5, when Bob requests the test ModA command, the RBDE initiates a task T_{Bob} and fires the corresponding test rule as a subtask. Before the activity of the rule is invoked, T_{Bob} acquires a read lock on the test suite S and on all the procedures contained in ModA (i.e., p1 and p2) and a write lock on the object representing ModA. Similarly, when Mary requests the command test p1, T_{Mary} acquires a read lock on p1. Now when Bob's task fires modify p1, it tries to acquire a write lock on p1, but discovers that p1 has already been locked by T_{Mary} in an incompatible mode, thus causing a conflict.

Once detected, conflicts are resolved by consulting the conflict resolution mechanism, which uses the consistency specification of the particular project to decide how to resolve the conflict. In the example, it might be allowable for Bob and Mary to edit and test p1 at the same time because they are cooperating together closely, and Mary knows that she is testing a feature of p1 that Bob's modification will not change. Her test would still be semantically valid in this case, but the special knowledge is needed for the RBDE to determine this.

```
COMMUTATIVITY-TROUPE:
    r1, r2, r3, r4;
    r1, r5, r6;
    . . .
```

Figure 6: Example of a Troupe of Rules

5   Conflict Resolution

Unlike in traditional database management, permitting non-serializable access to objects does not automatically mean that the consistency of the database will be violated, as demonstrated by the previous example. The conflict detection mechanism presented above detects all *potential* conflicts (i.e., non-serializable access to objects) and leaves it to the conflict resolution mechanism to consult the specific consistency requirements of the project and decide if any of them are actually violated by the detected conflict.

5.1   Troupes of Rules for Consistency Specification

In the domain of software development, non-serializable access to data and cooperation between concurrent tasks are required in many cases. The situations in which such non-serializable access violates the consistency of the project depends on the database operations implied by the rules in the particular project. The rules for different projects are different and thus the RBDE must be provided with knowledge about allowable interactions between rules in a specific project. The problem is finding a framework for specifying which interactions between concurrent tasks are allowable (i.e., do not violate consistency). The framework should specify the *granularity* at which different rules and rule chains can be interleaved. This specification framework can then be used by the conflict resolution algorithm to provide maximum concurrency while maintaining consistency.

We define project-specific consistency in terms of *control rules* that operate on the process model rule base. Each control rule has a condition that describes a conflict situation, and a repair that prescribes how to resolve the specific conflict. The conflict situation is described using the concept of *troupes* of rules. Troupes define sets of rules that share a particular semantic property. These sets are specified in advance (by the administrator who writes the rules describing the development process of the project), along with the data model and the process model. Each set is considered an instance of the troupe in which it is defined.

Troupes are like classes in that they prescribe methods, or actually one specific method, in the form of a control rule. It might be interesting to further extend the concept of class to troupes by introducing attributes of troupes and inheritance among troupes, but here we consider only troupes that define maximal sets of rules sharing a mutual property. For example, the COMMUTATIVITY-TROUPE in figure 6 defines several sets of rules that can all commute with each other (the knowledge as to which rules commute is provided by the administrator). In other words, it does not matter in

```
(ControlRule lock_conflict
  IF  (and (in-progress TASK ?t1 USER ?u1)
           (in-progress TASK ?t2 USER ?u2)
           (has-lock ?t1 ?obj ?lock_mode_1)
           (request-lock ?t2 ?obj ?lock_mode_2)
           (not-compatible ?lock_mode_1 ?lock_mode_2))
  THEN
      (if (and (exists USER_GROUP ?g)
               (contains ?g ?u1)
               (contains ?g ?u2))
       then
          (grant-lock ?t2 ?obj ?lock_mode_2
           ''Warning: user ?u1 also has ?obj locked'')
       else
          (reject-lock ?t2 ?obj
           ''Conflict: user ?u1 has ?obj locked''))

  COMMENT: ''Two users who are members of the same developer team
            (where USER_GROUP is a collection of objects, each of
            which represents a user) can share an object, while other
            users who are not members of the same team will not be
            granted permission to lock the object.'')

(ControlRule test_conflict
  IF  (and (in-progress RULE ?r1 USER ?u1 TASK ?t1)
           (start RULE ?r2 USER ?u2 TASK ?t2)
           (conflict ?r1 ?r2))
  THEN
      (if (exists COMMUTATIVITY-TROUPE ?t such_that
                  (and (member ?r1 ?t)
                       (member ?r2 ?t)))
       then (ignore-conflict ?r1 ?r2)
       else (abort ?r2))

  COMMENT: ''If the activity of the rule whose initiation caused the
            detection of conflict can commute with the in-progress
            rule with which it conflicted, then ignore the potential
            conflict since execution order does not matter.
            Otherwise, abort the later rule.'')
```

Figure 7: Examples of Consistency Control Rules

which order we run the rules that are members of an instance of this troupe; the results will be the same. Troupes provide semantic knowledge that can be used by control rules to resolve conflicts. Figure 7 gives two control rules. The notation in the figure is not the actual syntax of any particular RBDE language but is intended to demonstrate the idea of project-specific consistency constraints.

5.2 Consistency-Based Conflict Resolution

The conflict resolution mechanism uses the control rule base to decide what to do with a potential conflict passed to it by the conflict detection mechanism. For example, the conflict discovered in the example of figure 5 matches the IF part of the lock-conflict control rule of figure 7. In this case, the conflict resolution mechanism would check whether Mary and Bob are members of the same user group, whose members cooperate closely, and if they are, it will ignore the conflict; otherwise, the mechanism would reject Mary's request to test p1. The second control rule in figure 7 can be used to resolve a conflict that occurs between a rule just being initiated by a user and the in-progress rule in another task initiated by another user. The conflict situation of the control rule depicts this situation, while the repair part checks if the two rules belong to any instance of the COMMUTATIVITY-TROUPE, i.e., if the order of execution of the rules does not affect the results of the tasks.

If the conflict detection protocol detects a potential conflict that does not match any control rule, the RBDE will not allow the interaction that caused the conflict. Thus, in the absence of control rules, the RBDE enforces serializability as in traditional database systems. The control rules are considered additional information that is used to allow more concurrency than what serializability-based protocols allow.

6   Conclusions

We presented an approach to solving the problem of synchronizing multiple agents in rule-based development environments (RBDEs). We considered the interactions among multiple software developers concurrently accessing a common database in order to complete a development task. The development activities carried out by these developers are modeled as rules that read and write the database. The database represents the working memory of the RBDE. RBDEs apply forward and backward chaining on the rules to provide automated assistance to software developers.

We explained how concurrent access to the database by the rule chains initiated by user commands might cause conflicts. The primary challenge was to find a mechanism that supports both synchronization to ensure consistency and cooperation to permit concerted efforts. We defined the task, or rule chain, as the basic unit of concurrency control. We detect potential conflicts between concurrent tasks using a general purpose protocol, but then exploit domain-specific knowledge to determine which of these potential conflicts violate the consistency of the shared project database. Potential conflicts that do not violate consistency permit cooperation among the tasks.

Acknowledgments

Barghouti is supported in part by the Center for Telecommunications Research. Kaiser is supported by National Science Foundation grants CCR-9000930, CDA-8920080, and CCR-8858029, by grants from AT&T, BNR, Citicorp, DEC, IBM, Siemens, Sun and Xerox, by the Center for Advanced Technology and by the Center for Telecommunications Research.

We would like to thank Michael Sokolsky, who collaborated with us on the design and implementation of the single-user version of MARVEL. We would also like to thank Israel Ben-Shaul and George Heineman, who are working with us on designing and implementing the multi-user version of MARVEL. The single-user MARVEL version 2.6 is available for licensing to educational institutions and industrial sponsors; contact Israel Ben-Shaul, israel@cs.columbia.edu, 212-854-2930 for information.

References

[BK91]   N. S. Barghouti and G. E. Kaiser. Concurrency control in advanced database applications. *ACM Computing Surveys*, 1991. To appear. Also available as Columbia University Department of Computer Science Technical Report number CUCS-425-89, May 1990.

[CLF88]   University of Southern California, Information Sciences Institute, Marina del Rey CA. *CLF Manual*, January 1988.

[EGLT76]   K. Eswaran, J. Gray, R. Lorie, and I. Traiger. The notions of consistency and predicate locks in a database system. *Communications of the ACM*, 19(11):624–632, November 1976.

[Gup86]   A. Gupta. *Parallelism in Production Systems*. PhD thesis, Carnegie Mellon University, Department of Computer Science, March 1986. Technical Report CMU-CS-86-122.

[HL88]   K. E. Huff and V. R. Lesser. A plan-based intelligent assistant that supports the software development process. In *ACM SIGSOFT/SIGPLAN Software Engineering Symposium on Practical Software Development Environments*, pages 97–106, Boston, MA, November 1988. ACM Press. Special issue of *SIGPLAN Notices*, 24(2), February 1989.

[KBFS88]   G. E. Kaiser, N. S. Barghouti, P. H. Feiler, and R. W. Schwanke. Database support for knowledge-based engineering environments. *IEEE Expert*, 3(2):18–32, Summer 1988.

[KBS90]   G. E. Kaiser, N. S. Barghouti, and M. H. Sokolsky. Preliminary experience with process modeling in the marvel software development environment kernel. In *23rd Annual Hawaii International Conference on System Sciences*, volume II, pages 131–140, Kona HI, January 1990.

[KFP88]   G. E. Kaiser, P. H. Feiler, and S. S. Popovich. Intelligent assistance for software development and maintenance. *IEEE Software*, 5(3):40–49, May 1988.

[MR88]   N. H. Minsky and D. Rozenshtein. A software development environment for law-governed systems. In *ACM SIGSOFT/SIGPLAN Software Engineering Symposium on Practical Software Development Environments*, pages 65–75, Boston MA, November 1988. ACM Press. Special issue of *SIGPLAN Notices*, 24(2), February 1989.

[Nii86]   H. P. Nii. Blackboard systems. *AI Magazine*, 7(2 and 3), 1986.

[Per89]   D. Perry, editor. *5th International Software Process Workshop*, Kennebunkport ME, October 1989. ACM Press.

DISCUSSION

Presenter: Naser Barghouti.

Q. (S. Chakravarthy, University of Florida) : My question is, in conventional databases the granularity of conflict checks are predefined. Do you have any notion of extending that idea?

A. (N. Barghouti) : We're using a notion of locks that is similar to what the Orion system at MCC uses, which is composite object locks. It is based on a notion that has been developed before for conventional databases called granularity locking. In composite object locking, locking a sub-object causes the containing object to be locked in a certain mode which identifies that only a part of the object is locked but not the whole object. The granularity of checking for conflicts is the rule. The read set and the write set of a rule are known before we start executing the rule. If the read set or the write set of one rule overlaps with the write set of another rule, a conflict is detected at that level of granularity. Once a rule starts executing it completes and then we can only detect a conflict after it's done.

Q. (S. Kirn, University of Hagen) : I have two questions. The first is what are the lock modes you use. And the second thing is have you considered things like deadlock detection?

A. (N. Barghouti) : Okay, let me answer the second question first. No we haven't considered deadlock detection. The reason basically is, we could not afford to spend time on solving the problem of deadlock detection. We only have one staff associate working with me, so it's a two-person project. We talked about deadlock detection and then I attended the Sigmod conference last summer where Phil Bernstein, who is one of the big guys in databases, said that deadlock occurs in one per cent of accesses so it isn't really a major problem in practice. That was a comfortable remark for me, so we decided to ignore conflict detection.

The other question was about lock modes. So far we have been thinking of using the lock modes developed for the ObServer system at Brown university. We're thinking of having 16 lock modes. They're for composite objects and they range from shared locks to more extreme exclusive locks and everything in between. A lock that says you can write an object but not move it, you can move it but not delete it, you know, there are many kinds of locks. So we've identified 16 different, primitive kinds of locks that we need in order to do this. It's feasible that we might need less actually.

Q. (E. Dubois, FUNDP) : Is it possible in your system to attach some visibility to each agent with respect to the contents of the objects?

A. (N. Barghouti) : That's the part which is at the higher level. I talked about user sessions, but I didn't really say what those were. I'm not using the word "session" in the sense of the English word. I use it to mean a unit of work, that lasts maybe for days. This unit is a collection of activities that a user executes in order to achieve a task, such as debugging a module. That's what I mean by a "session". To each session, I attach activities that must be performed. The RBDE ensures that before the session ends you had to have done all these activities. It is like a checklist. I call them "obligations", and these obligations get created when rules are fired so they're dynamic obligations. So we identified those kinds of units for users. I use sessions as units of visibility, so it is possible for one user to work on objects during his session without having anybody else access these objects for the duration of the session.

Q. (E. Dubois) : Is it possible to develop your rules to express some preconditions on the types of agents who can trigger the rules?

A. (N. Barghouti) : We can express that a session operates in a domain, domain meaning a group of objects, a group of users and certain semantic knowledge that's available to it. So different sessions can be in different domains and there is domain specific knowledge. We can then restrict certain operation to certain domains through the control rules. So if you have a conflict, you can resolve it in one way (perhaps allow it) if it is caused by two users within the same domain, and resolve it in a different way (for example, disallow it) is it is caused by two users in two different domain. Domains can thus be used in the control rules to allow certain people to cooperate.

Q. (W. Chu, UCLA) : Do you allow your system to have inconsistent knowledge of data?

A. (N. Barghouti) : First of all we assume that all the rule sets are consistent. We don't do anything to detect logical conflicts in the definitions of rules. We are assuming at some point somebody is going to have a brilliant system that verifies the consistency of rule sets. That's one part of knowledge. For the other part of knowledge, the project components. Consistency is whatever the project administrator defines it to be in the rules and the control rules. If the control rules and the rules do not define something as inconsistency, the RBDE does not consider it inconsistent. In other words we do not have a global, predefined notion of what consistency is. We know that consistency is whatever the administrator has identified in the rules and control rules. Our protocols detect violations of this consistency. We don't have any predetermined notion of inconsistency.

The MCS multi-agent testbed: developments and experiments

James Doran
Horacio Carvajal
Y J Choo
Yueling Li

Department of Computer Science
University of Essex
Colchester CO4 3SQ
E-mail doraj@uk.ac.essex

ABSTRACT

This paper describes the MCS multiple agent software testbed which has been developed as a research tool in the University of Essex, Department of Computer Science. Recent enhancements to the testbed are noted, and experiments using it are briefly reported and discussed. The experiments particularly concern the relationship between 'situated' action and action resulting from 'predictive' or 'strategic' planning in multi-agent communities, and the impact of changing the content of agents' social models on their behaviour and collective effectiveness. The experiments are partly oriented to the study of human social systems in prehistory.

1. Introduction

A feature of Distributed AI research over the past few years has been the development of software testbeds designed to support complex experiments with multiple agents systems (Bond and Gasser, 1988). MCS is such a testbed which has been developed at the University of Essex, and which has distinctive features, most notably the use of a complex planner as an inference engine. The experimental use of MCS has been partly oriented to the study of human social systems.

In this short paper we shall (1) describe the more important features of the testbed, (2) outline some of the experiments using it, and (3) discuss intended future work and associated research issues. References will be given to more detailed descriptions of the core component of the MCS testbed (the IPEM planner) and to more detailed reports of the experimental work.

2. The MCS Testbed

The MCS testbed (Multiple-agent Core System) has been developed from the TEAMWORK2 system (Doran, 1989) and is relatively simple apart from its inference engine. In its design it is general rather than targeted at any particular application domain.

MCS differs significantly from other DAI testbeds such as MACE (Gasser, Braganza and Herman, 1987) and MAGES (Bouron, Ferber and Samuel, 1990) by being built around a 'state-of-the art' non-linear hierarchical planner, IPEM (Ambros-Ingerson and Steel, 1988), which integrates plan generation, plan execution and plan monitoring. This means that MCS is particularly suited to experimentation with the relationship between predictive planning and 'situated action' in multiple-agent communities. MCS is experimental rather than 'logicist' in its design unlike, for example, RATMAN (Burckert and Muller, 1990).

MCS is coded in Prolog (CProlog, NIP and Quintus) and runs in UNIX on Sun Workstations. It uses simulated concurrency rather than true multiple processing.

MCS will now be described from the inside outwards.

2.1. The IPEM Planner

The MCS testbed is built around the IPEM planner which is named for Integrated Planning, Execution and Monitoring. IPEM provides a simple and well-defined framework within which to integrate these processes.

Representation integration is achieved by consistently incorporating execution and monitoring information into a typical non-linear partial plan representation, using the STRIPS action representation, that is, preconditions and effects. The closed world assumption is not made. An important enhancement to the representation of an action is made in IPEM. There is now associated with an action representation an execution procedure for use when the action is actually to be executed (rather than manipulated as part of planning)

Control integration is achieved by, in effect, using a production system architecture. The partial plan (ie the plan being worked upon) resides in the working memory, and the production rules, whose antecedents and consequents are referred to as 'flaws' and 'fixes' respectively, embody the conditions under which particular partial plan transformations may be applied. These transformations include such things as the insertion of a new operator instance and the elaboration of an existing operator instance into greater detail as part of hierarchical planning. Such transformations are appropriately referred to as 'meta-actions'. Conflict resolution is achieved by the use of a scheduler which embodies the current problem-solving strategy.

The flaw-fix combinations which (1) select and execute a 'ready to go' domain action represented in the partial plan by an instantiated operator whose preconditions are currently satisfied, and (2) select and execute partial plan modification meta-actions which operate upon the plan itself, have been designed to be independently applicable. So the framework supports heuristic interleaving of planning and execution of plans in a simple and straightforward way.

The planner backtracks chronologically over all flaw-fix operations, apart from actual domain action execution.

An important range of control specification aids are provided which the experimenter may employ when specifying operators -- ie action representations, (in fact called 'schemas' within IPEM). These include priority orderings on preconditions, 'hold' preconditions, 'covered' (ie secondary) effects, and constraints which regulate operator expansions.

In sum, the most important features of IPEM are:

-(Extended) STRIPS style representation of actions
-non-linear planning
-hierarchical planning
-chronological backtracking
-integrated plan generation, execution and repair
-a range of control specification aids

2.2. MCS Agent Architecture

Each agent in the MCS testbed has independent access to the planner and has a set of plans and a set of goals currently being worked upon.

Each agent also has its own (Prolog -- but see later, section 3.2.1) database of 'beliefs'. We use the term 'belief' rather than 'knowledge' because an agent may well hold beliefs that are not the case and that are inconsistent with the beliefs of other agents. An agent also has available a set of operators comprising action representations in the STRIPS formalism together with associated action execution procedures as explained in section 2.1.

Finally, with each agent is associated demons which may be specific to the agent and which fire whenever their conditions match against beliefs in the agent's database (and immediately the matching is possible). The execution part of a demon may be any action or meta- action available to the agent. A system demon, common to all agents, sets goals for the planner. Demons provide agents with an important form of reactivity in addition to that inherent in the design of the planner.

There is a very simple interface between an agent and the remainder of the MCS agent community. Incoming information (ie messages from other agents, including messages from any environment agents which therefore notionally correspond to sensory input) appears as beliefs in the data base. The execution of domain actions by the planner sends messages out across the interface to other agents. A message to an environment agent corresponds to an action upon the environment (see section 2.3.1).

2.3. MCS Multiple Agent Community

MCS provides the facility to specify any number of agents, but experimental run times quickly become very large for more than, say, six agents. Concurrency is simulated by giving each agent in turn a 'flaw-fix' cycle, corresponding to the execution of a single rule in the planner's production system architecture.

As indicated in the preceding section, communication between agents is achieved by the execution by agents of actions (planned or reactive) whose execution procedures call inter-agent interface primitives -- which, in effect, write to the target agent's belief base. In particular, one agent may write a message to another's belief base which triggers the recipient agent's (system) goal-setting demon to set a particular goal to the recipient. Alternatively, communication may be via one or more agents treated as environment agents (see section 2.3.1).

MCS provides no features at this level by which a particular form of organisation (eg a ring, or a hierarchy) may be imposed upon the agent community. The assumption is that all such requirements are met by suitably structuring the agents' belief and operator sets.

2.3.1. Environment Agents in MCS

In MCS an agent regarded as an 'environment' agent is normally to be thought of as a simulation of a physical environment (eg of a warehouse, say, in which the non-environment agents, regarded as autonomous vehicles, are existing). As such it will it will do no planning, and its processing will be entirely a matter of demon executions. However, in principle an environment agent may also be set up as an interface to the real external world. No special facilities are provided for the creation of environment agents.

2.4. MCS User Facilities

The basic facilities provided for the MCS user are as follows:

- initial specification of agents and their contents (operators, beliefs, goals, demons). The experimenter must prepare an agent community specification file using a standard layout and syntax.

- monitoring at runtime. The user may interrupt the testbed, and, during the break, inspect the contents of all agents using a range of specially provided commands. A log file of all events is also continuously generated and may be used for monitoring.

- interactive updating of agents at runtime. Just as the experimenter may interrupt the system for monitoring purposes, so also the actual contents of agents (eg their beliefs and goals) may also be changed by the experimenter part way through an experimental run.

Note that the experimenter may create and destroy agents at runtime (as indeed may agents themselves).

2.4.1. Graphical Interface

A graphical interface has recently been added to the basic MCS system (Choo, 1990) providing window/menu/mouse driven interaction with and monitoring of the running testbed. It enables an experimenter to view the set of agents and the passage of messages between them, to vary the speed of execution of the system, and to intervene at any time to inspect and modify agents' beliefs, plans, goals and demons and also to inspect the contents of messages passing between them.

3. Experimentation

MCS has been and is being used to support a variety of experimental work. Such work typically involves loading into the testbed a particular community of agents (including, of course, their associated operators and initial beliefs), and observing their collective behaviour as experimental parameters are varied. By a suitable choice of operators and beliefs, and especially of the execution procedures associated with operators, agents may be set up to communicate in a particular pattern and to form a particular type of organisation. Specific experimental studies that have used, or are about to use, MCS are:

--a small scale implementation of a distributed sensing network for monitoring vehicle movements, based on that designed and studied by the DAI research group at the University of Massachusetts (Sim S K, 1988)

--a study of plan delegation in a multi-agent environment (using a variant of MCS called DePlan) focusing on requests as partially elaborated plans (Hopkins, 1989).

--a study of different types of reactive and planned action in a distributed problem solving hierarchy required to perform an (abstract) distributed production task (Li, forthcoming).

--the use of an extension to MCS, called MCS/SOMS, to study behaviour and problem solving performance in multiple agent distributed problem solving systems when the agents employ various types of social model (Carvajal, 1990).

--the use of MCS (and possibly MCS/SOMS) to support modelling of the processes of emergence of social complexity in the European Upper Palaeolithic period (the EOS project).

The last three of these experimental studies will now be described in a little more detail.

3.1. Distributed Problem Solving by an Agent Hierarchy

3.1.1. A 'Toy' Production and Distribution Problem

Motivated by anthropological studies of human exchange and production systems, Doran and Corcoran (1986) defined a 'toy' problem for a distributed set of agents. The essence of this 'toy' problem is as follows:

> There is a (spatial) distribution of agents over an area. Each agent has the ability to detect items in its locality and to move them. Agent localities overlap. Neighbouring agents can communicate.

> Items called 'resources' occur repeatedly but irregularly and in some degree unpredictably over the area. There are (recursively applicable) combination rules by which agents may combine resources (and products) into 'higher-level' products, some of which are consumable by agents. In general these rules will not initially all be available to all (or even to any) agents.

> The problem is to so design the agents (eg within the MCS framework) that they locate, transport and combine resources so that higher-level consumable products are generated, and so that these products are then distributed and consumed.

> It may or may not be a requirement that agents enforce a notion of 'fair exchange'.

There are, of course, many possible detailed variants of this 'toy' problem. They have in common that the agents must (be designed to) cooperate if they are all to consume successfully and the more they cooperate, the more they will consume.

3.1.2. Decision Hierarchies to solve the 'Toy' Problem

One of us (Y L) is addressing the following question, strictly within the framework of MCS. Given a FIXED set of agents in a FIXED communication hierarchy, what alternative agents' 'contents' (within the broad limits set by MCS) allow the distributed production and distribution task to be performed and in precisely what circumstances is each appropriate?

Three alternatives are immediately suggested by human systems. They are: (1) purely reactive or 'reflex' behaviour occurring only at the lowest level of the communication hierarchy, (2) totally centralised planning where all information is passed to the agent at the 'summit' of the hierarchy who plans for and delegates action to all other agents, and (3) planning at all levels in the hierarchy, but more abstracted from minor detail the higher in the hierarchy it occurs.

All three of these alternatives have been implemented and run in MCS. They do not, however, exhaust the range of possibilities. For full details see Li (forthcoming).

3.1.3. Discussion

A key question arising from this work is just when should purely reactive behaviour be designed into an agent, and when must more complex predictive planning be inserted? It is not easy to identify precisely when a purely reactive solution is no longer sufficient. Another important issue is how to derive suitable levels of abstraction (for use in solution 3 above) from the details of the problem specification.

The importance of this study from the anthropological perspective is that it makes more precise and detailed the observation that one external view of a decision hierarchy may correspond to a variety of different internal information and process contents.

3.2. Agents' Social Models and their Impact

3.2.1. MCS/SOMS

One of us (H.C.) has recently enhanced MCS (to form MCS/SOMS) by structuring each agent's belief base as a dynamic frame system. The frame system implemented allows the usual slot assignment and access operations, implements property inheritance, and makes the usual distinction between generic and instance frames. With slots are associated defaults, and constraints on the nature and number of possible slot fillers. The primary motivation in implementing this system was to study the properties and behavioural impact of agents' social models.

3.2.2. Agents' 'Social' Models

By an agent's 'social model' is here meant its (typically dynamic) representations of other agents and the groupings and organisations which they form or are believed (by the agent) to form. An agent's social model is therefore its representation of the social environment of which it itself may be a part (compare the equivalent structure in the MACE testbed, Gasser et. al. 1987). Social models may be partial or erroneous. They play a pivotal role in action choice (whether 'reactive' action or action in consequence of predictive planning) and in inter-agent communication. Limitations or errors potentially have major behavioural implications.

In MCS/SOMS an agent possesses generic frames for agents, groups, roles and organisations, and may therefore represent information about one or more instances of any of these. This may, of course, include representation of itself, and of any groups or organisations of which it may be a part. Table 1 lists the slots associated with frame instances of these four different types, and will give the reader an indication of the information held and the simple types of group and organisation at issue.

3.2.3. The Experiments

Within the context of the 'toy' production and distribution problem defined earlier (section 3.1.1), MCS/SOMS has been used to study the impact of cognitive limitation and cognitive economy (compare 'bounded rationality') in agents' social models on the extent to which and the speed with which the distributed task is performed.

It is assumed (and the agent community set up accordingly in MCS) that in the interests of cognitive economy the agents' social models contain (consistent) representations of non-existent groupings in the agent community. The agents exist objectively (ie from the point of view of an environment agent) but NOT the groups, which exist ONLY in the agents' social models. Memory is saved by individual agents (this is the cognitive economy made), because they 'remember' the supposed groups and their properties, instead of individual agents. The further experimental assumption is made that perceived group boundaries act as barriers in the production and distribution process in the following way. An agent will try to meet a simple request from (what it believes to be) a fellow member of a group, but will require a 'fair' exchange for a request coming from an 'outsider' -- and this will quite possibly impede meeting the request. Thus the impact of cognitive economy is linked via a kind of 'group loyalty' to the extent to which the distributed task will be performed.

The results obtained support (with qualification) the expectation that simplified representations of external groups save cognitive effort, but that the resulting 'perceived' boundaries impede effective cooperation (for details of these and other experiments see Carvajal, 1990).

AGENTS	GROUPS
-Name	-Name
-Capabilities	-Capabilities
-Goals	-Goals
-Physical Properties	-Type
-Summarised Plans	-Special Functions
-Group Membership	-Members
-Role Filling	-Group Membership

ROLES	ORGANISATIONS
-Name	-Name
-Capabilities	-Capabilities
-Goals	-Goals
-Filler	-Special Functions
-Summarised Plans	-Members
-Organisational	-Organisational
Membership	Membership

The indicated special functions which may occur within a group or an organisation are 'leader' and 'representative'.

Table 1 -- Attributes of frame instances in an MCS/SOMS agent's social model

3.2.4. Discussion

The anthropological significance of experiments such as these should be clear. The linkage between group performance, group boundaries and the conceptualisations of group members is a critical one -- as discussed by, for example, Cohen(1985).

3.3. The EOS Project

Around 20,000 years ago in Southwestern France a relatively simple hunter-gatherer society rapidly developed enhanced social complexity and a much richer culture, including world famous cave and rockshelter art. The causes and processes of this remarkable and unprecedented social development are obscure. The EOS project (a collaboration between the Universities of Essex, Cambridge and Surrey) is using the MCS testbed to examine a specific process model for the emergence of human social complexity in the Upper Palaeolithic of Southwestern France put forward by Paul Mellars of Cambridge University (Mellars, 1985). The primary objective of the EOS project is to give the essentials of the Mellars model a consistent computational interpretation and implementation, and to derive detailed properties by computer based experimentation. The results obtained will help interpret the evidence of the archaeological record.

The Mellars model takes into account environmental factors, increasing population concentration, more complex problem solving for subsistence, and changes in social perception and awareness. Figure 1 summarises it in diagrammatic form.

Population Concentration and Localised Environmental Resources

Crowding Stress
(more difficult distributed problem solving for subsistence)
(more structured social concepts required to avoid cognitive stress)

More Complex Social Organisation

Figure 1: An Outline of the Mellars Model of the Emergence
of Social Complexity in the Upper Palaeolithic
Period in Southwestern France.

Notice the linkage in the Mellars model between social conceptualisation and distributed problem solving. It is precisely at this point that DAI in general, and the MCS testbed and its experimental tradition in particular, seem to have something distinctive to offer.

4. Conclusions and Research Issues

The MCS testbed has many limitations. Apart from those of the IPEM planner itself (to mention just two: its inability to work with any representation of time intervals, and the absense of dependency directed backtracking), MCS is clearly overdependent upon the planner. Therefore, an important higher-level issue is the nature of the mechanism which calls and controls the incremental planning process and its 'reactive' alternatives within an agent. In MCS this mechanism is arbitrary and trivial. Demon firing always has priority over planning, whatever the tasks being performed by the demons. A less arbitrary way of choosing agent processes to run is required, perhaps related to the tasks to be performed by the agent community. Further, the concept of a demon needs to be extended to encompass more complex and long-running processes. Another and quite different deficiency of MCS is its lack of facilities for designing specifically environmental agents. Some of these issues are being addressed in the ongoing IED CADDIE project (Farhoodi et al, in preparation).

Although most of the experimental work mentioned is still in progress, certain recurring research issues have emerged. Prominent amongst them is the need to identify the circumstances in which agents being designed to cooperate in distributed problem solving should be designed to engage in predictive planning rather than purely reactive choice of actions. In the past it has often been assumed that complex predictive planning is desirable in the belief that the more powerful the technique always the better. But in practice this assumption leads to inefficiency within the system, and to a potentially unnecessary and irrelevant confrontation with some hard research problems for the system designer. Computational agents should be designed to use predictive planning only when they must and to the degree that they must. In particular we need to find ways systematically to determine at what level of abstraction predictive planning should be carried out when it is used. Reasoning about actions will almost inevitably involve some degree of abstraction compared with action execution. How much is an important design variable. We have very little understanding of the trade-offs.

Cognitive limitation and hence the need for cognitive economy seems to be a key issue. It forces us, as designers, to consider the trade off between approximation, with consequent error, and accuracy with consequent computational overload. The approximation can refer to the reuse of solutions to old problems which still seem more or less appropriate, or can refer to simplified social models as discussed earlier. We speculate that this trade off is at the heart of any precise theory of societies, whether human or purely computational.

5. Acknowledgements

The EOS project is funded by the Joint Council Initiative on Cognitive Science/HCI under grant (MRC) SPG8930879.

6. References

Ambros-Ingerson J.A. and Steel S. (1988). "Integrating Planning, Execution and Monitoring". Proceedings of the 1988 Conference of the American Association for Artificial Intelligence, St Paul, Minnesota AAAI, pp 83-88.

Bond A H, and Gasser L (1988). "Readings in Distributed Artificial Intelligence" Morgan Kaufmann: San Mateo, California.

Bouron T, Ferber J, and Samuel F (1990). "MAGES: A Multi-Agent Testbed for Heterogeneous Agents". Proceedings of Second European Workshop on "Modelizing Autonomous Agents and Multi-Agent Worlds". Saint-Quentin en Yvelines - France August 13-16, 1990. pp 219-239.

Burckert H-J and Muller J (1990). "RATMAN: Rational Agents Testbed for Multi-Agent Networks". Proceedings of Second European Workshop on "Modelizing Autonomous Agents and Multi-Agent Worlds". Saint-Quentin en Yvelines - France August 13-16, 1990. pp 241-257.

Carvajal H. (1990) "A Computational Implementation of Actors' Social Models Using the MCS/IPEM Software Testbed". M Phil dissertation, Department of Computer Science, University of Essex, Colchester, UK.

Choo Y J (1990) "Enhancements to the MCS/IPEM testbed". M Sc Computer Studies dissertation. Department of Computer Science, University of Essex.

Cohen M N (1985) "Prehistoric Hunter-Gatherers: the Meaning of Social Complexity". In "Prehistoric Hunter-Gatherers: The Emergence of Cultural Complexity" (eds. T. Douglas Price and James A Brown) Academic Press. pp 99-119.

Doran J. (1989) "Distributed Artificial Intelligence and the Modelling of Socio-Cultural Systems". In "Intelligent Systems in a Human Context" (eds Linda A Murray and John T E Richardson). Oxford University Press. pp 71-91.

Doran J. (1990) "Using Distributed AI to Study the Emergence of Human Social Organisation". Department of Computer Science Research Memorandum CSM-154, University of Essex, Colchester, UK.

Doran J and Corcoran G (1986). "A Computational Model of Production, Exchange and Trade". In "To Pattern the Past" (eds Voorrips A and Loving S) PACT Vol 11, pp 349-359.

Farhoodi F et al (In preparation) "The CADDIE Testbed". Paper to be presented to the 10th UK Planning SIG, Logica (Cambridge) Ltd, April 1991.

Gasser L, Braganza C and Herman N (1987) "MACE: a Flexible Testbed for Distributed AI Research". In "Distributed Artificial Intelligence" (ed M N Huhns) Pitman and Morgan Kaufmann: London. pp 119-152.

Hopkins C. (1989) "Meta-Level Planning for Multi-Agent Cooperation". Proceedings of AISB 89 Conference, Pitman & Morgan-Kaufmann, pp185-189.

Li Y. (forthcoming) M Sc dissertation. Department of Computer Science, University of Essex, Colchester, UK.

Mellars P.A. (1985) "The Ecological Basis of Social Complexity in the Upper Palaeolithic of Southwestern France". In "Prehistoric Hunter-Gatherers: The Emergence of Cultural Complexity" (eds. T. Douglas Price and James A Brown) Academic Press. pp 271-297.

Sim S. K. (1987) "A Partial Implementation of the Durfee, Lesser and Corkhill Model". M Sc IKBS dissertation. Department of Computer Science, University of Essex, Colchester, UK

DISCUSSION

Presenter: James Doran.

Q. (P. Bobbie, University of West Florida) : I have two questions pertaining to the exchange production system. Firstly, how do you put agents into different villages? And what is the basis of constructing your production in terms of various sources?

A. (J. Doran) : In response to your first question, the agents are the villages, the agents are not in the villages. In response to the second, we consider a set of agents, corresponding to villages or settlements, which interact to pass raw materials around, to generate new products, and to pass these products around in such a way that they all achieve their consumption needs. The particular 'toy' problems that we discuss in the paper, involving particular groupings of villages, were selected to help examine different possible types of behaviour. They were not motivated by any specific anthropological example, but do have regard to what we know about prehistoric human exchange systems.

Q. (P. Bobbie) : Is it feasible to put agents into some kind of clusters, perhaps intra-cluster problem solving?

A. (J. Doran) : Well, as I mentioned, there are facilities within MCS/SOMS to set up agents which build their own representations of other agents, groups and organisations and behave accordingly. But groups or clusters do not exist as agents in their own right.

Q. (P. Bobbie) : Presumably, if all the agents agreed about the existence of a group ....?

A. (J. Doran) : ....then effectively the group is there, because they will all behave accordingly.

For example, if a message is sent from one member of one group to the 'representative' of another group then that representative has to consult the other members of the group before making a reply. The kind of thing that happens is that the representative broadcasts a message to other members of its group. It will know the other members of the group, but the requesting group will not. The message will, effectively, say: "We have received a request for x. Does anybody think we ought to accept x? If so, what should we ask in return because this is not a request from one of us, it's one of them?" It's getting at the 'us and them' thing. We have run simple versions of this.

Q. (N. Mitchison, ISPRA) : It would seem to me here that one of the very interesting questions I'm left with overall is that this is in a context where agents do agree within groups. They will know to agree because they keep on getting messages and then pass them on and that makes them start to feel that they are part of a group. There's a machine learning question implied.

A. (J. Doran) : You are right and this is one of the things we are looking at.

Q. (M. Boman, Stockholm University, Sweden) : When you described your negotiation mechanism you said that it is usually the case that the other agents follow in line once they have agreed on one plan. Could you elaborate on how this is obtained in your simulation. For example, between villages, isn't it normal that in a negotiation, one village would like to have something in return for following in line.

A. (J. Doran): There are two contexts in which we mention negotiation.

First, when a request comes through to a particular group of villages then the receiver of the request will have to obtain information from the other members of its group regarding what to do about it. This is simply a matter of the request recipient asking the others,"Can we produce this? If so, what do you need in return that the requesting group, we believe, has got?". If the requesting group turns out not to be willing and able to provide whatever is required in exchange, then the exchange will not go through.

The other place where negotiation arises is in the context of the EOS project and is potentially much more complicated. Here there are a number of agents who are each trying to reach their own goals and they are concurrently trying to do so by formulating multiple agent plans on the basis of their knowledge of one another. So then there will have to be negotiation about which of the plans is the one, to be adopted, involving consideration of potential payoffs by the various agents. To make such a process converge sensibly looks non-trivial. We have not done it yet.

Interactions in Data/Knowledge Bases

Epistemic Logic
as a Framework for
Federated Information Systems[1]

Magnus Boman
Paul Johannesson

SYSLAB/DECODE
Department of Computer and Systems Sciences
The Royal Institute of Technology and
Stockholm University
Electrum 230
S-164 40 KISTA SWEDEN
Phone: (+46 8) 161678
E-mail: mab@dsv.su.se

ABSTRACT:

A set of axiomatic modal propositional logics of type *S4* called K'', realizing a federated information system, is described. The elements of K'', called nodes, each have their own epistemic operator, and a query algorithm giving the semantics for the multi-modal K'' is presented. Cooperation between nodes in K'' is described by means of a cooperation principle and by so-called negotiations, consisting of derivations in which some propositions originate in a different node from the one performing the derivation.

1. Introduction

1.1 Federated Information Systems

A <u>Federated Information System (FIS)</u> is a set of nodes in which each node is associated with a knowledge base consisting of propositions. The nodes are linked in a logical and physical network in such a way that each node has its own local database schema, and there does not exist any global schema which defines how the local schemata of the various nodes are interrelated. No node has full knowledge about what information the other nodes of the

---

[1] This work was supported by the National Swedish board for Technical Development (STU).

FIS contain and are able to share. Instead, each node has to control its cooperation with other nodes itself, deciding what information to import and export. The nodes may be heterogeneous, i.e. their languages may differ. It is also possible that the nodes share the same language, but their interpretations of the language differ. In propositional logic this simply means that different nodes are associated with different truth value assignment functions.

It is desirable to delimit cooperation between nodes to parts which are homogenous, or at least to parts for which translation functions between the languages exist. The latter problem has been investigated in [Baral-90] where maximal translation functions are obtained from the proof tree of the query. However, it is usually necessary to constrain cooperation further, in order to hide irrelevant information from every node. In the approach presented here, the translation problem is subsumed by the problem of constraining cooperation to the relevant homogeneous parts of each node's domain.

To be able to exploit the advantages of FISs described in e.g. [Heimbigner-85], [Johannesson-89], [Sheth-90], and [Ahlsén-90], as opposed to an ordinary distributed database system (see e.g. [Ceri-84]), one must employ some sort of formal representation for the information to be described in the system. One possible candidate for such representation is First Order Logic (FOL). Since the expressibility of FOL is to weak in this context (cf. [Thayse-88], [Levesque-90]), an approach which allows the system to answer queries about its own knowledge, as well as an easy way of describing cooperation between nodes, is called for. One such approach is to use FOL extended by epistemic logic, as proposed in [Boman-90a], and this path is followed here. This paper utilizes propositional modal logic only, even though extensions to FOL are occasionally discussed.

Distribution of control to autonomous nodes in a database context is less difficult in general than distributing tasks to agents in a Distributed AI system (see [Bond-88]). In an FIS, there is no direct need for planning and all the nodes can function simultaneously while in Distributed AI, agents often interact to achieve some goal. Since our sole purpose is to provide answers to queries, the problem of specifying a framework for FISs reduces to the problem of finding a natural and effective query algorithm. To the best of our knowledge, no such algorithm has hitherto been proposed.

1.2 Epistemic Logic

The epistemic modality operator **K** is a primitive knowledge-operator used throughout this paper and interpreted as follows. The expression $K(\Psi, A)$, or equivalently $K_{\Psi} A$ to use the notation of [Hintikka-62], means that the proposition A is "known" by Ψ to be true. The "knower", Ψ, will be referred to as a node in this paper due to the context of FISs, although it is usually referred to as an agent or, in the mathematical literature, a system. Formally, $K(\alpha, \ldots)$ is a different modal operator from $K(\beta, \ldots)$, $K(\gamma, \ldots)$, $K(\delta, \ldots)$, etc. We will thus study multi-modal systems in which the number of modal operators are equal to the number of nodes. Like all modal operators, $K(\Psi, \ldots)$ is not truth-functional. Instead, it maps a proposition into the values verified, falsified, and undecided. Verified means known to be true, and falsified means that the negation of the proposition is verified. If a proposition is neither verified, nor falsified, then the proposition is undecided. When a node is queried, a verification corresponds to a "Yes"-answer, a falsification to "No", and an undecidable situation to "Undecided".

The **K** does not stand for knowledge in the absolute sense of the word, but every node reasons as if its propositions were verified (cf. [Levesque-84]). This means that the axiom $K(\Psi, A) \rightarrow A$ holds locally in an arbitrary node Ψ, but not necessarily globally, i.e. among all nodes. Thus, the possibility exists that both $K(\alpha, A)$ and $K(\beta, \neg A)$ hold. This situation, with an <u>implicit inconsistency</u> in the FIS, is not unusual between real-life database systems with the same UoD.

In the following section, a framework for FISs is proposed. The first subsection defines most of the necessary terminology and formalizes parts of the idea of cooperation. This notion is discussed again in the second subsection, which explains the negotiation procedure between two nodes. The third subsection lists any node's contents, while the fourth gives the semantics for query evaluation in the FIS, and comments on the system's evolution over time. The final section comments on deficiencies, proposes extensions, and relates this paper to other research.

2. Epistemic Systems for Federated Information Systems

2.1 The Set of Systems K''

We now present a set of axiomatic modal propositional logics, and name this set K''. Each such logic is a set of modal propositions which we will continue to call a <u>node</u>. The choice of axiom schemata is (informally) explained and justified in [Boman-90a]. In the spirit of decentralization, K'' itself will not be discussed but whenever we discuss properties in the intersection of all nodes in K'' we will simply say that we discuss K''. We begin our description of K'' with a definition of <u>modal propositions</u> and then add two kinds of axiom schemata to allow reasoning with these.

Definition: Given proposition letters $p_0, p_1,...$
              modal propositions in K'' are defined recursively as:

   (i)   A proposition letter is a modal proposition;
   (ii) $\perp$ is a modal proposition;
   (iii) If A and B are modal propositions, then so is A $\rightarrow$ B;
   (iv)   If A is a modal proposition, then so is $K(\Psi,A)$,
          where Ψ is an arbitrary node.

   Ax-P: Axiom schemata on tautological form (to generate the tautologies of propositional logic using R-MP below).

   Ax-K: $K(\Psi,A \rightarrow B) \rightarrow (K(\Psi,A) \rightarrow K(\Psi,B))$,
          where Ψ is an arbitrary node.

Intuitively, the proposition letters are variables whose values are modal propositions which, in turn, are subject to the usual value-assignment function of propositional logic. The letters A, B, C,...,A_1, A_2,... are metalogical variables ranging over sequences of symbols belonging to the union of the languages of all nodes, while Greek letters range over nodes. A <u>substitution instance</u> of a modal proposition B is any modal proposition obtained from B by replacing all occurrences of proposition letters $p_0,...,p_n$ by modal propositions $C_1,...,C_n$ respectively. Ax-K is referred to as a <u>distribution</u> axiom schema, since it governs the distribution of $K(\Psi,...)$ over implication.

The sentences of any node's knowledge base can be classified in accordance with the below definitions.

Definition: The modal propositions <u>in</u> Ψ will be defined by
$$S(\Psi) = \{A : A \in \Psi\},$$

while the modal propositions <u>known</u> to Ψ will be defined by
$$K^-(\Psi) = \{A : K(\Psi,A) \in S(\Psi)\}.$$

The difference $S(\Psi) - K^-(\Psi)$
then defines the modal propositions <u>unknown</u> to Ψ.

We now introduce two rules of inference: *modus ponens* and epistemic necessitation, the latter stating that any node knows every theorem of K''. For these two rules we must also fix the notion of <u>derivability</u> in K''.

Definition: Let Γ be a set of modal propositions in an arbitrary node $\Psi \in K''$. The relation $\Gamma \vdash_{K''} A$ holds in Ψ iff A is the last member in a sequence $<A_1,...,A_n>$ of modal propositions such that for each i, $1 \leq i \leq n$, one of the following holds:
(i) A_i is an axiom,
(ii) A_i is a member of Γ, or
(iii) A_i follows from earlier members of the sequence by application of R-MP or R-N.

R-MP: The relation over modal propositions in an arbitrary node $\Psi \in K''$ containing all triples $<A,(A \rightarrow B),B>$.

R-N: The relation over modal propositions in an arbitrary node $\Psi \in K''$ containing all pairs $<A,K(\Psi,A)>$.

The subscript K'' will most often be omitted in the text. Given Ax-P and R-MP, we can generate all tautologies of propositional logic. A <u>proof</u> is a derivation with $\Gamma = \emptyset$. A <u>theorem</u> C in a node $\Psi \in K''$, written $\vdash C$, is the last member in a sequence $<A_1,...,A_n>$ of a proof in Ψ. The rule of <u>uniform substitution</u> holds in every node, i.e. if A is a theorem in Ψ, then so is every substitution instance of A. To make explicit the condition (i) in the definition above, we will present three more axiom schemata. The first of these can be seen as an assumption, namely the one that says that a node cannot know what is false.

Definition: Ax-T: $K(\Psi,A) \rightarrow A$, given any node Ψ.

The set of systems K'' will allow queries involving K. To handle this we need the epistemic <u>introspection</u> axiom schema:

Definition: Ax-4: $K(\Psi,A) \rightarrow K(\Psi,K(\Psi,A))$, given any node Ψ.

This axiom schema is often criticized in philosophy as non-applicable to humans, but for nodes, with their finite knowledge bases, the application of it reduces to a mechanical task. The <u>consistency</u> axiom schema, $K(\Psi,A) \rightarrow \neg K(\Psi,\neg A)$, turns out to be a theorem and can thus be excluded. Finally, we have the <u>mixing</u> axiom schema, which governs cooperation between nodes, i.e. the use of information originating in other nodes.

Definition: Ax-Mix: $K(\Psi,K(\Omega,A)) \rightarrow K(\Psi,A)$,
                given any pair of distinct nodes Ω and Ψ.

The demand for the nodes to be distinct is due to the fact that the axiom schema which has the same node substituted for both variables is derivable from Ax-K, Ax-T, and the rules. The consequent in any instance of Ax-Mix will be true only if the antecedent is true. But the antecedent´s truth value can not depend upon another instance of Ax-Mix, where it is the consequent, since that would only result in an endless demand for new instances of Ax-Mix. Rather, given that a node Ψ has access to a modal proposition A in another node Ω, something which is determined by whether there is an appropriate instance of Ax-Mix in Ψ or not, the antecedent in this instance, $K(\Psi,K(\Omega,A))$, will be true only if $K(\Omega,A)$ is true in Ω. The underlying intuition is that the set of modal propositions known to Ψ can be extended by the set of modal propositions known to any other node with which Ψ is allowed to cooperate. This is a way to allow physical distribution, on the pain of redundancy, and this <u>cooperation principle</u> is explained further in the rest of this section.

2.2 Negotiations in K''

A <u>negotiation</u> in K'' involves knowledge originating in exactly two nodes. This is not an actual limitation, since a negotiation between any number of nodes can be simulated by a series of bilateral agreements. It consists of one or more applications of R-MP on Ax-Mix, and it is an important step in providing answers to queries, since it is the queried proposition that triggers these rule applications. The node appearing in the consequent of Ax-Mix is called the <u>importing</u> node, and the node belonging to the outermost K-operator in the argument to $K(\Psi,...)$ in the antecedent is called the <u>exporting</u> node. A modal proposition resulting from a negotiation is called an imported modal proposition by the importing node, and an exported modal proposition by the exporting node.

By constraining any node Ψ by means of letting only some instances of Ax-Mix be part of Ψ's knowledge base, we can keep Ψ from being omniscient, i.e. from knowing everything. The instances of Ax-Mix do not have to be limited to controlling only which nodes Ψ can negotiate with; they can also control which modal propositions Ψ is allowed to import. This is achieved in (predicate) logic programming simply by having a constant denoting the modal proposition(s) that Ψ can import from the exporting node, and a variable indicating that any modal proposition can be imported from the exporting node. As an example, consider an FIS with four nodes where α is allowed to import any information from node β, no information from γ, and information only of the forms 'book('Ulysses')' or 'book('Finnegan's Wake')' from δ. Then the following instances of Ax-Mix would constitute a subset of α's knowledge base.

$K(\alpha,K(\beta,A)) \rightarrow K(\alpha,A)$.
$K(\alpha,K(\delta,'book('Ulysses')')) \rightarrow K(\alpha,'book('Ulysses')')$.
$K(\alpha,K(\delta,'book('Finnegan's Wake')')) \rightarrow K(\alpha,'book('Finnegan's Wake')')$.

Naturally this example could be flattened to propositional logic, but the ideal extension would include a method for automated theorem proving for full first order modal logic, as described in [Wallen-90]. Any realistic prototype would have to be made in a version of Prolog, though, hence the Prolog-like notation. This is further commented on in the concluding section. Since the number of nodes in an FIS is finite, and most often rather low, it is natural to state axiom schemata in each node, rather than constructing meta-level axiom schemata applicable to every node, as in a globally controlled system. This will allow us to exclude means of negotiation between some nodes in a natural way, as in the above example. The most common reason for such an exclusion is probably that the nodes differ in their value assignment to some relevant modal proposition or, in the FOL case, in their interpretation of some relevant term.

2.3 Node Specifications in a Federated Information System Constructed according to K''

We will now describe, for an arbitrary node α in the set of systems K'', what A in the definition of $S(\alpha)$ really is, i.e. which modal propositions can be <u>in</u> α.

* A finite set of tautologies, generated by Ax-P and R-MP.
* One instance of Ax-K, namely $K(\alpha, A \rightarrow B) \rightarrow (K(\alpha, A) \rightarrow K(\alpha, B))$.
* One instance of Ax-T, namely $K(\alpha, A) \rightarrow A$.
* One instance of Ax-4, namely $K(\alpha, A) \rightarrow K(\alpha, K(\alpha, A))$.
* A number of instances of the axiom schemata $K(\alpha, K(\Omega, A)) \rightarrow K(\alpha, A)$, which results from instantiating the two occurrences of Ψ in the definition of Ax-Mix with α. These instances will be α's mixing axioms. The number of instances depends on the constraints on α's initial possibilities to negotiate.
* A (possibly empty) set of modal propositions unknown to α.
* A set of modal propositions known to α, resulting from the cooperation principle: If $(K(\alpha, K(\beta, A)) \rightarrow K(\alpha, A)) \in \alpha$, and $K(\beta, A) \in \beta$, then $K(\alpha, K(\beta, A)) \in \alpha$, for any node β distinct from α, and any modal proposition A.

Since A and B are meta-logical variables, all of the first five kinds of modal propositions above are in fact axiom schemata, and α's actual content will be a finite set of instances of these, together with the union of the sets of the last two kinds. Thus, we have:

Definition: Let $S^*(\Psi)$ denote the closure of $S(\Psi)$ under $\vdash_{K''}$.

In a typical real-life situation, the data base administrator (DBA) will define the initial configuration of the nodes with respect to the mixing axioms, the physical distribution, and so on. The DBA will then extend all knowledge bases in accordance with the instances of the cooperation principle. After this initial phase is over, global control is no longer needed. Elements of the set of modal propositions unknown to the node will be added by the DBA, and as the node changes over time, it will export every new modal proposition to all nodes which are allowed to import it. (The importing nodes then prefix the exported modal proposition with their own K-operators, respectively, as explained in the following subsection.) The K-operators will not be part of this assertion-language. Moreover, some sort of inconsistency-check must be performed at the time of assertion, since we would not want to allow A to be added to a node if ¬A is derivable in it. Thus, K-operators will only be utilized by the user in queries. The answers to queries will be determined by derivability conditions, as presented in the query algorithm of subsection 2.4.

2.4 A Query Algorithm for the Set of Systems K''

First, we introduce three useful definitions.

Definition: Let $(?-A)_\Psi$ denote a query about the modal proposition A, posed to a node Ψ.

Definition: Let $\mathbb{I}(\Psi,A)$ denote the set of nodes such that every node Ω in the set has an instance of Ax-Mix, with $K(\Omega,K(\Psi,A))$ as its antecedent, which belongs to $S(\Omega)$.

Definition: Let $\mathbb{E}(\Psi,A)$ denote the set of nodes such that every node Ω in the set has an instance of Ax-Mix, with $K(\Psi,K(\Omega,A))$ as its antecedent, which belongs to $S(\Psi)$.

Intuitively, $\mathbb{I}(\Psi,A)$ consists of the nodes which could import A from Ψ, while $\mathbb{E}(\Psi,A)$ consists of the nodes which could export A to Ψ. Now, consider the query algorithm in **Figure-1**. The algorithm characterizes the semantics for query evaluation in K'', apart from the lines in the two

264

sections with IF-THEN-ELSE written in upper-case letters which concern node state transitions, i.e. heuristic constraints for the FIS.

Let $(?-A)_\Psi$ be given. Now,

if A has the form **KB**
then the system tries to establish $\Gamma \vdash B$,
  where Γ is a maximal consistent subset of $S^*(\Psi)$
    if $\Gamma \vdash B$
    then the system tries to establish $\Gamma \vdash \neg B$
        if $\Gamma \vdash \neg B$
        then the system answers the query by "Undecided" and halts
        else the system answers the query by "Yes" and
            IF **KB** is not in $S(\Psi)$
            THEN the system adds **KB** to $S(\Psi)$ and the system adds
            $K(\Omega,K(\Psi,B))$ to every $\Omega \in \mathbb{I}(\Psi,KB)$ such that neither
            $K(\Omega,K(\Psi,B))$, nor $K(\Omega,B)$ is in $S(\Omega)$, and halts
            ELSE the system halts
    else the system tries to establish $\Gamma \vdash \neg B$
        if $\Gamma \vdash \neg B$
        then the system answers the query by "No" and halts
        else the system answers the query by "Undecided" and halts
else A has the form B, and the system tries to establish $\Delta \vdash B$,
  where $\Delta = S^*(\Omega)$, for some $\Omega \in \mathbb{E}(\Psi,B)$
    if $\Delta \vdash B$
    then the system answers the query by "Yes" and
        IF B is not in $S(\Psi)$
        THEN the system adds B to $S(\Psi)$ and the system adds B to every
        $\Omega \in \mathbb{I}(\Psi,B)$ such that neither B, nor $\neg B$ is in $S(\Omega)$, and halts
        ELSE the system halts
    else the system tries to establish $\Delta \vdash \neg B$
        if $\Delta \vdash \neg B$
        then the system answers the query by "No" and halts
        else the system answers the query by "Undecided" and halts.

Figure-1

Given a query (?-A)$_\Psi$, the "Undecided" answer may result either from lack of any information about A in S*(Ψ), or from the fact that both A and ¬A are derivable in S*(Ψ). In both cases a three-valued logic is obtained, such that its connectives obey the three-valued truth tables of Kleene, defined in [Kleene-52], §64. The proof is straightforward.

3. Conclusions and Future Research

This exposition provides evidence for the conjecture that epistemic logic is well suited for describing FISs. It is limited, however, in that it concentrates on propositional logic, and one possible direction for future research is an extension to full FOL. Even though a complete formalization for FOL would be quite voluminous, it would not be very difficult. The presentation would be most readable as a cut-free sequent calculus (cf. [Wallen-90], Part II), or a semantic tableau (cf. [Smullyan-68]). We will concentrate on developing a prototype for propositional logic first, however, in order to exploit existing automated proof procedures for propositional modal logic.

Even though a formal framework for FISs can be seen as a formalization of a simple special case of distributed problem solving, this does not mean that distributed AI cannot learn anything from work on FISs. Any federated data base management system constructed according to K'' is suitable for extensions such as the ones suggested in [Chakravarty-90], and so it may be used for planning and more generic problem solving. However, these extensions are not as easily formalized and it may prove impossible to present them all in one unified generic framework, as noted in [Deen-90].

Semantically, each node in K'' is characterized by the class of reflexive and transitive frames, i.e. the axiomatization is sound and complete with respect to the class of models based on such frames. This proof is given for $S4$ e.g. in [Segerberg-71] and the extension to K'' is straightforward: the proof will be over an arbitrary node in the multi-modal case, instead of over the only node. By an analogous extension K'' can be shown to be decidable. The set of systems K'' is adequate for handling uncertain information, and was constructed for vague UoDs. For the forthcoming FOL version of K'', some of the results in [Levesque-84] for incomplete knowledge bases carry over immediately. Moreover, nonmonotonic FISs would be possible, even though K'' in its present form does not allow nonmonotonicity. Instead, provability logic seems like a good candidate, as noted in [Boman-90b], and this is something which is further investigated in a forthcoming paper.

Another idea to be investigated in the future is to make K'' more effective by allowing mutually inconsistent nodes to cooperate. This can be achieved by imposing an ordering on the nodes in K''. Intuitively, such an ordering would reflect the fact that certain nodes can be regarded as more accurate, or reliable, than other nodes. This could be captured from every node´s perspective, i.e. every node is connected to an ordering, or (more simply) from a global perspective, i.e. only one ordering exists. Since the nodes in K'' are not symmetric reasoners it would be possible to utilize the notion of bilattice, as presented in [Ginsberg-90], for these purposes. Again, K'' in its present form would be inadequate for such a probabilistic reasoning system.

Even though the theoretical aspects of FISs have been focussed in this paper, an effort has been made to always keep the practical use in mind. An example is the non-semantical parts added to the query algorithm. We would also like to point out that despite the fact that our terminology is not that of data base theorists, pragmatical aspects of data base theory have not been left out, either. As an example, (both static and dynamic) integrity constraints can easily be represented in K''. Moreover, data base schema design is not restricted in any way, since the FIS allows for heterogeneous systems to be part of K''; their homogenous subschemata, if they exist, can cooperate, while their heterogeneous subschemata simply cannot.

Acknowledgements

The authors would like to thank Paul Needham, Filip Widebäck and Henrik Boström for helpful suggestions and proof-reading.

References

[Ahlsén-90]   Matts Ahlsén & Paul Johannesson: "Contracts in Database Federations", in this volume.

[Baral-90]   Chitta Baral, Sarit Kraus & Jack Minker: "Communicating between
                     Multiple Knowledge-Based Systems with Different Languages",
                     presented at the *Working Conference on Cooperating Knowledge
                     Based Systems*, Keele 1990.

[Boman-90a]   Magnus Boman & Paul Johannesson:
                     "Axiomatic Epistemic Systems for Federated Information Systems",
                     in *Data Management*, pp. 195-213, Ed. Prakash,
                     Tata McGraw-Hill Publishing Company, New Delhi 1990.

[Boman-90b]   Magnus Boman: "A Survey of Provability Logic and a Note on its
                     Relevance to Nonmonotonic Federated Information Systems",
                     SYSLAB Working Paper No. 170, Stockholm 1990.

[Bond-88]   Alan H. Bond & Les Gasser: "An Analysis of Problems and Research
                     in DAI" in *Readings in Distributed Artificial Intelligence*, pp.3-35,
                     Eds. Bond, Gasser, Morgan Kaufmann Publ. Inc. 1988.

[Ceri-84]   Stefano Ceri & Giuseppe Pelagatti: Distributed Databases,
                     McGraw-Hill 1984.

[Chakravarty-90]   S. Chakravarty, S.B. Navathe, K. Karlapalem & A. Tanaka:
                     "Meeting the Cooperative Problem Solving Challenge: A Database-
                     Oriented Approach", in this volume.

[Deen-90]   S.M. Deen: "Cooperating Agents - A Database Perspective",
                     presented at the *Working Conference on Cooperating Knowledge
                     Based Systems*, Keele 1990.

[Ginsberg-90]   Matthew Ginsberg: "Bilattices and Modal Operators" in
                     Journal of Logic and Computation, pp.41-69, Vol.1, No.1, 1990.

[Heimbigner-85]   Dennis Heimbigner & Dennis McLeod: "A Federated Architecture for
                     Information Management" in *ACM Transactions on Office
                     Information Systems*, pp. 253-278, Vol.3, No.3, 1985.

[Hintikka-62]   Jaakko Hintikka: Knowledge and Belief,
                     Cornell University Press, New York 1962.

[Johannesson-89]   Paul Johannesson & Benkt Wangler: "The Negotiation Mechanism in
                    a Decentralized Autonomous Cooperating Information Systems
                    Architecture", in *Proceedings of the XI World Computer Congress*,
                    San Francisco 1989.

[Kleene-52]   Stephen Cole Kleene: Introduction to Metamathematics,
                    North-Holland 1952.

[Lemmon-77]   E.J. Lemmon in collaboration with Dana Scott (Ed. Segerberg): An
                    Introduction to Modal Logic, in *American Philosophical Quarterly
                    Monograph Series*, Ed. Rescher, Oxford 1977. Written in 1966.

[Levesque-84]   H.J. Levesque: "The Logic of Incomplete Knowledge Bases", in
                    Conceptual Modelling, pp. 165-186, Eds. Brodie, Mylopoulos,
                    Schmidt, Springer Verlag, New York 1984.

[Levesque-90]   H.J. Levesque: "All I know: A Study in Autoepistemic Logic", in
                    Artificial Intelligence, Vol.42, pp. 263-309, 1990.

[Segerberg-71]   Krister Segerberg: An Essay in Classical Modal Logic,
                    Filosofiska Föreningen, Uppsala 1971.

[Sheth-90]   Amit Sheth & James Larson: "Federated Database Systems for
                    Managing Distributed, Heterogeneous, and Autonomous Databases"
                    in *ACM Computing Surveys*, Vol.22, No.3, pp. 183-236, 1990.

[Smullyan-68]   Raymond Smullyan: First-Order Logic, Ergebnisse der
                    Mathematik und ihrer Grenzgebiete, Band 43, Springer-Verlag 1968.

[Thayse-88]   André Thayse et.al.: From Standard Logic To Logic Programming,
                    Chapter 4, John Wiley & Sons 1988.

[Wallen-90]   Lincoln A. Wallen: Automated Deduction in Nonclassical Logics,
                    MIT Press 1990.

DISCUSSION

Presenter: M. Boman.

Q. (J. Lenting, University of Limberg, Netherlands): Let me first say I'm not really into epistemic logic. I don't know very much about it but I was wondering if you know, you probably do, the story of the philosophers who are sitting below a tree. One starts laughing because he sees that the other one has a bit of bird shit on his head. The other one starts laughing. The third one doesn't laugh because he can conclude that the others know that he knows and so on. You said something like, if the Psi node discovers that the Omega nodes knows C, then he should broadcast to Omega that he knows that the Omega node knows C. Now, how do you know that it's not necessary for Omega to broadcast back that he knows that Psi.. knows that, and so forth? How do you know where it stops?

A. (M. Boman): Well, it's quite simple. Omega will broadcast the information further if and only if there is a third node which is interested to know that Omega now knows this fact. So if this node is called Gamma, then Gamma will add it to its knowledge base that Gamma now knows that Omega knows that Psi knows that Omega knows that C is true.

Q. (J. Lenting): But Psi doesn't need to know that Omega knows that Psi knows that Omega knows that C is true.

A. (M. Boman): No, but this doesn't affect the semantics. We have the possibility to sequentially search through every proposition in a node, it's an effective procedure, until we find something that starts with some sequence, say, "K(...,C)", if you see what I mean. If we find it, well, then this is an example of a fulfillment of the cooperation principle and so information will be broadcast.

Q. (J. Lenting): Have you tested the system, I mean mentally on this real example?

A. (M. Boman): What we've got is proofs of soundness, completeness, decidability and, in a sense, correctness. I'm not sure if that answers your question. We haven't got an implementation.

Q. (J. Lenting): I'm interested in the power of the system.

A. (M. Boman): I can't tell you because "the system" doesn't exist. We have described a framework for constructing federated systems; each system has to be validated separately.

Q. (M. Worboys, University of Leicester): A student at node 1 knows proposition P, and knows too the negation of that proposition. Now, supposing you've got some query Q. By this mixing axiom it seems that node 1 can know not P, so it therefore can know P and not P. Therefore if you use axiom T, you could therefore infer P and not P and then by propositional logic you can therefore infer anything. So, does that not mean that everything is unknown by your definition of unknown?

A. (M. Boman) : Firstly, we wouldn't want any node to know both P and its negation and we would like to design integrity constraints to prevent this from ever happening. Secondly, there is still the possibility to deduce things from an inconsistent node since we only, in the query, ever consider the maximal consistent subset. So what will happen is that it will be derivable and its negation will be derivable, so any query which has to do with P will be answered by undecided. But a query just to do with Q is not affected by the P and not P situation.

Q. (M. Worboys) : I just thought maybe Q would be calling up P at some point in the proof.

A. (M. Boman) : Yes, this can happen, but the restriction to the maximal consistent subset blocks the negation of P from being called up in the same proof.

Cooperative Query Answering via Type Abstraction Hierarchy

Wesley W. Chu, Qiming Chen and Rei-Chi Lee

Department of Computer Science
University of California, Los Angeles
Los Angeles, California

ABSTRACT

Cooperative query answering consists of analyzing the intent of the query and providing generalized, neighborhood or associated information relevant to the query. The key issues to accomplish cooperative query answering consist of supporting different knowledge representations at different abstract levels and providing inference between these levels. In this paper the *Type Abstraction Hierarchy* is proposed which is characterized by dealing with subtyping from subsumption, composition, and also abstraction views. Based on the type abstraction feature provided by this model, an inference technique for cooperative query answering is developed. Such an inference is performed by *abstracting* and *refining* the goal to generalize and specialize the query scope and to derive relevant answers with different generality, coverage, and approximation, or to link related subjects at certain levels by using different representations of knowledge given at different levels. A prototype system has been implemented at UCLA that demonstrates the use of this approach for such decision making and problem solving applications as conceptual query processing, neighborhood inference, and subject association.

1. Introduction

Traditional query processing provides exact answers to queries. It usually requires users to fully understand the database structure and content to issue a query. Due to the complexity of the database applications, incorrect queries are frequently issued and the users often receive no answers. **Cooperative query answering** is a process of analyzing the intent of the query and providing generalized, approximate, or associated information that is relevant to the query. In a cooperative query answering environment, queries can be imprecisely specified and accessing data is not limited to a single answer but can obtain relevant information of a wider scope, or even approximate information when the exact answer is not available. Thus, a cooperative query answering system may respond to a query by providing

(a) neighborhood information,
(b) general information, and
(c) associative information.

This research is supported by DARPA contract F29601-87-C-0072 and ONR contract N00014-88-K0434.

In order to facilitate cooperative query answering, it is necessary to associate one concept to another by taking into account the related factors. In fact, **association** is one of the essential intelligent mechanisms used to make decisions or solve problems. Indeed this notion has been studied in various semantic data modeling approaches [SMI77] [HAM78] [BRO81] [SU83] [ALA90]. The semantic links provided by those data models can considerably relax users from making their own programs to handle the relationships between database objects.

Equally important to association is the *knowledge level* where the association is represented. Many complex data intensive problems do not have clear representations at low knowledge levels, however they can be described at a higher knowledge level by more abstract object representations.

The use of maps is an evident example. A geographic object, such as "Los Angeles" city, has different representations on differently scaled maps. On a small scaled map it is shown just as a circle symbol, but on a larger scaled map it is represented as a graph. Different scaled maps are representations of geographic knowledge at different abstract levels. To solve a problem it is usually necessary to move the attention between these levels. For example, if we plan to go to a place in San Francisco from a place in Los Angeles, we would first move to a higher topological level. We would find the Freeway 101 as the connection between Los Angeles and San Francisco, since the knowledge "Freeway 101 connects Los Angeles and San Francisco" is represented at such a level. On the contrary, it is not reasonable to replace this knowledge by a large number of lower level rules listing all the particular places in Los Angeles and San Francisco that can be connected by the Freeway 101.

The above example shows the fact that *associations between related concepts are easily represented and traced at certain higher knowledge levels*. We can easily find more examples indicating this fact. For instance, a "system problem" can be viewed as the abstract representation of a number of problems such as a "disk writing problem", a "printing problem" and so on, it is efficient to give the rule at such an abstract level for relating a "system problem" with a "system manager" such as

"If there is a *system problem* then call the *system manager*"

rather than stating a number of specialized rules as

"If there is a *disk writing problem*" then call the "system manager".
"If there is a *printing problem*" then call the "system manager".

Thus, there are two key issues in providing cooperative query answering: the *semantic associations* and the *multi-level knowledge representation*. The first issue has been addressed in semantic data modeling, type hierarchy, and object-orientation. However, the second issue has been rarely addressed thus far. Although the notion of subsumption-based type hierarchy allows objects of a class to be treated as the members of its super class at a higher knowledge level, besides changing the type name it does not facilitate different instance values to accommodate the knowledge representations at different knowledge levels. In fact, this issue has been generally omitted by previous semantic data modeling and Object-Oriented Database (OODB) approaches. This motivated us to develop the **type abstraction hierarchy** to provide multi-level knowledge representation.

In this paper we shall first develop the notion of type abstraction and propose the type abstraction hierarchy to integrate the subsumption-based, composition-based, and abstraction-based type hierarchy notion for supporting the multi-level knowledge representations. Next, using the type abstraction hierarchy, we shall present an inference technique that is based on *query rewrite* to allow reasoning between different knowledge levels thus enabling us to provide cooperative query answering in a systematic way. Finally, we shall give examples to demonstrate the proposed methodology for cooperative query answering.

2. The Notion of Type Abstraction

Type hierarchy generally means the partial order for a set of types where a type at a higher position is said to be more *generalized* than a type at a lower position in the partial order, and the latter is said to be more *specialized* than the former. However, the term *generalization* and *specialization* may be interpreted from the subsumption, composition, and abstraction views.

2.1 Subsumption View of Type Hierarchy

The original view to type hierarchy taken by the object-oriented paradigm is *subsumption* [AIT86]. This view is theoretically associated with *many-sorted logic*, where classes of different types are considered as different *sorts*, and the universe of discourse is regarded as comprising a relational structure in which the objects are regarded as being of various sorts. Figure 1 shows a sort lattice. We can call the most specific sort as BOTTOM which is usually interpreted as the empty sort, and call the most general sort as TOP which is usually interpreted as containing "everything" in the discourse.

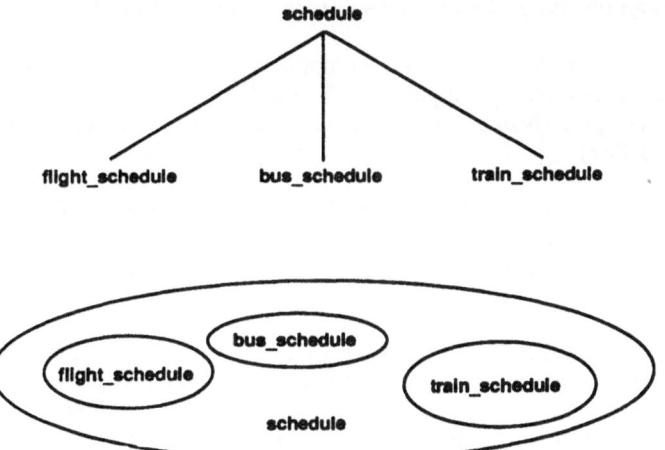

Figure 1   An Example of Type Subsumption Hierarchy.

When a sort S_1 is more general than another sort S_2, the position of S_1 is higher than the position of S_2 in the sort lattice. In this case, S_1 is referred to as a *super-sort* of S_2, and S_2 is referred to as a *sub-sort* of S_1, and the relationship between S_1 and S_2 is denoted as $S_2 \leq^\circ S_1$. The $\leq^\circ$ relationship is a *partial order*, that is, $\leq^\circ$ is reflexive, transitive, and antisymmetric, thus forming a partial order.

Because of the synonym of *sort names* and *type symbols*, the notion of concept subsumption captures the semantic relationship among *types*. However, due to its lack of revealing structural differences and constraints among objects, subsumption cannot be used for expressing the structural relationships among objects of various types.

2.2 Composition View of Type Hierarchy

The handling of complex objects in OODB's introduces the *composition* relationship among types, where a type is composed of other more primitive types. We should distinguish the multilevel type configuration from the type hierarchy mentioned above. However, type hierarchy can also be considered from a compositional point of view, in the sense that a generalized type has the *structure* commonly contained in the specialized types.

This view can also be formalized by the lattice theory under the **structural sub-type relationship** as described below. The concept that the super-type structure is a *generalization* of the corresponding sub-type structure, and the sub-type structure is a *specialization* of the super-type structure means that the super-type structure is somehow "contained" in its sub-type structures. For example, tuple types *(name, phone#, school)* and *(name, phone#, company)* are sub-type structures of *(name, phone#)*. If we assign a type name *EMPLOYEE* to the former and *PERSON* to the latter, we can clearly see that *EMPLOYEE* is a sub-type of *PERSON*.

Considering atomic, tuple and set type structures, when we say type T_1 is the *sub-type structure* of T_2, we mean one of the following:

a) T_1 and T_2 are the same atomic types.
      For example, type COLOR is a sub-type structure of itself.

b) T_1 and T_2 are *tuples* and every component of T_2 is the sub-type structure of the corresponding component of T_1 on the same attribute.
      For example, (Name, Sex, School, Grade) is a sub-type structure of (Name, Sex).

c) T_1 and T_2 are *sets* and the member type of T_2 is a sub-type structure of the member type of T_1.
      For example, {(Name, Sex, School, Grade)} is a sub-type structure of {(Name, Sex)}.

Note that we are not discussing from the usual PART_OF relationship point of view, but the generalization notion. In fact, the *structural sub-type relationship* is just the inverse of the structural *sub-object relationship* described in [BAN86]. Under the structural sub-type relationship, a super-type has a simpler structure than its sub-type. However, under the structural sub-object relationship, a super object has a more complex structure than its sub-objects. The set of all type structures under the structural sub-type relationship forms a partial order lattice, which is the *dual-lattice* of the lattice formed under sub-object relationship. We denote the fact that T is a sub-type structure of T' as $T \leq^* T'$ as shown by the example illustrated in Figure 2.

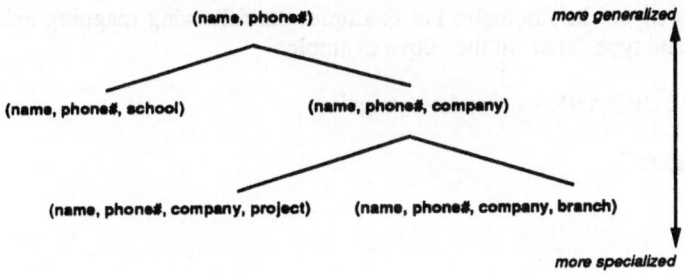

Figure 2   An Example of Type Composition Hierarchy.

The notion of composition of types thus captures the structural relationships among types. In fact, the *common structure* of a type over its sub-types is the intersection of the structures of its sub-types under the ≤* relationship. This notion is also not semantically rich enough for representing a complete semantic link between various types. On one hand, it cannot represent the semantics of the concept subsumption. For example, given the following two types:

  communication(name, address).

  phone(name, phone#).

from the subsumption point of view, "communication" is the super-type of "phone". Structurally they are not compatible since they contain different component types (i.e., attributes names: "address" and "phone#").

On the other hand, it does not distinguish between types that are structurally equivalent but conceptually different. For example, consider the following two types:

  student(id, name, sex).

  dog(id, name, sex).

These two types contain the same structure (id, name, sex), but represent two different concepts.

2.3 Abstraction View of Type Hierarchy

Let us now consider the *abstraction* view of type hierarchy, where a super-class is considered to convey a *more abstract representation* than its sub-classes, namely, the domain of the super type T' is abstract over the domain of the sub-type T. We denote such a fact as $T \leq' T'$. Under this notion, an object may be viewed either as an instance of a type T with a corresponding representation or as the instance of a more general type T' with a more abstract representation conformed by type T'. The sense of abstraction concerns not only the type intension, but also the instance extension, that is, the same piece of information can be represented differently at different knowledge representation levels. This view is generally absent in the current notion of type hierarchy.

Under this view, an instance may have different representations at different abstraction levels. For example, let us consider two atomic types "area" and "airport", where the former is the super-type of the latter. To indicate the location of BURBANK airport, we can either use the instance of type "airport" expressed as

  airport(BURBANK)

at the relatively lower knowledge level, or alternatively use the instance of type "area" expressed as

  area(Los_Angeles)

at the relatively higher knowledge level. In other words, there exist mappings between the instance values from a sub-class domain and the corresponding abstract instance

276

values from its super-class domain. For example, the following mapping exists between type "airport" and type "area" in the above example:

airport:BURBANK → area:Los_Angeles

as shown in Figure 3.

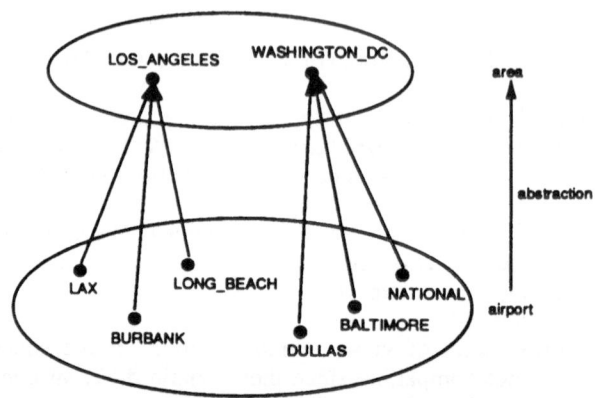

Figure 3   An Example of Type Abstraction.

Figure 4 shows another example where the instances of type "fare" for traveling by airplane, bus or train can have more abstract representations at a higher level as the instances of types "flight_cost", "bus_cost", and "train_cost" respectively. Going one level further, under type "cost" they can have even general representations.

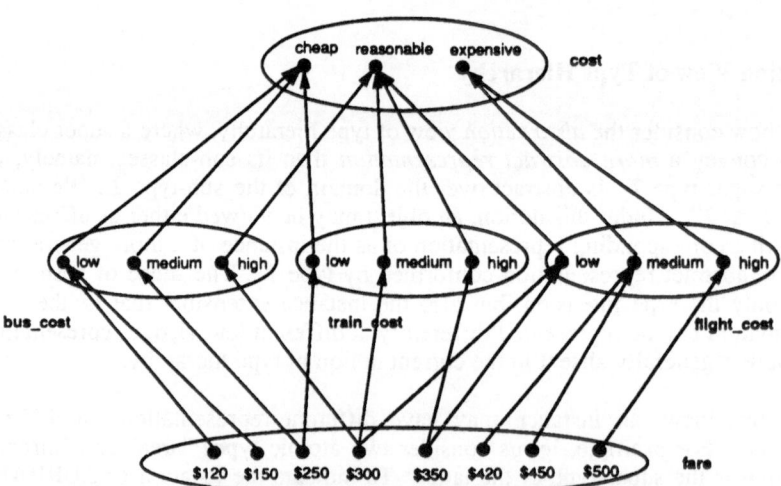

Figure 4   A Multilevel Type Abstraction Example.

The knowledge about different object representations at different levels is essential for transferring inference between different knowledge levels.

3. Type Abstraction Hierarchy : The Integrated View of Type Hierarchy

The introduction of the type abstraction together with the type subsumption and type composition form an integrated view of type hierarchy. In our proposed notion of **Integrated Type Hierarchy**, to capture the notion of *subsumption*, type names are used to conceptually subsume various sorts of objects, where Unique Name Assumption (UNA) on types is adopted. To capture the notion of *composition*, the structural sub-type relationship is introduced. To capture the notion of *abstraction*, different representations of an object at different knowledge levels is considered. Denoting the integrated subtyping relationship as $\leq$ for types T and T'. The expression $T \leq T'$ means :

the domain of T' is abstract over the domain of T (i.e. $T \leq T'$), or under the special case,

the domain of T' subsumes the domain of T (i.e. $T \leq^\circ T'$), and

the type structure of T is contained in the type structure of T' (i.e. $T \leq^* T'$).

It can be seen that *subsumption is a special case of abstraction*. Thus we shall refer to the type hierarchy underlain by the above integrated subtyping relationship as **type abstraction hierarchy**.

More formally we can consider a type as an atomic type, or as a tuple-type $T:(T_1,..., T_n)$, where $T_1,..., T_n$ are types, or as a set-type, $T:\{S\}$, where S is a type, the domain of type T be denoted as $dom(T)$. Then based on the type abstraction notion, a type T is a sub-type of a type T', denoted as $T \leq T'$. It is defined recursively as:

a) For atomic types T and T', if each value in $dom(T')$ represents one or multiple values in $dom(T)$, then $T \leq T'$.

b) For tuple-types $T:(T_1,..,T_n)$ and $T':(T_1',..,T_m')$ where $n \geq m$, $T \leq T'$ iff $\forall i \in \{1,..,m\}$ $T_i \leq T_i'$.

c) For set-types $T:\{S\}$ and $T':\{S'\}$, $T \leq T'$ iff $S \leq S'$.

For a given class, based on different views there may be multiple type hierarchies.

As an example, Figure 5 shows a type abstraction hierarchy where class "CC_JOURNEY" (CC stands for Coast-to-Coast) is partitioned into three sub-classes: "CC_FLIGHT", "CC_TRAIN", and "CC_BUS" whose elements are of types "cc_flight", "cc_train", and "cc_bus". These types are further refined to more specialized types. The schema of type "CC_JOURNEY", "CC_FLIGHT" and "DELTA_FLIGHT" are formally stated as follows :

CC_JOURNEY{cc_journey(departure_area, arrival_area, duration, cost)}.
CC_FLIGHT{cc_flight(departure_area, arrival_area, departure_period, arrival_period, hours, flight_cost)}.

278

DELTA_FLIGHT{DELTA_flight(flight#,   departure_airport,   arrival_airport,   departure_time, arrival_time, hours,
    fare)}.

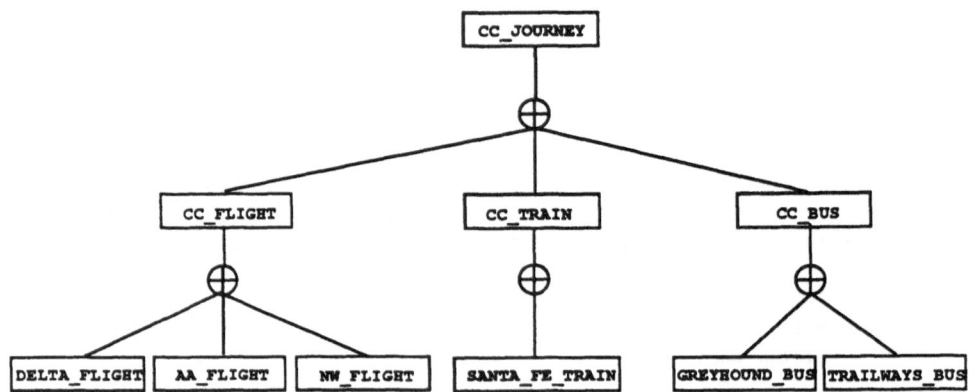

Figure 5   A Type Abstraction Hierarchy.

Now let us demonstrate step by step the generalized subtyping relationship between type "DELTA_FLIGHT" and "CC_FLIGHT".

Since

   departure_airport $\leq^{\wedge}$ departure_area,
   arrival_airport $\leq^{\wedge}$ arrival_area,
   departure_time $\leq^{\wedge}$ departure_period,
   arrival_time $\leq^{\wedge}$ arrival_period,
   hours $\leq^{\circ}$ hours,
   fare $\leq^{\wedge}$ flight_cost,

We have

   departure_airport $\leq$ departure_area,
   arrival_airport $\leq$ arrival_area,
   departure_time $\leq$ departure_period,
   arrival_time $\leq$ arrival_period,
   hours $\leq$ hours,
   fare $\leq$ flight_cost,

and then

   DELTA_flight(flight#, departure_airport, arrival_airport, departure_time, arrival_time, hours, fare) $\leq$
   cc_flight(departure_area, arrival_area, departure_period, arrival_period, hours, flight_cost).

which implies

   DELTA_FLIGHT{
   DELTA_flight(flight#, departure_airport, arrival_airport, departure_time, arrival_time, hours, fare)} $\leq$
   CC_FLIGHT{

279

cc_flight(departure_area, arrival_area, departure_period, arrival_period, hours, flight_cost)}.

Figure 6 gives an example showing an instance of type "DELTA_flight" which has a more abstract representation at the level of "cc_flight".

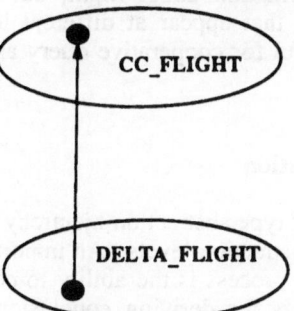

CC_flight(Los_Angeles, Washington_DC, morning, afternoon, 5, medium)

DELTA_flight(321, BURBANK, BALTIMORE, 10am, 6pm, 5, $450)

Figure 6   Abstract Representation of An instance.

Although the subsumption based type hierarchy is a special case of the abstraction based type hierarchy, the latter is suitable for providing links among those objects which have the same representation at a higher knowledge level. Figure 7 gives a comparison between Abstraction and Subsumption based Type Hierarchies.

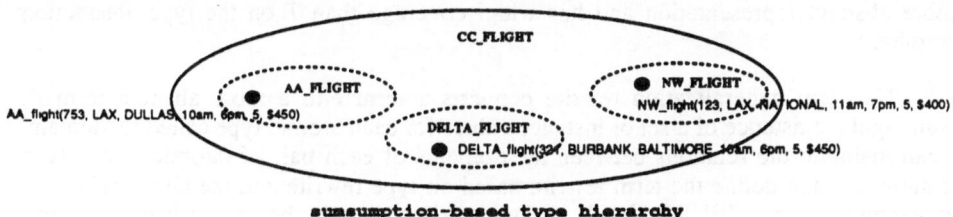

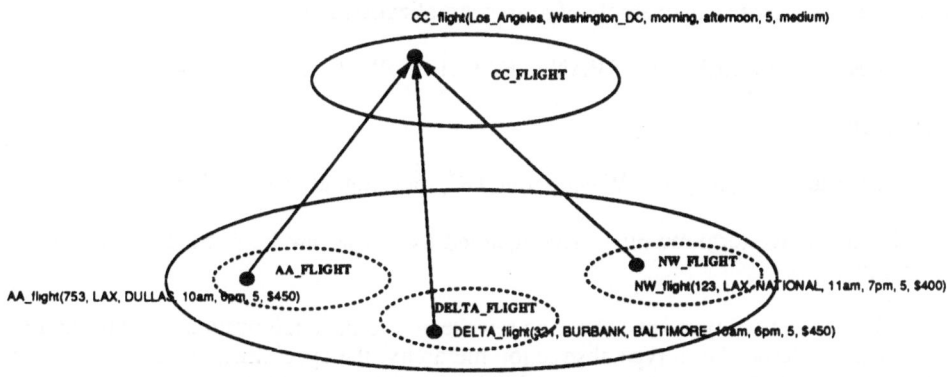

Figure 7 A Comparison between Abstraction and Subsumption based Type Hierarchies

To summarize, we have combined three relationships in our integrated type hierarchy: subsumption, composition and abstraction. The introduction of type abstraction offers the feature of enlarging or shrinking variable scopes by moving up or down along the type abstraction hierarchy. It is easy to understand that any concept described at a higher level has larger coverage than at a lower level. A class "CC_FLIGHT" only covers the coast-to-coast flight information, its super-class "CC_JOURNEY" not only covers the information about flight, but also covers the information about bus and train. Variables that appear at different levels may have different coverages. This feature is very useful for cooperative query answering as will be discussed in the next section.

4. Type Abstraction Based Goal Reformulation

One of the important characteristics of type abstraction hierarchy is that inference can be performed at and between different abstraction levels. An important requirement of the decision making and problem solving process is the ability to communicate and associate between different knowledge levels for deriving conclusions. Transferring between different knowledge levels is achieved by query generalization and specialization rewriting. Processing queries at different knowledge levels consists of converting object types, attribute names, and domain values involved in the query between different knowledge levels. These are all based on the mechanisms of *type rewrite* and *term rewrite*. By *term* we mean both instances and variables of types. There are two kinds of rewrites for types and terms: *generalization rewrite* and *specialization rewrite*.

The type generalization rewrite converts a type T to its super-type T', where T' is a more abstract representation and has wider coverage than T on the type abstraction hierarchy.

The term generalization rewrite converts a term t to a more abstract term t'. Assuming the existence of a set of instance values for each atomic type called its domain, we can maintain the relations between the domains of each pair of (atomic) super-type and sub-type, and define the term rewrite based on type rewrite and the above relations. For example, term "BURBANK" of type "airport" can be generalized to term "Los_Angeles" of type "area". Rewrite of a non-atomic term is made iteratively through stepwise rewrites of its component terms, starting from the bottom level atomic terms. Figure 6 also illustrates an example of term generalization rewrite, where the term

DELTA_flight(321, BURBANK, BALTIMORE, 10am, 6pm, 5, 450)

is rewritten to term

cc_flight(Los_Angeles, Washington_DC, morning, afternoon, 5, medium).

Note that the above term rewrite is accompanied by a type rewrite from "DELTA_flight" to "cc_flight".

The notions of type specialization rewrite and term specialization rewrite can also be defined similarly. For a type abstraction hierarchy, the specialization rewrite from an abstract type or term may yield a set of refined types or terms which provides refined information for searching the cooperative query answers.

Query rewrite is a technique for providing cooperative query answering which consists of two processes: *Query Abstraction* and *Query Refinement*. These processes are based on the above-mentioned type and term rewrite mechanisms. To implement query abstraction and refinement, we need to maintain the basic knowledge such as the information about the type abstraction hierarchy and the mappings between different representations of each pair of super-type and sub-type.

The *Query Abstraction Process* converts a query Q to a more abstract query representation Q'. The process consists of the following steps :

1. Find the appropriate super-type object through type generalization rewrite.

2. Convert the attributes to the corresponding types and vice versa (since attributes associated with the same type may be separately named). This may be necessary for objects at any level.

3. Transform attributes referred to in the query to those of the super-type object through type generalization rewrite.

4. Transform conditions referred to in the query to those related to the super-type object through both type generalization rewrite and term generalization rewrite.

The *Query Refinement Process* converts a query Q to more specific query representations Q1, Q2, ..., Qn according to the type abstraction hierarchy. The process consists of the following steps :

1. Find the set of sub-type objects through type specialization rewrites.

2. Provide conversions between the attributes and the corresponding types.

3. Based on each sub-type, use type specialization rewrite to transform attributes referred to in the query to those in the sub-type object.

4. Based on each sub-type, use both type specialization rewrite and term specialization rewrite to transform conditions referred to in the query to those related to the sub-type object.

The query modification, either upward or downward, is invoked recursively depending on the requirement and knowledge availability.

5. Supporting Cooperative Query Answering

The type abstraction hierarchy can be used to support cooperative query answering in a systematic way as will be shown in the following examples.

5.1 Neighborhood Query Answering

Neighborhood inference is a type of uncertain data inference (or inexact reasoning) which may not provide the exact answers expected by the user, but still contains information which may be helpful for the user. For example, if a user tries to reserve a DELTA airline flight from LAX airport in Los Angeles to NATIONAL airport in Washington is unavailable, then an alternative but similar flights of DELTA or other airlines may be given.

Neighborhood inference requires the transition of reasoning up and down to reach the neighboring objects. Given a query Q, the general processing steps are :

1. search the exact type of objects required by the query Q. If failed, then

2. move upward along the type abstraction hierarchy and rewrite the query to a more general one (generalization rewrite), i.e. $Q \rightarrow Q'$. Then,

3. move downward along the hierarchy and rewrite the query to a more specific query (specialization rewrite), i.e., $Q' \rightarrow Q''$.

Three kinds of tables are utilized for assisting neighborhood inference. They are the *type_hierarchy table* describing the subtyping relationship among types, the *attribute_type table* giving the relationship between attribute names and type names which allows attributes drawn from the same type to be differently named, and the *abstract mapping tables* showing the mappings of instances each pair of super-type and sub-type, or the corresponding instance values between a super-type and a range of sub-type (e.g. "morning" corresponds to "7am to 11am"). These tables describe knowledge representations at different knowledge levels, which are stored and managed in the database. Certain query language constructs additional to SQL are introduced, such as WITHIN for indicating set membership and BETWEEN for indicating a range with an upper and a lower bound.

For the above example, the neighborhood inference system first undergoes a *generalization* process from type **DELTA_flight** to its super type **cc_flight** (Coast-to-Coast Flight), followed by a *specialization* process from type **cc_flight** to its subtype **AA_flight**, **NW_flight**, and **DELTA_flight** itself to convey to the user wider ranged options, as shown in Figure 8. If all the subtypes of **cc_flight** are not available, a further generalization will be made to go up one more level to type **cc_journey** (Coast-to-Coast Journey) and then some specialization step is performed to go down to **cc_train** and **cc_bus**, and to its subtypes, if any.

```
SELECT * FROM DELTA_flight
WHERE departure_airport = "LAX" AND arrival_airport = "NATIONAL" AND
      departure_time BETWEEN <9am, 10am>
```

If the above query has no answer, the system can make the following efforts to respond to the query:

1. *Generalization Rewrite* : This step is to move upward along the type hierarchy to reach **cc_flight**. Due to the generalization rewrite process, the departure_airport "LAX" is replaced by the more abstract value "Los_Angeles" on departure_area,

the arrival_airport "NATIONAL" is replaced by the more abstract value "Washington_DC" on arrival_area, and the range of departure_time from 9am to 10am is generalized to the departure_period of "morning". Therefore, the query is generalized to

SELECT * FROM cc_flight
WHERE departure_area = "Los_Angeles" AND arrival_area = "Washington_DC" AND
    departure_period = "morning"

2. *Specialization Rewrite* : This step is to move downward along the type hierarchy to get the *neighborhood objects* of types **AA_flight, NW_flight** as well as **DELTA_flight** with the query specialized to the following, since all these meet the general conditions.

SELECT * FROM DELTA_flight
WHERE departure_airport WITHIN {"LAX", "BURBANK", "LONG_BEACH"} AND
    arrival_airport WITHIN {"NATIONAL", "BALTIMORE", "DULLAS"} AND
    departure_time BETWEEN <7am, 11am>

SELECT * FROM AA_flight
WHERE departure_airport WITHIN {"LAX", "BURBANK", "LONG_BEACH"} AND
    arrival_airport WITHIN {"NATIONAL", "BALTIMORE", "DULLAS"} AND
    departure_time BETWEEN <7am, 11am>

SELECT * FROM NW_flight
WHERE departure_airport WITHIN {"LAX", "BURBANK", "LONG_BEACH"} AND
    arrival_airport WITHIN {"NATIONAL", "BALTIMORE", "DULLAS"} AND
    departure_time BETWEEN <7am, 11am>

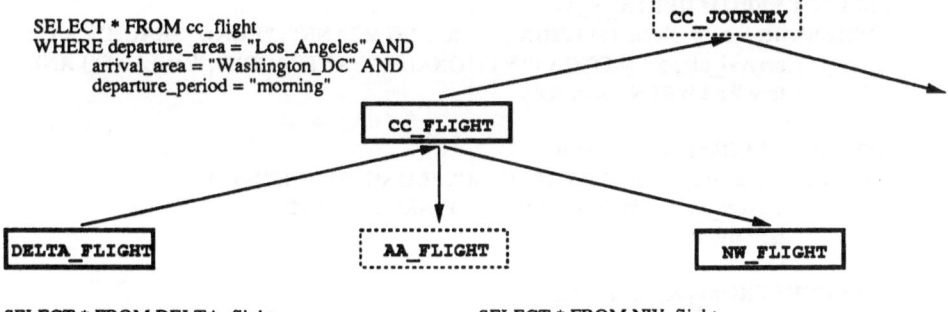

SELECT * FROM cc_flight
WHERE departure_area = "Los_Angeles" AND
    arrival_area = "Washington_DC" AND
    departure_period = "morning"

SELECT * FROM DELTA_flight
WHERE departure_airport = "LAX" AND
    arrival_airport = "NATIONAL" AND
    departure_time BETWEEN <9am, 10am>

SELECT * FROM NW_flight
WHERE departure_airport WITHIN
    {"LAX", "BURBANK", "LONG_BEACH"} AND
    arrival_airport WITHIN
    {"NATIONAL", "BALTIMORE", "DULLAS"} AND
    departure_time BETWEEN <7am, 11am>

Figure 8. Transfer a Query to the Neighborhood Objects

5.2 Conceptual Query Answering

Very often a user has a question in mind but does not know *exactly* how to formulate the query. For example, if a user wants to get information about traveling from Los Angeles to Washington D.C., but is unfamiliar with the airlines, buses or trains schedules, he does not know the best way to express a query. The proposed type abstraction mechanism is suitable for answering conceptual queries. With this approach, the user may ask a more general question about "how to travel from Los Angeles to Washington D.C. at a reasonable cost", as

```
SELECT * FROM cc_journey
WHERE departure_area = "Los_Angeles" AND arrival_area = "Washington_DC" AND
        cost = "reasonable"
```

With the *abstract type hierarchy*, such a query can be automatically refined to the following refined queries:

```
SELECT * FROM cc_flight
WHERE departure_area = "Los_Angeles" AND arrival_area = "Washington_DC" AND
        flight_cost = "low"

SELECT * FROM cc_train
WHERE departure_area = "Los_Angeles" AND arrival_area = "Washington_DC" AND
        train_cost WITHIN {"high", "medium"}

SELECT * FROM cc_bus
WHERE departure_area = "Los_Angeles" AND arrival_area = "Washington_DC" AND
        bus_cost = "high"
```

Note that in the above refined queries, **cc_journey** is "refined" to **cc_flight**, **cc_bus** and **cc_train**. Then these three queries can be further refined to

```
SELECT * FROM DELTA_flight
WHERE departure_airport WITHIN {"LAX", "BURBANK", "LONG_BEACH"} AND
        arrival_airport WITHIN {"NATIONAL", "BALTIMORE", "DULLAS"} AND
        fare BETWEEN <300, 400>

SELECT * FROM santa_fe_train
WHERE departure_station WITHIN {"LA", "LONG_BEACH"} AND
        arrival_station WITHIN {"DC", "FAIRFAX"} AND
        fare BETWEEN <300, 400>

SELECT * FROM greyhound_bus
WHERE departure_station WITHIN {"LA", "HOLLYWOOD", "LONG_BEACH"} AND
        arrival_station WITHIN {"DC_DOWNTOWN", "ROCHVILLE", "FAIRFAX"}
AND
        fare BETWEEN <251, 300>
```

and so on.

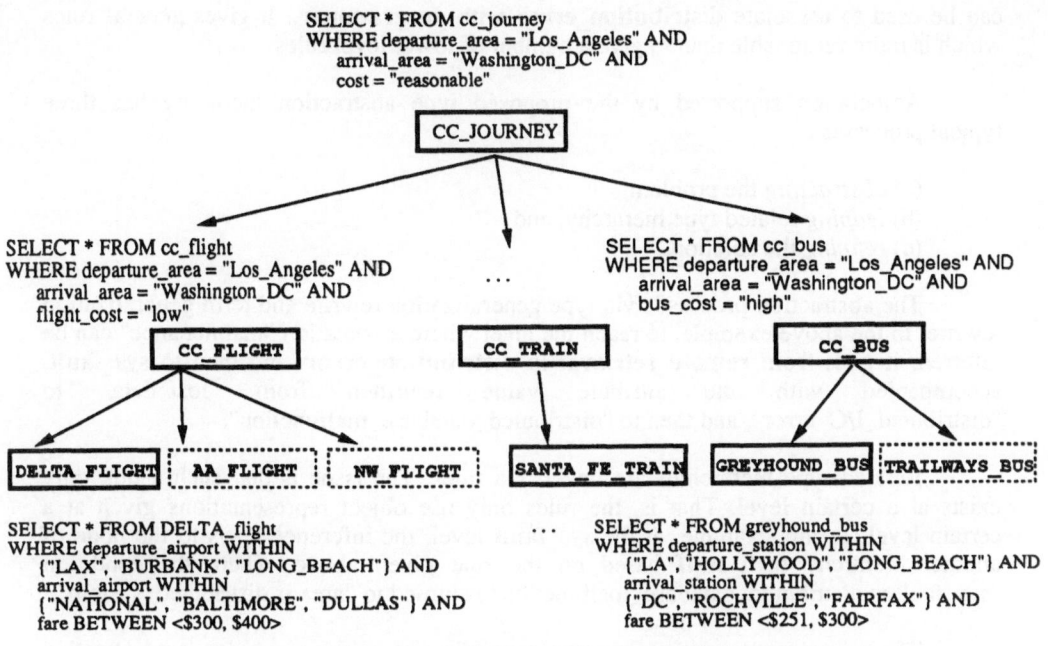

```
                        SELECT * FROM cc_journey
                        WHERE departure_area = "Los_Angeles" AND
                              arrival_area = "Washington_DC" AND
                              cost = "reasonable"
```

Figure 9 Refining a Conceptual Query

Thus based on the hierarchy of knowledge, a conceptual query can be processed to derive a set of more specific queries which can then be answered by the conventional query processing system.

5.3 Associative Query Answering

Problem solving usually requires the association of various subjects. In general association between related types of objects can be expressed by rules, therefore we can view these rules as links between these types. However, to express rules at a higher conceptual level is more clear and efficient than at a lower level. Furthermore, those links may be located at any abstract level, and in many cases the links between types are not located within a single type hierarchy but span multiple type hierarchies. The proposed type abstraction notion can be used to represent and handle associations between related subjects.

As a simple example shown in Figure 10, a **remote_retrieval** problem "lost_data" has no direct links to the researchers or programmers in the related fields. Instead, some general association rules can be given. At a higher level, the rule :

If system_fault is "distributed_database_malfunction",
    then call System_Development tech_staff whose speciality is "distributed_system"

can be used to associate **sys_fault** with **tech_staff**. At a lower level, the rule :

If distribution_error is "distribute_I/O_error",
    then call the programmer whose job is "network_programming"

286

can be used to associate **distribution_error** with **programmer**. It gives general rules which is more reasonable than to give a number of lower level rules.

Association supported by the proposed type abstraction hierarchy has three typical processes :

(a) *abstracting* the problem,
(b) *leaping* related type hierarchy, and
(c) *refining* the solution.

The abstraction process is via type generalization rewrite and term generalization rewrite. In the above example, to reach the level where association "maintenance" can be referred, it goes from **remote_retrieval** to **distribution_error**, and then to **sys_fault**, accompanied with the attribute value rewritten from "lost_data" to "distributed_I/O_error", and then to "distributed_database_malfunction".

Related type hierarchies are linked via rules. The issue is that such a link only exists at a certain level. That is, the rules only use object representations given at a certain level. In this example, at the **sys_fault** level, the inference leaps to the node of another hierarchy **tech_staff** based on the rule given above, where the condition "sys_fault is distributed_database_malfunction" is turned to "area is distributed_system".

The refinement process is via type specialization rewrite and term specialization rewrite. In this example, the refinement process leads to the solution "researchers whose field is database or network", or "programmers whose job is network_programming".

These processes are carried out automatically by the system. The user only states a request such as

ASSOCIATE maintenance WITH remote_retrieval
WHERE fault = "lost_data"

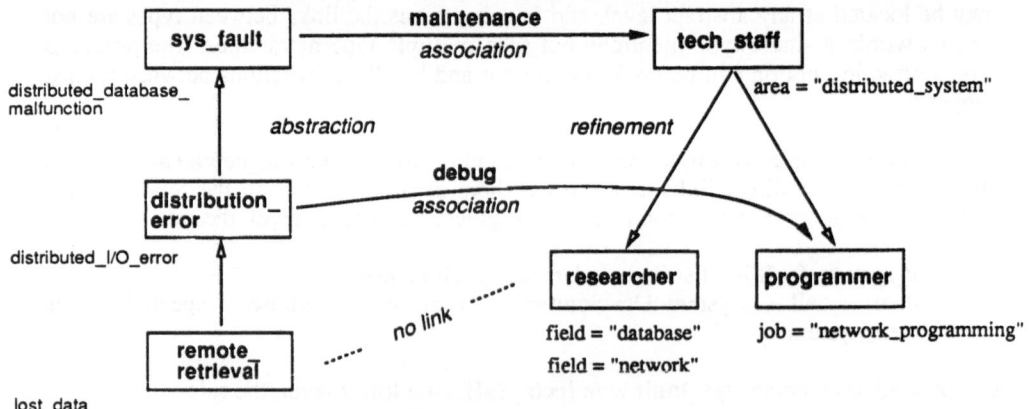

Figure 10. Associative Query Answering

This example indicates that an association links concepts represented at certain conceptual levels. To refer to associated concepts one needs to move up and down along the type abstraction hierarchy to find such links, since these links can only be found at certain conceptual levels.

In general, to support cooperative query processing through subject association, the system first moves up, if necessary, to reach a certain knowledge level where the association is defined. Then via the association link and rules it can transfer to another type hierarchy and refine the associated objects.

By using the type abstraction hierarchy, the rules may be specified at a higher knowledge level in terms of the object instances represented at that level. Considering the rule used in the above example,

If system_fault is "distributed_database_malfunction",
then call System_Development tech_staff whose speciality is "distributed_system".

Note that the instance "distributed_database_malfunction" referred in this rule is more abstract than the more detailed instances such as "lost_data", "transmission_error", and "disconnection". Thus using this rule is more general and convenient than using a number of rules referring "lost_data", "transmission_error", and "disconnection". As a result, the number of rules in the knowledge base system can be considerably reduced and thus the inference processes can be greatly simplified. Organizing knowledge based on the type abstraction hierarchy provides a systematic way to perform inference. Furthermore, such knowledge can be organized and managed by the database system.

6. Comparison with Related Work

The concept of abstraction has received much attention but has different meanings in different contexts. The proposed notion of *multilevel type abstraction* is characterized by representing the *instance values* (can be composed values) of an object differently at different knowledge levels. Using these instance values given at different knowledge levels, reasoning can be performed between different knowledge levels to derive information with various degrees of abstraction and coverage. Below we shall emphasize our notion of abstraction as *instance representation based* and compare it with the conventional notions of *classification, composition, and function based abstractions* found in the semantic data model. Particularly, we shall point out the differences between our approach and the OODB approach.

Classifying objects by grouping those with the common properties into a class is a kind of abstraction mechanism [SMI77] [HAM78] [BRO81,84,86] [SU83]. It allows the properties to be specified against the class rather than against each individual object, and provides a *class name* as an abstract title to qualify the class of objects. Such an abstraction does not concern the instance representations of the class of objects. For a class hierarchy, the notion of generalization is underlain by the subsumption relationship among classes . The corresponding *is_a* relationship only sorts classes but does not link object instance values. For example, the expression "A *is_a* B" means an object of class A is also an object of class B, without requiring its instance values in class A and class B to be represented differently. Therefore object classification does not provide instance representation based abstraction.

Composing several objects into a complex object also provides an aggregation-based abstract view over the component objects [SMI77] [ZAN85] [BAN87] [CHE88]. For example, a "car" can be viewed as the abstract representation of its wheels, engine and body all together, but not the abstract representation of any individual part. This kind of abstraction summarizes a set of related objects by identifying their aggregation as a single object, but does not provide alternative representations for the instance values of its component objects.

Functional abstraction is represented by the notion of Abstract Data Type (ADT) [GOG75] [GUT78]. The sense of "abstraction" of ADT comes from the principle of reducing the amount of complexity or detail that must be considered at any one time. This notion emphasizes representing types functionally in terms of axioms and implementing types by simpler types rather than dealing with instance representations. Further, our type abstraction notion provides a mechanism to represent objects at different knowledge levels directly by experience-based *plausible facts*, rather than by *algebraic axioms*. Such representation is often more practical and easier to be supported by databases.

In an OODB there exist two types of hierarchies: the class hierarchy which is considered from the classification (*IS-A*) point of view, and the object configuration hierarchy which is considered from the composition (*part_of*) point of view [GOL81] [BAN86] [BEE86] [TSU86] [ABI87] [CHE89] [KIM89]. As mentioned above, the proposed type abstraction view is not covered by these notions. Further, an OODB typically deals with information at two general layers: the *meta-layer* (intension) and the *instance layer* (extension). All the classes of objects at different levels of the class hierarchy are at the same instance layer so that one class may subsume another and a method defined for a class can be inherited by its sub-classes. The proposed type abstraction mechanism has extended such a two-layers limitation. An object can have its counterpart at a higher knowledge level but they are not at the same instance layer. Consider for example, at a lower level the age of a person, say 17, is countable by a certain function, however at a higher level of the type abstraction hierarchy it can be represented by a more abstract concept of age, say *young*, which does not have to be countable by the same function. For knowledge abstraction, there is no theoretical limitation on the number of layers for knowledge (or concept) representation. The knowledge represented at different layers may be *convertible*, rather than directly inheritable. Thus limiting object representation to only two layers, intension layer and extension layer, though adequate for handling data, is not sufficient for handling knowledge.

Finally we would like to compare our approach with the rule-based reasoning approaches such as [CUP89]. It is true that using rules can provide various links between objects. However, without a clean organization principle, the database and knowledge base tend to become two separated parts of a system and the inference using both data and rules becomes inefficient. The proposed type abstraction hierarchy provides a well organized framework for coupling data and knowledge, and supports cooperative query answering by the model based systematic methodology rather than by the ad-hoc rule-based reasoning.

7. Conclusions

The type abstraction hierarchy, query rewrite, and subject association are useful tools for supporting cooperative query answering. The proposed type abstraction hierarchy integrates the notions of subsumption, composition and abstraction and thus offers an integrated view of the type hierarchy with multi-level knowledge abstraction. Based on the type abstraction hierarchy, query rewrite and subject association can be used to provide reasoning among different knowledge levels to derive cooperative answers.

Data/knowledge base application requires complex tasks performed through the intelligent cooperation of multiple knowledge sources and agents based on the knowledge represented at various abstract levels. Since the object representative hierarchy can be handled by databases, and the type abstraction hierarchy can be coupled with knowledge processing, our proposed methodology is suitable for such applications. We have implemented a prototype cooperative database system at UCLA based on this methodology. Our preliminary experimental results reveals that this approach provides a systematic and efficient way for cooperative query answering.

References

[ABI87] S. Abiteboul, S. Grumbach, "Une Approche Logique de la Manipulation d'objets Complexes", 3e Journees BD3, Port Camargue, 1987.

[AIT86] H. Ait-Kaci, "Type Subsumption as a Model of Computation", in Expert Database Systems, Kersburg ed. 1986.

[ALA90] A. Alashqur, S. Su and H. Lam, "A Rule-based Language for Deductive Object-Oriented Databases", Proc. of the 6th International Conference on Data Engineering, 1990.

[BAN86] F. Bancilhon and S. Khoshafian, "A Calculus for Complex Objects", Proc. PODS'86.

[BAN87] J. Banerjee et al. "Data Model Issues for Object-Oriented Applications", ACM Trans. on Office Information Systems, 1987.

[BEE86] C. Beeri et.al, "Sets and Negation in a Logic Database Language LDL1", MCC Rep,1986.

[BRO81] M. Brodie, "On Modeling Behavioral Semantics of Databases", Proc. of VLDB'81, 1981.

[BRO84] M. Brodie, J. Mylopoulos, J. Shmidt eds, "On Conceptual Modeling", Springer-Verlag, NY, 1984.

[BRO86] M. Brodie, J. Mylopoulos eds, "On Knowledge Base Management Systems", Springer-Verlag, NY, 1986.

[CHE88] Q. Chen and G. Gardarin, "An Implementation Model for Reasoning with Complex Objects", Proc. of ACM-SIGMOD 88, USA, 1988.

[CHE89] Q. Chen & Wesley Chu, "A High Order Logic Programming Language

(HILOG) for NON-1NF Deductive Databases," Proc. of 1st International Conference on Deductive and Object-Oriented Databases, 1989, Japan. also in Deductive and Object-Oriented Databases, Elsevier Science Publishers B.V., 1989.

[CUP89]   F. Cuppens and R. Demolombe, "Cooperative Answering: A Methodology to Provide Intelligent Access to Databases", Proc. of the 2nd international conference on expert database systems, 1989.

[GOG75]   J. Goguen et al, "Abstract Data Types as Initial Algebras and Correctness of Data Representations", Proc. Conf. on Computer Graphics, Pattern Recognition and Data Structure.

[GUT78]   J. Guttag, E. Horowitz and D. Musser, "Abstract Data Types and Software Validation", CACM 21(21), 1978.

[HAM78]   M. Hammer and D. Mcleod, "The Semantic Database Model", ACM Trans. Database Systems, 6(3), 1981.

[KIM89]   W. Kim, "A Model of Queries for Object-Oriented Databases", Proc. of VLDB'89, 1989.

[SMI77]   J. Smith & D.C.P. Smith, "Database Abstraction : Aggregation and Generalization", ACM Trans. Database Systems 2(2), 1977.

[SU83]   S. Su, "SAM*: A Semantic Association Model for Corporate and Scientific-Statistical Databases", Information Sciences 29, 1983.

[TSU86]   S. Tsur and C. Zaniolo, "LDL: A Logic Based Data Language", Proc. VLDB 12, 1986.

[ZAN85]   C. Zaniolo, "The Representation and Deductive Retrieval of Complex Objects", Proc. VLDB 11, 1985.

DISCUSSION

Presenter: W. Chu.

Q. (S. M. Deen, Keele University) : I like your ideas but there are one or two points on which I'm not entirely clear. From the last few remarks you made, it seems to me that all these structures are built separately from the schema. If it is at the schema level you'll need the whole organization to act together to effect any change, which is a serious problem. And you also have an extensive query optimization problem. How are you handling all that?

A. (W. Chu) : Cooperative query answering is made through transforming one query to another to enlarge or shrink the scope of the query. Once the query has been transformed then you can use conventional query optimization techniques to handle the query processing. We provide, on top of an existing data schema, a type hierarchy specification based on the proposed abstraction notion which can be a table showing the domain values of a super-type and a sub-type. This provides an organized way to associate various concepts at different knowledge levels. For example, if I want to find a computer expert I should not go to the History department; I should consult the Engineering department or the Computer Science department. Further, if my question is related with database languages, I should consult the database group. Our proposed type abstraction hierarchy gives a well-organized structure to approach the user's goal.

Q. (S. M. Deen) : Are you building it for each user, each class of users or a group of users ? Given that, it would be a very complex structure and its design would take a large amount of time. Also you can get it wrong or you may need an extension. If it's an ordinary user you'll have a great difficulty in handling it.

A. (W. Chu) : To build such a system we need to analyze the domain of the required data. For example, answering the query on telecommunication and the query on airline reservation require different domain knowledge; their rewrite should be based on different type abstraction hierarchies. We provide the type abstraction information in the selected domains that users may be interested in. Queries on these domains made by any user can then be answered cooperatively.

Q. (S. M. Deen) : I think I understand. It is user-oriented?

A. (W. Chu) : Right, but more precisely it is domain-oriented. Type abstraction hierarchy provides a structure to organize concepts in various domains. The system conveys cooperative query answers to any user who queries on those domains.

Q. (J. Longstaff, Teeside Polytechnic) : It seems some of your queries were expressed in SQL where perhaps it would be more appropriate to use a sort of intellect type of query where the user doesn't have to know the structure of the schema. How much does a user have to know of your schemas and your hierarchy?

A. (W. Chu) : The reason we use SQL is because we're dealing with databases. However we will extend SQL by adding cooperative query answering features. The query rewrites are transparent to the user but the user should provide the original query with sufficient information to serve as the entry point of the type abstraction hierarchy. We need to know the users interest and select corresponding problem domains for building the type abstraction hierarchy, based on the user's typical queries and the type of answers they expect. As a result, when the user queries the database, the user doesn't have to know much about the build-in knowledge.

Q. (J. Longstaff) : Do you see a role for educating your users, by explanations or whatever, towards a common terminology for object entities or whatever based upon your names and your schema?

A. (W. Chu) : We plan to develop this system for the average level users and we don't expect them to know much about the schema.

Q. (A. Schafer, Mitre Corporation) : I wondered if you had considered using an object-oriented database?

A. (W. Chu) : First of all, we do integrate the abstraction notion with the object-oriented notions of subsumption and composition. However, our notion of abstraction is based on object instance representations, and the subsumption and composition notions are not concerned with that. If a class subsumes its subclasses, it does not imply any change on object instance values. Composing several objects together by identifying their aggregation as a single object also does not change the instance values of these component objects. Therefore, an object-oriented database deals with information only at two general layers: the meta-layer and the instance layer. Since forming an object-oriented type hierarchy does not introduce a new instance value, it is impossible to introduce an additional instance layer. However, in the proposed type abstraction hierarchy, instances of a super-type and instances of a sub-type may have different representations viewed at different instance layers, and such multiple layer knowledge representations are essential for cooperative query answering.

Q. (A. Schafer) : I'm not clear whether this hierarchy of abstraction is something implicit in the data modeling or you're adding additional semantic information into the database.

A. (W. Chu) : We add the additional semantic information to a conventional object-oriented system. While we organize a type abstraction hierarchy for cooperative query answering, we try to predict what the user will most likely be interested in, just as a travel agent should have knowledge about the traveler's concerns, the nature of the trips, business or leisure, and so on, in order to properly organize the customer's trips. After adding the additional semantic information, the system becomes more intelligent and capable of deriving co-operative query answering.

Q. (A. Schafer) : What is the benefit of using such a structured type abstraction hierarchy other than explicitly using rules ?

A. (W. Chu) : In supporting cooperative query answering, we attempt to provide an efficient and organized framework for coupling data and knowledge. Although using explicit rules can provide various links between objects, it lacks a systematic organization to guide the inference process.

Contracts in Database Federations

Matts Ahlsén
Paul Johannesson

SISU[1]
The Swedish Institute for Systems Development
Box 1250, S-164 28 Kista,
Sweden

Abstract

A model for information sharing in a loose association of
information/database systems is proposed. Such a system is referred to as a
federation, where the fundamental characteristic is the autonomy of the
member systems (the nodes). The model for sharing is based on the
establishment of bilateral agreements between nodes. These agreements are
represented by contracts, the terms of which define the rules for information
exchange. The model provides flexibility for resource sharing and for
cooperation in a decentralized setting.

1. Introduction

1.1 Rationale

Distributed information systems are becoming increasingly important as a result of
organizational demands and as a consequence of technical advances in computer
networking. In most approaches to distributed systems design, e.g., distributed
databases, a global view is adopted and realized thru global descriptions and constraints
which are often centrally maintained. A user (application) of a distributed database
perceives the system as a single logical database described by a global schema. Systems
based on these assumptions could in many cases become too rigid and a looser form of
association of local systems is preferable. This would consist of independent,
autonomous information systems (nodes) which cooperate in order to exchange
information with a minimum of global control and without a centrally maintained global
schema. In such an association the nodes decide themselves the conditions for the sharing
of information.

The fundamental requirement on an architecture for this type of loose association is to
compensate the lack of global structure and control, by providing facilities for
cooperation. This requirement may be met by combining mechanisms for information
sharing and authorization, paying specific attention to the autonomy of nodes.

---

[1] This work is supported by the National Swedish Board for Technical Development (STU).

Using these mechanisms nodes should be able to exchange sufficient knowledge about their database contents in order to arrive at agreements that define the authorization to share subsets of database objects. The set of rules that is the result of such an agreement is grouped into a logical entity called a *contract*. The purpose of the contracts model discussed in this paper is to define the meaning, use and representation of such agreements. The model is intended to serve as a platform upon which more elaborate schemes for cooperation can be built. The architecture within which this model is discussed is referred to as a *federated architecture*.

1.2   Context

To set the context for the discussion in the following sections, we here mention some aspects of distributed systems and properties of their designs. The research in distributed databases has been extensive since the end of the seventies [Ceri84][Özsu90]. The emphasis has been to provide a high degree of distribution transparency with sufficient performance. The common characteristic of many distributed databases is a global conceptual schema and a tightly coupled communications architecture. In certain cases this characteristic makes it difficult to provide autonomy for individual databases (sites). *Autonomy* is an important aspect of any distributed database (or distributed information system in general); it is a property of the constituent sub systems (sites) and refers to their independence of operation and administration. There are several possible alternatives to the tightly coupled architectures. Multidatabase systems, for example, represent a class of distributed database systems concerned with the integration of (possibly heterogeneous) independently operating databases. Most such systems strive for a global schema; however, some approaches to multidatabase management support cooperation between systems without presupposing the existence of a global schema [Litwin86].

The concept of communication between the sites in a distributed system can be replaced by the more general idea of cooperation. Cooperation in decentralized information systems is based on the idea of open systems [Hewitt84]. This concerns computer applications based on communication between subsystems that have been developed separately and independently, i.e. open-ended and incremental subsystems that undergo continual evolution. A class of decentralized systems close to this concept is represented by Federations, or Federated Information systems. This architectural model emphasizes the autonomy of nodes while providing possibilities for discretionary sharing. Recently, the area of Federated Systems, and databases in particular, has been given an increased attention, as a framework for dealing with issues related to autonomy as well as heterogeneity. A reference architecture for distributed database management, including Federated Database systems, is described in [Larson 90], which also adopts a taxonomy where Federated Database systems form a subclass to Multidatabase systems.

The initial contribution to the Federated Database model is the work by Heimbigner and McLeod [Heimb85][Heimb87] on the Federated Database Architecture. The architecture proposed consists of interconnected components and a federal dictionary. The components represent individual users, applications, workstations or other components in an (office) information system. The sharing of information between components is coordinated through bilateral "negotiations".

An interesting aspect of distributed systems architecture is *scaling*, which can be used as an instrument to decrease complexity while providing resource sharing. In a scalable distributed system [Konst90] nodes have the possibility to dynamically expand and shrink their domain of accessible resources (e.g. in terms of database objects). An open system based on a Federated architecture can provide a basis for scaling.

The model proposed in this paper is derived from that of Heimbigner and McLeod. One difference is, however, that it does not require the existence of a federal dictionary. The intention is to promote an even more loosely coupled type of network in that each member node will possibly only have partial knowledge of the surrounding system. Each node knows only those other nodes with which it has been acquainted, and may be able to access a subset of the database objects at these nodes. This is similar to the concept of the Partially Informed Distributed Database [Blakey87] where nodes only have partial knowledge of directory information. Cooperation in federated systems has implications on security and authorization; increasing security is one of several motives for decentralization [Gray86]. The contracts model can be seen as a generalization of an authorization model [Ahlsén88] applicable in a decentralized systems architecture.

A recent development is the attempt to merge (distributed) database management with knowledge based systems. In addition to the knowledge representation aspect, there is an emphasis cooperation between knowledge bases and on distributed problem solving [Kniesel90]. An example of a distributed knowledge based system is the KIWIS system [KIWIS90d]. The KIWIS system consists of a network of communicating knowledge bases. Each KIWI node is a complete knowledge base management environment including a knowledge representation language which integrates object-oriented constructs with logic programming, as well as advanced user interface tools. Each KIWI node also has the possibility to interface external applications, such as conventional DBMSs. To provide for cooperation between these knowledge base environments, the federated architecture and the contracts model described in this paper is currently being further developed and applied within the KIWIS Project. In the sequel, we discuss the federated architecture and the use of contracts in general terms.

2. Database Federations

2.1 Architecture

A database federation consists of a set of nodes which are able to communicate and share information. Each node is an information system consisting of three parts: a conceptual schema, an information base, and an information processor used to query and manipulate the information base and the conceptual schema. A federation forms a loosely coupled network, in which member nodes may enter and leave dynamically and where the communication paths may change. We do not associate any specific properties to the federation as such. Rather, we should view the "federation" from the perspective of a single node, and the possibilities given to that node thru its membership in the federation. Hence, the important point is the Federated Architecture which makes possible a certain form of communication and cooperation.

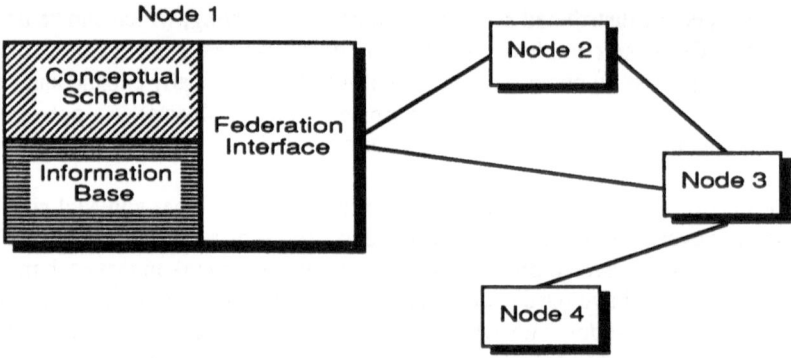

Fig. 2.1: Schematic view of Federated Architecture as a loosely coupled network

2.2 Autonomy

The most important property of the member systems in a federation is their autonomy. Autonomy in a distributed system refers to the distribution of control, and there are several possible classifications of autonomy [Özsu90]. We distinguish between three different forms of autonomy:

- *Semantical autonomy* means that the schema of a node does not have to conform to the schema of any other node, and consequently there is no global schema in the federation. The absence of a global schema means that there is no global extension maintained by the federated architecture. However, there still has to exist global knowledge, defining basic communication facilities and concepts.

- *Behavioural autonomy* implies that a node is not obliged to process requests from other nodes in the federation. This means that a node is in full control of its local resources.

- *Network autonomy* refers to the absence of a central authority in the federation to organize the interactions between nodes. Thus, nodes are not forced to be dependent upon intermediary nodes for communication.

The behavioural autonomy implies that from a certain node's point of view, the behaviour of the nodes in the federation is unpredictable. To overcome this problem, at lest partially, we assume that information sharing between two nodes can take place only if there exists an explicit agreement between the nodes concerning that information. Such an agreement is always established between two nodes, *partners*; the node which provides access to a part of its database is called the *exporter*, while the other node is called the *importer*.

Thus, the basic mechanism for sharing is thru the importation and exportation of database objects between the partner nodes of a contract.

We are assuming that when sharing information, the nodes make use of a common data model, i.e., the system is homogeneous wrt data model type. If some node would locally use another data model, there will arise a need for translation between this data model and the common one. However, we will in this paper not address the issue of data model translation, or other issues relating to heterogeneity. We assume that the common data model used in the federation is an object oriented model. Each object is assumed to have a set of properties, an identity and a state. The data model is also to provide set oriented query expressions. The choice of an object oriented model is not crucial, the fundamental characteristics of a federated architecture can be realized using any data model. However, the semantic expressiveness and structuring capabilities of object oriented models (e.g., thru specialization/generalization), are advantageous in overcoming certain problems caused by the semantical autonomy in the federation. Such problems include how to integrate information imported from other nodes with local information and how to handle inconsistencies in the federation.

2.3 Knowledge about the Federation

The network autonomy and the semantic autonomy imply that nodes must maintain their own local views of the federation. It is the responsibility of each node to acquire and maintain knowledge about the rest of the federation. As a result, a node will possibly only have partial knowledge of the topology of the federation and the application domains of other nodes. Specifically, a node has to keep track of the names and addresses of those other nodes it knows about, it must be able to find out what information other nodes are willing to export, and it must maintain information about all the agreements made with others. The information thus needed is modelled by a conceptual schema, referred to as the Cooperation Schema (fig. 2.2.). The Cooperation Schema is identical for each node in the federation.

Two important subsets of this information are represented by the *Federal Map* and the *Export Schema*. The Federal Map (object type NODE in fig. 2.2) is a local catalogue or dictionary that contains information on currently known nodes. For each such node the address and a description explaining its application domain are specified. The Federal Map will also describe the topology of the federation in terms of available communications paths currently known to a node. Further, it may contain information on objects which are available for exportation at other nodes.

The Export Schema is a description of those objects a node is prepared to export to other nodes; in the Cooperation Schema these objects are instances of the type EXPORTABLE_OBJECT. The objects in the Export Schema are not necessarily the actual database objects, but could be alternative descriptions of, or possibly views on, database objects. A description is here taken to be some representation that conveys the semantics of an object, not necessarily in the same language as its corresponding database representation. An export schema thus defines an interface for other nodes to the local database of some node. The schema can in this respect be compared to a View-Based

298

authorization mechanism on the local database, providing for possible transformations of structure (intensions) and content (extensions) of the local database objects. In general, the export schema will describe some subset of the local database, possibly the total database.

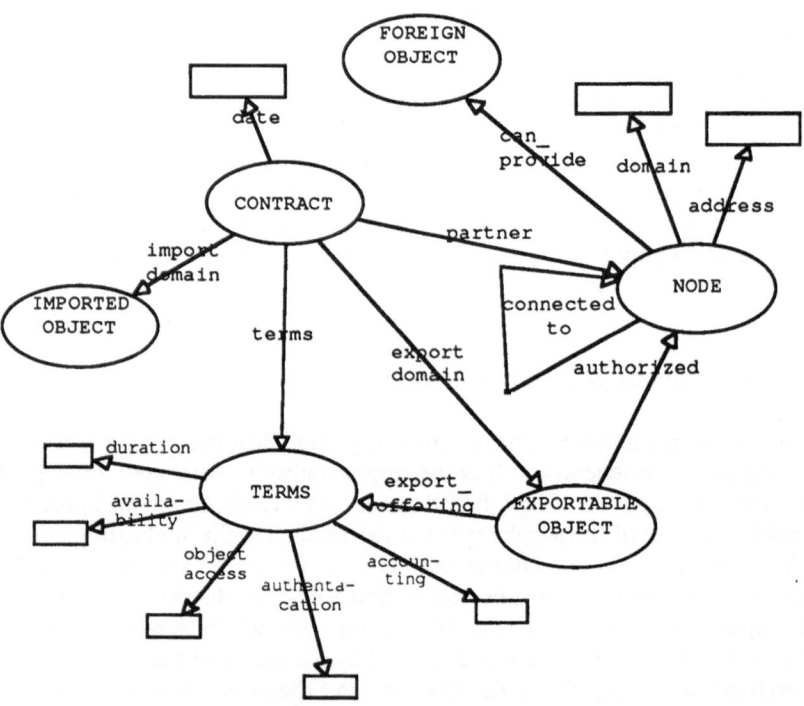

Fig. 2.2: Conceptual model of the Cooperation Schema.

Finally, the Cooperation Schema provides for the representation of agreements between nodes. Each such agreement is represented by a *contract* (object type CONTRACT in fig.2.2), which specifies the partners of the contract, the set of objects being shared and the terms, i.e. the rules under which the objects are made available to the importer. Every agreement is represented by two contract objects, one at the exporter and one at the importer.

Both the Federal Map and the Export Schema may be exported/imported, allowing nodes to acquire knowledge about the surrounding federation. The information described by the Cooperation Schema is represented at a node by the common data model of the federation, which makes it possible to query and manipulate contract information.

3. Contracts

3.1 The Meaning of a Contract

A contract is a representation of a bilateral agreement where one node, the *exporter*, is committed to make some subset of its database available to another node, the *importer*, according to a set of contract terms. The contract refers to a set of objects in the exporter's database, the *domain objects*, which are made available to the importer by transfers to the importer's database. The domain objects are chosen from the export schema of an exporter's database. The importer uses the contract as an interface definition to the exporter's database, and issues import requests. The exporting node uses the contract to monitor access to domain objects requested by a remote node by validating these import requests and by performing export actions, in this respect the contract is similar to a set of authorization rules.

The process by which an agreement may be reached, and a contract created, is controlled by the Contracts Establishment Protocol (see section 4), which allows nodes to perform a dialogue in order to decided the terms of a contract.

The basic property of a contract is the agreement it represents, which stipulates the *expected behaviour* of the partners. We must assume that a contract is mutually beneficiary for both partners and that this is the incentive for compliance with the agreed terms. Thus, it may also be a benefit to provide information to other nodes, not only to obtain information from other nodes. The nature of this benefit is application dependent. The behavioural autonomy of nodes means there is no guarantee that a partner will actually behave as expected, and comply with contracts. It is not possible to control this within the realm of the federation and the contracts model. Further, there is no third party for conflict resolution or to take action when partners do not follow contracts. Partners should instead have the possibility to detect situations arising from unexpected behaviour and take action accordingly, such as cancelling a contract. A contract is thus based on assumptions about the operation of nodes, most of which are beyond the systems control. The expected behaviour of a partner is however explicitly represented by the contract terms and the model thus emphasises the definition, representation and monitoring of these terms.

3.2 Contract Terms

The terms of a contract represent the rules under which a set of domain objects are made available to an importer. The basic principle is that all terms are negotiable, i.e., they are not pre-specified. The terms for a specific contract are dependent on the outcome of a dialogue between exporter and importer. This dialogue may result in the *establishment* of a contract, after which the terms are fixed. To be usable by the partners, the contract must also be *initialized* subsequent to its establishment. A contract has a duration in time, after which it is *terminated* and is no longer valid. *Any non-terminated contract is a valid contract.* Terminated contracts may be kept in a partner's database to provide a history and serve as templates in future contracts dialogues.

There are five different classes of terms :
• duration
  - initiation: initial event causing the contract to become valid.
  - expiration: the event for termination of the contract.
• object access: method to provide the importer access to domain objects.
• availability: acceptable degree of deviation from expected behaviour
• authentication: procedure for verification of a partner's identity.
• accounting: cost for establishment and use of the contract

These classes of terms are in general independent of the type of objects in the contract domain. We do not provide any additional terms based on the structure and contents of the domain objects, corresponding to authorization rules defined on subsets of the domain objects. Such restrictions can be achieved by the Export Schema definition. As a consequence there may be a larger number of contracts than if such rules were provided.

Initiation and Expiration

The separation of the establishment of a contract from its initiation, makes the process of deciding the terms for sharing independent from actually providing/obtaining that sharing. Once initiated, the contract can be used by both partners until terminated. A contract is terminated according to an agreed expiration term. The terms for initiation and expiration are specified by events or by a time interval both of which define the agreed period during which the contract is usable. Events can be time points or other events that may occur in either partner's database or as a consequence of the contracts dialogue.

Both terms can be specified by two successive time points. Alternatively, the initiation could be specified to occur after an *initiation time period* relative to the establishment of the contract. Should the initiation time period be zero, the initiation will coincide with the establishment, in which case the contract would become usable as soon as the contracts dialogue is finished. Initiation defined by events occuring in the exporter's database is probably the most useful. The importer may e.g. only be interested in accessing the domain objects when the populations of object types exceed a certain limit, e.g, in statistical applications. The exporter must then create and monitor a trigger that will initiate the contract when the necessary conditions are satisfied. In general, the initiation term allows several contracts (possibly for different applications) to be established, although only a subset are immediately initiated.

The Expiration term can alternatively be specified by a *period of notice* (PoN), the dual of the initiation time period. A node will then be notified by its partner (importer or exporter) about the termination, and when an agreed time period has elapsed both partners are freed from the contract. In this case the expiration term is specified by a time interval (equal to the PoN) relative to the notification event. Should the PoN be set to zero, the notification event will cause immediate termination of the contract. Expiration by means of a PoN means that the duration of a contract does not have to be fixed. Upon receipt of a notification for termination of a contract, the partners can use the PoN to prepare for termination, e.g., by notifying dependent applications.

Other application dependent events can also be used to specify these terms. We distinguish internal events from external events; the former are events caused by state changes in a partner's database, whereas external events are directly initiated by applications or users in the environment.

Object Access

The object access term controls when and how objects are imported and exported. This may be the most characteristic term of a contract in that it controls the information flow between the partners and has implications on both performance and timeliness. We assume that the data model provides set oriented query expressions. Such queries are used to transfer objects from the exporter's database to the importer. A transfer query is a query expression used by either importer or exporter to transfer subsets of domain objects from the exporter's database to the importing node, thereby providing applications at the importer access to domain objects. There are two alternatives for providing this access to the importer :

- by providing remote access to domain objects residing in the exporter's database.
- by tranferring copies of domain objects from the exporter's database to be stored in the importer's database.

The first form corresponds to remote querying, the second form is similar to the idea of "quasi copies" [Alonso89]. The two are motivated by the need for up-to-date domain objects, by performance and by the autonomy requirements. A consequence of autonomy is that transfer queries are side-effect free, i.e., remote updates are not allowed and the importing node can thus never modify the domain objects residing in the exporter's database[2].

Corresponding to the above two forms, the object access term may specify either of:

Direct access - the importing node may submit any non-modifying operation (query) on any object in the contract domain. This is always done on the importer's initiative. The importer may thus operate on the domain objects in the exporter's database but may not update them.

Snapshot - the exporter will provide the importing node with a pre-specified subset of the domain objects based on pre-specified events. A snapshot definition consists of two parts; a predefined transfer query expression that determines the subset of domain objects, and, the event that will execute the snapshot.

The generation of a snapshot is based on internal or external events in the exporters database. Such events could be time-points, time periods, or updates of domain objects

---

[2] The exporter may of course produce any side-effect as a result of an import request.

performed by the exporter. Concerning updates, snapshot generation can be restricted to special cases:
- the scope of an update of domain objects. The importer's application may only be interested in a new snapshot if the domain object have been updated to some critical limit.
- value deviation for quantifiable object properties [Alonso89]. E.g., a snapshot is executed when the new value of an arithmetic property deviates with a certain percentage or by an absolute value from the old one.

How the importer will handle results obtained by querying objects imported by direct access, is not controlled within the contract model. Further, snapshots are considered managed by the system[3], a new snapshot will be stored (possibly replacing a prior one) in the importer's database transparent to the importer's applications. A snapshot is an image of the domain objects in the exporter's database, and as such it cannot be directly modified by the importer.

The object access chosen for a contract is possibly transparent to a user (or application), but in some cases it may be advantageous to know the form of object access. A query involving objects imported by direct access could imply significant response time. The objects imported as snapshots may not be considered up-to-date at the time they are accessed. The choice of object access depends on whether it is performance or up-to-dateness which is most important to the local applications.

Availability

Due to the autonomy of nodes in the federation there is in general no way to force partners to comply with contracts, in fact there is no guarantee at all that established contracts are adhered to. The availability term is intended to give the importer (in a limited way) the ability to detect situations where the exporter can be regarded as not complying with the contract, based on expected responses to import requests.

The interaction between partners of a contract follows a simple protocol. An *import request* can be explicitly initiated by the importer, e.g., an application requiring access to some domain objects of a valid contract with direct access. An import request can also be the result of an event occuring in the exporter's database, in case of a contract with snapshot access. In response to these import requests the exporter performs *export actions*. An export action is a *response* or a *snapshot generation*. A response is either an *answer* corresponding to the result of a query on the domain objects, or an *exception*. An exception is an indication that the exporter for some reason fails or is unable to service a request. Exceptions can only be raised by the exporter and are intended to provide the importer with meaningful information on the nature of the failure. A snapshot generation is an operation performed by the exporter to transfer a subset of domain objects defined by a transfer query to the importer. As a result of an import request the importer may receive an answer or an exception. An import request for which no response is received within a specified period of time is a *failed request*.

---

[3] i.e., the software implementing the contracts model

The availability term specifies the "degree" to which the importer is prepared to accept exceptions and failed requests in response to import requests. This is an expression that relates the occurrence and frequency of exceptions and failures to import requests, e.g, the term may state a maximum of fails that may occur during a certain period of time. Availability is not relevant as a term in cases where the object access term specifies snapshot based on an event (other than time) at the exporter, since such events are local the exporter's node. If the exporter fails to comply with this term, the contract is considered terminated.

The specification of time-outs for failed requests cannot in general be a constant expression, since it is clearly dependent on the query expression in the import request and the properties of the domain objects of a specific contract. This will be a cost estimate function: contract x request -> time out.

Authentication and Accounting

As in any decentralized system it is important to provide nodes in the federation with a mechanism for mutual verification of identity. Authentication can be required in order to initiate a contracts dialogue, and to identify partners of existing contracts. The authentication term may be used to specify various standard techniques such as passwords or digital signatures [Denning82]. When using a password scheme the exporter provides the importer with a password in terms of a contracts identifier as a result of the contracts establishment. The identifier is used by the partners to authenticate subsequent object transfers within the contract. A more advanced scheme uses digital signatures based on public-key encryption.

The accounting term can be seen as an auxiliary term which can be specialized by nodes depending on their application domains. The term could be used to specify any reimbursement to the exporter associated with establishment and use of a contract. This term is mainly of documentary value since it cannot be formally controlled within the basic model.

4. Contracts Management

In this section we will consider the life cycle of a contract. When a node has localized some information it would like to import from another node, it will try to establish a contract with that node by initiating a contracts dialogue. The most basic form of a contracts dialogue has a very simple structure, [Heimb85], [Johann89a]. It can be seen as a two step dialogue, where the first step is a request from one node for a contract concerning a certain object of another node. The second step consists of the response of the other node indicating affirmation or denial of the request, where the affirmation results in the establishment of the contract. It is assumed that the responding node bases its decision on some pre-specified rules. These rules may take into account for example the export offerings defined for the object requested as defined in the Export Schema, or the extra cost for the exporter due to increased load on the system.

A need for more complex contracts dialogues may arise for several reasons. Firstly, it may be impossible to specify in advance how a node should behave in all situations that may occur in a dialogue. Secondly, it is possible that a certain object can be provided by several nodes, and thirdly, the pre-specified export offerings may not be satisfactory. This complexity motivates a more elaborated model of the contracts establishment process, which can form the basis for a computerized support system for the process. The Contracts Establishment process here proposed consists of the following four phases [Davis83], [Mazer87]:

- Announcement Phase
- Bidding Phase
- Negotiation Phase
- Commitment Phase

In the first phase a node sends an *announcement* to a set of nodes (fig. 4.1). The announcement specifies the object for which the node requests a contract and a proposal for the terms of the contract. This information is obtained from the Export Schemata of the concerned nodes.

In the bidding phase, any eligible nodes may respond by submitting *bids* to the announcer. In this case a bid from a node would be an alternative suggestion to the announcer concerning the terms which are to apply to the importation of the object. In thenegotiation phase, the announcer selects one of the bidding nodes and initiates a dialogue consisting of a sequence of steps where each step is an exchange of bids, successively modified to arrive at an agreement. The negotiation would be terminated only when the response is a definite affirmation or denial. In the final commitment phase, contract objects are created in case of an affirmative agreement, otherwise the establishment process is just terminated.

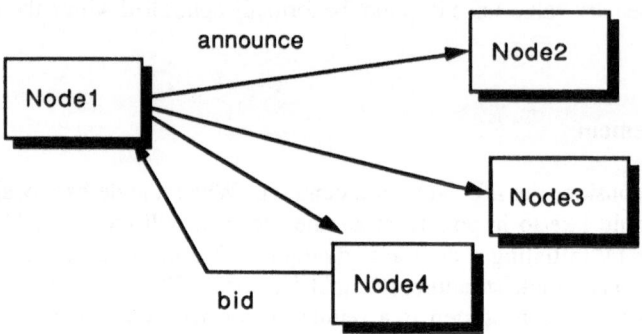

Fig. 4.1: Contract request by a (possibly limited) broadcast Announcement.

For the announcement phase to be applicable it is necessary that the nodes in a federation use a common terminology. All nodes in a federation should share a basic common language, which includes certain built-in object types and the object types in the Cooperation Schema. This language could also be extended with a set of application specific object types, that define common concepts in the application domain of a particular federation. The collection of these common types is referred to as the *common schema* of a federation. What distinguishes a common schema from a global schema in a distributed database system is firstly that a common schema does not specify any rules concerning the allocation of information among nodes, and neither does it contain any other types of constraints to which the nodes must conform. Further, the common schema may be partial, i.e. there may exist object types at a node, that are not contained in the common schema. Thus, the common schema is a dictionary that specifies the common terminology in a federation.

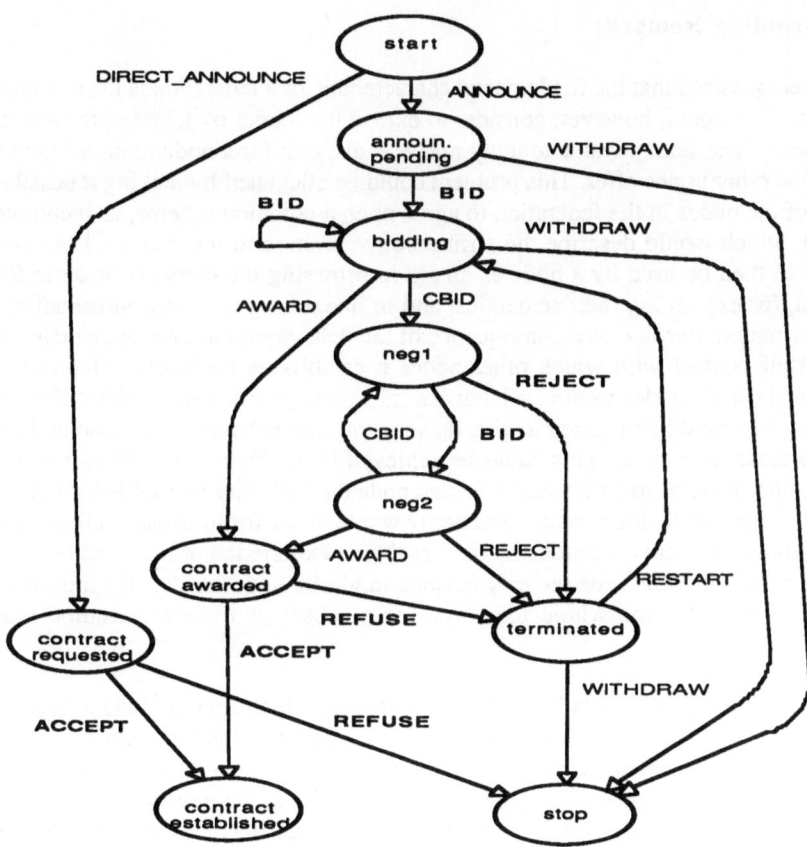

Fig. 4.2: States in the Contracts Establishment process described by a deterministic automaton showing the synchronization of Announcer (plain) and Contractors (bold).

The contracts establishment process can be described by an automaton (fig. 4.2). The automaton shows the synchronization of the messages from the announcing node (plain symbols) and those from the responding nodes (bold symbols). Note that the establishment process can be initiated either by a broadcasting announcement or a direct announcement. The latter case corresponds to the simple contracts dialogue outlined above, where the announcer sends its request to a single node, which then decides to accept or reject the request.

When a contract has been established and initialized, it will be used by the exporter to check the validity of import requests. An *invalid request* is an import request that cannot be handled by the exporter because no contract exists or the request does not comply with the contract terms. Provided that importers follow the expected behaviour, invalid requests should never occur. However, due to the behavioural autonomy of nodes it cannot be guarantied that nodes always operate within the model, which implies that invalid requests can appear. Consequently, such requests must be detected, but they will not result in a response.

5. Concluding Remarks

We have emphasized that the fundamental characteristic of a federation is the autonomy of the nodes. One could, however, consider to extend the model by relaxing the autonomy requirements. The semantical autonomy makes it difficult for a node to understand what information other nodes offer. This problem could be alleviated by making it possible for a subset of the nodes in the federation to agree upon a common schema, as mentioned in section 4, which would describe the terminology common to the nodes. The common schema can then be used by a node as an aid in browsing the contents of other Export Schemata, for explaining their semantics, and in integrating imported information with local information. Further, as a consequence of the behavioural autonomy, a node should always itself control with which other nodes it establishes contracts. However, it is possible that certain nodes would find it awkward to engage in a large number of contracts dialogues and would be prepared to give up some of their behavioural autonomy in order to reduce these dialogues. This could be achieved by making it possible for a node to assign another node as its proxy and give that node the authority to establish contracts on its behalf. Finally, relaxing network autonomy would allow for information flow controls in a federation. The network autonomy implies that re-exportation of imported information always is possible, which for security reasons might be undesirable. By introducing a supervisory node for the whole federation or a subset of it, re-exportation may be restricted.

We have outlined a Contracts Establishment Process which may include a negotiation phase. The aim of the establishment process is to support a situation similar to that of a DSS, where the task cannot be completely automated but needs user interaction. The task in this case is to get two nodes to agree on the terms for sharing a set of database objects, and the underlying assumption is that these terms are in many cases difficult to fully specify in advance. In a more advanced setting the contracts dialogues could be supported by a more complex negotiation component. The negotiation procedure could possibly take into account the outcome of previous contracts dialogues as well as knowledge of application domains and characteristics of other nodes.

The federated architecture is not a replacement for distributed database architectures, we regard it as a viable alternative when flexibility and autonomy are deemed important in the design of distributed system. The contracts model is a platform on which to build more advanced facilities for cooperation in the context of a federated architecture.

References

[Ahlsén88]   M. Ahlsén, "Specification and Control of Authority in an Object-Oriented System: Preliminaries", SYSLAB Internal Working Note 28, Department of Computer and Systems Science, University of Stockholm, Sweden, 1988.

[Alonso89]   R. Alonso and D. Barbara, "Negotiating Data Access In Federated Database Systems", in"*Fifth International Conference on Data Engineering*", Ed. pp. 56-65, Los Angeles, USA, IEEE Comput. Soc. Press, 1989.

[Blakey87]   M. Blakey, "Basis of a Partially Informed Distributed Database", in"*13th Very Large Data Base Conference*", Ed. pp. 381-388, Brighton, 1987.

[Ceri84]   S. Ceri and G. Pelagatti, "Distributed Databases - Principles and Systems", McGraw-Hill, New York, 1984.

[Davis83]   R. Davis and R. G. Smith, "Negotiation as a Metaphor for Distributed Problem Solving", *Artificial Intelligence*, vol. 20, no. pp. 63-109,1983.

[Denning82]   D. Denning, "Cryptography and Data Security", Addison-Wesley,1982.

[Gray86]   J. N. Gray, "An Approach to Decentralized Computer Systems", *IEEE Transactions on Software Engineering*, vol. 12, no. 6, pp. 684-692, 1986 June.

[Heimb87]   D. Heimbigner, "A Federated System for Software Management", *IEEE Data Engineering*, vol. 10, no. 3, pp. 39-45, 1987.

[Heimb85]   D. Heimbigner and D. McLeod, "A Federated Architecture for Information Management", *ACM Transactions on Office Information Systems*, vol. 3, no. 3, pp. 253-278, 1985.

[Hewitt84]   C. Hewitt and P. deJong, "Open Systems", in "*On Conceptual Modelling*", Ed. J. W. Schmidt, pp. 147-164, Springer, New York, 1984.

[Johann89a]   P. Johannesson and B. Wangler, "The Negotiation Mechanism in a Decentralized Autonomous Cooperating Information Systems Architecture", in *Proceedings of the 11th World Computer Congress (IFIP89)*", Ed. G. X. Ritter, North Holland, 1989.

[KIWIS90d]   KIWIS, "The KIWIS Project - Status Report", 9016, Esprit Project P2424 - KIWIS, University of Antwerp, 1990.

308

[Kniesel90]   G. Kniesel and A. Cremers, "Cooperative Distributed Problem Solving in EPSILON", University of Dortmund,

[Konst90]   D. Konstantas, "A Dynamically Scalable Distributed Object-Oriented System", in *Object Management*, Ed. D.Tsichritzis,pp.Centre Universitaire d'Informatique, 1990.

[Litwin86]   W. Litwin and A. Abdellatif, "Multidatabase Interoperability", *IEEE Computer*, vol. December, no. pp. 1986.

[Mazer87]   M. S. Mazer, "Characterizing Negotiation Protocols for Faulty Distributed Environments", in*IFIP TC10/WG 10.3 Conference on Distributed Processing"*, Ed. pp. Amsterdam, North-holland, 1987.

[Larson 90]   A. P. Sheth and J. A. Larson, "Federated Database Systems for Managing Distributed, Heterogeneous, and Autonomous Databases", *ACM Computing Surveys*, vol. 22, no. 3, pp. Sept1990.

[Özsu90]   M. T. Özsu and P. Valduriez, "Principles of Distributed Database Systems", Prentice-Hall, 1990.

DISCUSSION

Presenter: P. Johannesson.

Q. (M. Huhns, MCC): I notice in your paper you mention that the announcement is made in terms of a common language, or in terms of a common terminology, so you maintain a common schema. How is this different from a global schema which you state at the beginning you wanted to avoid having to develop?

A. (P. Johannesson): Our idea is that you can see this common schema as a dictionary specifying the common terminology of the federation. It is different from a global schema in traditional distributed databases in two respects: it does not contain any allocation information, and it does not specify any constraints to which the nodes must conform.

Q. (C. Kindermann, Technical University, Berlin): I find it very interesting that you have rules that deal with the initiation of contact and negotiating but you always use the term "terms" for those rules. So I'm interested in what kind of knowledge do you have? Is it more rule-based or more definition term-based like the ones I presented?

A. (P. Johannesson): Our intention is to use for implementation a rule-based language, more exactly it will be a language combining logic programming and object-oriented programming.

Q. (G. Kniesel, University of Dortmund): You described your cooperation schema and your federal map. Could you elaborate on what knowledge contained in this federal map has to be there from the beginning? I imagine you would at least have to know which nodes are in the system and which part of the knowledge comes as a result of negotiations and is incrementally added.

A. (P. Johannesson): It is certainly an important problem how the federal map is populated. The idea is that one first has to explicitly enter at least one node. Then one could import the federal maps from other nodes and thereby increase the number of nodes which one knows about. We envisage that the address attribute will initially be included in the description of a node and also the domain attribute which gives a short and simple description of the node, maybe in natural language about what information is contained in that node. Then you could perform a negotiation to get hold of the node's export schema and for this you will use the attribute "can_provide" which gives a much more detailed description of all the objects which a node is prepared to export. So initially you will have a very limited view of what types of information can be provided by other nodes, but there will exist mechanisms to examine it more closely.

Q. (G. Kniesel): And it is also part of a contract and it is like the other contract, it can be snapshots?

A. (P. Johannesson): Our intention is that it should be uniformly treated.

Q. (W. Chu, UCLA): Different nodes might call different objects by different names and the objects may have different granularities, so when you make the negotiation, do you have to do translations, or do you have interpretational knowledge?

A. (P. Johannesson) : It is a crucial problem of how you know what objects different terms denote. One solution to this problem is to provide some limited common terminology, what we call a common schema which would describe this. The difficulty lies in getting this partial global schema large enough without having to construct a complete global schema. This is a major problem which we still haven't addressed seriously, and we suspect it to be most difficult to achieve any substantial results here. Really, this is the complete schema integration problem.

Q. (N. Barghouti, Columbia University) : Have you made any comparisons between the overhead of communication in the federated database, such as the one you presented, where you have to basically send out many messages to initiate the contract versus a more traditional distributed database?

A. (P. Johannesson) : We are aware that there will be some overhead, first in communication as you said, and also, when a node gets a request it must check that there really exists a corresponding contract, which will also lead to some overhead. As yet we have not formally worked on performance or efficiency problems, but our belief is that they will not be very different from ordinary distributed database systems.

Q. (S. Sian, Imperial College, London) : You mentioned that the first step in the contract is that the agent browses around the network to find someone that knows and could supply the knowledge that it needs. Do you have a common way of expressing what information a node can provide to other people? I think it's probably easy to do it when it's just information but the moment you extend that to cooperating agents, they're trying to find a common formalism for expressing capabilities. It's probably a context problem.

A. (P. Johannesson) : Our solution here is still very simple-minded. We intended that each node could, for example, in natural language describe what type of information it can provide, and we haven't constructed any special purpose formalism for expressing that type of information.

Object Recognition and Retrieval in the BACK System

Carsten Kindermann
Technische Universität Berlin
Projekt KIT-BACK, FR 5–12
Franklinstr. 28/29, D–1000 Berlin 10
e-mail: kinderma@tubvm.cs.tu-berlin.de

Paolo Randi
Datamont SpA - Gruppo Ferruzzi
Datamont R&D Centre
Via Restelli 1/A, I–20124 Milano

Abstract

The development of information management techniques is an important task in building future intelligent systems. In this context we describe the integration of the terminological knowledge representation system BACK with a relational database management system. High-level schemata definition and access to the knowledge base are provided by BACK, while persistency is obtained by the database management system. Query processing is delegated to the RDBMS by compiling knowledge base queries into a single (or few) complex SQL query. The run-time compiler is based on a semantic indexing technique provided by the terminological representation system.

1 Introduction

Future information systems will be based on converging developments both in the fields of knowledge representation and database technology [Bro88]. On the one hand, conventional database technology has been found inadequate for non-standard applications, partly because the record-oriented data structures are inappropriate for keeping the information that arises in these domains. Furthermore, access to stored data requires the user to have detailed knowledge about the structure of the database. While knowledge representation systems with an emphasis on (logic based) inference mechanisms are expected to overcome these deficiencies, implemented knowledge base management systems currently lack most features typical for DBMSs. To cope with issues such as persistency, data security, or concurrency for heterogeneous, large scale knowledge bases, an enhancement of KBMSs by database technology is required.

Under the terminological knowledge representation approach based on the ideas of KL-ONE a number of *terminological logics*, or *term subsumption languages*, have been developed [PS⁺90, BS85] which allow the definition of knowledge base schemes centered around the notions of classes (called 'concepts') and binary relations between classes (called 'roles').

The BACK system [PSKQ89] is one of the more prominent representatives of systems following the terminological KR approach. Access to the KB scheme as well as to the KB content is provided by a uniform interface language that is conceptually distinguished in two parts: a terminological, or intensional, part to define concepts and roles, and to restrict the value range of roles and the cardinality of the set of 'role-fillers,' and an assertional, or extensional, part by which instantiations of concepts and relationships between objects are formulated.[1]

Terminological logics are distinguished from other approaches that employ the notion of classes (e.g. semantic database models [HK87]) by their inference mechanisms that deduce those propositions entailed by the explicitly told concept definitions and object assertions. Thus, terminological logics are more than just data models in the sense of data structures plus a set of data access/manipulation operations. Integrating database technology involves mapping one data model into another, and, as a second important issue, requires taking into account the inference mechanisms of the knowledge representation system in a sound way.

Database capabilities have so far been integrated into KR systems mainly by (a) extending the KR system with DBMS capabilities, or by (b) loosely coupling existing DBMS and KR systems (cf. [MFO90]). The former approach often adds DBMS capabilities in an *ad hoc* and limited manner, or requires repeated research on issues already dealt with in the DB area. For the latter approach poor performance has been observed resulting from a low level of integration and the limited use of the DBMS in the KR system. The solution presented in this paper tries to overcome these deficiencies by coupling the BACK system with a relational database management system in a tight fashion. The coupling may be characterized as follows:

- The "conceptual" KB scheme is formulated by the terminological part of the BACK language.

- The KB content is manipulated and accessed by the assertional part of the BACK language.

- A relational DBMS is used to obtain persistency for the objects created in the KB.

- The KB provides a special kind of semantic indexing of the information stored in the DB. In the following, we will refer to it as "conceptual indexing."

- Retrieval of objects is delegated to the RDBMS by compiling queries of the KB access language into single (or few) complex SQL programs.

---

[1]The formalism underlying BACK's assertional language allows non-disjunctive, variable-free, positive statements about the world. It provides a limited form of quantification over role-fillers, and employs the unique names assumption and the open world assumption, but allows the closed world assumption to be applied locally on role-filler sets.

```
esprit-eligible := company AND ALL(has-residence, cec-country).

sme          := company AND ATMOST(50, has-employees).

c-99         = company AND ATMOST(30, has-employees)
               WITH has-residence: CLOSE(italy).
```

Figure 1: The informal examples formulated in the BACK language.

Instead of accessing the data by streaming to the DBMS a big chunk of very simple queries, the conceptual indexing and the compiler for the KB queries enable one to fully profit from the efficiency at the SQL interface.[2]

After a short introduction to the terminological approach we present a scheme for mapping the BACK data model onto the relational model. Then we describe how objects are indexed by concepts modelled in the KB scheme. Following a characterization of different query classes we outline the design of a run-time compiler that translates queries in BACK's assertional query language AQL into SQL programs. Finally we conclude this paper by indicating further research, and by discussing the contribution of our work to the fields of future information systems and intelligent interoperability.

2 The Terminological KR Approach

The terminological approach is based on a clear distinction between intensional and extensional descriptions. This puts it close to the conventional distinction between *database scheme* and *database extensions*. On the other hand, the language designed for intensional descriptions is an expressive language and allows one to build complex descriptions. It thus constitutes a highly complex data model which includes a powerful reasoning machinery based on the language's formally specified (set-theoretic) semantics.

In analogy to the database terminology, the KB scheme is defined by expressions of the intensional description language, such as:[3]

> *An Esprit-Eligible company is defined as a company which has its residence in a CEC-country.*

> *A Small and Medium Enterprise (SME) is defined as a company with at most 50 employees.*

The concepts and roles defined in the KB scheme are used to introduce objects into the KB. Names serve as abstractions for their definitions. Thus by telling that some object c-88 *is an Esprit-Eligible company* the information that its residence must be a *CEC-Country* is inherited by c-88. This is a straightforward application of the

---

[2]In this paper we do not address the problem of maintaining the KB schema by a relational DBMS; a design of a relational schema for BACK's terminological component has been proposed in [BBST88].

[3]The informal examples from the world of ESPRIT projects are taken from [NP90].

concept definition as is also provided by other data models. The salient point of the terminological approach is that the definitions that form the KB scheme are used in an active way to classify objects by generalizing over their properties. For instance, from the following atomic facts it is derived that the object c-99 also instantiates the concepts **esprit-eligible** and **sme**.

> c-99 *is a company.*
> c-99 *has 30 employees.*
> c-99 *has its residence in Italy.*

To achieve this behavior systems following the terminological KR approach provide two major deductive inferences:

- *classification* structures the knowledge base scheme by determining the subsumption relation between pairs of concepts (on the basis of their structural descriptions) and by placing them into the concept hierarchy accordingly;

- *recognition* (or *object classification*) determines the concepts an object instantiates.

Both are based on the notion of "defined concepts:" Descriptions of concepts are formed by joining previously introduced concepts, or by restricting relations (roles) to other concepts w.r.t. range and number of fillers. A concept is marked as a "defined concept" to express that its description contains all necessary and sufficient conditions for an object to instantiate it.[4]

In the past, the role of terminological logics and of the classification service have often been discussed in their general significance for knowledge representation. In the following, however, we will see that terminological logics are especially suited for the management of knowledge bases.[5] In this context the role of classification and recognition has to be interpreted in a different way.

- Classification helps in defining the KB schema by detecting "forgotten" relationships among terminological descriptions and thus structuring the schema.

- Classification allows one to formulate queries in an arbitrary manner by mapping complex query descriptions to the indexing concepts constituting the KB schema.

- Especially in non-standard applications like CAD or CIM objects can often be described only vaguely by some of their properties. Recognition yields better characterizations for such objects by abstracting over their properties.

- Recognition builds up the conceptual indexing structure required for efficient object retrieval.

---

[4]Work on terminological logics has included studies on the decidability and complexity of the formalisms to a large extend (see [NP90] for an overview). For BACK, first results on the terminological reasoning have been reported in [Neb88]. Investigations on formal properties of assertional components have only been started recently. For a different dialect, [Hol90] shows that both subsumption detection and recognition are decidable and have the same complexity.

[5]A similar direction towards knowledge base management is taken by the work on CANDIDE [BGN89] and CLASSIC [BBMR89].

- Classification supports the recognition process by providing the functionality for handling abstracted descriptions of objects.

The first three aspects are oriented towards system usability. In the remainder of the paper, however, we will concentrate on the last two aspects and system internal-issues that arise when we make a KBMS based on the terminological approch cooperate with a relational back-end data repository.

3   Information Storage

Throughout the paper we assume the following simple, third normal form relational scheme be used to make the BACK knowledge base persistent. It consists of four relations: a relation managing instances of concepts, and three tables holding information related to roles. A precise description of the relational schemata is given with the following items (ConceptID, RoleID, and TermID are numeric identifiers refering to entities maintained in the terminological component, i.e., concepts, roles, and internal concept terms, respectively; Uc, short for *unique constant*, is a unique identifier assigned to each concept instance):

instances(ConceptID, Uc): Relates objects to the most special concepts they instantiate (and vice versa).

rvalues(RoleID, Uc, Value): Relates objects to their values[6] for some role.

rcard(RoleID, Uc, CMin, CMax, NumVals): Maintains the cardinality of an object's filler set for some role (minimum and maximum cardinality, and the number of explicitly known fillers). Note that roles are multi-valued, and that the cardinality of the filler set can be expressed without naming the values themselves.

rvr(RoleID, Uc, TermID): Holds those *value restrictions* for roles at an object that are not covered by the set of concepts indexing the object.

A general optimization criterion for designing efficient schemata that support assertional information seems difficult to define. The characteristics of a particular domain may, in fact, strongly influence the choice between various alternatives. We are currently investigating other relational schemata, such as hierarchical information structuring, or clustering of concepts around semantics based properties, e.g. 'prim-subsumption' (cf. [BR90, Kin90], and [NCL+89] for a related discussion).

4   Conceptual Indexing Through Recognition

Terminological logics provide a means to organize indexing along the "semantic" dimension, i.e. depending on the structure of the knowledge base. The idea of "conceptual indexing" is to set up pointers from concepts that constitute the KB scheme

---

[6]For the sake of simplicity, we ignore here that the internal representation of values may be of different data types such as integers and strings.

to the objects that instantiate these concepts. For each object the concepts it instantiates are determined. Among those concepts the most specific ones are selected to actually index the object. We call this process *recognition.*

Recognition of some object o involves processing the information contained in its description locally for o, processing the consequences for *adjacent* objects, i.e., objects that stand in a role-filler relationship with o, and abstracting the set of most specific concepts that are instantiated by o.

We can imagine an object's description to be normalized into a series of concept instantiations (unary predicates such as company(c-99)), and role-filler relationships (binary predicates such as has-residence(c-99, italy)). The recognizer implemented for the BACK system processes this information in the following way:[7]

(C) Concept Instantiations: A new concept instantiation is established by ANDing the new concept to the former description of the object. The resulting description is (temporarily) classified into the concept hierarchy, thereby testing its consistency.

(R) Role-filler Relationships: Establishing new role-filler relationships involves adding new fillers to those already recorded for the same role, propagating the new role-fillers upwards to superroles, and finally determining the cardinality of all roles involved. The abstracted cardinalities are added to the description obtained by (C) and are thereby checked for consistency.

(F) Forward Propagation: The internal description built up during (C) and (R) contains a number of *value restrictions (VRs)*, i.e., restrictions on the value range of roles that all fillers of these roles must satisfy. Therefore, all VRs are propagated to the new fillers established by (R); to the fillers that were known before (R) only those VRs are propagated that are newly introduced by (C) and (R). Propagating a VR to some filler means to recursively add the VR to its description and to recognize the filler.

(A) Abstraction: After successful termination of (F) all information is adjusted such that all concepts that are instantiated by the object being recognized can be abstracted. The object's internal description built up so far determines the searchspace for concepts to be tested. The searchspace consists of a well-defined partition of the concept hierarchy. A concept from the searchspace is abstracted if the object being recognized satisfies all restrictions associated with the candidate concept. Abstracting or rejecting a candidate concept each time allows the removal of other concepts from the searchspace. After the incremental processing of the searchspace has terminated all concepts are known that are instantiated by the object currently recognized. Among these, the most specific ones are selected to index the object. Restrictions that have been abstracted during recognition but are not expressed by the indexing concepts are recorded.

---

[7]A precise description of the recognizer can be found in [QK90]; differences to earlier implementations are discussed in [Kin90].

Generic Concept Description ⟨*btl-term*⟩	Derivation at Query Time	Enhanced Conceptual Indexing
primitive concept	Table Look-Up	Table Look-Up
defined defined concept concept	Complex Reasoning	Table Look-Up
complex term equivalent to TBox concept	Complex Reasoning	Table Look-Up
complex term *not* equivalent to TBox concept	Complex Reasoning	Complex Reasoning

Table 1: Characterization of query classes depending on the generic concept description ⟨*btl-term*⟩ and the implementation of the recognizer.

(B) Backward Propagation: In the same way the object currently recognized depends on its role-fillers and the concepts they instantiate, the result of its recognition may also affect objects that in turn have it as a role-filler. These objects eventually have to be re-recognized as well, although in a limited manner.

5 Characterization of AQL Query Classes

Information is retrieved from the KB by means of the assertional query language AQL. An AQL query mainly consists of a generic concept description ⟨*btl-term*⟩[8] of objects to be retrieved, and a sequence of restrictions ⟨*role-expressions*⟩ on the fillers of the roles valid for the objects:

GETALL ⟨*btl-term*⟩ WITH ⟨*role-expressions*⟩

Query processing conceptually is divided into

- *basic query resolution* that retrieves instances of ⟨*btl-term*⟩, and

- *application of the filler constraints* (expressed by the ⟨*role-expressions*⟩) on the result of the first pass.

While the latter may (in most cases) be directly compiled into a single SQL program, basic query resolution strongly depends on the ⟨*btl-term*⟩ and the implementation of the recognition process, as is illustrated in Table 1.

The basic query ⟨*btl-term*⟩ is expressed in exactly the same language as the one used to define the KB scheme. The most simple-minded way to implement basic query resolution would be to scan all objects checking whether they satisfy the concept description, i.e. whether they are *instances* of the query concept, and to return as the result set the set of instances of the query concept.

---

[8]BTL stands for "BACK term language."

318

	AQL Fragment	Resulting SQL Fragment
ANDWITH operator	⟨role⟩: ⟨value-expr⟩ ANDWITH ⟨role⟩: ⟨value-expr⟩	conjunction
AND/OR operator	⟨value-expr⟩ AND/OR ⟨value-expr⟩	conjunction/disjunction
constants	⟨role⟩:⟨constant⟩	SELECT uc FROM TO, rvalues WHERE rvalues.roleID = ⟨role⟩ AND TO.uc = rvalues.uc AND rvalues.value = ⟨constant⟩
CARD operator	⟨role⟩:CARD(⟨min⟩,⟨max⟩)	SELECT uc FROM TO, rcard WHERE rcard.min >= ⟨min⟩ AND rcard.max <= ⟨max⟩ AND rcard.uc IN TO
inverse roles	INV ⟨role⟩:⟨value-expr⟩	SELECT uc FROM TO, rvalues, ... WHERE rvalues.roleID = ⟨role⟩ AND TO.uc = rvalues.value AND rvalues.uc IN (compiled ⟨value-expr⟩)

Table 2: Compilation of AQL filler constraints. In the SQL fragments, let TO be the result of the basic query resolution.

Having built up a conceptual indexing structure, however, makes basic query resolution more efficient. A query is resolved similarly to the way a new concept description is handled, namely by classifying the query concept temporarily into the concept hierarchy. As a result either an *equivalent* concept, or the set of *immediate subsumers* and *immediate subsumees* is returned. In the former case, the result set is simply the set of all objects that are instances of the concept equivalent with the query concept, i.e., it can be determined by conventional look-ups in the appropriate DB tables. In the latter case, the union over the set of instances of the immediate subconcepts are included. Only the objects that are instances of the immediate superconcepts but not instances of the immediate subconcepts have to be checked.

Table 1 summarizes these results and illustrates the consequences for an AQL/SQL compiler. Table entries 'Table Look-Up' indicate that basic query resolution can be handled by a single SQL statement, while 'Complex Reasoning' refers to a derivative deduction of concept instances requiring an interlocked processing of terminological reasoning and a series of extensional tests by SQL queries.

There is a price to pay for such organization, however. Each new fact about an instance that is entered into the KB requires for the object—and perhaps for other related objects as well—a *re-recognition* to adjust the index structure. On the other hand, not building up the index structure makes object retrieval quite expensive. Whether an object instantiates a concept is then only deduced at query time, and the complex reasoning to solve a query becomes necessary for all but primitive query concepts. In general, when designing a recognition algorithm the problem is to make the class of queries that are solvable by mere table look-ups as large as possible without enforcing frequent alterations of the knowledge base scheme and subsequent updates of the knowledge base [Kin90].

6   Generation of SQL Programs

Basic Query Resolution

In describing how SQL queries are generated out of AQL queries let us start with the resolution of the basic query for those cases where it can be processed by a single SQL statement, i.e., when the basic query description is equivalent to an indexing concept of the knowledge base scheme. To get all instances of the basic query concept we have to look for all objects that—in the database—are indexed by the equivalent concept or any of its subconcepts (all and not only the immediate ones). The SQL query that corresponds to the AQL query GETALL ⟨*btl-term*⟩ thus is

```
SELECT uc
FROM    instances
WHERE   instances.conceptID IN (c, c₁, ..., cₖ)
```

provided that c is the concept equivalent to ⟨*btl-term*⟩ and $c_1 \ldots c_k$ are the subconcepts of c.

Application of Filler Constraints

Filler constraints following the WITH in an AQL query are applied to the result of the basic query resolution. Objects that violate any of the constraints on role-filler sets are eliminated from the result set. Most of the constraints can be compiled into a fragment of SQL code that—together with the code for basic query resolution—forms a single SQL query. For example, the query

GETALL c WITH r: rf-23

that asks for all instances of concept c that have as a filler for role r (among other fillers) object rf-23 is translated into the following SQL query:

```
SELECT uc
FROM    instances, rvalues
WHERE   instances.conceptID IN (c, c₁, ..., cₖ)
AND     rvalues.roleID = r
AND     rvalues.uc = instances.uc
AND     rvalues.value = rf-23
```

AQL Fragment		Resulting SQL Fragment
SOME subqueries	⟨*role*⟩: (SOME ⟨*class-expression*⟩)	SELECT uc FROM T0, rvalues WHERE rvalues.roleID = ⟨*role*⟩ AND T0.uc = rvalues.uc AND rvalues.value IN *(compiled* GETALL ⟨*class-expression*⟩)
THE subqueries	⟨*role*⟩: (THE ⟨*class-expression*⟩)	Run-time compiler check: (a) compile GETALL ⟨*class-expression*⟩, (b) execute the compiled GETALL query, (c) trap on |Result of (b)|≠ 1 else take retrieved instance as ⟨*constant*⟩

ALL subqueries	⟨*role*⟩: (ALL ⟨*class-expression*⟩)	SELECT uc FROM T0, rvalues v2
		WHERE v2.roleID = ⟨*role*⟩
		AND T0.uc = v2.uc
		AND NOT EXISTS (
		     (compiled GETALL ⟨*class-expression*⟩)
		   AND instances.uc NOT IN (
		     SELECT rvalues.value
		     FROM rvalues
		     WHERE rvalues.uc = v2.uc
		     AND rvalues.roleID =
		             v2.roleID
		))

Table 3: Compilation of AQL subqueries. In the SQL fragments, let T0 be the result of the basic query resolution.

Even complex subqueries like the SOME query in Figure 2 are translated into a single SQL query. Some AQL constructs, however, require parts of the queries to be resolved before the entire query can be generated. For instance, a THE subquery must refer to a unique object. This requires a check at run-time as to whether the result set of the subquery has cardinality one. Tables 2 and 3 contain translations for the most important AQL constructs.[9] A sample translation of an entire AQL query is given in Figure 2.

Queries that Require Complex Reasoning

The resolution of basic queries requires—for the recognition process described in this paper—a complex reasoning if the basic query is not equivalent to any indexing concept of the KB scheme (cf. Table 1). A procedure that solves this kind of query is composed of three fundamental blocks:

---

[9]Actually, the full AQL provides additional features described in [PSKQ89]. For the translation of further constructs see [BR90].

Determination of Immediate Instances: The instances of immediate subconcepts of the basic query description are in the result set of the query.

Determination of Candidate Instances: A set of candidates for the result set of the basic query is obtained by intersecting the set of instances of the immediate superconcepts of the query description, and removing from this set the set of definite instances determined by the previous step.

Instance Selection: The query description is distinguished from its immediate superconcepts by a list of role restrictions. These restrictions are tested on each of the candidates collected by the previous step. Objects satisfying all restrictions are included into the final result set.

Two kinds of restrictions are tested on candidate instances, and their filler sets for roles, respectively: (a) *number restrictions (NRs)* that concern the cardinality of the filler sets—they may again be handled by a single SQL query (the same way the CARD operator is handled, cf. Table 2), and (b) *value restrictions (VRs)* that require determining whether all fillers of the restricted role at a candidate are instances of the restriction—testing VRs involves look-ups in the rvr DB relation, or a kind of *query time* recognition of role-fillers in case the information in the rvr relation does not suffice to prove that the restriction is satisfied.

As long as the basic query description is distinguished from its immediate superconcepts only by a list of NRs, the basic query can be resolved by a single SQL statement. As soon as a VR is involved, however, determining the complete result set may become very complex.

7 Concluding Remarks

The development of elaborate techniques for information management is an important task in building future intelligent systems. One of the main achivements of DBMS has been to free programmers from problems of (physical) data handling. A similar abstraction is required on a higher level. Appropriate means of dealing with classes, objects, complex dependencies, rule-like knowledge, etc., will lead to systems which finally might be called "knowledge based," whether these be (stand-alone) information systems or intelligent problem solving agents in a cooperative environment.

It seems promising to apply the techniques developed in the field of terminological logics to the design of knowledge base management systems. The descriptional means provided by the approach allow for dealing with an application domain in a natural way, and at the same time lead to techniques that may be applied to the internal reasoning and retrieval process of a KBMS (cf. [NP90]). There is increasing interest in this area. Terminological KBMSs are investigated for the potential role they might play in a cooperative problem solving environment (e.g., the CANDIDE system [BGN89], a semantic database model influenced by the terminological approach, for the architecture outlined in [CNKT90]). Furthermore, in [CCL90] an approach to *cooperative query answering* is presented that is based on the use of type abstraction

Which are the instances of c1 that have as a filler for role r1 any of the known instances of c2, and that have between one and two fillers for role r2?

Formulated as an AQL query:

GETALL c1 WITH   r1: (SOME c2)
              ANDWITH r2: CARD(1,2)

The resulting SQL query:

```
SELECT uc
FROM    instances, rvalues X Y, rcard
/* Basic Query Resolution */
WHERE  instances.conceptID IN (c1, c3, c4, c5)

AND     X.roleID = r1
AND     Y.roleID = r2
AND     instances.uc = X.uc
AND     X.uc = Y.uc
AND     X.value IN

/* Solution of the Subquery GETALL c2 */
        (SELECT uc
         FROM    instances
         WHERE  instances.conceptID IN (c2, c6) )

/* CARD Constraint Application */
AND     Y.uc = rcard.uc
AND     rcard.roleID = r2
AND     rcard.cmin >= 1
AND     rcard.cmax <= 2
```

Figure 2: Sample translation of an AQL query. c_i denote concepts, r_i denote roles. Assume that concept c1 has subconcepts c3, c4 and c5, and that c2 has a subconcept c6.

hierarchies. The requirements formulated on these hierarchies are satisfied by most of the systems developed under the terminological paradigm. More generally, intelligent interoperability requires agents to be able to communicate [Bro88]. Standard interfaces as are employed in lower-level computer communication seem necessary here. The well established and almost pre-normative state of work on terminological logics makes them a good candidate for this purpose.

The work presented in this paper contributes to this overall goal. We described the integration of a terminological KR system (BACK) with a relational DBMS. The means for high-level schemata definition and access to the KB are provided by the terminological logic in BACK, while persistency is gained through the relational DBMS. Query processing is delegated to the RDBMS by compiling KB queries into few but complex SQL queries. The run-time compiler is based on the conceptual indexing structure maintained for KB objects.

The development of the BACK system has been underway since 1985. At the TU Berlin we just released the fourth system version which is again written in Prolog. It implements the recognizer and the interface to the relational DBMS described above. A first prototype of the AQL/SQL compiler has been developed at Datamont SpA, Milan. It is only now that we have started to study performance characteristics of the compiler and the resulting SQL queries which in turn depend on characteristics of the KB scheme (such as its density) and distribution of objects among KB classes. And, as mentioned above, further investigations are required on alternative schemata for the storage of KB content.

The results of our work will be further exploited in the ESPRIT II project AIMS (P5210) in which an Advanced Information Management Server is being built. One objective of the project, among others, is the development of techniques to deal with preexisting heterogeneous data sources including multi-media data.

Acknowledgements

This work was partially supported by the Commission of the European Communities within ESPRIT Project 311 (ADKMS). We would like to thank Christof Peltason, Albrecht Schmiedel, and Tatjana Oster for their comments on earlier versions of this paper.

References

[BBMR89] A. Borgida, R.J. Brachman, D.L. McGuinness, and L. Alperin Resnick. CLASSIC: A Structural Data Model for Objects. In *Proceedings of the 1989 ACM SIGMOD International Conference on Management of Data*, pp. 59–67, Portland, Oreg., June 1989.

[BBST88] S. Bergamaschi, F. Bonfatti, C. Sartori, and P. Tiberio. Relational Data Base Design for the Intensional Aspects of a Knowledge Base. *Information Systems*, 13(3):245–256, 1988.

[BGN89] H.W. Beck, S.K. Gala, and S.B. Navathe. Classification as a Query Processing Technique in the CANDIDE Semantic Data Model. In *Proceedings*

324

of the International Data Engineering Conference, IEEE, pp. 572–581, Los Angeles, Cal., February 1989.

[BR90] E. Bertino and P. Randi. Task 5.4.2: Mapping AQL into SQL Programs. Deliverable 2 Amendment Phase ESPRIT Project 311, May 1990.

[Bro88] M.L. Brodie. Future Intelligent Information Systems: AI and Database Technologies Working Together. In M.L. Brodie and J. Mylopoulos, editors, *Readings in Artificial Intelligence and Databases*. Morgan Kaufmann, San Mateo, Cal., 1988.

[BS85] R.J. Brachman and J.G. Schmolze. An Overview of the KL-ONE Knowledge Representation System. *Cognitive Science*, 9(2):171–216, April 1985.

[CCL90] W.W. Chu, Q. Chen, and R.-C. Lee. Cooperative Query Answering via Type Abstraction Hierarchy. *In this book.*

[CNKT90] S. Chakravarthy, S.B. Navathe, K. Karlapalem, and A. Tanaka. Meeting the Cooperative Problem Solving Challenge: A Database-Oriented Approach. *In this book.*

[HK87] R. Hull and R. King. Semantic Database Modelling: Survey, Applications and Research Issues. *ACM Computing Surveys*, 19(3), 1987.

[Hol90] B. Hollunder. Hybrid Inferences in KL-ONE-based Knowledge Representation Systems. In H. Marburger, editor, *GWAI-90. 14th German Workshop on Artificial Intelligence*, pp. 38–47, Springer-Verlag, Berlin, 1990.

[Kin90] C. Kindermann. Class Instances in a Terminological Framework – An Experience Report. In H. Marburger, editor, *GWAI-90. 14th German Workshop on Artificial Intelligence*, pp. 48–57, Springer-Verlag, Berlin, 1990.

[MFO90] D.P. McKay, T.W. Finin, and A. O'Hare. The Intelligent Database Interface: Integrating AI and Database Systems. In *Proceedings of the 9th National Conference of the American Association for Artificial Intelligence*, pp. 677–684, Boston, Mass., 1990.

[NCL+89] B. Nixon, K.L. Chung, D. Lauzon, A. Borgida, J. Mylopoulos, and M. Stanley. Design of a Compiler for a Semantic Data Model. In J.W. Schmidt and C. Thanos, editors, *Foundations of Knowledge Base Management*, pp. 293–343. Springer-Verlag, Berlin, 1989.

[Neb88] B. Nebel. Computational Complexity of Terminological Reasoning in BACK. *Artificial Intelligence*, 34(3):371–383, April 1988.

[NP90] B. Nebel and C. Peltason. Terminological Reasoning and Information Systems. In D. Karagiannis, editor, *Artificial Intelligence and Information Systems: Aspects of an Integration*, Lecture Notes in Artificial Intelligence. Springer-Verlag, Berlin. To appear.

[PSKQ89] C. Peltason, A. Schmiedel, C. Kindermann, and J. Quantz. The BACK System Revisited. KIT Report 75, Department of Computer Science, Technische Universität Berlin, September 1989.

[PS+90] P.F. Patel-Schneider, *et al.* Term Subsumption Languages in Knowledge Representation. *The AI Magazine*, 11(2):16–23, 1990.

[QK90] J. Quantz and C. Kindermann. Implementation of the BACK System Version 4. KIT Report 78, Department of Computer Science, Technische Universität Berlin, December 1990.

DISCUSSION

Presenter: C. Kindermann.

Q. (M. Huhns, MCC): Have you coupled your inferencing system with this query compiler so that rules access the assertional and terminological knowledge through this compiler?

A. (C. Kindermann): The rules I mentioned before have a different status here. They are applied to infer further information about objects and to make them instantiate other classes as well. So far the system is used more as an information system where users directly access the terminological and assertional knowledge. At the moment it is not coupled with other reasoning components, but in perspective one could imagine a rule based system that gets things out of BACK's knowledge base. I wrote some little toy examples in PROLOG where PROLOG clauses queried the BACK system for information and then further processed the data. But I guess that to couple BACK with a rule based system in a realistic way some other aspects have to be considered first. For example, for the compilation of an application program it may be useful to have the ability to compile the queries at the time the rules are compiled.

Q. (A.L. Furtado, IBM Brazil): Would you make some comments on the performance of your system?

A. (C. Kindermann): I couldn't give exact figures on the actual behavior of the AQL/SQL compiler because it's just a prototype, and my colleagues in Milan have only started now to experiment with it. But I recognized for an earlier implementation of the system how inefficient it is not to build up the indexing structure. So, with respect to this older implementation, the performance was improved by indexing objects appropriately, and by reducing the number of SQL queries through the compilation as I have described. On the other hand, the performance of the recognizer is not fully satisfactory at the moment. Processing a source file that contains a few hundred object introductions or modifications takes quite a while.

Maybe I should add that I'd like to see a reimplementation of BACK in an ordinary language, like C or C++ for instance. And in the follow-up project there will be one project partner who will be mainly concerned with this issue. So, we made good experiences in building our prototypes in PROLOG; a lot of things can be written down very fast, and this was very helpful in experimenting with new features. But once you know what your system should do, you could do much better if you had arrays or destructive assignment, and things like that. So, we believe that parts of the performance problems stem from the Prolog implementation, and that with a reimplementation in C the performance would go up.

Author Index